ThΣ King Θf ΣRΘtiΣa™

8

L[Θ]RD JENNINGS

Book 2 of 2

☦.Ḳ.Φ.Є. Publications
PUBLISHED BY LARRY WILSON, JR (DAPHAROAH69); GOULDS, FLORIDA

ISBN 978-0-578-06680-6

COPYRIGHT © BY ALIYAIH, SUNJARAIH AND LARRY C. WILSON, JR.
IN THE EVENT OF MY UNTIMELY DEATH: Demetrius Mozell and john Wilson are overseers of my books, images, and legacy, which I will leave to Aliyaih Hernandez Wilson and Sunjaraih Hernandez Wilson., unless otherwise stated, in writing, by me personally.

LIBRARY OF CONGRESS CATALOGING-IN-PUBLICATION DATA HAS BEEN APPLIED FOR.

Edited by Dapharoah69, The King of Erotica™

COVER DESIGN BY DAMON

Meak Productions Agency represents Dapharoah69, The King of Erotica ™

Fran Briggs, Publicist

This book is a work of fiction. Names, Characters, places, incidents are either the product of the author's imagination or are used fictitiously, and any resemblance to actual persons, living or dead, business establishments, events or locales are entirely coincidental. Without limiting the rights under copyright reserved above, no part of this publication may be reproduced, stored in or introduced into a retrieval system, or transmitted, in any form, or by any means (electronic, mechanical, photocopying, recording, or otherwise), without the prior written and signed permission of both the copyright owners and the above publisher of this book.

Books by Dapharoah69:

The King of Erotica 1: THE THRONE (Short Stories only)
The King of Erotica 1: THE THRONE SPECIAL EDITION
The King of Erotica 2: THE CROWN
The King of Erotica 3: SWORD V.I.P.
The King of Erotica 4: the DeTHRONEment of a King
The King of Erotica 5: WAR:Dr.O.[Be]
The King of Erotica 6: BATTLE PLANS
The King of Erotica 7: PH/A\ROAH
The King of Erotica 8: LORD JENNINGS
Some Men Wear Panties
Call Her Queen Hatshepsut

Anthologies

Mocha Chocolate
Voices From Within
The WSN Anthology

Part 2
Lord Jennings

Luke 21:14-19 (King James Version)

[14]Settle it therefore in your hearts, not to meditate before what ye shall answer:
[15]For I will give you a mouth and wisdom, which all your adversaries shall not be able to gainsay nor resist.
[16]And ye shall be betrayed both by parents, and brethren, and kinsfolks, and friends; and some of you shall they cause to be put to death.
[17]And ye shall be hated of all men for my name's sake.
[18]But there shall not an hair of your head perish.
[19]In your patience possess ye your souls.

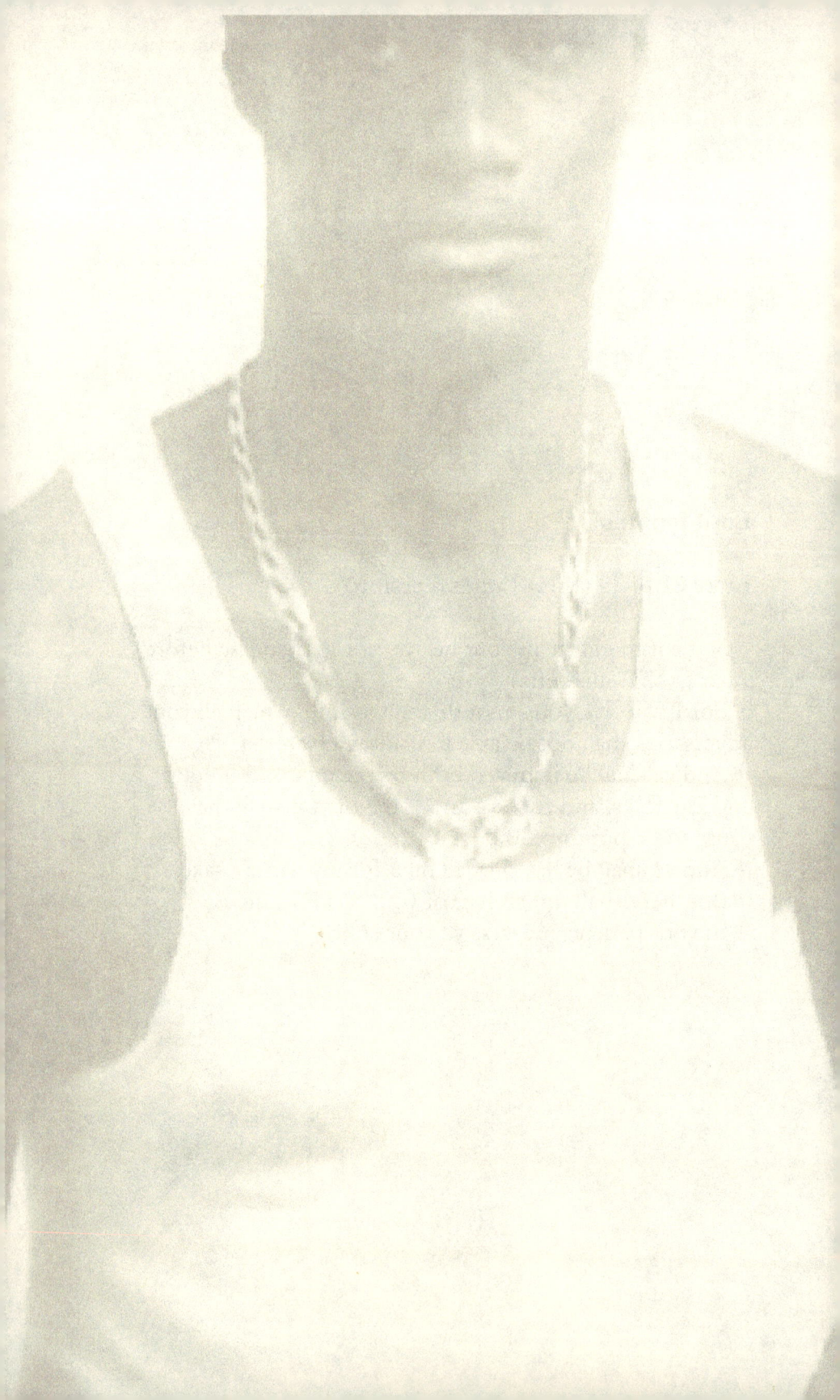

ORDER OF OPERATIONS
IDENTITY THEFT

BOOK COVER BY DAMON	
POETRY	PAGE A
KING:FACE	PAGE 21
CHAD RENDER	PAGE 33
LETTERS FROM CHAD TO PHAROAH	PAGE 43
PRISON OBITUARY	PAGE 61

THE UNIVERSITY OF HELL:
PRISON DIARIES

PRISON PART 1 THE CORONATION	PAGE 63
PRISON PART 2: RAPE	PAGE 143
PRISON PART 3: SUICIDE	PAGE 147
PHOTOS	PAGE 157
EARTHLY WISDOM	PAGE 177
FAMILY IS A HOAX!	PAGE 181
DAMN!! YOUR BREATH STANK!	PAGE 191
MASTURBATION MEETS DEATH	PAGE 197
DEAD INSIDE (POEM)	PAGE 201
HURRICANE ANDREW JOURNAL	PAGE 207
WHITE PIECE OF CHALK	PAGE 212
GRUDGE AGAINST THE CHURCH	PAGE 221
I SEEN YA' TRICKIN', BABY!	PAGE 243
GROWN FOLKS TALKIN'	PAGE 251
CHARACTER DEVELOPMENT	PAGE 263
MICHAEL MYERS	PAGE 275
CHURCH SMURCH MY ASS!	PAGE 287
AM I YOUR GOD?	PAGE 293

Lord Jennings and Pharoah Pt 1	Page 315
Aggravated Assault	Page 321
Lord Jennings and Pharoah Pt 2	Page 333
Mabel	Page 335
Problem Child	Page 347
Ying/Yang	Page 357

ThΣ $t®ippΣr Dia®IΣ$

You Na$ty Boy	Page 377
The Pator' Chamber$	Page 379
The Main A$$embly	Page 385
Promi$cuity	Page 393
Weakne$$ of The Fle$h	Page 401
$tripper	Page 405
The Ri$e of the Lu$tful Bea$t	Page 413
The Debut of Pharoah the Robot	Page 417
Dome$tic Violence	Page 427
Mama Deare$t	Page 437
The Anger of the Bea$t	Page 445
Daddy, The Illu$ion	Page 449
The Wooden Box	Page 453
NIGGAHS	Page 457

ThΣ UnitΣd StatΣs A®my Dia®IΣs:

U.S. ARMY Obituary	Page 465
The United States Army: PROGRAMMED	Page 467
Dimension	Page 504
The Final Obituary	Page 547
Lord Jennings Vs Pharoah Armageddon	Page 549

Poetry:

Chess:

By Dapharoah69, The King of Erotica ™

I pull out the…board,
and set up my…pieces,
we jump from cross/
words to
jigsaw pieces,
yet all these games
lead us both
to hop/
Scotch
to the Henny
in[TOXIC]ate:
my brain
just to prepare myself
for you:
This mighty fine bed,
disguised as a table
I lay a[CROSS] the plush quilt,
naked and able,

willing and labeled,
licking my lips,
as you begin
with your lips
to
/desce
nd/
King poignantly hides queen
queen uses pawns to
provoke the k[NIGHT]s
swirling inside my mentality,
Testing my patience,
sliding diagonally,
horizontally,
to seduce the bishops,
which is why I don't have faith
in the church anymore,
they're too busy castling
my Temple, mowing my lawns,
erecting my edifice,
to have, with such delicious wine
the body of my edible sacrifice,
carefully and cleverly disguised
as what one called Cum: Munion:
two up and one down,
waaay down to the pit of
my urgent desire...
knights and rooks beckon
from inside me
the disquieting freak,
silenced through ...
bibles and scriptures,
so I make love to the messenger
to recreate the mess[AGE]
I don't mean to be rude

but what was it?
The Book of John, Chapter 1:
Verse two reads,
oh, I forgot, I can't focus!
tongue kiss my [TEST]:icles,
while I try to focus on the [BI]~ble,
take it from my hands,
throw it across the room,
I say over and over:
we
shouldn't
be
doing
this!
you are a higher up in the church
someone everyone truly respects…
Strategically replace me,
as you snatch away…
another pawn,
patience is a virtue,
yet I'm not virtuous,
slide across my spaces,
tarnish my armor.
diagonally thrill me across
the dinner table:
then pawn me to cash me,
pull me to recycle castling:
slide with me, within me,
deep inside me,

on top of me,
sweat, laugh, bit my bottom lip,
taste my saliva,
doesn't it remind you
of my edible sacrifice?

One down, two over,
my Temple begins to crumple so:
lick me at an angle,
suck me until I explode
three more pawns for you to
snatch up and spit out
rook collapse into the
spirit of knights no longer standing,
brandishing my mentality,
testing my in[TELL]igence,
make love to my patience
to impregnate the queen.
Touch me, tease me,
camoufl[AGE] your moves to
Uncover my hidden grooves:
I'm trapped,
slide diagonally,
suck me at an angle,
I aim to pl~[EASE},
but I don't want to...skeet in your eye:
Intelligent, patient, virtuous:
say my name,
look me in the face my Queen:
Stale M~[ATE].

King:fce™

Sex + Stranger = Russian Roulette™

This is Larry Wilson Jr's tenth (that's the number AFTER 9, haters!) book. Eye had to split my autobiology (autobiography) into two parts because the original manuscript was simply *too* enormous to stuff in one book. Eye was going to eliminate a few chapters, but my fans spoke. They said leave every *single* page and goddamn it *that's* what eye gave them. Every stinking page.

Am eye proud of myself, you ask? Um, no! But eye am blessed and ever thankful to God for the journey. A friend close to me called me a writing machine. No, folks eye am not a robot. Eye have veins, feet, nuts and a big dick and if you thinking TMI then TMI these nuts and shut up. This is my goddamn book, you up tight ass clowns. Eye don't have wires and bolts and shit like that. While some of you FAKE CHRISTIANS and ATHIESTS DRESSED AS CHRISTIANS were out fucking, eating pussy, sucking dick, clubbing, taking full advantage of Ladies in Free before 11 PM at Miami Knights, shooting up the neighborhood DJ and *robbing* muthafuckahs…Larry C. Wilson Jr. was writing his poor heart out because he had nothing else going on, because I was homeless, down and at my lowest…and doing something constructive with my time shouldn't be a bad thing. It kept me from robbing muthafuckahs, and kicking in doors with a ski mask on my face to make ends meet. I am not a violent person, nor have I ever been. And I never will be.

My daddy didn't want me and Mama threw my tall lanky ass away without a second thought because eye'm bisexual and *won't* marry a woman and make a baby so all eye have was writing. Did eye lose sleep over it, yes but eye lose sleep writing about it. And that was it. So don't flatter yourselves Mama and Daddy. That's how eye stay outta trouble. Don't get me wrong. Eye love women and eye love pussy, too but eye love Niggahs too and eye won't suppress it for nobody. Not even Mama. She fucked who she wanted to fuck in her lifetime (had her fun) without regard to me or my feelings so eye'm having MY FUN on MY TERM$.

 She didn't owe me any explanations. Eye didn't owe anybody anything and they didn't owe me shit. Ain't anybody *obligated* to take care of my grown ass but *my* grown ass. So eye will FUCK who eye wanna fuck. This is *my* dick. What the fuck ya'll worried about it for? When half ya'll asses went behind your wives backs trying to get in my Fruit of a Looms. Now I didn't even wear them anymore. Go eat your girlfriend's swagga-jacked pussy and stay up out my face with her moisture on your lips when you kiss my neck. Frankly, eye don't even have time to watch the News because the media lie to you all day in and day out and the News teach you to lie and stick your noses in somebody else's business and you really believe that bullshit. Well, eye don't. The country didn't believe in GAY MARRIAGE, yet half the muthafuckahs making the laws suck more dick and get fucked in the ass more than loaded videos on Xtube.com. Half the country didn't even believe in God, but threw God in my face to systemically control me. Bite it, bitches. Jesus loves the Pharoah, this I know for the BIBLE has told me so. Well, the part that wasn't an edited addition.

 You know eye'm pimpin' this literary shit to keep your attention on the negative so you figure out how to work through bullshit for the positive. Most folks fold and surrender without a preface or preamble when it comes to adversity. Me? Eye simply stare in her haggard face and write another book. I might fuck her if the pussy good.

 Sometimes my computer screen was *Adversity*. Staying up 14 hours a day with little sleep, taking four hour breaks and up and doing the writing thing again sometimes [the computer screen] aggravates me. I glared at it, frown, sigh, smile and wink and when it dawns on me I'm smiling and winking at my characters and relating to another male character and the way eye describe him and the women eye write about with bubble asses going after their own while robbing muthafuckahs for their own made me frown, get angry and want a vendetta so eye write about men spreading diseases (*Luscious* in *Some Men Wear Panties*) to bluntly teach whatever message eye'm conveying. StimYOUlate then EdYOUcate ™.

Eye create promiscuous church goers who fuck each other wearing golden masks to golden masks in a higher level of a ménage a trois called an Orgy (The King of Erotica 1 The THRONE!) to shock, break down, stimYOUlate then edYOUcate; and while your dicks get hard and your pussy fucks up your brand new pair of fifty dollar panties—when Kmart's $9.99 pack would have sufficed—Melissa Jackson (The main bitch from my first book) sucks and fucks through paradise and she *doesn't* know a few of them were infected with HIV and spreading it.

And when you experience this via reading, you lose your erection and your pussies dry up Sahara Dessert Style and you realize in your own life you need to make your lovers wear recently purchased condoms or *you* could bring them, ladies (know your man; know who you give up the pussy too). Or practice abstinence. Be willing to talk to your lovers about your concerns. Better yet, get to know someone and have meaningful sex when and after you *learn* the person you're with. Sex + Stranger = Russian Roulette.

But even with *that* some stores got a two for one sale on condoms, but don't be fooled. Get 'em free at your local clinic.

Everything that's free ain't necessarily good. Check the expiration date on those kinds of condoms (and free condoms, too). They have a First Out, First In Rule with their inventory. During a two for one sale they getting rid of that about to expire in two days condom (First Out) to make room for that Up to Date condom (First In) and that condom gonna run you about $15.99 for a box of Magnum condoms.

Eye bluntly teach this in my work. Looks could be deceiving. And whoever still thinks they can look at a person and guess they have HIV…um, they are just…they are …crickets in the brain.

Unreachable. A few of *those* kinds of people wound up with HIV or some other STD's. I knew a few of them myself. Different methods of spread most people never thought about because they so worried about the gays. Bitch what you so worried about the gays for? Some *straight* men got muthafucking AIDS or HIV too, bitch.

Worry about your muthafucking selves! So *what* a man sucked a dick. Mad they ain't sucking yours? Wash that stinky dick then maybe a roach will entertain the thought. Just because eye'm bisexual didn't mean eye wanted a goddamn man. Sometimes eye want some pussy you insecure ass Niggahs. Pussy brought me here so why would eye turn my back on it? Eye love pussy too much.

A lot of women ate pussy but you glamorize that kinda gay shit with your late asses. Listened to Ludacris "My Chick Bad!" a little too much. Muthafucking *PHAROAH* Bad. Period. Eye'm badder than half the bitches out there and eye'm 33 years old. Eye walked in a room your man's dick gets hard and he's the furthest thing from my mind. You got a problem with him looking at me too much eye'm not leaving the restaurant, you ain't *Grand*. Better eye check your man.

And if a woman got something to say then you better stop your "man" from looking at my ass when you turn to slap palms with your girls.

Look at my tall sexy ass. Eye fucking your irises from those book covers and didn't even know your dry weave ass existed. Beckoning you to come read some stimYOUlating shit. Your man mad because you stay up day in and day out trying to finish reading my books. He wanted some pussy but had to take a cold shower. *Duh* he secretly read my books in private to see what it was all about.

Now he hit me up on Facebook begging to fuck me.

Eye didn't care who liked my writing or not. And eye didn't give a fuck about your criticism either. As long as you get something from it then my job was done. Eye've matured a lot. Couldn't get in my boxers that easily anymore. If eye didn't love ya' then you don't get any.

Now that's hard. Even Usher boasting about a woman being into a woman and this so called straight muthafucker raising a son. What kinda example was that setting?

Eye answer to no one. And eye can fuck who eye wanna fuck you on the low bitches. And if you were so against it…if its against how you were raised then fuck Niggah STOP STOP STOP begging me to suck your dick, and as a matter of fact eye don't want your short stroking dick tonight. Go fuck your don't-got-a-clue-or-she's-in-denial wife.

Trashy dick couldn't even make me yawn. Ain't your child support payments kinda late this month? You tope spending child support money on me your child could eat.

Just stick your tongue in it and tell it to my anus.

Get educated on HIV/AIDS and take a brush up course free of charge on Google.com to stay abreast of the disease. Don't say eye didn't warn you people about folks purposely spreading HIV. They would fuck and suck you into an infection and leave your ass alone, spent and baffled.

Education was the key. If you didn't know that a) semen, b) vaginal secretions c) BLOOD and d) Breast Milk had the highest levels of HIV then baby you need to pick up a HIV pamphlet and start over.

Eye say that bluntly because HIV didn't give a fuck about me, *you*, your kids or *your* late ass; didn't care about your unborn kids, your Bridal Shower, your wedding; or your third grade teacher—the one with those God-awful glasses and that stale ass wig; HIV didn't give a shit about your husband or wives; and HIV ran rampant in the Church and every time there was a dance show *everyone* came for support; but when Pa$tor did a show about HIV...*crickets* filled the church singing in unison. Only 5 people showed up.

Two of them left because it wasn't as thick or as jam packed as they thought it would be. So phone number scouting was out. The Pa$tor didn't even show up and he was the emcee. So they wore their Sunday best and spend hundreds on threads, shoes and hair do's for nothing. Their goes next Sunday's tithes. Pa$tor probably gonna think "*Goddamn* collection plate kinda empty today!"

Papa wanna go to the Miccosukee in Miami-Dade County and gamble. Try to win some money.

So he grabbed the microphone with such a stern expression and said, "Remember God said to give cheerfully. Be a cheerful giver."

He glared at Susan because he paid for that pussy before; why she ain't put nothing in the tithe plate?

"Don't give outta obligation," he snapped at her, taking a quick drink of water while the lead Usher admiringly pat dried his handsome yet contorted face with a damp rag that, seconds ago, held on to the remaining remnants of coolness; *now* its damp and hot and making him sweat more.

So he takes out five hundred dollars from his wallet and put it in the collection plate and the congregation applauded, standing up and he waving his hands dismissively, like, "Naw, don't praise me praise God. I'm a cheerful giver. Put my own money in the collection plate."

And when eye was 15 eye didn't clap at all. Eye walked up the aisle, stopped in front of him with my arms folded because eye was FED UP with church lies and people stopped clapping and eye was tapping my foot on the thinning green carpet and eye cut my eyes before eye rolled them and said, "Your horny ass ain't no cheerful giver."

Gasp, gasp and gasp. Eye went on. "You paid for Susan's pussy 'cause she told me!"

The oh so attentive Pa$tor's wife was stunned, walking around the pew; knocking Sister Mary's *Songs Book* from her wrinkled, bejeweled hands. Sister Mary didn't know one song in that book and been reading those songs for 15 years. Humming her ass off with too much make-up.

"WHAT?" Pa$tor's Big Titty wife said.

Eye glared at her. Come on, chick. Shaking my head. Chile. Boo. *Casper*, sit! Like you didn't know. Walkin' round church trying to be Casper the Friendly Ghost instead of being a dutiful Proverbs Wife.

"Rumor has it 'round the church that Pa$tor hadn't fucked you, dreamed of fucking you or *thought* of fucking your hamhock eating ass in years. Don't act so shocked. Reaching ain't cute. Both of you stayed married for the 'kids' sake,' but your kids were now grown adults about to graduate college. Somebody got some 'splannin' to do! That shit don't sit right with my teenage ass."

Pa$tor hopped off the stage and grabbed me by the arm.

"Leave this church. With your filthy mouth!"

"God said come as eye am, hypocrite! AND YOU CALL MY MOUTH FILTHY?" Eye said powerfully, getting in his wife's face. Hoe didn't scare me. Niggah my daddy has *never* been there for me so getting saucy ain't g'on fly with the Pharoah. He pointed at the door and congregation members whispering at me harshly and eye rolled my eyes, faced them and said, "Ya'll talking all that shit but Pa$tor didn't say that when eye sucked his dick the other day, talkin' 'bout don't tell nobody and ya'll talkin' shit?"

Instant fail. Church went up in an uproar. Eye got the microphone and said, "Talk all that noise now? Nobody got *nothing* to say. Ok, eye do."

Eye pointed at Tom. "Eye had your grown ass."

Eye pointed at a thirty-two year old black dude that was infatuated with me. "Eye had you. Didn't last ten minutes, but whatever."

I pointed at three other men and four female adults.

"Can you say Orgy? But everybody got something to say about Pharoah. This church is a joke and you want me to take it seriously and everybody sucking and fucking everybody. I don't wanna come here anymore!"

HIV didn't give a fuck about the nuns, the elders, the congregation nor the business men in million dollar suits nor NFL stars nor NBA stars nor sports agents, journalists, nations or emperors or Hollywood stars.

Somebody in EVERY bracket eye just named has AIDS or HIV or herpes. But money buys silence when you're rich and cures never released to the general public was the ultra rich's playground.

But to the poor folk like us (me included, a struggling erotic writer who was so much more than sex), had to fill out ADAP papers and see your Case Manager in person during the last full week of your dosage and get your blood drawn and get your T4 cell count (your numbers) every three months; and do paperwork every 6 months to be renewed just to get HIV medicine. And they trying to tell me this was an uncontrollable disease when the very medicine eye took was monitored, documented and signed off for. Eye believe there was a cure. This was a money cash cow business, this HIV stuff. Goddamn control. Sad. Eye'm glad eye'm learning how to work through adversity as a struggling writer so when eye do get millions (if its God's Will, not mine) eye would know that money wouldn't change a thang 'bout Larry C.

Eye write realness. Like Donald Goines fucking the shit outta Jackie Collins with Joan Collins' pussy on the brain humming Beyawnsay's "Frekum Dress," *cumming* while an episode of ZANE the Sex Chronicles played on "Mute" in the background on the plasma TV four shows away from the tube blowing.

No time to fake the funk with my writing. Eye wrote exactly what the hell eye wanted to say. Lyrical release, getting pressure off my mind and depleted from my brain before eye blow a fuse so eye write for hours to meet the supply and demand of my heart. Eye thank God for that.

No water in my goddamn book. Straight Moon shine, Henn Dawg, Grey Goose on the Loose intoxicated vocal word play via my goddamn books. Just because you're reading SOME of my private thoughts didn't mean you will get to know them. Just read, and when you start to figure me out eye'll chameleon that ass; meaning change up on some new shit and leave you scratching your head when I snatch your wigs; so while you try to guess why my favorite color was black and last week it was blue eye'll still be rocking blue clothes till you figure out black was never my favorite color because I am black.

I may love myself, yes, but sometimes I am NOT my favorite person. Especially when someone crossed me. You gun for me bitches be prepared for battle. I fight alone. That's when my alter ego cums to play. And The King of Erotica will suck and fuck you if that means fucking you up in the middle of your nut. Its business for you 'cause you got your nut. Its personal to me because eye didn't get a nut because I fucked you up. Positive thinking leads to optimism, but of course your oppressors want you to think you're not capable of anything and if you think your family won't hurt you eye suggest you open your eyes. If eye would have listened to naysayers, haters and family that told me eye wasn't smart enough to write…well, you wouldn't be reading THE KING OF EROTICA 8: LORD JENNINGS now would you?

Thought so. Eye appreciate you buying or reading PHAROAH and taking a glimpse into my life. It's not all of it because some things eye kept to myself and didn't wish to share. So now that you're reading Lord Jennings, which happened to be the name of the shrink that counseled me, get something from it. While you read this book eye will be enjoying Miami Beach, eating crab legs, jack off a few times and enjoy life till eye finish writing A Lonely Christmas book 3. You wanna know what eye've recently been through…save me as your screensaver and *study* the picture of me in the blue Airforce coat with an open palm resting over my right eye. Resting. It's not pressed *on* my right eye. Now blink. Give a killer smile. Get your award. Thank God later. That's what some of you think about me.

So look at your screensaver. The icons to the far right hand of your toolbar shows your place in society but society didn't know your place. Your computer toolbar is reminiscent of military rank or insignia on your military uniform. The more you achieve the more decorated you become. Everybody couldn't have cobblestone streets, be famous, suck down expensive bubbly with stars or dine with the Elite. Eye didn't even do that but eye was certainly invited to wine and dine with the Elite and they even offered to pay for it but eye know well enough to know that everything ain't free and when someone offer you something free of charge bet your ass the price comes in a form you may not be too prepared for. Does it look like I've sold my soul? Hell naw. I ride with GOD, JEHOVAH, AND JESUS (not Hey Seus but Jesus), baby. So eye work for everything eye achieve. You think major publishers aren't pissing their pants to get me to sign over The King of Erotica? Yea, they are. Eye turned down $1.5 million dollars in September of last year and another $2 million a month ago. They want all my rights, wanna put white people on my shit and _Caucassionize_ my shit. Yea this was *my* book so eye made that word up. Eye'm black. Why would eye want to Caucassionize my shit?

You should see my computer tool bar. Eye could be a goddamn five star general. Platinum everything: from Spy Ware to a thousand dollar photo shop program my fans bought me. My fans sponsor any and everything eye need. All they want me to do is write. That's how eye roll and eye didn't boast or brag about it. When eye go around friends eye didn't boast or bring up eye am The King of Anything. Eye stay mum. My friends bring it up themselves and even then eye down play everything. Sometimes eye just wanna be Larry.

Eye was made in God's image and so were you. Buddha, Allah and Gandhi *wished* they made me. *God* made me and the God *eye* love and serve name was JEHOVAH. NOT JAYHOVAH BUT JEHOVAH. Eye could NEVER praise a fucking rapper. Not in this lifetime. Eye have the full Armor of God and it's the best outfit eye have ever acquired. Everyone wasn't fit enough to wear that kinda armor. The full Armor of God wasn't just my armor but that's where eye store my mental armory. May no weapon formed against me prosper baby. Jesus died for my sins! Know what that means you conservative Catholic bitches? That means he died for my bisexuality as well. He died for homosexuals, the transgenders and the lesbians too. He didn't say on the cross "Eye die for the adulterers and the men sleeping with fifty women and the women who can't control their twats but not the gays."

SHOW ME IN THE BIBLE JESUS SAID HE DIDN'T DIE FOR THE GAYS? THOUGHT SO! HE DIED FOR ALL SINS! And if you're gay, bi, DL or a lesbian don't let society tell you your sexuality was an abomination. Because its not. Be who you are destined to be and love yourself and if they didn't like you pray for them and move the hell on and if you didn't believe in God then blessings be unto you. You have the right to serve who you choose, but eye choose to serve God in all his glory.

This ain't True and False or Multiple Choice. Who are you to tell someone who they can and can't marry? Half the men in legislation making laws against gays were secret fags themselves. Eye slept with three of them. Eye should know.

And some of you Pa$tors out there fucking around on your wives with anything that has a warm hole…don't get me started on you phony fucks. People preach all day long about being gay was wrong but half you Facebook pa$tors (and regular so called neighborhood Pa$tors) keep trying to fuck me behind your wife's back. And wasn't TD Jakes son caught in the bushes by police a while ago having "gay sex," according to the news? And that shit died down in less than two days. Money talked. Now eye'm talking and eye got bills to pay.

Lord Jennings was about to start. Satan, Jesus died for my sins and died for the sins of man. Stop confusing the public with your music, movies and books saying otherwise. Satan is real people. And so is God. We are at spiritual warfare right now and the time has come to choose a side. Eye chose mine. Eye sides with God. The King of Kings, Lord of Lords. Yea eye curse, yea my flesh was weak, yea eye masturbate, yea eye sometimes smoked weed but guess what? Eye'm a sinner, and so were all of you. Satan, did Jesus die for your sins Hmm, eye wonder. But you all big and bad. The Devil is a liar. Satan, you tricked me for a long time. Half my life you sent people in my life that tried to hurt me ever since eye was a small child. And eye still wound up being Bestselling author Dapharoah69.

Toodles, you all. Enjoy Lord Jennings and think about what eye said. Chose a side. You don't have much time. Christians, learn to forgive others. Stop putting it off and adjusting it to your own timeline. You know why, Christians? Tomorrow wasn't promised. You die tonight, tomorrow, in the next second, minute or hour and you haven't forgiven people for what they've done to you, or if your hearts are filled with hatred, don't think you'll inherit the Kingdom of God.

Try the flames of Hell.

Tell me about Chadrick Render
And the incident in Oregon
That landed you in prison

Lord Jennings

This was one of the most depressing chapters eye would ever write in my life. Eye have written many books and created many characters, but my own life was something eye never thought eye'd actually document, even though eye fantasized about doing so numerous times. The first time eye attempted to write my autobiography was when eye was incarcerated at the Inverness Jail in Salem, Oregon back in 1997. Mom told me eye should try to write a book after eye sent her a collection of poetry eye'd written and eye used to go to the Law Library, telling officials I wanted to work on my case yet I lied, hiding my writings in my paperwork. It became my obsession, writing that was. Eye wrote my first book, titled *A Lighter Shade of Men*, and sending it home to mom on my way to the Big House (prison, after eye was convicted of Attempted Sodomy in the first degree, and the lesser charged dropped), my books were lost in the mailing system and eye suffered a deep depression. I think one of the guards stole my book.

Before eye get into the charges and what happened eye will first set up the entire ordeal. My first visit to Oregon, a state eye'd never been and a state eye would visit on vacation and leave on probation, was an educational one. Eye learned then that your own kind would destroy you, especially if you were a foreigner in their neighborhood and state. Portland niggahs didn't like Down South niggahs, and they let that be known after being phony, laughing and smiling in my face. Once I became comfortable, that's when they attacked.

Chadrick Daquan Render was my best friend for 15 years and my brother at heart. He was the Keeper of my inner secrets and he protected them with the heart of a warrior and eye never asked for the protection but he so willingly gave it. A pint sized bundle of blackness, don't let his size fool you. Every time eye walked in a room his face lit up like a Xmas tree. Talk about a loyal friend, he was that. Athletic, handsome and he loved the ladies and treated them with respect. Before I visited Oregon, eye was going through problems at home, just getting out the Army with a dishonorable discharge and being back in Mama's house, a place eye wanted to desperately leave, did a number on me. Eye was still heartbroken over Chantelle having an abortion behind my back while in the Army, stationed at Fort Hood, Texas. Chad helped me cope. The fact that I was talking to her empty womb thinking my child was growing inside gave me a lot of sleepless nights and Chad and I stayed up for hours on the phone crying together. He felt my pain. He helped me get through the tough time.

At the time Mom was involved with a dude named Jimmy, who worked for the FEDS on the same institution grounds as she, FCI Miami. Eye didn't like him very much. In fact eye couldn't stand him back then.

After mom helped him out, even got a leather chair on her credit for his apartment, eye guess his bills caved in on his manhood because next thing eye know my 8 year old sister was waking me up out a dead sleep.

She was worried. "Pharoah! Pharoah! Get up, boyee."

Aggravated, I was mad as hell. Waking me up. I hated that shit. "What, girl?"

"Who is that man in Mama's kitchen in his draws cooking shrimp for breakfast?"

I sucked my teeth. "Probably Laron."

"IT AIN'T LARON, BOYEE! It's a grown man! Eye never seen him before."

OK. She got my attention now. Beign I was the man of the house, eye got up and walked into the kitchen, wiping sleep out my eyes. Eye had to get up anyways. Eye had to go job hunting, since Uncle Sam wasn't sending me guaranteed checks every two weeks anymore.

Inhaling cooking shrimp and eggs, eye saw him. Muscular body, ass a little on the flat side and eye said, "Excuse me, who are you?"

He looked at me with those thick lips and sparkling eyes. "Hey, Pharoah."

I looked at him sideways. "How do you know my damn name?"

He smiled, stirring the shrimp, sizzling in my ears. "You're the oldest, right?"

"Yea, man. Now who are you? Are you in the right house? You're in your draws around my fucking 8 year old sister?"

"Eye mean no harm. Eye'm your mother's boyfriend. Eye just moved in."

Eye narrowed my eyes. "She doesn't have a man." Eye felt betrayed. "She moved you in and didn't even prepare her own kids. Typical."

"She's grown, Pharoah she doesn't have to tell you anything."

Oh, boy. Here we go. Try'na control me already and it ain't gonna happen. Black cocky bitch ain't been in my kitchen two hours and he trying to pull some damn heat. "That may be true but put some shorts or pants on! Your half naked ass around my goddamn sister ain't cuttin' it. Tell my Mama *that*!"

He was grinning, stirring the shrimp. Eye said, "Who cooks shrimp for breakfast? Eye guess you got it like that?"

"Eye surely do. Eye do work for the BOP."

"Eye know who you are now. You showed up here one day when Mom and Sweet (my cousin) was painting the living room. You were the one who claimed to have followed her home because you took one look at her and was all in love, and she fell like a dick in loose pussy for that bullshit."

"Watch your mouth."

"You ain't my goddamn daddy."

"Eye'm your step daddy," he said, emptying the pot of shrimp on a plate.

"In your dreams, muscle neck," eye mumbled. Eye didn't have to time argue with Mama's boy toy. He was what, man #2 since we been in this Hartford Square ass house in Naranja. The first piece of shit, Sam, who was in the Airforce came and went and eye was glad because eye was tired of losing sleep from Mama OH GOD OH GOD through the walls, like eye didn't have goddamn ears. Eye knew she said all that. Eye used to press my ear against the wall laughing my ass off at the little leprechaun try'na make Mama's toes curl. What was it with Mama and midget niggahs? Now a new Sheriff was in town and eye would shoot his ass real quick he try me.

The trouble had just started.

Over their dizzying relationship eye was never close to the man, but my brothers loved him mainly because he had video games. Wowee. Who gave a shit? Eye wasn't easily won over when it came to a man Mama dated because, when they hurt her eye was the one who had to see her tears, and watch her write lyrics from CD's on paper to give to those worthless cock suckers. Eventually, at least eye thought at the time, Mama chose him over me. Made like eye didn't exist and eye was blindingly jealous. So eye retaliated and Chad convinced me to move to Oregon and eye did so in the next few months. Mama and eye were not on speaking terms and we basically hated each other.

Mama and this man were up and down. In love one day, arguing the goddamn next. He took Mama all over town looking like a Cuban with a hair cut (he loved Spanish women and damn sure had my Mama trying to look like one and eye HATED IT! Only Mama didn't realize it) and the next day they were at it again. He's arguing with her and she's arguing back, over everything from a man in a picture with Mama with his hand above her ass (Jimmy SWORE his hand was *on* her ass, and his jealous ass got his panties in a wad), to a video surfacing of a half naked bitch with her tits hanging out popping pussy on camera and he claimed he made that tape BEFORE he moved into our house but that leather chair Mama got for him on her credit turned that undercover truth into the lie it was.

And she still kept him. What did it for me was hearing him on the phone one night with one of his ex fuck buddies or Baby Mama, telling her what he missed doing to her, and that he wanted her to send him naked pictures to his P.O. Box and eye woke up Laron, my brother and said, "Oh my God! That double crosser!"

"What are you talking about?"

"Jimmy cheating on Mama!"

He was wide awake. "*WHAT?*"

"Hell, yea! Listen." Eye put the phone on speaker, with the MUTE button pressed.

"What kinda pictures you want?" the bitch asked him.

"Eye want pictures of that pretty pussy," he said.

"You miss this pussy, don't you?" she asked.

"Oh hell naw," said Laron. He was steaming. "And eye liked him. Eye thought he was cool."

"Eye never liked the bitch."

When the phone call ended we called Mama at work and we told her what we both heard.

"Oh hell no!" she spat icily. Eye didn't know how Mama got home so fast from the prison but she did, coming through the door with a purpose. Eye was so happy. YES! Another one bites the dust. Pack your shit and GET O-U-T!

She was yelling and screaming, "Who was that bitch you were on the phone with?"

He was like a dear trapped in head lights. "What are you talking about?"

"Pharoah and Laron told me they heard you talking to some bitch on the phone! Eye didn't know you had a P.O. Box! She sending you goddamn pictures, Jimmy?"

"PHAROAH!" he yelled and eye ran out the door with my brother. We ran across the street by the gas station (CITGO, it was after, what, 11, 12 a.m. at night, and we hid in the bushes.

"He ain't finna Teenage Mutant Ninja Turtles my ass with those thick ass arms," eye joked and Laron was laughing.

"Eye say we go back."

"Hell naw."

"Come on. Two against one!"

We went back.

Jimmy and Mama argued for the old and the new.

The next day eye felt crummy. An eerie feeling befell me and eye couldn't shake it. Eye was glad Mama found out about the double crosser and he was gone.

Eye opened my eyes and was startled, jumping outta my skin.

Jimmy was in the doorway, dressed up nicely. He smiled.

"Get out!" eye shouted. Eye hated him so much.

"Eye see you were eavesdropping."

My eyes were blood shot red. "Get out, double-crosser."

"You see that's just it," he said, gloating. "Eye convinced her you were making it up. Your Mama and eye are still together." He winked.

"Eye hate you, bitch!"

He laughed and walked off. Eye walked into Mama's room. "So he gets to stay?" eye asked rhetorically.

"Yea, he does. Why did you and Laron lie on him?"

"WHAT?"

"You heard me! You need to get out my house! You're supposed to be in the Army. But you fucked that up."

"Eye heard him, Mama!"

"YOU NEED TO STAY OUT MY BUSINESS!"

"Mama!"

"Eye don't wanna talk to you Pharoah! Get out my face!"

"Mama!"

"NOW!"

"He lied to you!"

"You and Laron lied. Lie again eye'm throwing you out my goddamn house!"

"Eye hate this shit."

"Get out my house, Pharoah."

"If he stays, eye stay." And eye went to my room and closed the door.

She opened it. "Don't close no doors in my goddamn house you don't pay no bills. You need a job."

"Whatever."

She slammed the door closed.

Eye called Chad on the phone and of course eye filled him in and he was like, "Yo, that's fucked up, Baby Boy."

"Tell me about it Red Eyes."

"You should come to Portland."

"Eye've *never* been there."

"For real, dawg. Come up here with me. Eye miss home, though. And it will be hard with you up here because you are the only link eye have to talk to my family behind Junior's back."

"What your cousin, well your so called *guardian*, do now?"

"Can you believe he pissed in my shoes because he doesn't want me going out with Komingo?" Chad's African girlfriend.

"That's foul." Eye was shaking my head.

"He hates her and he controls me. He told me if eye won the state championship in wrestling he would let me go see my mother."

"And what happened?"

"Eye won it, and he reneged, said eye couldn't talk to her. Calls my Mama all kinds of names. Yes, she does drugs but so what? That's my mother and eye love and miss her so much."

"Eye'm sorry, dawg. Eye can't even stand my Mama right now."

"So are you gonna fly up?"

I smiled. "Yea, eye am."

He was so happy. "Eye'll help you buy the plane ticket. You can stay as long as you want. You're family."

"Ok, eye'll get on it."

"Eye am thinking of joining the Blood gang."

I choked on my spit. What the fuck? "WHAT?"

"Pharoah, don't trip."

I was infuriated. "DON'T JOIN THAT SHIT! They will kill your entire family you try to get out."

He laughed it off. "It's not like that."

My eyes were wide with fear. "YES IT IS!"

"Eye want your blessing."

I rolled my eyes. "To join a gang? Eye had a rough life but eye'm not joining a gang, Chad."

"Please, Pharoah."

"Nope. Hell no. Eye love you dude. But join a gang friendship is OVER!"

He was hurt. "You don't mean that!"

I was devastated. "Yes the fuck eye do!"

"Baby Boy."

Eye hung up the phone in his face.

And turned the ringer off.

After buying my plane ticket a few days later eye called him and let him know eye'm on my way to Oregon.

He was happy. "Hell yea. *Piru's in the house, Blood! What's your set?*"

"What the fuck does that mean?" eye asked, confused.

"Nothing, dawg eye'm just glad you're coming up to P-Town!"

"Eye can't wait."

"It's me and you, brothers for life."

"You *knowwww*! Eye am going to mail you the flight itinerary. You gonna pick me up?"

"In the white Cutlass hell yea, dawg."

"Bet.

That night eye thought about my future. Eye was all of 19 years old, fresh out the Army, no sense of direction, and needed a job. Maybe Portland would be a great start, not knowing Oregon was a racist ass state.

Eye pulled out Chad letters and read them over, happy with my decision to visit a place eye never been let alone heard much of. It was an invigorating experience for me, running away from home again and hoping for a new start.

Eye loved Mom but eye hated that man she dated. Why didn't he just move out and leave us alone? Eye have been the one consistent man in Mama's life, and with Jimmy there eye was starting to hate.

Them both.

Letters to Pharoah
From Chadrick Render

Well Blood I thought enought West 4 DLB's in this shit Blood. A West 4 with that Girl you use to go with, A Blood I Don't need to meet her B-cuzz if she can break my Nigga's heart she aint worth meeting let alone looking at Blood. B's 4 & 4 Fuck all crabs gangs (L). A But West Been 4 the reason I say West all the of the time is B-cuzz that's were the Bloods hang, and the Crabs hang on the (Eastside) the Fuck side. a so what's Been up with you lately, l just got your other tape so a nigga's on lock down shited that what yall think im a player 4 life like yall said on that tape L-dog Westside 4 life. a are you going to do that 4 a nigga you know when you go to the youth fair, get me a shirt with my picture on it, yeah on the front and on the Back l want my mom's name or something l tell you later and know l don't want no girl's name not even lowergo's name on my shit Blood. a But a nigga is just chilling doing nothing really, yeah yall was tacking a lot of shit on that last tape But that's okay B-cuzz l liked it But im going to Beat your home girl shit 4 hard day.

CHADRICK RENDER

Sunrise
Oct 23, 1976

Sunset
July 27, 1997

"Oh" tell Kelvin thanks for the picture it looks really good. Hell I wish Mark could draw like that let alone look up to me the way my shorty does Mr. <u>Kelvin</u>. A West ☦ with Puffy anyways, and when are you ☒ trying to come ☦ here on spring break or something well when even if you are let a nigga know in advanced or if you're going to surprise me let J.R. them know okay alright. Damn I needs to go over Savann house and get my Carmera from him so I can take my ass some pictures and shit Blood. a I wrote Yoshi a pretty nasty letter B-cuzz she wanted one I didn't get as nasty as I could have But it was nasty enough 4 her.

  a But a nigga's got to go alright, alright then
    W/B when ever you can see ya
      B's ☦ <u>Blood</u>.

My best friend Chad
My house, Naranja. Hartford Square
1996.

Letter #2

West & Larry a long time Hu! Yeah I
know a but don't trip B-Cuzz I'm still
here Lil Nigga. A tell my Babies thanks
4 the pictures & the letter I Luv it. A
So what's new Blood, nothing here But
problems. My Cousin J.R. Should "B" Back
16th at 8:00 AM But I'll "B" at
school, But I Don't give A Fuck. Damn
Larry Why do we catch all the Fucking
Drama from mom's and Bitches, I know
why B-Cuzz we are the Fucking Best Blood
My Big wrote me not to long ago and
I wrote Back, then he didn't write no
more. Blood I guess Life Just

Chad at Adrianne (the love of his life) Emmanuel's house.

wasn't 4 us. Niggas like us you want ever come by again Lil Nigga, A I'm going to send ya some pictures that's on (Piru Luv) we are Homies, better yet are Brothers yo! and Fuck everyone else. Baby Boy don't worry at all this shit B-cuzz God Luv's us and that shits real. A I might send Yoshi A picture 4 X-mas Just B-cuzz I still like her I Lil. But I'll give you 1st drips on the pictures. Well see ya Love ya! Lopes 4 Blood.

Letter #3

aug 15, 1996

What up Baby "L" what's been popping nothing much here. Damn you be writting your ass off a but I like that. "Oh" why didn't you ~~call~~ call me back yet Why Man!!!

Q when are you going to be getting out of the army and when you do get out what are you going to do. But anyways what's been happen with you "oh" I haven't forgotten about your pictures I just have to find you some okay. So what is your mother saying about you getting out or did she ~~say~~ say anything about it gpt. damn I really don't have anything to say so I'm going to close this ~~ugly~~ ugly letter sorry. Bye, Bye love you lots

54 | Prison

Letter #4

2/20/97

West † larry west Been Happening with you Blood. ain't shit here But Bad times I sending you a lil something. yes I gave Puffy some 2 to "B" on target Blood. I'm sending you these so "B" happy okay. I really don't have much to say But could you do me A lil something Could you give one of these pictures to My auntie. thanks a lot. I would do it Myself But I'm out of stampes right Now you know. Damn its like everything I want to use My stampes 4 something like this I don't have none sorry Man. Well I hope you enjoy this picture I'll send you some more later when I get them out okay. So let puffy have 40 2 B-cuzz you will B getting yours soon trust me on that Blood. Love ya Chadrick Daquan Render.

"CHAD"

C
H
A
D
R
I
C
K

My best friend forever.
You will NEVER be replaced, Red Eyes.
Eye will keep your memory alive!

These trials are only to test your faith
To show that it is strong and pure

It is being tested
As fire test and purifies gold
And your faith is far more
Precious to God than mere gold
So if your faith remains strong
after being tried by fiery trials
it will bring you much praise
and glory and honor on the day
when Jesus Christ is
revealed to the whole
world.

1 Peter 1 vs thr the 7th verse

Home Going Service for:

Sunrise:
September 1987

Sunset:
July 1997

Prison

Pharoah C. Wilson, Jr's Freedom
March 1998
11:30 a.m.
Oregon State Penitentiary
Sweet Home Baptist Church
69 S.W. DOOMSDAY Lane
Rev. Dr. God vs. Satan

<u>1 Corinthians 6:18</u> *Flee from sexual immorality. Every other sin a person commits is outside the body, but the sexually immoral person sins against his own body.*

A Time to be Born: Pharoah Wilson, Jr has survived four bitter miserable years of rape only to grow up a confused teenager. Learning to hate himself, he fell into a dark vortex of problems dealing with people twice his age that used his young body for carnal pleasure. That would lead to his own freedom being snatched away by the very men that killed his best friend.

A Time to Grow: Educationally, Pharoah loved reading, writing and researching but in his heart, mind, body and soul he was dying. No one listened to his pain yet everyone had something to say about what he was doing wrong, calling him a faggot and rejected him because of his lifestyle that he never brought around those he loved. Those he loved persecuted him when he needed them the most.

A Time to Reflect: Pharoah Wilson snitched on the men who he thought murdered his best friend Chad and he received death threats on his life but he never stopped cooperating with the police. His faith in God was starting to get cloudy as he rejected the Bible and Pastors to find his own way in the world. But going into Hell labeled "Prison," he would rediscover God all over again and his faith never waivered.

A Time to Die and be mourned: On a very sad morning, in March, after his mother made him take a plea bargain, Pharoah sucked up the pain and false accusations, swallowed the death of his best friend and entered a place called Prison where everyone wrote him off and said he would be raped and die in the darkness. Pharoah Wilson died…and left behind the ashes of yesterday…

The Coronation
The King of Erotica
In the making:
PR[I]S/O\N

Someone asked me what "made" me gay. Nothing "made" me anything. Situations eye was in, traumatic things eye was forced to endure, certainly influenced me, but even when eye was being raped as a child eye made a choice to succumb to it, to enjoy it, and to become addicted to it. Yes eye was addicted to the sexual abuse. Our choices lead us along the path. Sure, eye wasn't mentally or physically prepared to comprehend or handle what eye went through, and it wasn't right by a long shot. But at certain points of my childhood eye used to ask him for it, because eye grew to enjoy it, and even then eye didn't know it was wrong. Four years of rape when eye was a child certainly influenced it, molded my young mind like a potter does wet clay and whatever shape was formed, its put in a kettle and hardened and glazed and fixed up and celebrated on a mantel. And by the time it ended when eye was ten years old, eye had grown to enjoy and like what was done so eye lived my life chasing my anger throughout my teenage years, sleeping with people twice my age to replace what was no more. That's all eye'll say. Eye'm bisexual. Eye've been this nearly all my life. Eye love men and women equally. And whoever eye choose to be with knows my orientation. Eye'm man enough to be honest and let whoever eye deal with choose to take it further. Everyone is different; accept people for who they are. All gay and bi men are different individually. Don't mash me together with other gay or bisexual muthafuckahs because

NONE OF THEM was Pharoah C. Wilson goddamn Jr. Everyone's pain was their own. Generalizing a group of people into what you wanted them to be was a form of discrimination. The prejudiced in the gay community was astounding. The HATE eye've experienced in the gay community never bothered me. In fact eye could give a fuck if a gay or bi Niggah liked me or not. Eye'm learning to love me. You can't even get gays to agree on anything outside of BeYAWNsay Knowles in online forums with all the bashing that goes on if you don't like their favorite musical entertainer, style of dress or choice of food. The ONLY being that can decipher the human species is God, the Creator. If you don't believe in him then that's *your* Free Will and *your* choice. If a person is gay, bi, or transgender embrace people for who they are. And stop stuffing them in a generalized box because we're ALL different.

In my life eye have been tried for purity for a very long time. Years, in fact, dating back to when eye started watching the Jackson 5 cartoons on Sunday, just before Church. And probably months before *that*. Eye grew up watching Mama smile when she had it all, pat herself on the back when she held down sometimes two jobs to make it work and was married, with a husband who always had secret bitterness that eye wasn't his son. But at the time eye didn't even know he was my step father; eye always *assumed* he was my biological father because he bought me McDonald's every Friday and took me to Toys R Us and always hugged and showed me love. So imagine my surprise, after this man groomed me, turned around and brutally raped me and took it all out of power, control and selfishness.

But as a kid eye was not to know this. He blocked my blessings by testing the purity of my soul. He tried to break the unbreakable because my Mama always prayed for the safety of her children. So a realm of protection surrounded me but the more and more Mama stopped praying, the very moment she cut off God by reducing her prayers to breakfast, lunch and dinner that protection, that realm weakened, and he violated my comfort zone and came all over my ass cheeks when he was done.

And this manufactured me. How could eye pray to God when eye didn't know him yet? When you're 6 years old you still didn't know the world was bigger than your bedroom, the bathroom and Mama's living room.

Eye never stopped believing in God because eye was forced to like him and to love him and eye didn't know him. Eye hadn't made the choice to worship God or believe in Scientology at that age because eye didn't know such a choice had to be made. How could eye when the theory at the time to me didn't exist?

And eye would carry this misconception throughout my life. Pray to a God eye didn't know and never saw, and eye could remember a few times eye prayed for him to show me his face without peeking around the darkness and over the years he had.

He showed me. He showed me when my uncle's daughter took my virginity and opened my eyes and he showed me when she wound up pregnant when eye turned 11, revealing and destroying the myth that storks carried babies 'cause honey if they did then my cousin was a big, black ass stork.

Where's her beak and where are the feathers. Eye could remember feathers in my hair when eye used to eat her pussy, from a hole in one of Mama's pillows on her water bed, back when sleeping on water was today's version of Jesus or Peter walking on water, but don't take your eyes off Jesus if you do. You'll get swallowed by whales.

And my older cousin swallowed my virginity like a good plate of greens and cornbread. Always wearing long floral dresses to fool the elders but when she pulled it up making my dick hard she didn't have on *any* panties and she would beat me with an extension cord if eye didn't eat her pussy to her expectations and if eye didn't fuck her, topping the last performance. Eye feared her so much that when she came around eye was unnaturally quiet and barely said two words to her.

God showed his face when eye slept with people twice my age. "Baby, wait till you marry to have sex. Keep yourself pure," Mama used to tell me and eye was already fucking.

Yet older people in the 'Hood that were married were fucking me and watching me fuck them through the reflection of mirrors, doing it on the washer, dryer and the nightstand.

Eye was barely 14. He showed himself again, after being raped in Perrine by The Pail Man (from PHAROAH), and God showed himself again a few weeks later when I was beat up and dragged into the bushes by the Circle (pink duplexes behind Lee's Grocery store) by two bullies who eye always hated. Even when they raped me, they couldn't fuck. The times eye wanted to laugh, but eye didn't because a) it wasn't a laughing matter and b) eye still had the mentality that eye was put here for men to misuse and mistreat me. It was molded into me for four years. Um. Eye survived. It didn't kill me; it made me stronger. God showed himself in every major situation in my life in the form of my sanity and survival; but eye denied his presence because eye was too busy chasing my self-hatred and the weakness of my (the) flesh. God showed himself AGAIN when Mom and eye fell out when eye was 19, because, back then, eye thought eye was grown. Eye thought eye knew more than my mother and eye bought a plane ticket and flew to Oregon to stay with my best friend, running from my problems. Eye needed to get out of Mama's house, and eye was determined to do just that. God showed himself in that situation by allowing Satan to attack me, just as long as he didn't take my life, for disrespecting my mother. My days were numbered and I didn't even know it.

Eye had never been to Oregon, and eye was glad eye went. Eye hadn't been on that side of the world (well eye was born in Salinas, California but eye had no memory of that) and eye needed to see this. Eye remember when the plane arrived in Portland, Oregon, in 1997. It circled a huge mountain topped with snow. It was one of the most beautiful things eye had ever seen in my life. Chad was at the airport to pick me up and when we saw each other silliness met silliness again and we were ranking on people like in the old days and talking about everybody and hugging so much we just couldn't believe we were in each others' lives again.

    He changed, though. And not in a bad way, no. His voice was more polite and he was in college. Eye was proud of him, that he was going to Portland State University. He recently made the newspaper in high school. That he played three sports and still had like a 4.0. Big upgrade from the Perrine, Florida days, when his grades were about to take that unnatural plummet to hell. Eye remembered eye used to do his homework, while he thought about selling drugs. Chad's passion was simple. He wanted to be a better man than his father, and he wanted to make enough money so his mother didn't have to ever work again. Chad also wanted a daughter. He wanted to terrorize his daughter's Prom Date when the time came. When he first told me eye was laughing so hard eye almost threw up.

    And he was sent to Oregon to better his life and wound up getting murdered there. That's the irony. No matter where you live you have an entirely new set of dilemmas and problems. Eye'm so glad he never sold drugs, no matter how much he wanted to. Something in Chad never let him give up or stop fighting and that rubbed off on me. Eye never met a more humble person. He practically raised himself since he was ten years old. And that's why we were so close. We kept each other going. The one thing Chad always longed for, that his guardian's tried to keep from him, was his mother. Chad confided everything to me. And some things eye won't say, because if he specifically asked me to keep it between me and him, even in his death, eye will HONOR his wish. But the few things eye do reveal Chad really didn't give a fuck if it got out. It was no secret that Chad's mom did drugs at the time. Chad used to be angry about it, but he never judged or disrespected her. When Chad was sent to Oregon, he said he didn't want to leave his mother, but once he realized he needed a future, something his mother could be proud of, he went. Leaving life as he knew it behind. All his friends. His upbringing. Goulds.

Chad didn't go to Oregon for Chad. Chad went for his mother and never told anybody his true intentions, but me. His Mama was his secret life source. This drove Chad to the brink of destruction. Chad didn't like South East Portland, which, pretty much, was the good part of town. North East Portland was a place his guardian's warned him to stay away from, but he would wind up over there anyway. That's where most of the blacks were, and eye didn't care how you tried to live around white people and dance to their music and eat their food. Part of you will always gravitate towards your own kind. Wrestling became Chad's passion. Sure, he also played football, and excelled, but he loved to wrestle. This little pint sized best friend of mine, about 5 feet 4, throwing Niggahs on their big asses like it wasn't shit. He rose up the popularity list. His wrestling got him a national spotlight. A spotlight he never anticipated. He used to write me letters and send me pictures and post cards. His guardians always pushed him to be the best and do the best. And eye believed in this, until eye went to visit Chad in Oregon and he revealed the shade. He revealed the lies. He told me one thing that not only pissed me off, but eye cut his guardian's off, without even telling them.

They lied to him. Chad and eye were sitting in his room one day. He was showing me all the wrestling photos. All his accomplishments. Of course eye was proud of him, but Chad could care less about those accomplishments. He down played them.

"Why, man? You should be proud."

"Eye'm not, Pharoah." Eye always liked how he said my name. Always made me smile.

"Why?"

Eye was still flipping through pictures. He told me to take the ones eye wanted. Shit, eye wanted them all.

"You know they lied to me to get me to win."

Eye slowly looked up at him. He told me this before but I didn't say anything. "Lied about what?"

He smiled bitterly and sat next to me. Eye put the book up. Pictures could wait. He looked under the door to make sure passing shadows weren't lurking. When it was all good, he looked in my eyes. "They promised me eye could see my mother if eye won the wrestling championship. Eye put my all into it, even in practice eye sucked up what made me a winner because in the back of my mind eye knew eye could see my Mom. When eye won the wrestling championship they did everything in their power to ensure eye didn't get to talk to my mother."

"Ah, man, yo. Are you serious?"

Hot tears fell down his face and he hugged me and eye hugged him and he said, "Eye just want to lay eyes on my mother, Pharoah and they keeping me from her."

Eye died inside. Chad longed for Mom. He loved his mother unconditionally. Eye didn't care what she did in life; he had his mother on a pedestal, and his favorite Aunt Tanka on a pedestal. Tanka's kids were Chad's universe. Jason, Erika and Kim. Chad pretty much raised them as if they were his children. His brother Wand, who was locked up (at the time) was Chad's source of inspiration. Chad adored his big brother, and just because he was in prison didn't mean shit to Chad. That's his brother and he was going to stick by him no matter what. Chad always asked about Jason, Erika and Kim and part of him was mad eye was in Oregon because eye was his link to talk to his family when eye was at home. Eye used to call three ways so he could talk to his family, and he told me to never let his Guardian's find out.

Chad and eye stayed up all night talking once eye got settled at his Guardian's home. His cousin, who went to junior high school with my Mom and his Filipino wife, eye didn't like her at all, was Chad's *worse* nightmare he told me. When they greeted me eye was cordial and doing all the little shenanigans Mom taught me, but once Chad and eye went in the room and eye set my bags and suit case down, his drawings all over the wall, and my picture in his mirror, he said, "Don't fall for that shit, Pharoah."

"What do you mean?"

"They are fake. They will smile in your face and stab you in your back."

"Then why are you still living here?"

"Eye have nowhere to go."

"What about your girlfriend? How does she feel about it?"

"Komingo?" Mingo was African, and her African mom was married to a white man, and living large in Portland. "Nah, eye tried. Komingo's parents even told me eye could live with them."

"And what happened?"

"My hot tempered cousin." His Male Guardian. "He threatened to show up on her door step raising hell if eye did. So eye'm trapped in this house. Can you believe one time this man actually pissed in my shoes so eye couldn't go out with her."

"Wow, eye remember you told me that in one of your letters and on the phone."

"Eye'm trapped in here. They try to control everything eye do. So some shit eye do they will never know."

"And what's that?"

He was quiet, staring at me. Swinging a red bandana around on his finger.

And it still didn't dawn on me.

Chad's *favorite* color was red and his nick name was Red Eyes. He had two key chains made with Baby Boy (me) and Red Eyes (his) that read "Best friends forever." Eye put one of the key chains on my keys and began to enjoy Portland.

It was *so* different there. Portland natives called soda "Pop" and eye got in plenty arguments over it whenever eye went to a fast food joint and asked for a soda. They looked at me like eye was a Martian. One cashier asked, "Sir, what is a soda?" And eye was like "Um, Sprite, Pepsi…"

She smiled, dismissing my comments with a wave of her hand. "Oh. You mean you want a Pop."

Eye slapped my forehead in mock horror.

When my best friend was murdered eye was devastated. Eye think that was the single most hurtful thing eye have ever gone through in my life. My best friend stuck by my side since childhood and he died without me by his side. Eye had no clue he was murdered until the next day. Eye saw it on the news. And when he face flashed on the screen eye tried to dig up the earth itself. Eye didn't eat or sleep right for weeks. Eye withdrew into myself. Eye stopped loving and caring for any and everything. Eye used to confide in him all the time and he always had my back and was very protective of me.

Eye remember back to July 27, 1997. The day and year he died. We had a good day. Eye had his gold rims installed on his car for him, since he had to work and eye was driving around feeling good because he felt good. Eye had just gotten fired from Circuit City because they found out eye was stealing merchandise, and eye was because eye was selling it to have money to survive. My mother said eye wouldn't make it on my own and she said hell would freeze over before we spoke again so eye had a point to prove. Eye told myself eye would NEVER call her for help. So stealing and selling merchandise provided for me temporary relief, till eye was caught and eye didn't apologize for it.

But on July 27th, eye was enjoying spending time with my best friend, not knowing it would be the last day eye ever saw him alive. Talking about this thirteen years later seems so foreign to me. Tears fall down my face remembering the pain and grief of losing my best friend. But eye remember driving Chad's car, getting the rims installed, then getting his stereo system (eye bought for him) installed. Eye was enjoying (at the time), for a second, another man's car as mine and once eye took it to him at his place of employment (Belmont Terrace, a nursing home—he loved working there, and the elderly loved him!), eye had never seen his eyes glow so brightly.

He loved that pearl white Cutlass. It was a 70's model, and you couldn't tell him anything about that car.

When he saw the rims on his car he smiled so big eye melted. "Is this my baby," he said, running his hands over the hood of his car. "Sitting on the all gold cheeses!" "Cheeses" was his word for gold rims. He looked at me, giving me a big hug. "Thanks, dawg! This is what eye always wanted! My car totally fixed up! The Hoes g'on hate me! Eye love you, dawg."

"Eye love you too, bruh!"

Things were going along swell until one of Chad's friends came to visit him, to see his car. And *that* friend brought *another* friend Chad and eye didn't know.

Confused, Chad looked at me. "Who is that niggah with Toine?"

"I don't goddamn know!" eye said, eyeing the other dude suspiciously. "Eye'm visiting Portland. Eye don't know who any of your friends are."

"*Toine* is my friend. But eye don't know that other Niggah."

Chad agreed to take us all for a spin in the car. So when ole boy made his way to the front seat eye walked right past him and said, "The back seat is back there."

Chad, laughing, said, "Yea the front is for my brother."

Nuff said. Stuff was pretty uneventful. Four black men driving around N.E. Portland, blasting music and having a good time. Chad was so happy his car came together. One of his wishes (he once told me) was to have his car fixed up, so he can say it's his and then he wouldn't want to live anymore. Be careful what you ask for, eye told him.

Chad's friend, Toine, asked him, "Yo, homie. Fam. We should go pick up these two bitches across the way."

Eye was down. Shit, eye flew across the country, from Miami to Portland to kick it with my best friend so eye knew eye was going.

"Ok," he said, unsure of himself.

"Eye'm going," eye said, sure of it.

"Um, no you're not," Chad said, blurting it out.

Eye looked at him sideways. "What?"

"Yea, man," Toine said. "Just us, man. So there's room for the girls."

"Niggah this is my best friend and my best friend's car and Eye'm not going no fucking where." Now eye felt betrayed by my own best friend.

Chad was telling me, again, "*No*, you can't go with me to get these bitches," with two niggahs in his back seat that had him marked for death.

Eye would find out the next day that Chad saying "No" saved my life. God showed himself verbally, through the wavering soul of my best friend. Because if Chad would have said "Yes," we both would have been shot at the place he was told the two Hoes lived, and the place was abandoned.

God showed himself through accusations of sex abuse against a kid. Eye still couldn't believe people would sink so low. Eye was only 19 years old. A year past 18, and already my own kind turned against me, had my best friend killed, showed no emotion, lied, lied, lied, then tarnished my image because eye was the only one cooperating with the police to bring them closer to the murderer.

Then God showed himself again when they put me in the same prison with the goons that killed my best friend. What type of racist fucking state does that? Um, fucking Oregon. Four percent black and half of them in jail, under Ballot Measure 11. Measure 11 was a law that high jacked Niggahs, giving them a mandatory 8 years day for day or more for getting your black asses out of line in Oregon.

Stay in your place. They tried to pin that shit on me but it didn't stick because they didn't have DNA evidence or NOTHING to tie me to this so-called bogus ass crimes, but they won through my ignorance because eye didn't know the so-called Public Defender (or Public Pretender) begged me to plea bargain just so he could collect a big paycheck. As far as eye know my lawyer could have been a snitch from a jail cell in a Burberry suit and sent to court to represent you or get you to sign a plea bargain, even if they have lack of evidence and a bunch of circumstantial bullshit.

OK. Eye'm black. Tarnish my name, reduce it to 11517837 and call it a fucking day.

Eye had a solid alibi and someone, an unexpected friend named Tracy, stepped forward and wrote me a letter. He told me everything, how my so-called victims were related by blood to the very one that helped get my best friend murdered. I was in shock. Eye showed my lawyer this letter so the lawyer agreed to talk to Tracy. Tracy said it was part of the conspiracy, that Chad was murdered, that we knew, and the plan was to take me down as well for "snitching." And when eye started cooperating with the police, that angered the members of the Blood Gang even more to either take me out or to shut me up. So eye was marked for death. Eye felt good, because eye told Mom of the witness who could prove eye didn't molest a kid, and my lawyer felt good about it as well. That was my smoking trump card, and instead of thanking God eye thanked Tracy and everyone but God.

Wouldn't have taken me 3 seconds to thank the Lord. But it wasn't even on my mind or in my heart. So God vanished, and when he did the enemy took it all.

Even Tracy's reputation.

One day, in one of the dorms at the Inverness jail, eye was sitting with the infamous Tom Curtis at one of the dinner tables, watching the news. Inmates loved the news. They were on it. They knew who did what before you even got there. He asked me did eye write anything, since eye used to sneak to the law library and type my stories and hide it in my paperwork so it wasn't confiscated. Eye told him eye had. Tom smiled, skinny ass. But he was good people.

"What about poems? You got some?"

"Yea, eye do."

"Eye need one for a girl."

Eye shook my head. "You sound like all the other dudes in here. In the past month eye must have written over a hundred poems. Luckily eye keep a copy to prove eye wrote it."

He was quietly watching TV.

"Tom?" Eye was studying his face.

He was pointing at the screen. "Isn't that your boy Tracy, your witness?"

Eye slowly looked at the TV, the breath caught in my throat. Yes. He was on TV. And the next few words eye heard made me close my eyes and say "Oh, God."

And a scandal has unfolded. Tracy Ross, a 17 year old high school student, was really a 30 year old man imposter. More details at 7.

The room was spinning. "No, this can't be happening. He's 30?" eye asked, watching Tracy's life dissect right before my very eyes. Huge tears fell. Eye couldn't breathe. His picture flashed on the screen, and the high school he attended imposing as a student made me wanna puke.

"Oh my God, Pharoah. Welcome to Oregon, dude. Chad's murderers want *your* ass in jail. They just secretly called the police and exposed all his shit so he's discredited from getting on the witness stand. Man if anything proved your innocence, it's this latest development. If you weren't innocent this wouldn't be happening. He was getting away with posing as a *seventeen* year old and illegally selling cars across the Canadian border. Now he's on his way to jail."

Eye wasn't hearing him. Eye lay my head on the table and refused to open my eyes. God showed himself. You put anything before me eye will take it away. Including my freedom.

And my only key witness.

The next few months unraveled horribly. Eye lost Tracy as a key witness, as his life played out all over the news for weeks. Eye couldn't believe even eye didn't know he was really 30. Hell eye didn't even know he was going to high school. He damn sure didn't look 17, so how in the hell he pulled that off? Then the news showed his real picture from an old year book. Eye was simply taken aback. Eye lay in my bunk, watching the news heart sick. He had fake documents, fake birth certificates, fake military papers. The whole nine. Whoever put in that secret snitch phone call exposed all his shit. Eye didn't understand. Maybe because eye was just 21 years old and the year eye became legal to buy alcohol was the year eye was locked up and would stay locked up for the next four years.

What kind of people had eye made my friends when eye was visiting Oregon? These were the people Chad took me around and introduced me to. Eye didn't like them at first but Chad *assured* me they were good people and when he died they really showed me what they really thought of him. They hated him.

And hated me for being so close to him.

Eye was still going to court. Eye would stand up and be a man. But my manhood was slain when Mama took the wheel, and she wasn't bullshitting. She made all the decisions for me while locked up.

Mama and the family intervened. Family intervention. Before eye was to go to court, the judge summoned me. I was shackled and transported to the court house. Once eye arrived, eye was ushered in the judge's chambers. She called Mama on the speaker phone. My Mama, a FED, on the speaker phone in Oregon from Miami, told me to take the plea bargain or basically lose my family from my fucking stupidity.

Eye was angry. Very angry. "Are you on their side, Mama?"

"No, baby. But this is a crime against a kid and the people who had your best friend murdered are all behind this and we can't prove it. Those motherfuckers know you didn't do that. Where's the DNA evidence? They don't have any DNA evidence and they know it."

When she said it the lawyer and Judge lowered their heads. Didn't say anything. And eye was staring at them.

"So why should eye sign a plea bargain, Mama? Eye didn't do this. If eye did eye would man up but Mama you are the one who always told me to stand up for what's right."

"This isn't play school, Pharoah. You made this bed."

"Eye know that. All eye did was the right thing. Cooperating with the police to find Chad's killers. He was my best friend. Eye couldn't just sit by and do nothing! Eye shouldn't have to be punished for that!"

"Everyone on the jury will be white. Your judge is white. Your prosecutor is white. Your lawyer is white. You are in a predominantly white state. Eye warned you not to fuck with Oregon. You go there on vacation and leave on probation."

"Mom."

She said more sternly, "You are black with no record. Your Mama is a FED and not a welfare case, they already mad about that. That your Mama has some sense. They have no evidence, none, Pharoah. And they know this. Where is the DNA? If they had DNA they wouldn't be asking you to plea for a lesser charge. They would stick it to your ass. But that's white people. They love destroying our black sons. They are probably gloating now."

Funny thing was *no* one in the room protested what she said. This made me shake in my chair.

"If you go to court you are already hung. Your defendants are bitter blacks who had your best friend killed and are after you for talking too much. Take the plea. You can be a dumb ass, and lose, doing 8 years day for day. No good time. You won't be the same, Pharoah." She was near tears, eye knew this had to be destroying her.

"Mama, eye'm going to court."

"TAKE THE FUCKING DEAL!" Eye sat straight up, quiet. The judge smiled. Victory in her eyes.

My hand shaking, and my own self talk telling me NO DON'T DO IT PHAROAH, God showed himself when eye signed. Hot tears streamed down my face and for an instant eye saw empathy in the judge.

Eye didn't sign just a plea bargain, pleading no contest, eye signed a pact with God that eye endorse seeing you for years yet putting mortal man and my own sins and carnal pleasures and immaturity and recklessness before GOD, but now my life begins.

Now begin the terrible climb back from an infamous piece of shit to grace.

And when eye get there eye must say Thank you God.

When eye did time eye didn't shed one fucking tear. Eye refused to cry. When eye felt myself about to cry eye would bite down hard on my tongue and it'd go away. If eye could survive four years of rape and four years of high school eye could and would survive this.

Eye was Nassau, Bahamian; we didn't fold when facing a dilemma. But now wasn't the time to embrace Bahamian values, when you just signed a pact with God that eye would never lose faith in him and never let it waiver ever again.

Eye needed to be embracing God. But that didn't mean eye wasn't still a sinner because eye was young. Eye was an old soul but eye wasn't a 40 year old. Eye was still 21.

Doing time was rough. Eye could not believe eye was going to prison. My decisions and the choices eye made in life got me here. Eye never blamed anyone for my problems, eye always owned up to them. Some more reluctantly than others, but now eye'm in prison for a crime against a child when eye love children and eye didn't know how to embrace that. So eye didn't.

Eye gave it to God. By then it was out of my hands, but eye had to go through the motions to prove to myself eye was worthy of life.

When eye was bussed from the dorm of the Inverness jail to the infamous Oregon State Penitentiary, maximum security, eye was shaking my damn head. Eye wasn't a violent *or* a hateful person, even though eye've hated my own self for years. So eye never understood why they sent me to a maximum security prison.

Being shackled in a white jumpsuit, eye felt the lowest eye had ever felt. My mother did this for a living, dealing with federal inmates but this wasn't the cozy FEDS with sparkling windows and marble floors.

This was state prison. Nothing sparkling about that. Eye shook the entire time. Eye was so in fear eye was about to call out for my mother, but the mistake of calling out for mortals was the sole reason eye fell from grace. Eye still hadn't called out to God.

So eye did. Eye closed my eyes and talked to God the entire time. Telling him eye didn't know what to do or what to say.

And within seconds my nervousness vanished.

My arrival at OSP was scary. Eye was in prison. Eye couldn't believe this shit.

When eye arrived, eye think there were about four other people with me. We agreed to make a pact, that, despite our crimes, we were all young and we would be like brothers. And we would hold true to that motto, even when doing time got rough with predators walking the yard, scalping, trying to find the weakest of the bunch so he could move in his cell and rape him all night. Eye was also told to stay away from an inmate named Chicken George and Clayton. They said Clayton liked to apply baby oil on his naked body during count time so the guards could see his meat and that Chicken George hog tied his young victims and gave them old man dick till they passed out.

Eye was warned of all this before eye got there. So eye knew what to look out for. But it's one thing to look out for it before you got to prison. Because once eye got there eye found out it was bigger than just looking for it. This was a place designed to tear you down and destroy you, being amongst the bitter, cold and angry with a concrete jungle was the scariest thing of my life. The scariest time of my life.

Eye was anxious to start doing my time and get on with my life.

But eye shook like a hooker in front of the state senate. Gotta tell how Bill Clinton's cum got on my good Easter Sunday dress.

Getting off the transportation bus in shackles, eye felt like a slab of meat. Being introduced into mind control slavery.

Eye was stronger than eye gave myself credit for. Eye was still 13 Bravo Field Artillery *whooooaaaa* and eye was still a motherfucking soldier, whether eye was out or not. Military thinking had become my whole thought process as eye entered that Concrete Jungle surrounded by thirty feet walls.

Guard towers surrounding the place. When eye told one of my friends back at the Inverness Jail (12926272, the number eye was reduced to), that they were shipping me to OSP he was shaking.

"Oh, no! That's a Mad House! Oh, God Pharoah eye pray for your safety."

Eye had God deep in my heart. Eye feared no one, not even man.

But that all changed when eye was on that bus, being lead to the Blair Witch Project: PRISON.

My life has been reduced to this.

Eye was very upset with myself, that my decisions led me here. Despite it all, eye blamed nothing and no one but myself.

Eye may not have done the crime eye was accused of, but as of that day eye stopped making excuses. This was real life, not TV. This wasn't a stage play with directors and casting managers and background lights and scripts.

Eye saw all the prison movies. Almost always you saw the submissive one being approached to be fucked or raped.

So eye was a Miami-Dade County Niggah, Goulds up in the Salem, Oregon camp.

After going through the transition, given light blue long sleeved shirts and blue jeans bearing an orange OREGON iron on, eye got dressed. They gave me some ugly ass shoes.

One of the guards, a short male, looked me over.

He smiled and eye lowered my head.

"Hey, there," he said, walking up to me. "You must be Miami."

"You know me?" eye asked, afraid to look up. Felt like eye was being singled out.

"No, eye don't," said officer Wadley. "But eye heard you are an amazing poet. My friend works at the Inverness jail. He told me to look out for you, that you have a raw talent for words."

Eye looked up and smiled. "Really?"

"Yea, Officer Gaston."

"Oh, yea. He good people."

"Something is off about you."

"Off?"

"Yea. Looking at you, you don't belong in a place like this."

"Tell me about it. Famous last words."

"OSP isn't all that bad. Eye hope you weren't scared up before you got here."

"Yea a friend was telling me it's the mad house."

"Here's the ropes, Miami. Stay away from the tobacco trade. Don't snitch, mind your business, and always eat. Eat all you can."

"Why?"

"You'll understand if it ever happens to you."

For some reason that made sense.

Σ

Eye was given a cell in D-Block. There was honor Block A, and C block, you have to have a job to be in A or C, and there was a waiting list for A Block. A lonnggg waiting list.

An honor block and a waiting list in prison, laugh out loud, sounded like section 8 sucking of the welfare line.

There was a long pill line as eye crossed the beige so-called marble floors. Air smelled of depression, lights dimmed of imperfection casting ghosts, not light upon those awaiting medicine.

Eye was holding my property and my clothes, my squeaking shoes against the floor disheartening.

They looked like zombies in the pill line.

One inmate, a big Niggah, went slap off.

"Eye want my motherfucking meds!"

Oh, yea. Wouldn't be talking to him.

Eye kept my head ducked.

When eye was approaching D Block, eye walked into the unit, huge as hell. Eye looked up. Cells seemed to go on for miles.

"Oh my God. Be with me. Eye just entered the lion's cave."

Eye was walking past cells on the second tier. Another officer showed me where to go.

The Block officer, Miss Storm, looked at me, with dents all in her face.

"She used to be a stripper," said the guard. "She got good pussy too."

Eye was laughing.

"What?"

"You are crazy. That ugly thang used to strip?"

He gazed into my eyes. "Eye used to own the club."

Walking up the tier, the block officer opened my cell. A few inmates, who didn't have jobs, or were indigent, were looking at me. There goes the whispers.

"Damn that Niggah fine as fuck."
"Look at his eyes."
"Hey, pretty lady."

Eye paused at the bars and slammed my boots against it, he jumped a hundred feet back, throwing up his fists, "Bitch you touch me eye will go postal on your monkey ape looking ass."

And walked off.

What the fuck am eye doing? Might as well play as crazy as the men in the pill line so word travels about me fast.

Eye walked in the cell, and a troll looking Niggah got off the bottom bunk.

The guard said, "Get ready for Chow, Miami."

Eye faced the guard with fear in my eyes, dropping my shit on the floor.

He mouthed "Good luck."

Why was he whispering?

Suddenly, eye knew why.

Guard separated himself from inmate.

We're back on opposite sides.

He had a job to do, and eye had one to do.

Eye turned and faced the midget.

"Wassup, Niggah?" he said. "What's your name?"

"Miami."

"Mighty chummy with the guard."

"We went to school together. Couldn't stand his dumb ass," eye lied.

He laughed; eye barely smiled. Tried to look Ford tough and was soft as white on melting snow.

Eye opened the bottom drawer and threw in my things.

"You got the top bunk, tall ass Niggah," he said, a tattoo by his eye. Of a tear. Oh, boy. Gang banger. They were like shit stains throughout the institution.

You were either a Blood. Or a Cripp, at least that was what it appeared to be.

Eye would later learn about Vice Lords.

And the Aryan Nation.

Skin Heads.

"What you in for?" Inch, my new cell mate asked.

"Being young and goddamn dumb," eye joked, and he started laughing. Eye wasn't ready for him to know why eye was there. Eye was still accepting it myself.

And to think Chad's killers got off with making up lies on me. And Sheba, my so-called friend telling cops eye told her eye was raped. Yea, eye did tell her that but her fake, late ass was just mad that all those attempts to throw her dry ass pussy at me failed when she found out eye threw this asshole like pussy to those Niggahs.

Rejection was the marshmallow man thumping through the inner city of her mind like the Ghostbusters's movie.

Eye sat on the bottom bunk with him. He glanced at me.

"You're different."

"Different how?" eye asked. He was trying to figure me out.

"Eye don't know. You seem reserved, to ya'self."

"Yea, eye am very anti social."

"You ain't on that shit are you?"

Bwahahahaha, funny. Eye wanted to laugh like count Dracula.

"Naw, Eye'm on that cough syrup like you."

"Oh, Niggah!" He pulled out the cough syrup. "Hell yea, dawg. Sippin' on some sizurp."

"Oh my damn, three 6 mafia."

"It's the 666 Mafia," he corrected.

"Evil bunch of Niggahs, huh?" He poured some in a cup, taking it to the head. Then another cup, then another, then another.

Damn.

"Give me some of that," eye said, taking 2 teaspoons of it. That's all.

"Feeling that shit?" he asked, zonked as fuck.

"Yea, eye really feel it," eye joked, rolling my eyes. Eye didn't feel shit and wasn't trying to.

The cell popped and a soul-lacerating bell rang. Oh, God, the sound drove me crazy and made my skin crawl.

"Time for CHOW!" screamed the guard.

Eye got up and followed the line movement.

Once in the Chow Hall eye got in line, and refused to look up, my heart beating out my chest. Eye was about 175 pounds, a small afro going and my scalp dry as fuck. Dandruff forming, and eye didn't have shampoo, just those little bars of soap. The rest of the stuff eye had to buy off the canteen.

Plus eye had to call home, so eye could tell Moms eye was here and safe.

Something told me to look up and eye did. Looking around, eye saw nothing but white men.

Eye shook with fear and ducked my head.

They were mean mugging me hard.

Hesitantly, eye looked up again.

One of the men had a huge swastika on his arm. The Chow Hall was segregated.

Another skin head, red neck was behind me.

He pushed me. "Move it, Nigger. Line in motion. They don't serve coons over here."

"Watch your mouth, buddy!" Eye snapped, turning to face him. *Buddy? Eye sounded so goddamn gay what the fuck was that, Pharoah?*

"Oh you standing up to me nigger?"

"Yea, spick." eye turned and walked up to one of the servers. No one on the food line was black. All skin head motherfuckers.

"What do you want, Nigger? Eye ain't serving no colored boy!" He slammed the spoon down, and the other skin head said, "The fried chicken isn't in this line. Goddamn you ugly bitch how they says it in that one nigger movie written by that nigger bitch YOU SHOLL I'Z UGLAY!"

Before eye could respond an older black man, well kept, neatly trimmed, approached me.

He took me by the hand. He had friendly eyes.

"Young black man, the brothers are on this side of the Chow Hall."

"*Get that nigger in his place, monkey face.*"

"*Coons belong in the woods to be hunted and shot for supper.*"

"*Niggers eat coons, too!*"

Eye followed the brother to the Black Side.

Eye knew deep down in my heart eye would write this account one day; eye just didn't think it would be so soon. Well, it's been 12 years now. After getting my food, string beans, fried chicken and soda (they called POP), eye sat next to the brother who led me over here. His name was Earl. He has been locked up over 20 years and still had his sanity. He introduced me to another man named Big Saint. Eye met Punch, Skeeta, Bam and a host of other Niggahs. Eye knew instantly eye wasn't what the pacific northwest preferred.

Eye was a Goulds Niggah. Eye held my head high.

"Damn eye don't mean to sound so gay but you have a nice smile," said Stressla, the intelligent, bald headed brother of the group.

"Thanks…"

"How long you been here?"

"Just got here a few hours ago," I said, thinking, *Why are you being so goddamn nosey?*

"Where you from?" he asked and I just stared at him for a few minutes. Half the inmates in the Chow Hall stared at me, waiting for the answer.

"Goulds. That's in Miami, Florida."

He stared at me blankly. Never heard of Goulds.

"Goddamn! *Miami!*" he said with a smile.

"Welcome to Miami!" someone sang, referring to Will Smith's big hit.

Eye smiled.

"What you in for?" Stressla asked.

Eye looked him dead in the eyes. "Attempted Sodomy."

They gazed at me. Laughing.

"Yea, right."

"You don't look like you ever stole a candy bar."

"What are you really in for? Credit card scams? Pussy boy crimes?"

"Talk all the shit you want, at least eye got a release date."

That shut his ass right on up. Eye picked up my tray.

"Eye'll take my chances eating with the skin heads."

Eye walked back to the other side, the Niggahs looking at me like eye was crazy. The Skin Heads glared at my skinny ass.

"Oh, no. The coon is back."

"What's the matter? The chicken taste like black pussy? You know black asshole is like imitation crabs, ain't pussy but damn sure smell like one ahahahaha!"

Eye sat down at a table of three, pushing their books on the floor.

"You know what?" eye said. "Eye just wanna eat my fucking food. Don't have time for all this bullshit. If Eye'm a fucking coon bitches you're skinned dogs when you get wet. Stay away from the water Scrappy Do."

Eye ate my chicken in peace once they realized eye was no longer scared.

Chile, eye was frightened as fuck.

But eye had a Poker Face long before there was a Lady Ha Ha.

I meant Lady Gaga.

Eye moved out of Inch's cell in D Block to another cell when eye got a job a few weeks later. He was a good cell mate, but he abused cough syrup a little too much for me. Eye was now in E Block with some dude named Big Cease who got off on counting everything in the cell. From magazines and attire to the actual cell bars. I kept to myself in that cell. We didn't even speak.

Eye hated D Block, OMG, and getting out of Death's Block was one of the best things that happened to me. And that ain't no goddamn accomplishment.

Refused to die in Oregon. At this time eye didn't know that the fucks that murdered my best friend were going to be put in the same facility as me.

If you weren't working or doing something constructive, like snitching on other inmates (one thing eye NEVER did was snitch), you couldn't go to C Block and eye so wanted to move there. Make my stay in prison as comfortable as eye could make it.

Pharoah always kept himself out of prison business 'cause prison business was closed to the world, but running rampant behind those thirty feet brick walls that been up since, what, 1903 or some shit like that?

So taking away an inmate's mail, personal belongings, labeling it contraband, takes away some of their hope to live, especially if they got life. Hell Section 8 housing was starting to look like families stuffed in little houses like jail cells, making you pay a little a month for a bed.

When eye got work it was in the Cafeteria. Eye was there less than a week and wound up getting a proposition to work as a tutor on the Education Floor, which was one of the high paying jobs at about $60 a month (SIXTY DOLLARS A MONTH, MASSA!). Eye wasn't trying to work in the cafeteria. Hell naw. Eye cooked for my Mama and siblings for over 12 years. Wasn't about to cook another four years for thousands of inmates. But getting the job on the Education Floor would come right on time…

Eye made it to the yard.

This was an entirely different world from what eye was used to.

A huge concrete track. Benches lining the gates.

A crummy ass golf course. The weight pile had Niggahs on it looking like prehistoric dinosaurs.

A group of Niggahs approached me and eye put up my fists.

"Calm down lil niggah."

"Oh this one got a set."

"He'll fight, eye like that."

Eye didn't put my fists down. Eye backed up so the fence was behind me.

"Who are you? Eye don't know who you are!" eye said, my eyes narrowing dangerously.

"Calm down lil niggah, shit. He a soldier," said a tall, well-built inmate with easy going eyes. But eye didn't trust it.

"Uncle McAdoo has summoned you," an older inmate said, and eye was like eye don't give a fuck. Nobody summons me.

"And he rarely summons anybody," said the shorter inmate with an attitude.

"Who is that?" eye asked.

"Follow us," they all said.

Eye followed them to the middle of the yard, to what appeared to be a concrete slab. McAdoo, a much older brother, was one of the most respected men in the institution eye would learn.

McAdoo stood up and eye felt like a Ninja Turtle about to address Master Splinter.

"How are you, Miami, right?" he asked.

"Yes, Miami."

"That's where you're from?"

"Yes."

He was skeptical. "Oh, yea? What part?"

"Eye was raised in Goulds, but eye currently lived in Homestead, before eye was arrested."

"Shit. Eye been to Homestead before, is that right? Eye was in the military."

"Really?"

"Homestead Airforce base, right?"

Eye was smiling. "Yes, we stay on 127th Avenue."

"By the little gas station."

"Yes!"

"Eye like you, Miami. He cool, ya'll." He gave me a package in a brown paper bag.

It had soap, toothpaste (real toothpaste, and not that institutionalized shit), a long toothbrush and the bare necessities.

"Only thing eye ask," he said, "is for you to help the next brother who comes through those doors."

Eye shook his hand.

He would be my guardian angel throughout my 4 years 9 months.

After that encounter it took me a long time to go back to the yard. A couple weeks later my cell was popped open and eye was told to go to work in the chow hall. Like hell. Eye didn't wanna work in there anymore; bad enough eye had to be in here against my will.

Eye went to the yard instead, meeting new folks. Eye had in my hand my folder, and eye started a book called *The Scorned House of Blue Scars*.

At the Inverness jail eye wrote a book called *A Lighter Shade of Men* but some of the chapters were lost when eye mailed them out.

Eye swear someone in the mail room stole my book.

No time for that now.

Eye sat at one of the tables and eye began to write about Aalexandria Cummings. A single black woman with it all, except a man.

At that point eye knew eye didn't want to write a chick book. But eye started it out with Thelma, Jane (white girl acting sistah) and Aalexandria. She met a doctor named Marlo at her best friend's Gertrude's engagement party. Gertrude was married to fine ass Louisiana boy De'Andre James.

Eye already fell in love with the characters.

When eye was done writing the books opening with those god awful small ass gold pencils, eye read over it.

If eye had thirty arms, hands, fingers and toes, eye still couldn't count the number of men eye sucked, fucked, pussified, bewildered, mystified, conned and Mummified looking for love or searching for some rare form of it and here eye am at age 29, got it all, brand new socks and draws, and still got a leaking roof in a $90,000 condo, a fucking Chrysler 300 M and a leaking roof. Damn shame eye had expensive shit throughout my condo in Blueberry Hills, Lauderhill, Florida and a bitch still had to whip the buckets on a rainy day to catch the water from my leaking roof.

Eye was satisfied. Eye'd tweak it later.

The sun shined brightly. Two males sat in front of me. One said, "How are you."

"Eye'm good," eye said with an attitude.

"What are you writing?" asked the other.

"Ah, its nothing," eye said, folding the paper.

"A letter? Oh, Eye'm Bobby." He was one cool white boy, looked like Drew Carey.

"And Eye'm Tre," said the taller one.

"We're road dogs," said Bobby. "What's your name?"

"Miami."

"Your real name?" asked Tre.

"Pharoah C Wilson, Jr."

"LCDUB!" joked Bobby and eye was grinning.

"L-C-Dub, 'ey?" I said, tired as hell.

"Yea, eye'ma call you that. You seem real cool, family. Why you over here by yourself?"

Tre studied me.

"Just to myself and my thoughts."

"That's just it. Everyone here got a hustle, and you're a free thinker?" Tre asked.

"Yea, eye am like that eye guess." Eye pulled out my paper, spread it on my folder and kept writing.

Tre looked over. "Oh, shit. He's a writer."

"Let us read." He took the papers and I smiled. Bobby read what eye wrote and eye held my breath. Eye mean it was about a chick.

"You got skills, dawg," Bobby said.

Tre said, "Lemme see." He read over it, nodding his head. He couldn't stop reading the page.

"Not bad. Good shit. Good grammar. And you can spell."

"Ha ha," eye said.

"No, man you don't understand. The prison is filled with wanna be writers," Tre said.

"Like Sleepy," Bobby interjected happily.

"Sleepy?" eye asked.

"Yea, his name Anthony. He writes books."

Eye had to meet Sleepy. "For real?"

"Yea, he got skills," said Bobby and Tre nodded in agreement.

"But the boy can't spell worth a damn," Tre went on warmly.

Eye was laughing. "Who is he?"

Tre pointed at him and eye looked across the way. He was about 6 feet, sleepy-looking eyes and his pants sagged.

His swagger was off the chain. He spoke to everyone, Chicos, Mexicans, whites, blacks.

Eye stood up and walked right up to him.

He tucked his chin back, looked me over and smiled, extending his hand.

Eye shook it, squeezed it firmly.

Yea, eye ain't no punk.

"Eye know you?" he asked.

"No, but eye hear you're some kind of writer."

"Yea, eye am an author."

"When can eye read your work? Let me determine that?"

"Eye'm the best writer here."

"You ain't better than me."

"Eye write that street lit," he said.

Eye faked a yawn. "Over and done with that kind of shit, when are you going to *dare* to be different?"

People literally stopped talking.

Then they said, *"Sleepy's good."*

"He writes good stuff."

"Niggah you can't even write."

Eye stared him down. "Whatever you wrote eye will top it, shatter it and walk across that shit."

Eye called him out. "Oh, yea? You write anything?"

"Follow me."

A few Niggahs followed us, smelling drama and it wasn't even that kind of party.

When eye got back to the table, Bobby and Tre spoke to Sleepy.

He had a blue wool skull cap pulled low above his eyes.

Eye handed him the paper with the book eye started.

"One page?" he asked.

"Yea, eye got confidence in that one page."

"And he say he's better." Everyone laughed, except Bobby and Tre.

They looked at me.

He began reading out loud, "If eye had thirty..." He kept reading, entranced by my words. He hopping up and down, fist over his mouth, wide eyed.

He read the back and his minions were like, "Can we read that?"

"Shit, he writing about a bitch. Is she fine, Miami?"

"Yea, she got big tits and good pussy," eye said, observing.

"Does she have a man?" an inmate asked. "Write about me. A gangster who wants to get out the lifestyle and go to college to care for his breezy."

Breezy was another word for "lady."

Eye was taking notes.

"Ok, eye can do that. What's your name?" eye asked.

"Capone. Mone Brown."

Eye analyzed him further. Clean cut, definitely a smooth talker. He was the kinda man Hoes threw their panties at.

He damn sure had a pimp appeal, like he pimped Hoes so my walls went up.

Eye reverted my eyes, didn't let him look in them too deeply.

Con artist, too smooth, eyes bounced when he spoke which means he thought shit up as he went along.

"Eye can put you in the book."

Another guy, named Marlo, dark skinned, said, "Damn, can eye be in the book?"

"Eye have a character named Marlo already."

He was grinning. "Must be destiny."

"Ha, ha. He's a doctor in the book."

"Ok, and he has to be from Louisiana? Eye'm from there. Calliope projects."

"Ok, will do."

"Don't jive me. Eye wanna read that shit."

"Well Eye'm writing by hand."

Sleepy said, "Eye'll see what eye can do. Let me talk to some people."

The stage was set for the rise of:

DAPHAROAH69.

A few days later my cell popped.

"Wilson!"

Eye peaked my head out.

"Education floor!"

"Education floor?" Eye put on my shoes and headed out.

Eye asked one of the inmates where the education floor was. He pointed at a stair case, and opening the door and looking up eye was like goddamn, these are a lot of stairs.

But eye made the climb, not sure of why eye was summoned. Eye didn't know eye was making the climb into the beginnings of my bestselling author destiny.

Eye had a high school diploma, and eye had to drop out of college when eye came to jail.

When eye reached the top floor (goddamn my legs were sore), eye came face to face with a poster hanging on the wall.

DON'T WANT PRISON TO BE A ROTATING DOOR.
JOIN A COGNITIVE PROGRAM.

Eye took the poster down, folded it and stuffed it in my pocket.

Damn sure didn't want prison being a rotating door in my life.

Eye approached the main Desk, run by inmates. Everything was run by inmates. Guards sat back like African chiefs observing and correcting when necessary.

"And you are?" a big, white, burly inmate asked.

"Miami. Eye was summoned up here."

"Oh, yea. Eye heard you're a writer. Eye'm an avid reader. Maybe eye can read your work."

Eye shook his hand. "Eye got you."

"Mrs. Marsters called for you."

I scrunched my face. "Mrs. Marsters? Who the hell is that?"

"She's a sweet old black woman. Tough as nails. Married to a white man."

"Oh, ok. But why she called *me*?"

"Just wait and see."

When eye walked in her office eye noticed a petite, tiny older woman, graying hair, knowledgeable and thin glasses over keen eyes. The Oracle.

Eye felt her wisdom, it rolled all over me.

"Are you Pharoah?" she asked, not looking up from the book she was reading.

"Yes, eye am."

"Eye hear you are some kind of writer." She slowly flipped a page.

"Who told you that?"

"Anthony."

Eye smiled. "Yes, eye am."

"Will your work entice me like the book eye'm reading?" She flipped another page, quickly devouring the words. "As you can see eye haven't looked up from the book yet."

"Yes, my words are enticing."

"Really?"

"Yes."

Books were all around her. Stacked on the desk. On the shelves behind her, surrounding her.

"Eye used to be one of the Salem newspaper editors. Eye have a Masters degree. And eye don't read crap."

Then and only then did she close the book, looked up and said, "Do you have a portfolio?"

Eye looked at the folded paper in my hand. "No, but eye have this."

Eye extended my hand, and she looked at the paper like it was a ton of shit and she was wearing white.

"And you're a writer? Please. Anthony isn't even as good as he said."

"Ok, eye don't need the third degree."

Eye spun and was leaving.

"Bring me the paper. That's a direct order."

Ok, she's tough as nails, but eye gotta switch ball change up for her ass.

Eye slowly walked up to her, one of two gay men, her student aides and tutors, glanced up from typing his vampire tale, based in *London*, on the computer.

The other, Charles, a real geek looking motherfucker with Jagged Edge teeth and blackening gums, looked up at me as well. The brainiac.

Eye handed her the paper. She looked it over.

Eye put my hands behind my back, the "at ease" military position, the thumb across the other, and watched her.

She adjusted her glasses.

She began reading.

Quietly, to herself. Calmly reserved. Eye was on pins and needles.

She said, "Aha. Hmm."

She flipped the paper over. Read some more. Touched her forehead. Looked at her watch.

She looked up. Eye took the paper and started for the door.

Yes, eye embarrassed myself. Eye wasn't a writer, eye didn't know why Sleepy set this up.

When eye reached the door she said, "Pharoah."

Eye paused, not looking back.

Jerrid, one of the tutors, vampire boy, waved Bye Bye with a sly smile.

Eye flipped the bird at him and he mouthed, "Bite me, you inexperienced writer."

"Face me."

Eye looked at her.

She was standing. Looking heavenly, radiant.

"There's your computer right there." She pointed at it. "There's your dot matrix printer, old school but doable. We have a newsletter called Outer Visions. You will serve as a contributing writer. Eye can get you a Journalism credit through Chemeketa College."

"Thank you. Wow." Eye felt like Harriet Tubman wanting the sugar lump out of the bowl for a touch of heaven.

"Eye know you hated my little story. Sorry for embarrassing myself."

"Oh, yea. That's another thing. That one paper was better than the book eye was reading. Feel free to write your book on that computer at your leisure. If eye'm on the clock, you can write all day, as long as you want, till count time."

A whole new world opened up.

And my mentor Tommy Marsters was there to help me on my literary journey.

Only eye didn't know eye would actually succeed.

She edited my first book, *The Scorned House of Blue Scars.*

It took me three months to finish, because eye didn't know how to write books. Eye thought there was some sort of special formula for writers.

Seemed something unattainable.

Everything eye wrote she edited. At first my paper bled from all her red markings.

But she explained them, never trying to change my voice or writing style, because she loved it.

Eye kept my promise and put my boys in my book, but eye did it Dapharoah69's way.

But the first thing she told me was, "You are describing everything, and that's good but its not."

"Explain."

"You wrote here, 'Eye picked up the Oil of Olay soap and turned on the cold water and the knobs were somewhat rusty and after my shower eye put on Suave lotion.' The rusty shower knobs was a stroke of genius, but Oil of Olay soap and Suave lotion you didn't need to describe. Just say soap and lotion. Let the reader substitute their favorite soap and lotion right there. *Include your readers!* Don't exclude them."

Eye took it to heart.

Over the next few weeks proved to be productive.

Jerrid and Charles and a third tutor, Mark Marshal, an artist, handled the tutoring while eye was writing my book.

Mrs. Marsters whipped me into shape. Replaced the carburetor under my hood and eye was running like eye was brand new.

Eye started writing home, typing my letters, truly thankful eye could type stuff and write my book.

And eye had an amazing editor who told me my strong and weak points.

Over the course of my first book, eye was seeing her red markings less and less.

On one of the chapters she said eye was an "excellent character study. Eye could write from a dog or cat's point of view and would be devastatingly accurate."

That touched me.

Jerrid was getting jealous.

He'd been writing his vampire saga forever and a day before eye came, and there eye was pumping my book out like it was already there, and Mrs. Marsters couldn't wait to edit it.

She was editing Jerrid's book less and less, and he silently hated it.

And she focused on my book. She was the only black woman or black teacher working on the floor and eye was the only black tutor.

When eye completed my first book eye celebrated by releasing it on The Yard, giving an inmate at a time chapter by chapter so they could read it.

But it was hard to keep up. The folders found everyone's hands and the story exploded all over the Oregon State Penitentiary. It was hell keeping up with all my shit!

But what eye wasn't prepared for was a group of skin heads called the Aryan Nation seeking me out, hunting me down and once they did, all hell broke loose.

Something eye wasn't prepared for.

Eye put my chapters inside one three ring binder, so eye didn't have all forty chapters in 40 different places. The book was so good inmates were reading any chapter they got their hands on and feigning for the other chapters afterward.

Aalexandria, the character, was causing quite a stir in the penal system.

Then the guards were alerted. They stopped by my cell one by one.

"Eye wanna read that book everyone is talking about."

So eye had to print out an additional copy. Eye mailed my floppy disk home and told Grandpa to put it up, and to not open the envelope, and he did just that, so eye was protected in the event late bitches tried to publish my work.

That did it. Another guard stopped by, a white man with a lot of tattoos.

My cell was popped.

"Pack your things."

"Where am eye going?"

"To C block."

Yes.

Leaving Inch in D Block to move with Big Cease in E (Echo) Block wasn't a good move because, in addition to counting bars and tile, Big Cease was into all that selling tobacco shit and eye didn't want to be around that.

C block was a work block. If you didn't have a job you weren't celled up in there.

They were much bigger, way bigger, with a lot more room, and eye fell in love with a motherfucking cell block.

Somebody fucking shoot me.

There was a spot for a TV and eye instantly knew eye wanted one.

My cell mate was a cool ass niggah.

Before eye could say my name he said, "You're the writer, Miami."

"Yea."

"What a goddamn honor!" He shook my hand. "Any of your stuff published?"

"Naw, man. Eye don't wanna be no published author."

"Why not man?" Hanging all around the cell were black men from black history.

He had self help books everywhere. *Ebony, Essence* and *Jet* magazines.

On the TV was BET and eye was like oh my God. Damn. In jail?

"Eye don't know. Eye'm not no James Patterson."

"Nah, you better than James Patterson. You better than all those big timers."

Eye was laughing. "Yea, right."

"Shh, shh, listen."

"Who is that yelling?" I asked, narrowing my eyes.

"Hear what he saying?"

Eye was listening. Sounded like laughing. Hysterical.

"Miami a goddamn fool! Ya'll read this shit? Aalexandria, damn eye wanna fuck this bitch she my kinda bitch!"

"Wait till you get to the part her doctor boyfriend Marlo finds out the man he performed his first liver transplant on is his biological daddy! That he was the product of rape. His daddy was a skin head, what a fucking twist!"

My new cell mate, Dee Boo said, "And you were saying? They are talking about your books more than they talk about the big timers or Sleepy's sorry ass book."

"Eye still don't wanna be no published author. Eye'm not writing any other books."

But eye had already secretly started writing *Superstars*.

Eye gave Mrs. Marsters the first two chapters already.

Eye was walking around the track because the education floor was closed on weekends. And eye didn't feel like being cramped in the cell, plus that gave my cell mate some alone time. We had it worked out. When eye wanted alone time he went to work or on the yard to the weight pile. When he needed alone time eye found the library, eye hardly went to the yard.

Eye was walking around the bend of the track when eye saw a white guy with tattoos all over his arms, body and back laughing to the point he was chocking.

Eye rushed over to him. "Mister, are you ok?"

Eye started pounding his back, and he coughed up some meat and noodles.

"Thanks," he said, then took one look at me and said, "Oh, Gawd. A Coon helped me?"

"Eye'm not a goddamn coon, bitch."

He jumped up. "Who are you calling bitch you uneducated nigger?"

"Whatever, man Eye'm gone."

"Yea, get your faggot ass away from here. All you black niggers are fag fucks."

My eyes grazed a folder on the table. It was yellow. One of my stories. How did it get out of the binder?

"Eye see you are reading my story eye wrote."

He got quiet. He sat down and rubbed his palms across the top of it.

"Yea. Right. Nigger you wish you wrote this."

"Eye did."

He gazed at me for a few minutes, and eye glared him down.

Suddenly. He burst out laughing. "Oh, shit you're trying to trick me. April Fool! Ha ha ha!"

"You know what sir one day eye will be a published author," eye said, unsure of it, but anything to show this honky tonk ass white man down.

He laughed even harder! He jumped up to his feet, grabbed the folder and walked over to his Aryan Nation boys. They all tattooed up, cursing worse than blacks and chewing snuff, which was illegal in prison and contraband, but eye didn't give a shit what they did with their time.

"Guess what boys?" He pointed at me. "This coon burnt butt monkey said he's gonna be himself a published author!"

They roared to life, laughing and tripping over each other.

"Yes, ok and eye am Clark Kent, bitch!"

They laughed even harder. Eye was smiling.

"Have you even written a book?" another inmate asked.

"Yes, the folder you're holding. Eye wrote that."

"Yea, right. A white man wrote this," he said.

"Um, no he didn't. Eye wrote that."

"Bullshit! Eye happen to like this story Eye'm reading. A black bitch married a man with a KKK father. That's some…"

Eye was smiling. Eye handed him my ID card, with my name on it.

"Pharoah Wilson." He said it slowly.

"Turn it to the back page," eye said.

His boys watched him. He did so.

His eyes were wide. "No. One Pharoah Wilson is the author of this? This is like the thirtieth chapter eye have read, and my boy read this, too, Nigger what do you know. You are a talented sonofabitch."

One of the men tried to shake my hand but when eye extended my arm he snatched it back. "Eye hate black people. Eye never talked to a nigger in my life where *eye'm* from."

"We're one in here, man. A state number. Separated from our families, away from our loved ones. Right now there is no black and white."

They were quiet. One of them, eye'm guessing the ring leader, started to walk off and eye grabbed his arm and he snatched it back and grabbed my neck, "Fuck Nigger you crazy touching me?"

Eye kneed him in the balls, "Bitch don't fucking touch me."

A few brothers rushed over, including Uncle McAdoo. Eye was happy to see him.

"Nephew, you're ok?" Uncle McAdoo asked.

"Yes, eye am."

He looked at the Aryan Nation boys. "We got a problem?"

"Now Mac you know we started doing time together."

"And we never liked each other," he said, pushing me behind him. "Eye am in here for fucking murder, bitches." He had fire in his eyes, like a father protecting his son.

"Remember what eye did last time. Eye will gut a bitch and cut his head off and kick it down the road. You know how the fuck eye roll."

"We meant no harm."

"But the nigger grabbed me."

He turned to face me. "Miami, there are just some things and some people you never talk to in prison."

"Eye got you." Eye walked off. Eye have never been called so many niggers by a prejudiced red neck dog smelling crackah in my life. Let him come to Goulds with that kinda shit.

"Miami," Uncle Mac called out and Eye kept walking. One thing Eye would never do again was give a damn. Eye couldn't change the world, especially not a prison.

"Miami!"

Eye walked towards the outside activities building, sulking into myself.

"Miami."

Eye looked back. It was one of the Aryan Nation boys.

"Let me have a word with you. Alone."

We were sitting on the concrete slab, the weight pile behind us. The sound of weight rising and dropping, the clanking of iron meshed with grunts and moans filled our ears.

"Listen, nigger…Eye mean, bro. This is hard for me, you know…but something you said was true."

Eye was offended, but I remained mum. "And *that* is?"

"Inside these thirty foot walls we are all the same, a state number. Separated from our loved ones." Trembling, he handed me a photo of a gorgeous woman with a little baby girl. I could tell he fought himself to be cordial to a "Nigger."

"Wow, she's a fox. And cute kid," I said, meaning it.

"Thank you. You know," he said, in his little red shorts and bare-chested, "You are the first nigger…Eye mean bro Eye ever showed my family too."

Eye handed him the photo back. "Well Eye'm flattered."

"Eye have a friend in here named Sony, he one of the math tutors up stairs."

"Never heard of him," eye said, because eye mind my business.

"He is Mr. Gregson's tutor. Eye think he tutors math."

"Eye'll check it out."

"Eye was raised to be the way Eye am, son. My father hated black men so much he used to hang them and Eye used to watch without a care in the world. Eye wasn't born to hate. Eye took on the trails of my folks."

"Eye understand." Eye thought about my sexuality. If he wasn't born to hate surely eye wasn't born gay.

"But eye do know this. Everything has a changing point, and eye can tell you what is changing, at least with me, but may not sit well with the boys."

"What's that?" eye asked.

He took my hand, and eye felt his muscles flinch, like he wanted to snatch his hand back quick, fast and in a hurry.

"You are one talented motherfucking black brother! Fucking A right, man. Eye read that story and man oh man. If Alexandria was a white woman eye'd have to get that whore and make her my baby Mama, isn't that how the brother's say it?"

Eye was laughing. "Yea, man. Thank you. Eye am no author. Eye just write."

"What inspires you, and what's your real name?"

"Eye'm Pharoah. Eye don't know what inspires me. Eye lose a part of myself every time the sun set."

"Why do you say that?"

"Because eye become another part of myself when the sun rise."

He released my hand. "This is what eye'm talking about. Never before have someone like you come through here. Bro, you remind me of a friend eye used to have in high school."

"Really?"

"His name was Billips. He was timid as a sheep, but smarter than a fox."

"Sounds like he was a loner."

He looked into my eyes. "He *was*. Look, rumor has it you are in here for attempted sodomy."

"Yes, eye am. And eye…"

"Bro, let me show you something."

Eye started to back away. "Are you going to try to kill me?"

"Bro," he said, as eye realized he no longer said Nigger. "You are a gift from God almighty. And for me to tell a brother that is beyond reproach, but it's on my heart. Eye may have been raised for war and hate, but you are a talented young man. And one day eye feel in my heart you will be a published author."

Tears fell down my face, and eye wiped them away. "Thanks."

"No problem." He put his arm around me. "Come on, let me show you something."

Eye followed him into C Block. He was in Sub C, the cells below the other cells, and eye followed him to the end. The guard popped the cell, and looked at me sideways. He started to press the radio to say eye was in an unauthorized area, but the Aryan Nation dude shook his head no, and the guard relaxed. Eye followed him inside. He had all kinds of shit hanging up. Eye could tell he been in this cell for over ten years. His entire life was in here and for some reason eye felt at home. The word **ILLUMINATI** on a huge poster caught my attention. With a picture of the Beatles on it, throwing weird hand gestures.

"Have a seat," he said. Eye sat down. The cell closed.

"My cell mate is my lover," he said, "But we don't show any type of affection out on the yard. We hardly even embrace. We are painfully quiet about our relationship."

"Eye understand. It's safe with me."

"He and eye will die in here, and he's my whole world. Eye could never see my wife again."

"Does she visit?"

"No. She married my brother and just gave birth to his daughter. That's the picture eye showed you on the yard. It sliced my heart in two, so eye know heartbreak."

"Thanks for sharing that with me, but why me?"

He looked at me, then reached on the top shelf to take down a manila folder. "Eye like you." He sat down on the opposite stool, and dumped newspaper clippings on the table.

"You started to tell me about why you're in here," he said, finding what he's looking for.

"Ok..."

He opened the newspaper clipping. "What does he mean to you?" he asked.

Eye looked down, taking it. My heart hit the floor when eye saw Chad's picture. Tears fell. "Oh, God." Eye broke down instantly, and the funniest thing happened. He gave me a loving hug.

"He was your best friend, wasn't he?"

Eye couldn't utter a word.

The cell popped and eye followed him up the tier.

"Something tells me you were set up."

"Eye was. Eye was even marked for death."

"Prison don't treat rats too kindly, but in your case, brother, you did what you thought was right."

"Yes. Eye didn't snitch on anyone, eye merely cooperated with the police. Hell eye was even a suspect."

"You wouldn't hurt a fly, that much eye do know...do you have any siblings?"

We were walking past the guard, and up the stairs, going back to the yard. "Yes. Four. Eye'm the oldest."

"Sweet. Eye bet they adore you."

"Yea, they do."

"Have any pictures of them?"

"Yes, Eye do."

"Maybe you can share them with me, like Eye shared mine with you."

"That would be cool."

We shook hands.

When we got back on the yard eye followed him over to the Aryan Nation boys. They had a huge spread on the table. A cleaned, ripped open garbage bag. On it mounds of Doritos, on top of it cooked Top Ramen noodles, like a pizza. One of the younger members poured on the refined beans, then another poured on the cheese, then the chopped meat.

Smelled yummy. My new friend looked at me. "We can't cook like the bro's but damn it we do all right!"

There was a boom box playing a song Eye never heard before.

"What is that playing?"

"Rock music my friend. System of a Down. It rocks, huh?"

I loved the beat. "Yes, it damn sure does." Eye was bobbing my head. "Sounds good."

"Yo, boys! The author likes our music!"

"Yea!"

"YEAAA!"

"Rock on, Miami!"

The member that cursed me out for grabbing his arm jumped in my face and stared me down. Eye looked away. Eye knew this was a little too made for TV.

"Yo. Eye hate to read but eye read a little part of your typed book," he said like he was having open heart surgery without anesthesia.

"Oh, yea?"

He extended his hand. "Eye may not join the million man March, but brother, you got it. You got it, and you are a bad man with the writing. Don't stop. Don't stop for no one."

"Thank you."

"You're free to join us for some grub."

He handed me a cup and a spoon.

"Thank you!" The other brothers on the Yard looked on in shock. Uncle McAdoo nodded with a smile, winking.

He said, "Let the author get his grub first, boys! Take all you want."

He pats my shoulder. "And take your Uncle Mac some, too."

"Eye will. And thanks, man."

"Eye want next on that book. Can you write a story about a redneck piss head hick like myself from Grant's Pass, Oregon who get all the girls pregnant and have to play musical pussy lips at the hospital."

Eye was done, laughing so hard eye dropped my cup.

"Eye'm for real, Miami."

"We'll see, man. We'll see."

Eye helped over 170 people get their G.E.D's. All inmates, who had their heads high when that G.E.D. opened some doors for them when they got out. But the real challenge would be, even with education, you have a felony record so what are you gonna do? Say you don't got one and take your chance of being found out and fired or take the chance to be tuned away by telling them straight up, no bullshit, from the beginning, so when you're hired, by being given a second chance, you can't get fired for dishonesty because you prayed to God then went to your interview and God was with you the entire time.

How do you know? When you smiled and thanked the interviewer for their time, baby that was God.

That's all the interviewer needed was to see someone smile, after the bad interviews he's done and the number of times people cursed him out because he said, "Don't call me. Eye'll call you.

But inmates didn't look at the big picture like that. They looked at it as an accomplishment, which it was, but also, some could never use it when they have life in prison. What was a G.E.D. gonna do when you got life in prison?

Eye can tell you what. And one of the Lifer's once told me.

"Getting my G.E.D. may not open the prison doors, but it opened the doors of being incarcerated in my own mind so when eye read a book, or book after book, with my mind eye am out of prison and experiencing the story eye am faithfully reading about so when eye read the Bible, eye start to see things with my mind, and realize that even Jesus was jailed, even he was persecuted so if he can rise from death after being nailed to the cross then eye can keep my mind out of prison and my body in this cell and know God hasn't forsaken me."

That got me doing some things to enrich myself. Eye met two bad people my whole prison term.

The men eye met were cordial and nice, some were quiet and tried to pretend to be crazy but Pharoah never fell for that crazy shit.

Scream, shake your head real fast and do the Hammer Man across the OSP lawn. Yawn. Niggah. Try some *other* crazy shit. Where eye'm from those kinds of people never became a threat. And at OSP everyone called me "Miami." Don't get me wrong. Some niggahs didn't like me, yet those were the same Niggahs chasing me, begging to fuck me in my ass, then act like they didn't know me on the Yard. Damn. They got Down Low Gay Inmates as well. But ain't no closets in Prison, unless you're a Pimp, doing 9 years and eye opened the utility closet on the Education floor a few months before Christmas and saw a well-known Pimp fucking another supposed Pimp in the ass. The two biggest Pimps at OSP fucking and making cocks and nuts swing like an Action flick was revealed when eye told just one person on the Yard what eye saw. To get it off my mind.

And it was all over the Yard in about an hour. It was one of the biggest dramas OSP had seen in recent years.

Blimp and Tony Curry Chicken George. Two Pimps that pimped all over the world, Girl, were fucking in the closet. Moaning like Buffaloes were fucking them and so off cadence eye was mad just because they couldn't fuck. Rocking and shit, like a R Kelly Slow Wine.

Ain't doing shit.

When they saw me eye slammed the goddamn door closed. They been fooling all the listeners at OSP that liked a well told story, yet a Niggah from Miami, Pharoah caught their asses and it became a huge scandal. Even eye couldn't believe it got so big.

One of Tony's friends, a so-called boxer, was so upset at the revelation of his friend being caught doing the do that he tried to punch me in the face when eye wasn't looking. And eye turned, on that Miami, Goulds, Florida swagga, Nigga, threw a two piece that dissected one punch times three and that Niggah was like Oh, Shit and retreated.

There were Niggahs running out from pay phone booths leaving their girlfriends and wives hanging like sitting ducks waiting for a fucking bullet, rooting and cheering me on.

Ole Boy was known for knocking niggahs out.

Eye had to make an example out of one. And *that* set the tone. Don't *fuck* with me, bitch. Eye ain't the baddest muthafucka in the world, but if you beat me Eye will fight your ass all day everyday till Eye take back the title.

Eye was raised that way.

My popularity went through the roof. Niggahs that didn't like me were buying me commissary and getting me what Eye needed to lighten the load on my Mama's wallet.

A Gagster Niggah asked to move in the cell with me and he made sure Eye had soap, lotion, tooth brush, the best tooth paste and the most expensive shit on the commissary.

And all he wanted me to do was re-enact that one, two punch at Tony's right hand man, and he would buy me what eye wanted.

He died laughing. Eye mean, every time eye did it…it was funnier and funnier to him. But that was a moment Eye would never take from him. He had life. And that laughter Eye gave him Eye wouldn't trade for all the diamonds in the world.

We were good until one night, he asked me to sit on his bed. Eye did, since eye had the top bunk. He looked into my eyes. Sitting in his draws and Eye avoided his eyes because Eye heard them whispering to my ears. This Niggah wants to fuck you. Eye loved how you threw that punch but Eye looked in your eyes and a saw a wounded bitch that needed a real man to fuck him good and make him feel safe.

Eye turned away, gasping. "Eye know you ain't asking what Eye think you're asking."

"Eye'm a Vice Lord, he said. "From Chicago. My daddy pimped niggahs in wigs. Hell, Eye pimped a few of them myself and eventually won over my daddy and put his ass to work, too. So Eye love handsome ass niggahs. Pretty niggahs. And the way you threw that punch Eye want you to reenact it on this dick."

Eye leaned towards him and kissed him, he was rubbing my thigh, his uncontrollable breathing slowly suffocating me. Because if Eye kiss you and you can't fall into place, get in sync and breathe in cadence with me then you ain't getting the booty.

So Eye got him hot and jacked him off.

And put his ass to sleep, getting in my bed, crying from the weakness of my flesh guiding me and said, "God, please forgive me, Father. Eye know not what eye just did. Eye'm starving for affection."

Amen.

Between going to the Education floor for work and rarely going to The Yard, that applied to the Chow Hall as well. We got a monthly schedule of things to be cooked for breakfast, lunch and dinner so eye pretty much *knew* what days eye was going to eat and what days eye wasn't based on the menu.

All that beef stroganoff bullshit? *Ew,* Niggah. Not Pharoah! Eye wasn't eating that bullshit! And they seemed to serve that nasty shit every other day. Eye fasted instead. Until Mom sent me a $150 here and $150 dollars there and Eye stoked up on Top Ramen, sausages and junk food.

And chips.

One day Eye got into it with Vee, my cell mate, the Vice Lord. Eye was getting tired of this dude, begging me to jack him off every night.

Niggah, your fucking wrist broke? My Mama sending me money, Eye'm buying my own shit, got my own supply Niggah who wants Zest when Mama sent me enough for Ambi soap, that good toothpaste and to buy my own TV.

He jumped up from his bed, turned and punched me twice in the face and eye was shocked. Eye jumped out the bed and head butted this bitch and threw a two piece.

Bitch. What the fuck. As much as Eye been practicing, reenacting that one two on Tony's friend, you dare try me Niggah?

"Fuck you! You ain't shit. Bitch. That's why Eye fucked you."

"Fuck Niggah. Eye have been jacking you up. You didn't even sniff my ass, bitch you weren't good enough so who the fuck you think you talking to Vice Lord?"

"Go to hell! Eye'ma beat your ass."

"Bitch, try!"

"SHUT UP!"

"Why? Because you don't want muthafuckahs jacking your little ass unflattering dick every night? Shit should be a *cock*, as thin as it is. They should have a *law*. A law for dicks. If it is 6 below, it is classified as a cock. From 7 to whatever, baby, you got a big ass dick!"

He spat in my face, bruised from me stepping on his manhood and snatching a so-called fake ass Gangsta out the closet. People laughing and clapping and somebody yelled MAN DOWWWNNNN MIAMI FUCKING MAN DOWN!

They normally and unusually screamed MAN DOWN when someone was shanked (stabbed) or beat up real bad.

So eye guess when Vee's reputation got stabbed by my words people were like MAN DOWNN!

"Get your shit and get out my cell."

So eye took the pillow case from my pillow and put all my shit in it, my extra prison uniform, and everything and screamed, "LET ME OUT THIS MUTHAFUCKING CELL!"

When the reality of so-called Gangsta crying befell me eye became silent. What was he crying for?

He looked helpless. "Daddy! *Please* don't leave me. Mama swears she won't fuck that man again. She promised,

Daddy! *Don't* go! You always said you wouldn't break up the family."

Something didn't make sense.

"Eye gotta go," Eye told him. "GUARD LET ME OUT!"

"Please, Daddy! Eye'll let you jack my dick again! Just don't leave Mama. She won't find out, Eye swear."

And Eye didn't know why but Eye wrapped my arms around this Niggah, a Niggah that spat in my face and held him and let him cry on my shoulder.

"Daddy," he began, rubbing my back. "Eye forgive you for breaking up our family. You said you gave it to God and you repented, so you came to me to ask for forgiveness. And Eye do forgive you, dad. Eye do. And eye forgive myself."

God showed himself to me again.

When it dawned on him that we were hugging, he pushed me off him.

"What the fuck, Miami. Why you hugged me?"

"What?" eye asked, in shock. Now eye'm confused. He was like two different people.

"You heard me? And man why your shit packed? Man, eye'm sorry for spitting on you, man. Eye thought you were my dad. Eye spit on him when he walked out on his family."

He started taking my shit out the pillow case. I scratched my head, confused. "Man we're fam. Eye don't want you jacking me off. Eye'm sorry for taking out on you what my father had done to me."

"It's ok."

"No its not. Man if eye want God to forgive me for my crime and my down falls eye have to learn to forgive."

Eye sat on his bed and said, "My God."

On the Yard the next day, Eye called home, talked to the family, then left to go run some laps. But Eye fell out of it that fast and decided to walk. Clear my head. Think about my future. Am eye gonna make it out of here alive? Am eye going to die here? Four years and nine months was a long ass time. Plus eye get good time. And eye never got wrote up and eye never went to the Hole. Eye felt eye was doing well.

Another day gone was another day to mark off my calendar. In prison sex with men was so big they tried to hide it. One night Eye saw Officer Billy Dame fuck one of the so-called-thug-Niggah-inmates on his bunk. All in the open. A guard fucking an inmate like a bitch; OSP guard Niggah deep inside tight thug asshole, his eyes rolling to the back of his head, moaning his wife's name.

Calling the Niggah Samantha Gooding and shit. Yea eye heard it, shit eye'm right there a few feet away, cell smell like Cool Water Cologne, Old Spice and straight dick and grimy ass.

He then pulled out, slapped the thug's face with his dick (some shit on it) *then* his ass cheeks, spread his cakes apart and decided to use his tongue for the icing. I wanted to throw the fuck up. Ugh! Didn't you see shit on your dick?

He tongue fucked the thug and he staring at an Ice Cube picture hanging on the cell walls ripped from some VIBE magazine article and tears falling down his face. What got me was the guard moaning, "AHH FUCK NIGGAH DAMN! POP DAT PUSSY ON MY TONGUE!" loud as fuck, and the Thug grunting like Porky Pig and the DL Closet Thug Niggah was fine with a dick bigger than the guard's dick. But the guard fucking the big dick thug Niggah with pathetic dick. Eye shook my goddamn head like *"Damn* he wasting all that good black thug dick. But eye'm straight. Eye get fucked eye don't do the fucking. Hell to the no."

So why all this yelling and grunting, ass slapping, dick swishing asshole unlike wife's pussy and no one saying anything. No inmates opening their mouths. Surely, they were at their cell bar doors listening.

Some licking their lips, four other white men separated two by two in individual cells sucking and quietly fucking but didn't make a sound; a few niggahs were beating their dicks, legs trembling below the knees and one of the niggahs had an old white man eating his black asshole. Niggah had to be about 25, 26 and the old white man you can say was older than prune juice. Old white prude tongue fucking the hell out of the Niggah, struggling to keep his ass cheeks apart.

On the white man's head was "Eye'm a Child Molester." The Niggah had a page cut out on his face like a mask. Of Macaulay Culkin.

Eye stood there in shock, afraid to move. What did eye just step into? The Twilight Zone. All this shit going on, a cell block goddamn orgy damn near and all this noise the guard and thug making and nobody screaming, cheering, alerting other guards or yelling.

Eye stared at this dude and he somewhat stopped jacking his dick and he looked up into my eyes from the first floor. Eye was on the second tier.

Eye noticed he was in the PC unit, where most the big time rapist, serial killers, stars and reject parole revoked child molesters were kept.

He kissed at me and eye flipped the bird at him. It was then it dawned on me that the niggah with the Macaulay Culkin mask was a guard himself.

Down illegally in the PC unit making the old white Caucasian child molester suck his dick, eat his asshole and beat his white ass to make him suffer like he did to those children. And they were HIS children eye would later learn. And his children were now GROWN and he was STILL molesting and raping them before he was locked up for life.

Eye shuddered when eye found that out. That one could be so cruel, heartless *and* cold. That's like my step daddy (well, ex step daddy) putting me through four years of rape, and kept fucking me through my rebellious teenage years and when eye became an adult he was still fucking my ass and face.

No, that didn't happen like that (it stopped when eye was ten, and my cousin Lily started it next!). But eye looked at the situation that way to better understand it. And eye understood perfectly.

At some point the child molester father grew to like and love and enjoy what he was doing. He fucked up emotionally and now it was an emotionally psychological problem. And eye had to wonder did his grown children hate it, gave in like me and start to inevitably enjoy it. Like what eye experienced as a small child.

What did they do and say when he did what he did? Did they go to bed crying at night like me, wishing they were dead and calling on God and never getting him because no one, not even my parents, told me that believing in God and Jesus was a Free Will Choice God gave to all?

No wonder he didn't come when eye called on him. Because eye wasn't saved as of yet (eye was 6! How the Hell was eye supposed to know eye needed saving when my parents hadn't told me eye was born into sin? Eye didn't know the world surpassed my living room or school and definitely didn't look past my bedroom because ex step daddy was fucking me to sleep.)

Eye was forced to love him and Mama tore my ass up if eye didn't get up for church. She beat me all the way to the car. GO TO CHURCH! TAKE YOUR ASS TO CHURCH!

And she really beat me when eye said, "Mama, you're not coming?"

And she gave me every goddamn excuse to stay her red ass home. She went to church Easter Sunday though. In her best low heels, dress and that curly perm was off the chain.

Then eye further questioned that God-loves-me-but-never-met-him theory because eye was like how do you *love* something or some being or somebody and you never even spoke to or saw him before.

In that case, since we were made in his (God's, but derived from the strongest seed from Daddy's cum) image, why don't eye love my classmates?

And eye couldn't stand half their dumb asses.

Somebody lying somewhere, eye thought as a kid. And eye made it a mission.

To one day find out.

So eye knew then that guards ain't shit. They were probably church-going guards. They *had* to be. They were married to conservative, Biblical white bitches (oh yea! They in church every Sunday for Mass) and now throwing shade by punishing people who already been convicted of their crimes. Who died and made those guards God? Somebody surely fooled them. So my guard went up instantly to the muthafucking police wanna be OSP guards. A bunch of ass clowns.

Eye stood there watching the guard and the thug niggah fuck. Flip-flopping and shit, fucking each other. Guard couldn't take much dick, thug dick too big so they switched balled chained up once more and the guard had the wheel. When the guard saw me eye ran to my cell; but no one was at the guard booth to pop it open. Eye knew the guard wasn't in the guard booth. Because he popped ole boy cell and was fucking him in the ass.

So eye was caught out there...

Niggah guard (after getting dressed in the child molester's cell) looked up at me and eye looked down at him. The guard fucking thug boy, eye'll call him Offer Dumb Fuck (because he certainly was a dumb fuck. No, literally) smiled at me and eye shook my head.

"Eye didn't see nothing," eye said, coming up with a well devised plan.

To my advantage.

My dick was hard as fuck (goddamn *go soft!* GO SOFT!*)* but *damn* it! My mind was STILL on God.

Because God revealed himself in this entire ordeal. Eye was seeing things incarcerated that eye didn't see on the streets as a free man. Before I was incarcerated I was cocky and thought I had the world by the balls. No. Those kinda niggahs would fall and fall hard because God was so real and so true he made any and everybody, kids and animals too, bow down.

And at one point in your life you have bowed to God; you just didn't realize it. Eye didn't care where you were from or what you had going on. It happened at least once.

That's God's existence in a nutshell. Right there for you. You didn't even know or understand God yet you STILL fell to your knees praying during a traumatic experience to Jehovah. And you're bitching and groaning and complaining because he didn't come on time for your bitch asses *this* time? You didn't even appreciate when he was there for you on time the *previous* time. You *question* God, when your faith and endurance, even when you didn't believe in him and was doing your own thang, has disappeared into selfishness? Your tears and pleas and the fact you were crying out with your heart through your lips via the tongue and *not* your tongue via the heart has been sent *back* to hell where it came from because you used to lie to God and he knew you were lying and you go out and do the same shit yet again.

But he continues to forgive.

In this instance, eye was in a Catch 22. The Guard wanted to fuck me and eye wanted him but I signed a pact with God when I signed that plea. So I compared both sides. God's love GO HARD 24/7. A dick? Hard. Um, yea ok. It's long, big and thick. What's the battery life of a good scrumptious dick? What's the miles per gallon on his nuts (they looked a little small. Too small for my tastes).

What's the battery life on each square inch of a dick? That means the average niggah nut in two minutes when he ain't gettin' any pussy so when he up in me he gonna last, like, what *ya'll* do the math, don't just read my autobiography use you damn brains.

He'll last about 30 minutes till his official dick goes soft.

God goes hard 24/7 with a mustard seed of faith, if you just try it out? So eye decided to pick up the Bible and eye turned a blind eye and he popped my cell and eye went inside and the cell bars closed with a loud CLANG noise and eye glanced at the lotion bottle.

More temptation. Now eye wanna jack my dick. But eye couldn't. Or could eye?

Eye'm licking my lips, struggling to keep reading the Bible, lotion bottle on my mind at the same coordinates as the images of the Guard's dick deep inside Thug Boy's asshole making me wiggle my toes and my legs started to tremble then shake with fear and trembling at the very thought of looking away from God. Not right now. Eye was in prison. Hell on Earth. Why did you think the government kept building them?

Duh! Hell on Earth all over goddamn Earth. And Christians talking 'bout eye'm going to hell bitches eye'm already in Hell on Earth University called OSP. Didn't get any fucking worse than this.

When eye was younger, when eye wasn't saved and when eye didn't love or believe in him he never showed up when eye called because eye called on my Mama first. That's a false idol in the eyes of God. Nothing and NO ONE before him. He meant business, folks. And eye learned the hard way.

You knew my life now up until this point of the chapter (unless you cracked the book open and you were immediately on this part then eye would suggest you read from page 1). Eye called on Mama, didn't believe, wasn't saved, didn't say with my lips and tongue that eye believe in Jesus and he died for my sins after admitting to being a sinner. If you don't do that you could pray all you damn want. God ain't gonna show up. He knew what's in your heart.

And you calling your Mama and Daddy first? Over God? Put NOTHING ABOVE HIM!

And now, after suffering all that abuse and heart ache and self hatred eye was in prison struggling to keep my faith in him; after confessing that eye love him and that Jesus died for my sins and eye got baptized at Church when eye was 14 life got much harder for me.

God brought me through the rain and the storm and eye was now struggling to stay faithful, falling to the sins of my flesh, sins against the Body of Christ.

After eye signed that plea bargain (pact with God) eye promised to stay true and faithful and to turn to him through any and everything and GOD revealed himself in that because eye have the FULL ARMOR OF GOD!

Know how powerful that was? Eye walked through the Valley of the CHOW HALL OF DEATH, mean mugged skin heads, ate on their side of the Chow Hall, beat on the bars with my boots, threw that one, two piece Popeye's meal at the so-called Midget Boxer on the Yard after eye caught two Pimps fucking each other. Eye had it out with a Vice Lord who later broke down after eye jacked his dick for months and he spat in my face then begged Daddy not to leave Mommie. That Daddy promised he'd never break up the family.

And he was a grown ass man on some childish teenager bullshit. So jacking off was out. Eye even trashed the lotion bottle.

And continued reading the Songs of Solomon.

A few weeks later eye saw the Guard that fucked Thug Boy. He was at the Main Box or whatever that shit was called and eye needed to get in my cell. Eye avoided his eyes because he damn sure was trying to get my attention.

Eye walked up the tier.

"YO!"

Eye spun on my heel. "WHAT, NIGGAH?"

He raised a finger mid air and signaled for me to come to him.

"Eye'm in my 20s dawg, eye ain't no goddamn teenager."

He kept fingering me to *come here*. So eye went. Just getting off work.

Eye reminded him of what eye saw.

He laughed like something was funny and eye looked around him and didn't see Casper the Ghost tickling him so why was he laughing?

"Fuck you Miami Bitches!" he spat evilly, staring me down. Trying to put the fear of God in my heart and eye farted just to make a goddamn point. Stinky fart, too. Niggah fanning his nose and shit.

"What?"

"What is it? 305? Ya'll ain't 'bout dat dere. Eye'm 'bout making dat paper. Yea. Eye'm married to a white bitch but eye'm from L.A. Used to be in the Cripps. Moved away, got a new start, met a white Hoe with money and got this here job. This is the West Coast, Niggah. Ain't no Miami shit poppin' off up here. Trick Daddy? That's hard?"

Eye smiled. "Yea. Trick is hard, bitch. Leave Trick Daddy out your mouth, pimp. Don't talk about Trick in my face dude, eye'm serious. He got more money and Hoes than you can count. And Tupac gotta West it Up when he was born on the East Coast to give L.A. a goddamn Mascot, bitch?"

The smiled died from his face. "You disrespecting me?"

"Eye saw you fucking that thug. Eye saw your goon guard buddy making a child molester tongue fuck him while beating his dick to *you* fucking said thug boy. So eye got all the trump cards. Eye'll spare thug boy, but fuck the police?"

"You think you got all the trumps cards?"

"Eye do."

"They won't believe you. Eye'm always to work on time, always the first to arrive and the last to leave and eye'm always doing overtime."

"Duh. Isn't thug boy your bitch?"

He got dangerously quiet. "What?"

"You're in love with him. Niggah if eye had ass that good eye'd fuck my wife with two minute dick to save that second and third and fourth nut for your prison faggot bitch, too."

"*That's it, Niggah! You're* going to the hole."

"Do it. Or have you forgotten who my mother works for. The FEDS. Eye'll tell her what the fuck you're doing and we'll see who believes who and Mama a working mother that make money and they take over half in taxes so she quick to sue a punk bitch!"

"Well eye saw you on the tier, my co worker saw you on the tier and eye didn't see you catching me fucking said thug boy so it's your word against mine. My co worker got my back. That's two to one, Pharoah. Faggot ass. Eye swear. And as you can see..." He held up his badge. "Eye'm one of them."

"Fuck the other side, Niggah."

"Fuck you Miami niggahs. Bitches. Eye'm the law, convict." He spat in my face and eye closed my eyes. "Who you think the Warden gonna side with?"

I wiped his spit from my face. I glared into his eyes.

And he winked his eye at me. "Go to your cell. You're under a restriction. Eye should write your faggot ass up."

"You write me up eye will put your business all over the goddamn yard."

"Eye hate your bitch ass!"

"And eye love you, unfortunately God says eye have to love the handicap."

"Cell in. That's a direct order, bitch."

Sure, dude.

Keeping my mouth closed eye retreated to my cell.
With an evil smile on my face.
I was turning dark, and fast...

The next day my cell was popped and my cellie was called to work.
Eye walked onto the tier, heading for the guard box.
"Wilson? You're under restriction," said the Guard on Duty.
Eye smiled. Heading to him.
"Not if you got a job. And eye work on the Education Floor."
Eye walked past him.
"Pick your mouth up off the floor. Have a good day, sir. God bless you."
And fuck you too, bitch.
Two to 1 my ass.
Eye got God. It's Infinity +1 to 2.
With God eye had the Home Court advantage.
Eye always have GOD as a backup plan.

Eye caught the guard again. The fifth night eye saw Officer Billy Dame fuck one of the so-called thug Niggahs on his shift. All in the open. Same time, same bat channel. Pow! Bang! *BOOMING* Thug pussy. A guard fucking him like a bitch.
Eye stood there, again, *watching*. Dick hard, mind wondering but never leaving GOD, yet my legs buckled.
He stopped fucking thug boy and they both looked at me. Strangely.
Eye waved with a Goulds, Florida smile. "Hey, Officer. See me now?"
Eye let the hunter see the hunted.
Eye ran to my cell but no one was at the guard booth to pop it open.

Because he popped ole boy cell and was fucking him in the ass again. When the guard ran out to me (not rushed this time), fixing his shirt and he said (not whispered) "Eye can fuck you, too!"

"Nah, dude. Eye'm cool."

"Come on Miami," his black ass said, licking my ear. "Let me get in that ass. Eye heard it's good. Got niggahs spitting in your face and shit. Eye fucked every pretty boy at OSP in the 3 + years eye've been here. Eye put money on their books using druggie bitches from the 'Hood and they keep making this dick spit, since eye work almost double shift everyday and eye am always away from my family and my wife.

Eye shook my head and said. "Eye won't say anything, man."

"Eye hate Miami bitches but eye want some Miami Pussy."

"Sorry. Eye don't let House Niggers fuck me."

"Eye find that hard to believe."

"That's because you keep it hard in that thug's pussy."

The Thug inmate frowned and eye rolled eyes daring him to get rowdy with me. Eye'll pull his motherfucking card and cancel that bitch.

"That ain't what eye heard about Ole Boy and Tony, two pimps fucking in the storage closet on the educational floor. Eye heard you pulled their cards all over the place. You're a fucking hero."

"Is it really that big?"

"YES!"

"Eye won't say anything. Just leave me alone."

"Eye know you won't," he said, grinning.

Eye rolled my eyes again. Eye didn't know what he meant by that, but it really didn't matter because he was a garbage niggah spitting garbage for words.

Ten minutes later my cell popped.

"WILSON, PACK UP TO MOVE."

They moved me out the cell and into my own.
On the *other* side of C Block.

My new cell mate was Craig (I changed his name). A bald headed black gangster from Portland. And he was actually good people. We hit it off fantastically. He never tried me sexually nor did eye try him. He was like my big brother. He didn't judge me and if he had extra, so did eye. What we brought to the cell we shared.

And that taught me, that even in prison, brothers can live together during to lowest of times, yet still make it comfortable for the other person by being open hearted, kind and generous, even in prison. He loved working out on the weight pile and listening to his radio and his favorite song was: "*Eye need a Project Chick. One who can suck my nuts. And come and suck this dick.*" That wasn't the Cash Money lyrics, but he changed them and made me laugh.

We were the best of buds.

Nominations to hold office in Uhuru Sa Sa (Swahili for Freedom Now) were cast, and a few people nominated for Secretary, since eye now worked on the Activities' Floor, first as a volunteer for HAAP, HIV/AIDS Awareness program, and then to Executive Director of Office Operations when Charles, the founder, was released from prison. The program was the only one of its kind in the United States, and we sent information on HIV and AIDS and the dangers of other STD's to institutions all over the country.

And now eye was Co CEO, making $50 a month. Mrs. Marsters retired and it was like my grandma died.

Eye cried all night when she left. Eye would never forget her, ever. And eye was also a math tutor with another teacher. A white man. Named Mr. Gregson.

Waiting for Uhuru Sasa nominations, eye had all my books in multi-colored folders my new Boss Mr. Gregson, brainiac, had ordered for me. Mrs. Marsters told him eye was a writer so he never interfered with my writing. Since eye was a math tutor, eye didn't do as much teaching as skin head Sonny. Sonny, such a cool dude, taught math and eye was writing my book called *The Blonde Bombshell* that may never see the light of day. Eye may never publish that book, that book was written solely to help me hone my craft. Story dealt with a local stripper turned multiplatinum singer, actress and screenwriter that battles a lunatic serial killer that escaped a mental hospital and was killing her Hollywood friends.

When eye got to my cell eye would add a new folder to my book legacy stash on the top shelf above the cell's entrance.

Eye was proud of all my writing. People talking about my books, got people on the Yard reading them and giving me praise and corrections officers stopping by for something to read while on the clock.

One day after eye got off work (had a long day) my cell was raided by three guards.

"Step outside the cell Wilson!" one guard said forcibly. Eye looked at him like, Chile, puleaze. Eye took my goddamn time.

"What? What are you doing?" eye asked.

Another taller guard was taking my folders and my books and some of them had my shit stored on disk. OH NO!

"No, you can't take my shit!" eye said, my heart stopping.

"Having folders in your cell is contraband and we're confiscating it!" the Tall guard barked, getting in my face and shoving me against the wall, with my arms trapped in his tightened grasp.

"What do you mean?" eye asked, looking his dumb ass square in the eyes. Motherfucking flash light cop bitch! Fuck you!

He laughed in my face. "It's going to get destroyed…"

Σ

Eye sat on the floor like somebody kidnapped my children and killed them. Then eye lay on the floor dead to myself, dead to the world. They took my soul. My soul was in my writings, writing that kept my mind out of prison. None of my books were about prison. NONE OF THEM! My books were about history and incredible sex and family deception, books that were thought provoking, bringing guards and inmates into my mind, into my world and they read how eye viewed the world and the Word and how eye mentally challenged things.

And all of that was gone.

A week has passed and eye hadn't been to work. Eye faked like eye was sick and made myself vomit and they left me the fuck alone. Eye hated myself and hated life. Why didn't eye leave my books at work where they would be safe? Easy. If eye was rolled up and moved to another institution they wouldn't let me go up to the Education Floor and get the product of my hard work. Then somebody else would steal it and publish it. Eye didn't look that stupid.

So eye brought them to the cell with me, where they'd be safe. And the guards used authority and came in my cell and took them.

Savage bitches.

My cell popped.

"Wilson! Hearings."

So eye had a hearing, and it was rather quick.

Convict Niggah, yea that was me, #12926272.

Stuck up Crackah. Well cut. Handsome, mid forties. Well groomed, tailored and dressed. Staring down my nose like he didn't get buggers, bitch.

"Mr. Wilson."

"Its Number one two nine two six two seven two. You don't know me like that to be calling my goddamn name."

"Tough one."

"Eye want my books."

"What gives you authority to use OSP computers…"

"State computers, dumb ass."

"To write what you call books. Eye saw what you wrote and its bullshit and trash."

"The skin heads don't think so."

"They just want to fuck some black snatch."

"Fuck you. Eye want my books."

"They have been destroyed."

A lump formed in my throat, like a mother just finding out her favorite child has died in a car accident by a drunk driver under age with a fake license.

"Ya'll destroyed my hard work?" Eye asked, tears forming in my eyes at the anger that begin to boil with my stomach acids and eye got heart burn. Eye was about to fuck this crackah up. And he wouldn't enjoy it.

"Let's get this clear, young man. You don't have no luxury in prison. You are not to use state computers and you are not to print using state printers for your entertainment."

"Fuck you bitch!"

He laughed. "Take your faggot ass back to C block."

Eye steamed all the way to my cell. Eye couldn't believe he gloated about my books being taken. My boss gave me permission. Mr. Gregson said eye could write for as long as eye wanted. That white man had my back. Eye told him what happened and he went to bat for me but they told him my books have been destroyed and eye cried myself to sleep.

Saying, "God *please* don't let it be true! Eye won't believe it! They couldn't have destroyed something you gave me. A gift for words. If they destroyed my books then why do eye still feel optimistic and determined to continue writing?

The next day, around 4 p.m., my cell popped.

Captain Lacey summoned me to the property room.

Oh, no. They changed my job probably to janitor just to make sure eye'm not around computers.

"Hey, Wilson."

Eye was dead to the world. Didn't look up or at him. Didn't care to. Eye said nothing.

"Wilson."

Eye said nothing, holding my stomach and eye puked on the floor and puked and puked, the force from the pull had my stomach muscles sore as fuck.

"Wilson!" He gave me a mop, and pushed some fresh mop water towards me. "Clean it up. That's a direct order."

And eye cleaned it up, huge tears falling down my face. How could they destroy 34 books like it's nothing?

Eye looked up and he handed me an index card.

"What is this for?"

"Write a name and address on there and don't tell nobody but eye switched boxes with a fake box and they threw out a box of old books from OSP's Library."

Eye blinked three times. "What?"

He picked up two huge boxes and set them on the counter. "Man *listen* here."

"MY BOOKS OH MY GOD!"

"Listen, Wilson. Eye was going to throw it out but eye read what all the prison hype was about when it came to your book and my Lord the way your mind thinks young man you write such incredible stuff. Eye'm a fan."

Eye shook his hand. "Thank you so much man this means so much to me and eye thought eye lost them forever. Thank you Jesus!"

My hand trembling from anxiousness, eye filled out the index card with my granddaddy's address and two boxes of my books were sent to him for safe keeping.

Paid for by the state, baby.

Thanks Mr. Lacey!

When it came time for nominations, my friend Craig was getting out of prison, and eye hated to see him go because eye had to find a compatible cell mate, but he needed to go and continue his climb from shame to grace. It ain't what you go through. It's how you get through that counts.

Eye had to put together a speech, and convince Uhuru Sasa members to vote for me for one of the highest positions: Secretary.

The speech for president and Vice President went well. My dude, Skeeta, who eye call my cousin 'cause we close like family, was running for President, and will win it. Very business minded.

When my name was called eye went up to the podium. My hair was growing out (eye had plats). Eye took center stage. Eye lay my papers on the podium, neatly typed before me. Eye said a quick prayer.

Amen.

"Hello, Eye'm Pharoah Wilson and eye know eye am the best man to be secretary. Eye type 62 WPM and as quickly as eye type memo's and faxes eye can stand up and defend the beauty of Uhuru Sasa."

Eye won them over already.

"...*Don't* vote for me out of favoritism, vote for me if you feel eye am the best candidate for the job and eye already told you eye'm the best so think like a winner and pick a winner. Thank you."

They clapped and whistled. Eye felt good about the voting.

Till this one muthafuckah stood up. "Eye oppose. Eye oppose till you tell us if it's true."

"Is what true?"

The Rapist asked me, "Is it true you caught Tony fucking my dawg, the Pimp, in a closet on the Education Floor."

OK. God was testing me. Time to see his presence.

Everyone was quiet because they wanted the answer. Shit, shit. You a Goulds Niggah! *Own* this moment.

Eye smiled, bowed and said, "Eye respect your question but at this time my speech is completed. Time has *expired*. And eye choose *not* to entertain the question. *Thank* you."

And everyone clapped, standing up and The Rapist looked like the ass he was.

Eye stared at him like, "Yea, bitch, check mate. Eye'ma Goulds Niggah."

Eye won Secretary.

Things were looking up for me. Eye stopped calling home so much and focused on myself behind those thirty foot walls. Eye made my life worth living by writing books, and staying to myself. Being the Secretary was fun because eye got to vibe and bond with the President, Skeeta (Damien Neyland, my dawg outta Portland), Issac, and Stressla.

Damien was the most business minded Niggah eye ever met. Eye think he was in for murder, but he has truly changed for the better. It reflected in his business sense and the very respectful way he spoke to people. Eye learned a lot from him that eye apply to my career right this very day in 2010 as eye type this with White Zinfandel Arbor Mist chilled at my side.

Clad in Phat Farm sweat pants (eye jammed in around the park earlier) a long sleeved gray NIKE shirt and black Nikes and Niggah socks (means eye didn't have any socks on).

But all things, good things at least, must come to an end. Before eye went through a falling out with three inmates, eye was selected with a hundred or so others to be in Bruce Willis and Billy Bob Thorton's movie *Bandits*.

Eye was so excited. Eye didn't think eye would get picked when eye took off my shirt to pose for a Polaroid picture. Producers combed through applications we filled out and eye made the cut.

Eye was so excited Eye was about to get my first taste of Hollywood from in prison.

When eye was coached by the director, while they were about to shoot "The Boxing Ring" scene, eye was sad because eye didn't get picked to be an extra in that particular scene.

After the director and his side kick called out names, eye walked off.

"Hey, you," said the director, Barry Levinson.

Eye turned to face him. "Yes."

"Pharoah Wilson, Jr, right?"

"Yes."

"Come on, man. You're picked to be up close to Bruce Willis and Billy Bob!"

Oh my God!

Thank you Jesus!

And 14-15 hour shooting days began.

Doing the same thing over and over. Eye had on red shorts, black shoes, white socks and a blue skull cap over my braids.

Bruce Willis OH MY GOD! Was in the ring, in boxing gear getting ready for his scene.

It was SO COOL! BRUCE WILLIS WAS THIRTEEN FEET AWAY FROM ME!

So close eye could smell the sweat of his hard work. He did the scene fluidly. Such a Die Hard star he was.

We had to do the same thing over and over. Eye was really excited when Billy Bob Thornton came in the room. He spoke to everybody and eye died. Eye think he was married to Angelina Jolie, when she was just dick sucking lips then, keeping Billy's blood in a locket around her neck.

Barry Levinson stopped filming a few times, looking directly at me. "Pharoah. Act like cameras aren't in here. You keep looking in the camera smiling!"

"Sorry!" He was so nice. Shit HOLLYWOOD!

Billy and the director went over the scene. Bruce, during breaks, sat down with a makeup artist reapplying his makeup. He looked so goddamn scrawny, not at all the buff dude eye saw in *Die Hard*.

And he kept looking at us out the corner of his eye like he was disgusted, like we were going to snatch his little ass and eye was like aw shit dude you ain't all that now. Eye haven't even seen Die Hard. None of them. Just the commercials.

Barry Levinson snapped his fingers and screamed BAKGROUND! Meant we had to do our extra part, making like we were training while Bruce was boxing. ACTION! Billy Bob rushed into the boxing room. Telling Bruce they took garlic off the commissary.

Bruce, according to the script then got frantic and started punching the hell outta the man in the ring and Billy Bob Thornton screamed ANGER MANAGEMENT! ANGER MANAGEMENT!

It was perfect!

CUT!

The director was cool with that.

When we wrapped for the night, a man took a few Polaroid pictures of the set so it could be decorated exactly how it was during tomorrow's shoot.

What an experience. The next scene was the break out of prison shot. We had to play basketball on the court while Bruce and Billy sneak to a cement truck to break out of prison. Eye saw the different camera angles. One shot had the camera just on Bruce and they had to act as if both were being filmed. CUT. Then the next shot the camera was just on Billy and they did the same acting. HOT!

When Bruce and Billy got to the cement truck to break out of prison we had to run, cheering, towards the gates, leading them on. They even did a shot with a camera on a motor cycle and the camera man on the motorcycle kept up with the cement truck. WOW!

After that scene Bruce was his usual retreating eye'm scare of ya'll self and Billy Bob came over to speak to us.

OH MY GOD! Everyone shaking his hands, pushing me out the way. Eye couldn't get to him. He was signing any autograph the inmates wanted telling us he did time before and that there was life after prison.

He looked me deep in the eyes and smiled and eye melted OH MY GOD!

"Come here young man."

A few inmates mumbles something out of hate and eye smiled, star struck. He shook my hand OH MY GOD and he said, "Who do you want me to make your autograph out to?"

"To Pharoah with Love."

"Who is Pharoah?"

"Me, silly!" Eye could not stop smiling.

"This is the last autograph eye'm signing today, Pharoah. You getting out soon?"

"In a couple years."

"Something different about you," Billy said. "What you do to occupy your time?"

"Eye write books."

He shook my hand once more. "Never give up. Who knows. One day you might be a bestseller."

And that's exactly what happened. Thanks Billy Bob Thornton! When the movie wrapped our money was deposited on our inmate trust accounts. A hundred something dollars. Since we were inmates we couldn't get the high pay scale, but eye was cool with that because eye got to shake Billy's hand and get an autograph.

Eye sent my free BANDITS hat and shirt to my brother, and sent my BILLY autograph to Tamera.

Then disaster struck me.

When eye wasn't even prepared.

Darkness came.

Eye was on the Activities Floor, doing Uhuru Sasa business.

After typing up a BLACK FIRST article for the inmate population in Uhuru's News Letter, eye decided to take a little break from writing.

So eye stood up and headed for the Studio; a place where certain inmates made rap beats and rapped their well-produced music. Damascus (Doo Doo) was the best goddamn rapper eye had ever seen. A young cat eye grew close to. He was one of the coolest Niggahs in the world and he loved my writing and eye loved the way he wrote raps and spit his verses and his flow made TI look like shit but of course eye didn't think T.I. was out during that time and this dude was like 23 or something like that.

Sometimes Big Zin, cool ass niggah and a helluva producer and rapper, laid down tracks and eye got to hear them. Big Zin was good people.

But that particular day Big Zin wasn't up there.

An inmate, Anthony (the Pimp eye caught banging the other Pimp in the educational floor closet), came up to me, smiling. Eye couldn't stand this snake. He used to pimp men and women all over the world. And this niggah had it bad for me. He told me he was going to spit rap (game) till he gained control of me.

"You're the *finest* bitch in the institution," he said. "Eye got to have you."

"Well you can't have me, dude damn. Let my pores do their job and sweat me naturally."

"Look. Go back by the studio. One of your homeboys called you, told me to come get you."

"Who?"

"Big Dog, your lover."

"He ain't my lover."

"Please. That Niggah eating that sweet boy pussy. And he lucky. Eye know he sticking dick to that sweet asshole."

"Bye, Anthony."

Naively, Eye went to the studio to see what Big Dog wanted. When eye got back there eye was ambushed. By three Niggahs, Anthony included. One punched me so hard in the face eye flew into the wall. One was a red bone Niggah with a sick need that needed attention. Another was a tall dark skinned Niggah that didn't love himself and raped niggahs to build his ego and recharge his power and Anthony was just a late faggot. Eye didn't scream because eye was from Goulds, bitch and we owned up to a battle. My heart quickening, eye said a quick prayer to God, knowing eye wore his full armor.

"*Hey* Miami!" said the bald one, the ring leader with a black chiseled body rivaling a Greek God. Fucking beautiful, but right now wasn't a very beautiful moment. His dick hard from anticipation, he unbuttoned his pants and pulled his dick out. Eye remained quiet, observing those Oregon niggahs. They never spoke to me before. Why they try'na spark a conversation now?

My game face sturdy, eye said, "What do you want with me?"

The red one said, "It's about that time Miami."

Anthony said, "We gonna fuck the shit out that pussy. We tired of dreaming about it. Niggah eye want a shot of pussy now! NO LUBE!"

"Hell naw, bitch! Ya'll gotta fight me and fucking take it!"

The black one, eye'll call Black Stallion, jerked his dick, then slapped it against his hand to get it extra hard. Cute ass. But he wasn't getting no ass today.

"Eye wanna cum in your asshole, Miami."

"Fuck that! Let's rape this bitch Niggah. NO MERCY!" said Anthony.

"Eye want some booty hole with your sexy ass. Eye always wanted a shot of Miami pussy," the red one said, his huge dick hard as hell.

My guard went up. Everything my ex step daddy did to me came flooding back. Eye was shell shocked, panicking. About to have a nervous breakdown and they fed off it, tormenting me. Saying what they were going to do with me. We hate Dade County, bitch! Were gonna put three dicks in your pussy they promised. Eye was gonna *love* it, said Anthony. The humiliation of my childhood, the embarrassment was too much. Tears fell down my face and eye quickly wiped them away Eye was a warrior. Prepared to fight.

Eye lowered my head, my eyes on the devil's spawns.

"Ya'll gotta fight me. Eye'm not coming off my ass, sorry bitches."

"He called us a bitch," said Black Stallion. "Eye'ma kill this faggot when eye'm done fucking him!"

"Don't resist us, Pharoah. If you do we are gonna fuck you longer and harder."

"Bitch!—suck it!" eye yelled.

The red one lashed out at me, *grabbing* my arms and the black one was behind me, "Yea gimme this ass!"

Eye flung the back of my head into Darth Vader and eye head butted the piss colored Niggah in the face.

They both stumble back, disoriented.

Eye was a bit disoriented myself.

Did Black Stallion, Anthony And Red Man rape you?

Lord Jennings

Two arms wrapped around my body from behind, holding me tight, and Anthony hastily pulled my pants down. Eye was trying to break free and eye refused to fucking yell. Fear bit at me ferociously but I needed to survive. They looked like killers, and I refused to believe this was it for my life. Like Hell. If they wanted to fuck they had to fight me for it. Every ounce of fight I had they had to exhaust.

    Black Stallion punched me in the stomach and the light skinned one pushed me on the floor, holding my legs and Anthony held my arms and they punched me in the ribs and in the back and eye felt paralyzed. I'd never known so much pain.

    Eye thought of the officer eye met when eye first arrived at OSP.

    "*Something is off about you.*"
"*Off?*"
"*Yea. Looking at you, you don't belong in a place like this.*"
"*Tell me about it. Famous last words.*"
"*OSP isn't all that bad, I hope you weren't scared up before you got here.*"

"Yea a friend was telling me it's the mad house."

"Here's the ropes, Miami. Stay away from the tobacco trade. Don't snitch, mind your business, and always eat. Eat all you can."

"Why?"

"You'll understand if it ever happens to you. And if it does you shit all over those motherfuckers, Pharoah."

The instant Black Stallion tried to push his dick in my asshole eye let muthafucking go.

Eye started shitting all over his ass and he jumped fifty feet back, swinging fists, disgusted.

Eye just kept shitting, the sounds felt like my favorite rap jams as they poured into my ears. Shitting on myself, muthafuckahs you wanna fuck me cum get this shitty booty muthafuckahs.

Eye got up and slapped Anthony with shit.

"Ya'll want some ass?" eye yelled, throwing shit at Black Stallion and it was all in his face. He started vomiting all over himself. Disgusted beyond his wildest dreams. Nah, bitch you ain't dreaming. I'm ya worst nightmare, bitch!

Sipping in vomit and shit, Anthony tried to run.

"Oh, no piss colored Niggah!" I yelled at him...

Angrily, eye ran behind him and slapped shit in his mouth and he fell on his back, kicking and gagging, trying to spit shit Niggah you ain't no rapper you a bullshit artist rapist muthafuckah!

Anthony was so disgusted he squirmed on the floor, gagging and making himself vomit and eye squatted over him and shit, just fucking boo boo boo boo all over that Niggah.

Goddamn, what did eye eat? Fuck. He pushed me on the floor, and I lid in my own shit but I didn't give a fuck. They were trying to rape then kill me and these so-called OSP guards fucking off and ain't doing their jobs so I'll do it for them!

Al four of us slipping and sliding, and I staggered to get up but I got a rush of adrenaline and I stood up, ran at Black Stallion and eye kicked him in the rib cage, repeatedly, trying to pull my pants up.

He's grunting, holding his side, curling up.

Anthony grabbed my foot and I slipped against the wall, but caught myself.

Eye kicked Anthony and that's when the Red Bone Niggah tried to run at me and eye pivoted on my heel and slapped him with shitty hands.

Whop, bitch!

Pow! Bam! Boom, bitch!

He slipped in shit and fell on Anthony.

"How about some golden piss!" I was so lost within myself part of me started to turn darker than the color black.

Eye pissed all over their asses, looked to the side and saw a push broom.

While Anthony, Red Bone and Black Stallion sliding in stank shit, trying to get up eye stuck the broom stick up Black Stallion's ass and kicked his bitch ass in the face.

Blood spurted from his thick lips.

And the minute the light skinned Niggah tried to scream I pulled the broom stick out Black Stallion's flat ass and eye shoved the shitty broom stick in his mouth, his head snapping back from the force of it on his tonsils.

"How that shit taste, bitch!"

Eye beat their asses with the broom for dear life!

And dropped it, pulling up my pants, shit all over my clothes.

And left the Activities Floor so fast I couldn't breathe.

What was the boiling point of doing time? Did it ever break you down?

Lord Jennings

SU/I\C/I\DE

After eye got back to my cell after taking a shower and washing feces and fear off me, eye turned off the light, leaned against the wall and slid down to my ass. Closing my eyes, eye was breathing in deep, wide eyed and my hands in the form of fists. Eye didn't want to be anymore. Eye simply didn't *want* to *be* anything. Eye shook with rage but burdened down with the blues. Eye wanted to scream, rant and yell but decided not to because they would think eye was crazy and they would dope me up in the SMU (Special Management Unit) so why bother? Eye didn't feel like being pumped or forced to take institutional drugs. They could be giving us some incurable shit, using us as lab rats so fuck it.

Eye missed home and eye missed my freedom. Eye was having Vietnam flashbacks about my freedom, and life on the other side of the thirty foot walls. Why didn't eye listen to Mama and *why* did eye have to be so fucking hard headed. Dumb ass bitch. Now you're a convict and they all gonna laugh at you! My hands shook with fury and eye started perspiring. As eye got angrier and angrier, withdrawing into myself, losing sense of reasoning, the blackness zapped my color and in return gave me anything my heart desired; as long as eye used it in the comfort of the darkness.

Eye hated myself so much eye hadn't realized the sun has set and it was well after 10:30 p.m. Eye sat here in this spot, didn't fart, eat, shit or piss at all. Didn't think of it, didn't want to do it if eye thought of it. Count time came and went and when the guard walked his faggot ass by he simply looked in on me, checked off his inventory list, and moved on to the next cell.

Eye miss HOME! Oh my God! *Let* me out this bitch! Prison has finally broken me down. Eye can't be strong anymore. Eye forgot how to.

Eye'm shattered and broken right on down to the core. The final transition of soul from body interjected into my mental immobility. My inner self. Eye didn't want to live anymore and putting my hands in front of my face eye didn't want these hands anymore. Could eye get a refund on the purchase, Lord?

Eye looked at my feet and suddenly didn't want them anymore and surely not my body. *Grown* muthafuckahs been using my asshole and my goddamn dick LONG ENOUGH! Eye turned out to be a promiscuous muthafuckah. Couldn't control my flesh because eye was never taught how to take care of my individual self.

This was the end! Goodbye, world! Hey young world my ass, Slick Rick. Muthafuckahs reading me bedtime stories have given me nothing but grief and nightmares that played like full Hollywood movies through my mental frame of mind for the 8 hours a night eye sleep.

Eye couldn't believe my life has resorted to this. All eye've been through have become troubled waters.

Eye couldn't sleep. Just lost my lover, Big Dog. He was told to pack up and they moved him to a lesser security facility. Eye was heartsick because eye kept our affair hidden for so long, and now eye couldn't hide it anymore. Eye broke my own goddamn rule. *Never* get attached to anyone. They could be moved at any given moment. You'll learn that fast when doing time. Stay as unemotionally attached from Niggahs as you can!

Eye was in love with an incredible man in my eyes, *but* because we're convicts society labeled us scum.

Two state numbers submerged into love. Eye knew eye was going to die in prison and the realization made me hop up and vomit in the silver commode. The thought of never seeing my mother destroyed me inside. The thought of never seeing my only sister graduate high school or see her pretty self all dressed for her Prom sickened me. Eye already missed Laron and *Jarshawn's* high school graduation and looking at the pictures Mama sent me only made me die inside because eye couldn't see or talk to them so in my mind eye destroyed the images of family so eye could meet my maker with ease.

Eye wasn't going to tell anyone so nobody tried to save me. When you cried out about suicide you weren't going to do it. No, you wanted attention and eye didn't want attention so eye was going to snub my fucking self.

By the time eye thought of time it was 2 a.m. in the morning. Whole cell block asleep. Nobody up at all. Few TV's glowed from several cells but all was quiet. Too quiet. The silence fell on my ears with a ton of unease. Eye heard a few murmurs and moans, and the guy one cell over from me had an orgasm and his cell mate kept saying, Yes, Nigga...cum deep in that boy pussy!"

Depressed, eye turned on hot water and lit a small candle I took from the Activities Floor (contraband) but who cared if it was contraband when eye was about to kill myself.

Eye turned on the hot water and steam colored the mirror. Darkness and the glow of the candle twisting the night away beautifully. Eye was one with the radiance. Of the low. And the darkness. Misery filled my heart and overflowed into my bleeping soul. Sort of here, gone, here gone. Here, gone the next second here, gone the next second.

The steam. Moisture on my face and arms. Nipples erect. The blurs on the mirror now fog. Eye looked into my misconstrued reflection. Eye raised a finger, studying myself, my void, emotionless eyes…growing wearily dark. Eye was a grain of sand mixed with rice in a salt shaker.

Eye drew the all-seeing eye in the middle of the mirror, thinking of Africa; my fingertip moist from the interference of steam/fog interaction.

"Eye hate you." Eye told my reflection. The reflection of my left eye aligned with my illustration. Eye was about to steal time from myself.

"Eye have hated you for a very long time, Pharoah," eye said to myself, meaning every fucking WORD! "Your past loathes you. Your future doesn't think you're strong enough to make it. Eye am an inmate: 12926272 to be exact. The state's property yet they say we freed from slavery. Bullshit. Now eye couldn't free myself from self-hatred. Forever branded," eye went on, raising the razor to my right wrist, tears falling down my face and dripping from my chin, falling into the sink water, mixing with heat and steam.

Eye cut open my wrist, the pain not even making me wince. Eye was too far gone, retreated too far into myself, past my soul, backing away from the light source, the glow of the Holy Ghost distant and fading every time eye took a step back.

"Eye'm in love with a state number Niggah. He's gone, probably met somebody else and digging that Niggah out. Packed up and left with hardly a hug to commemorate the relationship. When the bars closed with him on the opposite end carrying his property forever separated us. Disturbing my self-rehabilitation. Now eye was a wreck, couldn't stop trembling. Rubbed my asshole trying to spark a conversation with my dick and it didn't feel the same. Eye could still taste him on my tongue, my lips begging for a piece of the essence.

"Eye hate you, Pharoah."

Eye traced the all-seeing eye with my blood. And then eye punched the glass repeatedly until it cracked down the center. Eye kept punching.

"Eye hate you, Pharoah! Eye hate you! Eye don't wanna be here! Eye don't wanna write anymore! Fuck this shit!"

"*Miami,*" an inmate called out from the cell above me.

"FUCK YOU! FUCK OSP!"

"*Pharoah, bruh please listen to us man, you a helluva writer. Don't give up, man!*"

"Eye can't do this anymore!" My blood spiraling down the drain with the running water.

"*Miami, man you have so much to live for,*" said a white inmate from the cell opposite mine.

"NO EYE DON'T! Eye'm a convict. We're all convicts! The enemy has won!"

"*Miami. Eye love your writing, man. Not trying to sound like a pussy ass Niggah, man. Don't you understand? Eye am never getting out, Miami. Your writing is all eye have to look forward to Miami eye don't have a family. Mom is dead, daddy dead, brothers dead, sister, dead, wife, dead, children, dead. Died during the last fifteen years eye been incarcerated in this very cell.*"

"*Fuck that shit!* All that writing ain't *shit!* Eye'm fooling my goddamn self. Me, an author, Yea, right! Eye will never be published! NEVER!"

"*Miami,*" said another inmate from the cell below.

Eye grew silent. A few more inmates woke up, harsh whispers filled my ears.

"I'M A NIGGA AIN'T NO SECOND CHANCES FUCK THAT WRITING SHIT FUCK THAT SHIT NAACP DON'T WANNA KNOW ABOUT ME WHAT THE FUCK LEAVE ME ALONEEEE!"

"Man, Miami! If you stop writing eye will kill your ass, fuck Niggah. Represent your black culture, Niggah. You hear me Niggah?"

"Miami, hang in there man. At least you got a release date."

While eye continued getting words of wisdom, and praise and threats on my life if eye turned my back on myself and my writing, eye silently turned to the light yellow metal wall. Closing my eyes. God. Eye've wasted your time. My life was a complete joke. Look where eye am. Eye am nothing, God. Nothing! Nothing about me was worth talking about, thinking about or saving. Jesus died for nothing, God eye am so sorry he gave his life for me and eye didn't deserve it. Eye give up.

Eye'm not a manuscript. *Jail house writing* my shit was called. Eye threw my manuscript in the toilet, water swarming the bottom half of it and eye started flushing. Over and over as my wrist slowly clotted, and blood stopped coming out. Dark red and hardening into a thick scab. The rush of cold toilet water soundly filled my ears.

Eye flushed the toilet again. Whispering harshly *"Eye don't wanna write eye don't wanna write eye don't wanna write eye don't want this writing shit!"*

Eye didn't have a gift. Eye'm no goddamn author. Eye'm no Tom Clancy and no James Patterson and no Sidney Sheldon! Those inmates were toying with me. Hey. Joke on Pharoah! Eye faced the wall. Eye give up, God. Right here right now. Eye give back the gift, didn't want it you could give it to someone more deserving. Eye would never write again! Eye reached up towards the top shelf. My hands shook. Eye took a Sharpie (contraband). And did what my heart told me to do.

Write.

You stole the stars from the sky.

Eye wrote it with big letters.

You froze the sparkles in my light brown eyes.

Something opened up in me, something real deep that was rushing to the top of the light for air, for just a quick GASP.

Eye welcomed the company. Eye was smiling through my tears, writing, loving what eye was writing and needing to write; it was *imperative* that eye keep writing because if eye stop writing eye was going to wither without writing then die with no future writing to immortalize.

Eye will never ask you why
Because my soul may turn on me and hide
There's no passion left within me
My truths won't even set me free
Eye have no start to finish from
So eye will be exactly. What. You. Want. To see.

Eye was lowering myself as eye wrote along the wall; writing so fast my head was spinning, focused and concentration, driving my words and sectioned them off where needed.

Eye continued writing the poem down the wall. My hand moving a mile a minute. Eye was nearing the end of the wall but eye kept writing. Running out of space.

Eye sat on my naked ass and wrote on my left thigh.

Now you wanna battle me
Jealousy against envy

On my right thigh.

Eye'm just Armor without a Knight.
Eye have no life.
So turn around and ride off into the moonless…

And on my forehead:

Night.

Eye stood up, slowly approaching the mirror. The water turned cold. Eye turned it off. Wasted enough of taxpayer's money and didn't give two fucks.

Above the mirror eye wrote:

Armor without a Knight

Eye got on my bunk, crawled into a ball and cried myself to sleep. The blood fully clotted in my swollen wrist. Before the Sand Man brought me a dream I whispered, "God, please kill me in my sleep. Forgive me for my sins. Amen…"

Funniest thing happened…

Eye awakened the next morning when the bells sounded and the guard yelled "CHOW! MORNING CHOW!"

The morning bell rang once more. Alerting inmates that the cells were about to close. Eye covered my eyes. Eye wasn't hungry and eye just wanted to be alone.

The bars closed back. The guard walked the tier and eye pulled my blanket up to my chin.

"Glad to see the future bestseller making it through the night."

Eye looked up.

It was Vencio.

Eye smiled. "Yea, eye did."

"Don't give up on your fans. Even though your fans are fellow inmates. You got men reading your shit, Miami. You are inspiring fucking inmates to be better than themselves, don't you realize that Pharoah? All of us love you dude. You aren't supposed to love in prison, but we love you dawg. We won't let anything happen to you, do you hear bruh? *You're* dedicated *and* you're humble. You smile everyday in a fucking dark place and that makes us smile. Not to mention niggahs chasing your ass all over the yard."

"Ha, ha Vencio."

"Promise me this," he said, taking my hands through the bars. He kissed them both.

"Yes."

"When you become famous don't let *anything* or no group of people turn you from God."

"Group of people?"

"Yes, group of people."

"What group of people?"

"If you're ever famous, you'll know bruh."

He got dangerously quiet and eye shook my head, confused but decided to drop it.

"Promise me, Pharoah!"

"Eye promise, Vencio."

He squeezed my hands. He never took his eyes off the all seeing eye dried in blood on my mirror.

Eye would never understand why. At least not at that moment.

But as the years passed and the books dropped, it would make perfect goddamn sense.

Perfect sense.

ME AND MY HOMEBOY, BOOT CAMP, FT SILL, OKLAHOMA SEPTEMBER OF 1995. UNITED STATES ARMY.

PHAROAH POSING BY BRAVO BATTERY 1ST AND 33RD, FIELD ARTILLERY

Ha ha this is one of my favorite pictures. We were cleaning our M16's. Me and the rest of the Army Goons.

Me and my friends at Gunner's Inn, a couple weeks before we graduated from AIT, 1995.

BRAVO BATTERY 1ST AND 33RD WARLORDS WHOOOOOAAAAAA!!!!

ME MR. CHI-TOWN

| DAPHAROAH69

My graduation picture UGH I hated it OMG!

Me and my ex girlfriend

ME AND THE SEXY WOMEN AT MY PROM. MY DATE, TAM, CAN YOU SAY YAWNNNNNNNNNNNNN.

UGH I HATED WORKING FOR RGIS INVENTORY OMG!

| DAPHAROAH69

Me and a dear friend from Lane, South Carolina 1995. I love the elderly.

Me at the New Buildings in Homestead, Gossip Central.

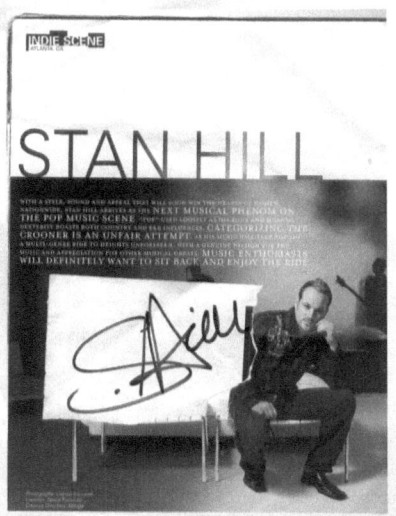

I SAW STAN HILL PERFORM IN THE ATL. HE WAS INCREDIBLE, AND I GOT HIS AUTOGRAPH!

YESSSS AND I GOT JANET'S AUTOGRAPH IN 1993, JANET TOUR (MY FIRST CONCERT) AND I NEARLY DIED! I WAS 15 YEARS OLD!

| DAPHAROAH69

My Militant look!

My smooth ass in front of Mom's house and the second is of me on the park with the Dog Collar around my neck.

Me and my afro in 2003

Me sitting on my Lincoln Continental during Hurricane Frances

| DAPHAROAH69

ME AT THE GOULDS CHURCH OF CHRIST

ME AND MY SERVER AT RED LOBSTER. SUCH A SWEETHEART!

Making use of this don't work ass motorcycle.

Dapharoah69

BITING THE CUFFS AWAY HATERS.

MY THAT'S THE WAY LOVE GOES MOMENT LOL

My two amazingly beautiful nieces. I will protect them at all costs.

Me and my niece Aliyaih

| Dapharoah69

ME AND MY NIECE SUNJARAIH, MY BOO BOO.

YEAAAAAAAAAAAAA THEY GOT LIKE THE COOLEST UNCLE SINCE POLAR BEARS EATING MELTED SLUSHIES WITH ICE CUBES.

ME AND ALIYAIH, HER FIRST DAY OF SCHOOL; AND ME AND MY NEICE AT THE MALL.

THE KING OF EROTICA. YEA BITCHES THAT'S RIGHT.

| DAPHAROAH69

Ummmm me and my babies!

Me and my bestfriend at Wal-Mart goofing off.

Me, my bestfriend Demetrius Mozell and Tyrone Payne, My brother.

Me and my brother. His graduation flick, South Dade High School

| Dapharoah69

ME HOLDING THE KING OF EROTICA BOOK 2: THE CROWN PROOF COPY.

ME, CARLTON AND MY FEMALE FRIENDS, SOUTH BEACH.

Me and my Dog Collar.

Jaime's birthday bash. Look at Cole's ass try'na be gangsta. And Brit Brit looking cute.

| Dapharoah69

ME DANCING WITH A NEW FAN AT THE ATL ITLA PRIDE, SEPTEMBER OF 2009. I TURNED DOWN A $1.5 MILLION DOLLAR CONTRACT A DAY BEFORE.

ME AND TWO NEW FANS. THEY SO KAYUTE (CUTE) OMG!

Tell me about your Earthly Wisdom

Lord Jennings

Back in the day (my Promiscuous Years), eye messed up and eye didn't realize eye messed up or how messed up eye truly was till eye became an adult and gradually matured. Maturity wasn't something you snapped into. Maturity was like olives. You had to acquire the taste. Some people didn't like the taste of olives and eye used to hate the taste myself. Frowning at the thought of olives and wanted to vomit from the smell. But one day eye tasted maturity and eye've been maturing ever since.

  Eye depended on my earthly wisdom when eye was going through hell and back. Dealing with backstabbing family and deceptive lovers had me turning to everything and everybody but God. Eye thought eye could do everything myself on my time table. Eye depended on earthly wisdom to make sound decisions and not God's grace.

  My life was so 2nd Corinthians. Blindly following God and doing a half assed job at it and didn't even understand

The Holy Ghost nor spirituality. That was my addiction. Eye read the Bible for sport because eye knew it was a conditioning tool crooked folks used to keep me obedient and controlled. And eye memorized and recited scripture for imaging purposes in church. My thought process back then was simple: how could eye believe in something eye couldn't see and say that eye love it above all else, even above my own life, mama, brothers and family when my own family didn't even love me if eye did *anything* for myself outside of them or for someone else? Hadn't my daddy Larry C Wilson, Sr, born in Riverdale, California November 1, 1955 (with a brother named Alton Clark and a sister named Beverly Clark out of California) done the same exact thing to me? Déjà vu. How could daddy love me and he hasn't laid eyes on me in over 30 years?

How could eye truly say eye love my father when eye didn't remember if eye ever laid eyes on him or not? Eye was about 14 months old when Mama left him. If he passed me on the street eye'd be *Where's Waldo* in a sea of faces. Even if eye tripped over his foot and said "Eye'm sorry, Sir!" and looked deep into his eyes we would still be unrecognizable and complete strangers. There would be no honorable mention or recognition. Eye was made in God's reflection and so was Daddy so looking in his eyes eye wouldn't see anything familiar for miles.

We're detached from God through sin and apparently God has cursed man with tending the fields.

The white man would eventually figure out how to tax generational curses next.

There was already a tax on pussy.

File income tax on what the woman pushed out on delivery beds and after the child was delivered parents or the parent give him or her a name and the government affixed a social security number. Once they digitize social security cards we will be microchipped and have to manually punch our socials with fingerprint recognition to get on or off the clock.

Something wicked this way comes. George W Bush's daddy already said a New World Order was soon coming, its all over You Tube. And eye hope you folks get it right with God soon...

After surviving the things eye have eye now depended on God's Grace to pull me through those dark days of adversity. The world already showed me love through letters and emails defending my authority over turning down $1.5 million and shunning the Gag Order a "major" publisher was trying to affix on my lips. But eye read contracts and eye read it thoroughly.

My critics attacked me once upon a blue moon like Paul in 2nd Corinthians. There was so much drama in 2nd Corinthians eye'm starting to think eye was Paul in a past life.

Paul instructed the Corinthian believers in the faith and addressed several problems there, according to the Caucasian written Holy Bible. Eye never trusted a muthafuckah with a flat ass and a Colgate smile.

And in this life eye did just that. Instructed my fans, my believers, to give all praise to God and not me when it comes to these books. Don't thank me for the success eye've had. It's not mine, its God's. Eye'm just doing my job, telling my testimony and hoping somebody will be lead to Jesus.

And, *Lord<* my fans are very supportive. God, my fans praise your Holy name especially after surviving so much. And eye was still God-fearing and humble; treating people the way eye wanna be treated. Eye still fall on my knees and say *Thank You, Jesus* for the gift of writing books. Eye love it. And eye wouldn't change giving people hope for the world.

Or for earthly wisdom.

Why do you say your family is a hoax?

Lord Jennings

Eduhate™. *What is that you ask? Edu. And Hate? Eduhate is the opposite of educate. When you raise your kids through proper education to grow into a thing of negativity and hate then that's eduhate. Professors always rush the lesson for a check but the scientist usually takes his time with his studies and career. Those kind of men don't work for checks or live check to check. They sign checks.*

This part of the chapter I come to realize one simple thing, and boy was this a wakeup call for me. Whoever said Home was where the heart was must have been a runaway hiding out in the Aunt's dining room, behind the China cabinet because that couldn't be farther from the truth. As much shit as the some of (but not all of) my family put me through growing up, increasing the load God already had on me, never putting on me no more than I could bare, yet family play God and put their expectations on me and my self-confidence waivered and my inner voice demised. So I used to sit up at night and just cry. Because even as a kid I knew something wicked this way comes. My *elders* told me when I was 8. And my great-grandma Olive also warned me.

"Look, son," my grandpa said, his eyes stern, holding my glare down to a minimum gaze. "Life is hard, Son. I know you've been watching the *Snorks*, He-Man and the power of She-ra, I meant Greyskull but all that Disney Land shit cost money to enter. Ain't nothing peaches and cream in this life. Its all about hard work and determination."

I took that to heart. So I lived my life doing more dancing to music and entertaining, but what I was really doing was observing; observing my family and church-going friends that claimed they were so God-fearing and bashed me for being who and what eye was.

Belinda was a faithful attendee in the church and was a publicly embattled *Holy* woman; but look at this bitch over there hollering at our third cousin Weasel. They supposed to be family, even though he was five years older than her; shit, *that* didn't mean *anything* to those two incestuous bastards. The way they all up on each other I just KNOW he did something to that girl before she was 18.

Sleazy bastard. Yet when I come to church she was always in my face. Looking me up and down. McDonald's hash browns on her breath. Same heels she had on at the Club, at the recital, at the baby shower and wore back to the club. Why she always going to baby showers and then to the clubs to forget watching the first dance at the recital, oh shit at the Bridal Shower and then to church every time she go to a baby shower?

She trying to make sure the Daddy in every situation didn't realize that their son's eyes were not identical to his but the spitting image of his best friend, first cousin or brothers because when those you're close to meet your lover trust they gonna try that pussy to see if they can get it. But the catch was they gotta have a good job, drive a nice car and make decent money. Fucking a bitch with money and getting an outfit and some new shoes and gold teeth makes a Niggah feel like he came up in the dope game. But when he finds out a few of those bitches bought you those clothes with her husband's credit card, bought her outfit and heels with said credit card and depended on her other man, the side line Ho for survival, then you feel pimped, stupid and outlandishly foolish because another man's bitch got your soft ass tamed.

How you gonna come up in the dope game high off your own supply, eliminating another five dollars you coulda had in your pocket yet tell yourself you're a pimp? And when that lover leaves your ass you're dancing to R Kelly Slow Wind to remember how he grinded in that ass.

When you calling your old pimp twenty years later to see if there are any job openings then you got a muthafucking habit or a problem. Either way. It ain't Pharoah's problem.

So why bash me because I went from a four year rape survivor, suicide contemplator, false accusations, jailed for helping police with my best friend's murder when drug dealers secretly created scenarios with said police to stop me from talking but I was talking while I was walking, homeless, on parole and broke to becoming the first self-published author to place three different books in the Barnes and Noble.com Top 100 bestsellers list at the same time? To being featured in E Lynn Harris' Literary Café, to E Lynn holding my books up with such a radiant smile. Look at the glow of his eyes in that photo. Matched the glow of his teeth with devastating accuracy. Destiny met destiny. My pupils were the master of ceremonies for the Passing of the Trophy through the irises of the Master to Student brick layer.

I know I must pave the way for something using his blue prints but remaining Pharoah C. Wilson. I don't wanna be the next E Lynn Harris and whoever tried or tries to be the next E Lynn Harris will fail miserably because you failed the minute you inspired to be someone you can never be versus becoming the man you were destined to be by using common sense, your education and experiences to make a name for yourself; to give your testimony so you can inspire aspiring writers, artists, singers, rappers and songwriters? Every wrist has a sway. Mine matches the sway of my back.

That's what I did when I called my book The King of Erotica. I carved my own destiny. So what, I was in the porn industry for 5 days to make my money. I didn't enjoy it, I was thinking the entire time "I'm doing this to raise money for my own publishing," and I faked like I was moaning, and was pissed from all this Cut, that ain't right and goddamn it stop the film there are too many people in the background with background lights from the director.

Why were there so many people in there when it's a fuck scene but when we shoot the foreplay scene half the people leave from lack of participation?

That was my motto. Bitch don't talk about it, be about it! You want a book out then Niggah you put that muthafuckah out and you say something worth reading in it you fucking hear me! You be a voice for the silenced. You write your life in your characters and you give them strength, hope and throw in some conflict and when your fans ask you what inspired you tell them "I tried to be something I wasn't instead of being myself and making my own decisions and I wound up fucked up, ridiculed and scorned. But I made it. I endured that shit."

Publishing houses shouldn't have rejected me without reading my book first, that goes for family too. Just wrote me off and didn't believe in me. If I would have had the blessings of family or a chance from a publishing house then I wouldn't have to do porn at the time to pave my own damn way. I sacrificed who I was to become the man I was destined to be. Isn't that Evolution? We all have done something we didn't wanna do to get to where we gotta be but of course for every positive there was a negative bitch saying "No, Sir. Nope. I never did what I didn't wanna do to get to where I wanted to be."

"So how do you know you've truly *arrived* if you never

left the 'Hood in search of the round world? And that's why you still fucking with Hood Rats in the Projects. Always telling a muthafuckah what you will never do. So why you selling dick to your sister's brother so he can pay his car note and have a little left over to cover his cell phone bill?"

Yup, one of my cousins was doing that right as eye typed this, but had the gall to call me names. Bitch suck it. Who really hides in the closet these days? Niggahs coming out like it's the In thing to do. What if a Niggah was hiding in the pantry or the garage? Shit, I was hiding in my Mama's closet. Hiding when she came home early and that man had just gotten through raping me. I was so upset I tried to hide behind the row of shoe boxes on the floor, filled with your receipts you were keeping till hell froze over.

So when he started having sex with Mama I crept out the bedroom without closing the closet door, nursing anger and frustration.

So stuck on the closet and you didn't see a bitch sneaking out of the house with his clothes in his hands and naked.

And as for my books…when I sent query letters to publishers, if they would have read it then threw it in the pile with the other books from the other people who didn't even type it up that would be one thing. I wasn't one of the people sending in a book written with pens and color pencils. At least I could tell them when the shit hits the fan and I get famous that I did warn you ahead of time of me and my talent. I sent a few publishers the *entire* manuscript and not to the other company and I remained loyal to the word of my query letter, but you already had another offer on the table.

One of those publishers told me I was getting published but secretly threw my shit in the trash, had me waiting for months with a pipe and a dream and wound up getting pipe from the dude I was with to make me nut and forget I was ever a fool for a publishing company who want all rights, not first publishing rights and wanna draw you up a contract with a gag order in it, that I could never say I was the King of Erotica and you thought I would endorse 1.5 million dollars for my life's work?

They must have thought a brothah didn't know a thing about contracts and taxes. After taxes I'm lucky to bring home $900,000. And if I told anybody I wrote the books the publishing house would take my black face off and put the white boy in loose unzipped jeans on my cover. They'd say and advertise that he's was The King of Erotica, staring, from the cover, at the ladies' with a hard dick; after that, the publishing house could sue me for the other $900,000 and now I would have *no* rights, no copyrights and freedom of speech in the constitution wouldn't get my work back. Constitution was written by gays in white wigs and pointy toed shoes.

That's how they came up with don't ask, don't tell me Abraham Lincoln was a fag when he wrote the Emancipation Proclamation? No wonder there's no equality between the DL Niggahs, the Bisexual Niggahs or the Feminine Niggahs. Didn't he get assassinated in a theatre yet we as blacks always jump on the whites in theatres when they show racial films such as Malcolm X and Roots?

Just don't tell my wife, they say.

I didn't know this was poker.

Bitches I AM the King of myself; I KNEW I was the King now and every man, gay or straight, trying to prepare the coronation with the debris from a dumb ass *never* gets recognition. But a dick head damn sure opens doors when your hands are full, bitches. That's how I looked at adversity. As a bitch I could fuck and pray it's not a man in drag.

If you bring a broke Niggah or a broke Ho around your family that inspires a bitch to get a goddamn job. Bitches hate to be broke. I meant Niggahs hate to be broke. So if they gotta sell dick to the highest bidder recession remains a thing of the past. Because his mind was on his money so how could money really be on his mind when he staring and paying for ass all day. That's hustling, I say.

And my family ain't no exception. So to find out I was gay, and no longer bringing the pretty girls around, they bashed me hard. "That Niggah gay. Told ya'll he was gay. Fuck, man. And that was a jazzy Hoe he brought around here two months ago. Man what I woulda did to that pussy. Can't do that shit to no muthafucking man, bitch."

Um, muthafuckahs. That *was* a man in drag. Looked like a real woman, huh? I guarantee his nuts are bigger than yours and he wears panties and bras. If that's true how come one out of the three gay guys I used to hang around described your dick size, the size of your balls and knew about that small tattoo of a Scorpion behind the head of your dick?

You trying to hide something?

And to an older female cousin…used to always have my name in her mouth. Chile…I *always* knew your older son was your so-called baby Daddy's best-friend's baby, but since his mind always on money and never taking his time he didn't stop long enough to really think about the situation he was in.

I used to ask myself that. When things were familiar you release something peculiar. But I got tired of bitches talking shit about my mother when she was there to defend herself.

"Um hmm, where ya' Mama?" one of my cousins once asked me, a few years ago.

I had an attitude. "At home sleeping. She's tired."

"Tired? She needs to be tired. Working all the goddamn time. Never hang out with the girls any more. I remember she used to come over to your Aunt Rose house and she used to have this smile, this glow about her. Yea. *Now* the red bitch acts like she doesn't *know* anybody. She won't even lend a bitch $5."

"Well, you're talking to the wrong person. If she don't wanna hang out find you some new friends or get a goddamn hobby. When you depend on people for your happiness I wouldn't hang around your dumb ass either so you can keep my Mama name out your mouth, bitch."

The same family that stood in the way of my dreams, trying to destroy, *stop* or stagnate me, take your pick, was the *same* family I had to watch closer than my friends when my books took off and they talked and bashed me, even when my books were added on Amazon.com (and a gazillion other online retailers) in Japan, Europe, The United Kingdom, Germany and Canada. Some of my family were like "How did this loud mouth faggot make it this far in the book game?"

Didn't you think that hurt when I found out? But you know me, Dapharoah, excuse me Pharoah, have been suffering in silence since I was 6 years old so every year I was destroyed and violated I unlocked a puzzle to piece myself back together through unbiased eyes so when I did graduate high school with a diploma I was a little stronger than half the kids my age, because I had something they didn't.

An OLD soul.

At least my grand daddy once told me that, the most intelligent man I know.

Its funny how so many people tell me some bad things about my grandfather yet he stays trouble free and has a good marriage. After all these years he still cherishes his wife, who I called grandma, but knew she could never be or replace my Grandma Alice because I never met Alice or looked in her eyes so looking in my new granddaddy's wife's eyes didn't remind me of my Grandma Alice.

That's how you misconstrue some shit.

Suddenly I knew and understood that people all over the world were buying my books. Maybe not by the millions (sometimes I start to regret turning down that 1.5 million dollar contract, but then again that's just the after math of a rash decision so it's all good) but every book I sell reminds me of progress so if I'm willing to hustle myself to get my sexual message out there then I have equal opportunity rights to turn around and put that some of my characters have diseases, ailments, were gay or bisexual, in the closet fiends that bash openly gay guys and raid bath houses during Gay Pride; so while they are publicly scandalized you got the time to destroy the sex you two had on the Video Phone, burn the pictures and delete the evidence, never revealing you were having an affair with the subject. Where was the confidentiality in this country?

You're drinking water to quench my thirst while my blood continues to push beer, weed and other ailments from my brain. Yet blood is thicker than water. If you add water to it, stretch it out and become something weakened and implausible, you're just a man of color because the black of your skin slowly and gradually tarnishes every time you use the white man's skin products. Talk about bleaching skin. *Go* ahead; keep buying that buy one get one free lotion. Ain't nothing cheap in this country, including lotion. So beware. You know the trick? You know the gimmick? Since its buy one get one free, take down the suggested price, raise the retail price from $4.99 to $7.99, doesn't add up when you get the buy get one free but at least we recouped 45% of the funds so we're still good.

Anything better than nothing ain't always good if he smoking a crack pipe and fooling the public.

You need to know this about the world before you buss a nut, squirrel. Busting nuts and getting pecans has always been the In thing to do. Because man these days learn from their sons, the ones they abandoned back in the day chasing good pussy, yet your son in your absence survived rape, survived raising his younger siblings and remained man of the house, showing you how a man really was supposed to be. That's why I wish to find and meet my Daddy. So I can shake his hand, say Devil I rebuke you, and turn on my heels, Shalom, and never look back again to remind myself of the sale.

So you don't wake up a year later, scream from a dream and look at your hands to remember how far your roots and your blackness actually go, wanna be white boy.

Tell me about an awkward date

Lord Jennings

I was going on a date. Well, not really. In his mind it was a date. I was involved with someone and in love, and yes he knew that and I told him that but he still wanted to take me out, since I didn't go out at all when I was writing, so this was his way of re-introducing me to the world. A world I was trying to escape.

I really liked this boy, but eye was with someone that truly made me happy. I write 14 hours a day, 6 days a week. Fall asleep writing. Wake up, thank God for waking me up, take my HIV medicine after praying over it and I write. I write everything. The smell of Downy fresh in the air as my clothes wash in the machine and the scent of fabric softener sheets tumbling with my drying clothes.

The hum of the dryer pours into my ears when he hit me up on my cell for a date. Fine Niggah.

"Damn, King, you write all day."

"I'm Pharoah. God is the King, not me."

"But you're the book writer. My Mama praises your book. Read it five times already. Her and my grandma fighting over the book and shit. My Grandma read you went through four years of rape and lost her mind. She rushed to her closet and pulled her gun. Crying and shit. Damaged because your books inspired her to write again. And she said she wanted to kill the man who raped you. I never seen grandma stand up for shit after her husband died."

I was touched. "Maybe I can meet her."

"I thought you would never ask."

He drove me over to meet his family.

And I was nervous. People tend to sum me up by the books I write. They don't understand that I'm three people when I write.

Dapharoah69, the author that pieces stories together like the wind blows.

Pharoah Wilson, the gentle giant with a quick temper, validated himself sexually and didn't love himself to his fullest potential and The King of Erotica JUST DON'T GIVE A FUCK!

His Mama had stars in her eyes. House Pine Sol'd down. Sinks cleaned with Comet. Food cooking on the stove. Trying to convince me there wasn't a sign of dysfunction in her house.

Chile. It was everywhere. In her choice of framed photography. Her son's baby pictures but no updated framed pictures.

Pictures of his Mama in short skirts and eccentric hairstyles at the club doing club poses with the Niggahs. Well I called it a female doing "prison" poses at a club. Mimicking what her baby daddy sent her in photos from the Big House. Man was a big time dope dealer.

He had it all and I guess she still thought they were in their hey day, when he was never going to see sunlight again. When was she going to understand that some of those clubs (and especially the clubs she frequented) was a woman's prison? Alcoholic incarceration? There's a reason women (not men) get in free and drink free all goddamn night. Promoters and deceptive niggahs wanted ya'll asses drunk that's why they wore Easter suits at the front door ushering your asses inside so when you awakened the next day good and fucked (in both holes) don't ask God "Lawd, why me?"

"How are you, King?" she asked, kissing my cheek. Doll was clad in dollish clothes. Hair tight. Nails long and chic. Purple panties barely contained behind a very short skirt she hasn't worn since the late 80's.

"I'm good, Ma. Nice to meet you."

I raised her arm and spun her around. "NICE MAMA!"

"Thank you! You're a good, *good* man. And what you went through as a child, son call me Mama. I won't let nobody hurt you."

"I appreciate that."

"COME EAT!" she said, taking my hand and pulling me to the table. "I cooked fried chicken, corn bread (I put sugar in mine, hope you understand), mashed potatoes and homemade gravy, baby. My gravy ain't store bought."

She fixed the plate, set it in front of me and gave me a beer.

I wasn't hungry. I had the urge to write. It hit me hard, and the sight of food did a number on my stomach.

I stood up. "Can I wrap it to go home with me? I write a lot and barely eat. I can eat it later."

"Sure. Sure. I don't have that many plates but sure."

She was a little disappointed. So I bit off the chicken (YUCK! What the fuck she put in this?), and gave a winning smile.

She clasped her hands together, scrunching her face for my approval.

"Damn this shit taste good." I bit it again, and spooned mashed potatoes in my mouth (ugh! NO SALT IN HER FOOD!)

"You like it?" She's clapping, hugging her son.

"Yes. You can cook your ass off."

"Thank you! Take a plate for your Mama."

My Mama ain't gonna eat this nasty shit! She trying to make Mama shoot my ass for bringing her tasteless food. When you fuck up fried chicken then bitch you can't cook.

But I didn't tell her that. I kept it in.

Grandma merges from the room. "What's all this ruckus out here?"

"Hello, ma'am," I said respectfully. When you're a guest in someone's home YOU spoke first.

"Who you? Get out my house. Why ya'll bringing sorry ass Niggahs in my house? GET OUT BOY!"

I started for the door. Old bitch. Bye.

"Mama," said my friend's Mama. "That's Pharoah Wilson, the author, The King of Erotica."

"THAT'S WHO?" She looked at me. "No its not!" She rushed in her room, grabbed my book and waltzed up to me barely keeping her dentures in her mouth.

She held the book up next to my face.

She dropped the book on the floor, her hands trembling. "Oh my sweet lovely Jesus in heaven."

She grabbed my hands and started singing old Negro hymns. She then started kissing my face and I smiled.

I was floored.

Her voice was filled with so much pain, untold pain. I wanted to understand her pain but I never sung a Negro spiritual or hymns and singing those boring ass church songs at the Goulds Church of Christ didn't count.

She kissed my hands. "Ya'll offer this young man something to eat?"

"Yes, they did," I said. "Taste good."

"Now I know you lying, Niggah," she said, pulling me to the kitchen. "That nasty ass chicken and salt less mashed potatoes my daughter cooked two days ago was leftovers."

She pulled out the plate from the oven. It was wrapped in foil. She handed it to me.

"I cooked this last night. I cook for myself. Season it to your specifications and pray over it for nutrition. Why worry about salt in your food and high blood pressure when you got God, son. Food was made to eat, not be monitored. Don't listen to those skinny crackahs on TV selling you a diet plan. Who the fuck is Jenny Craig anyway? I'm a black woman. I ain't try'na be a skinny white bitch. And just because she cook with Aunt Jermimah didn't mean she knew about black food. God don't monitor food. His people fast, cut food away for a specified amount of days. They ain't worried 'bout no goddamn salt. Eat."

I took the plate. I kissed her cheek. "Thank you."

"You keep writing those books. Your books made me look at my gay grandson with some respect. Because of you I found out my sister molested him when he was 9 years old. Your book is the voice of the silenced."

I kissed her hands.

And me and her gay ass grandson went on our date.

If you're on a date and it starts out with you and your date sitting on the opposite side of the table across from each other and ends that way then it's time to cancel the rest of the date, get a new date and call it a loss.

If the person don't come over and eventually sit by you then that Hoe just wanted a free meal and wasn't planning on calling you again. Unless you got a shitload of money then a bitch will give you phony pussy to stay in your wallet.

You didn't have to listen to me, Niggahs.

That's what happened with me and ole boy. We talking and all I could think about was writing.

He telling me his goals and I pull out my pen and a folded blank paper from my wallet and I started *A Lonely Christmas*.

I was writing and writing. When I ran out of space I took out my cell and text myself the rest of the outline for the story.

He was taken aback. "Pharoah. You're writing bruh."
Eye looked up. "Sorry."
"You're supposed to be on a date."
"I know," I said. "And I got a man, remember?"
"So why you're writing?"
"Because. That's what I do. I write."
"Snap out if it Pharoah! This is supposed be an enjoyable occasion for us both."

I looked lost but smiled anyway. "Ok. I enjoy writing on this paper and texting myself stories."

He looked away, his temples twitching with anger.

I felt sorry for old boy. I folded the paper and put it in my wallet. As text messages came in by the numbers (my text story outlines) I sat by him.

"You feel better now?"

He turned to kiss me. "Yes."

"Goddamn your breath stank!" Oh, shit. I didn't mean to say that. But his breath was stank as fuck. Goddamn. Brush THEN gargle, Niggah.

"My breath ain't stank."

"Like hell it ain't. Grown ass man with halitosis breath, the sequel."

"I should beat your ass."

"I should beat your ass for letting me come over here to be bombarded by your witch hunt ass breath. If this was Halloween I'd understand your breath being dressed as *Shit*. But goddamn it!"

I stood up and walked towards the door.

"Pay for your food!"

I turned and looked at him.

"Make sure you order Colgate for dessert and eat that shit till it smells minty fresh."

And I was out the door.

"Make sure those dishes are spotless when you're done washing them."

Tell me about Hurricane Andrew, how it affected you and your life during your sophomore year at Boyd Anderson High School.

Lord Jennings

Masturbation meets Death

BLUEBERRY HILLS CONDOMINIUMS.
FORT LAUDERDALE, FLORIDA.
1993

My family and eye have moved out of the Inverrary Hotel and now lived in Blueberry Hills Condominiums. Eye hated this neighborhood with a passion but of course we gotta do what Mom says. Eye missed Goulds. Didn't wanna live in Broward County.

    I lived for Janet Jackson's JANET album. But don't get it twisted; I loved ALL of her albums. I was too young to appreciate Janet Jackson, her first album and Dream Street, her second. But I was 9 when Control came out and 13 when Rhythm Nation dropped. Every album she released was the soundtrack of my life. Being raped I wanted to take Control of my life and stop the abuse and when Rhythm Nation came

I was living in the Circle behind Lee's Grocery Store in Perrine, surrounded around prejudice, ignorance, bigotry and a slew of depressed adults who couldn't read a WIC coupon, so illiteracy was a reality.

When the JANET album dropped, I had just come from seeing the movie (Poetic Justice) with Mama, and she took me to the mall and bought me the album.

Oh my God! I stayed up day in and day out learning the "IF" video.

I became so good I won six dance competitions in the tenth grade. I have a huge Janet Jackson scrap book with everything Janet in it. My friends say I'm crazy, but they can kiss my black ass. I love Janet Jackson.

I think she is the finest woman in the world and certainly the most talented. Madonna doesn't have shit on Miss Jackson.

And I'm only 15 years old. I just don't see myself playing Vogue or Like a Prayer. I don't wanna dance to that shit.

Give me Rhythm Nation any day! If Madonna was a black woman she would not be as huge as she was.

Peep game. I was straight up, straight forward, and just plain blunt. I get it from my Mama. The only thing I got from Daddy was a maybe I would be there to help your Mama raise you. His hard on kept him pressed for pussy that kept him forever lost in a game Adam and Eve originated. I was not going to apologize for being real. And I don't think like most 15 year olds. I had to grow up way ahead of my time, seen things before I was 13 I shouldn't have seen till I was a grown man, but life dealt me so much devastation and I never really had anyone to talk to about it.

When you were real there was no room for fakeness. Everything I said or did come from great thought. I pondered every decision like Oprah signing her own checks.

I had an acid tongue! No I haven't always been that way. In fact, growing up I was a shockingly quiet, introverted little nappy headed Niggah hell-bent on listening to everybody from The Pet Shop Boys, Duran Duran, Teena Marie, Prince, Michael and Janet Jackson, my personal favorite. Michael had the hottest jacket out back in the 80s, with the zippers all over it from the Beat It video. Mama never bought me one; I had the Michael Jackson doll instead.

But every one of my friends had the Beat It jacket, and I felt out of place. So I grew into a deeper shell, because I seemed the only asshole with a Michael Jackson doll and not the jacket. So I was picked at badly.

He's a faggot.
Look ya'll, he can't afford the jacket.
He has a doll! Ah, Pharoah! Your Mama must be on welfare.
Even the girls have the Michael Jackson jackets and they don't have dolls, punk!

Janet Jackson's *Control* came out when I was 9 years old, and blasted from every Cadillac, Chevy and Ford careening up the block. And Boy George, George Michael, Patti Labelle, Sugar Hill Gang and AC/DC. Mama didn't allow hip-hop in our house, back then. In fact she detested it, told me hip-hop wasn't Sam Cooke, Barry White, Otis Redding nor was it Diana Ross and the Supremes, Millie Jackson, Betty Wright and Aretha Franklin. I embraced all music, growing a very eclectic mind.

I used to write my own lyrics to my favorite songs. I remembered being 8 years old, jamming to Whitney Houston's *Saving All my Love for You*. Now what the hell did I know about love at that age? Most kids were fascinated with the *Smurfs*, *Scooby Do* and *He-Man* cartoons. I was, too. But I was *also* into something else.

Unfortunately, I was heavily into sex. I was somebody's sex slave. I was being tormented and taunted, forced to be silent by the very elders I looked up to in my bloodline. I was lying to the people I love the more I kept the secret.

I hated myself. My self-esteem was brutally taken from me; I hated life, people, and things. I hated time. I was told to keep it buried deep within my family, to never talk about it, to forget it happened.

I was told to keep the white man out of it, leave the police to bark up someone else's tree. I was taught to pretend it didn't happen; that it was a figment of my imagination, that it was all in my head. Yet my rectum ached daily, with the most excruciating pain I would ever know.

I was into crying myself to sleep when the lights went out, praying that God helped me, to protect me. After all I was only 6 years old. But every time, during the wee hours of the morning, the boards would creak and I would wake up sobbing quietly.

Waiting for the bedroom door to open. And when it did, Satan was there to greet me; he seemed to be 8 feet tall. I could remember how he looked, how he smelled.

A grown man I used to love and trust would defile me because of a rumor, the rumor being that Mama was using him, only married him so she wouldn't wind up on the streets of Goulds.

And for her mistake, if that was indeed true (which I doubted), I was punished, unknowingly to my Mama because he vowed to kill me and my Mama if I ever talked. So I kept quiet. He used to superimpose into the shadows spitting the darkness from chapped lips and sexually raping me until I lay, spent, silent, crying, breathing hard and digging my nails into my pillow, hoping I never woke up again. But of course the Good Lord snapped his fingers and I woke up anyway. I never understood why.

When the sun rose on my face and those little shapes were formed on my skin from the sun light beaming through the lacy curtains, I slowly opened my eyes and I would just cry so hard, sometimes in pain. It hurt to walk, it hurt to run in school, it hurt to play kick ball in P.E at Pine-Villa elementary school.

I remembered I was May Day King in school. May day, I forget the logic behind it, but there was a May Day Queen. Shawana.

I felt special when I was crowned King.

I remember the lyrics I wrote listening to Whitney Houston, the biggest singer in the world. I didn't know life was preparing me for a lyrical battle, lyrical man hood training.

I was being prepared for something greater.

I opened my book bag, pulled out a scrap piece of paper, a pencil chewed up with my teeth marks, habit of mine to chew my pencils, and I wrote.

Every night
I wait for you.
Every day
a different episode.
I wait for you
to bring it back,
take me away
leave me dead
dead inside
from a love I can't find
a love I don't
understand
feelings of weeds growing
from the depths of my soul
you're in control
while I save it all
for the one my future holds.

I was 9 years old when I wrote this, reading everything from dictionaries, thesauruses to newspapers, books and anything else that kept my mind out of my abusive home. I went to elementary school chipper and faking it, telling myself I couldn't let my friends find out what I was going through. I didn't want to face the ridicule, the shame. They already slammed me for having a Michael Jackson doll and I'll be damned if I give them ammunition to blast me again about something else.

Bad enough I was the tallest Niggah in school. Kids thought I actually stayed back because I was so tall. I was the same height as seventh grader. I always hated to be tall, but I accepted it because members of my family told me I was meant to be a ball player.

Football and basketball I was good at, but I gave up because, once Mama divorced the Evil Demon, I had to stay at home, play Mama, Daddy and Grand daddy to my brothers, cooking and cleaning, sewing loose buttons on shirts, moping and watching siblings that weren't my own children just so Mama could work, to make ends meet.

I would start dinner by 6 p.m., have them fed by 8 p.m., help them with their homework by 9 p.m., have them in the bed by ten p.m., even though Mama specifically told them to be in the bed by 8. But she worked and I was the Head Niggah in Charge so I let them stay up another hour. I spanked their asses like I was their Daddy. Extension cords on their behinds kept their asses in line. I didn't want to do anything that put Mama's house out of order when she came home.

She never depended on a man to do shit for her; good dick never brought her down to Dumb Blonde standards.

Good dick or not Mama always put her children first, but at the same time she worked so much. She was gone from home 80 percent of the time. When I was being raped and abused, even by the neighbor's kids Reynard and Junior, she had no clue and eye never gave her a clue out of fear for her life.

I remembered Junior, who was about 2, maybe 3 years older than me. I was about 7. We were out in the front yard of the wooden house we lived in Goulds. I was in

Dynamite's dog house, our German Sheppard. The first dog that loved and protected us fiercely.

Junior's Mom stayed in the first house on the block and had the same last name as my favorite singer, Janet.

I had on a Spider man shirt and some jean shorts. Mom was in the house with her husband and my brothers and I was hanging with Junior because looking at my step daddy depressed me.

"So, Pharoah. I heard you like baby dolls."

I was pulling up grass. "It's a Michael Jackson doll."

"That ain't what I heard," he said, massaging my shoulder.

I looked up at him. He was looking deep into my eyes. He was heavier than me, way bigger. I was skinny like a toothpick, just tall as hell.

"What did you hear?" eye asked, my heart racing.

"I heard you're gay," he said, rubbing his dick.

"Huh?" eye asked, playing dumb.

"Gay," he said more sternly.

"What is that?" eye asked dumbly.

"When men like men."

"Well, I guess so. A man has sex with me all the time. I just can't tell anybody because he said he'll kill my Mama."

He started smiling, his eyes darting all over my body

"Is that right?"

"Yes, Junior. You can't tell him." I started trembling. Why did I say anything?

"I won't tell him," he said, unzipping his pants. "I won't tell him if you suck my dick the way you suck his."

"No, man. I can't he'll kill me. He said I can't do anything with nobody else."

He crawled out of the dog house and said, "I'm going to tell him. Is he in the house now?"

I nearly broke out in hives from the fear. "Please, don't. Please! He said he'll kill my Mama."

He crawled back in the dog house and unzipped his pants. "And suck my dick well."

I went down on him with tears falling from my eyes. He grabbed the back of my head and started pissing down my throat and I gagged, trying to pull back.

"Swallow my piss bitch or your Mama dies right now."

I swallowed his piss and when it was over, I had never run so fast in my life.

I ran and hid in the bushes, sticking my finger down my throat, making myself vomit.

And cried till I fell asleep in the bushes.

The same bushes I was once raped…

Shaking it all away, I'm 15 years old now, sitting on the third floor of the Inverrary Hotel. Jackie Gleason, the famous star, died in this hotel and this was my home for the next few months. And I'm sad because I loved Southridge High School, and wanted to go back but had to settle for Boyd Anderson here in Ft. Lauderdale and I hated this school because hurricane victims were picked at. Thankfully I had an amazing friend and her name was Leandra Hayes. She was in my Biology class. The most petite, prettiest girl in all the world. I have a crush on her. God, I do. And Nicole Samuels and Trena Fletcher were two other special friends of mine.

While helping my brothers with math and spelling, I realized I was too mature for my age. I knew things and was doing things meant for a twenty-four year old by the time I was ten. I was plagued with being black and having good looks but I was never fixated on myself; especially after being raised to hate myself and to think I was ugly.

Deep down I knew I looked very nice, but people always tore me down even if I said I thought I was handsome. So I stopped saying it and started saying "I'm a muthafucking loser."

My handsome looks were confirmed when one of my school pictures (at Boyd Anderson) was hung in the main jewel case for the whole school to see. I had never encountered so much hate. The photographer told me my photo was striking, and that my eyes told a story. I rolled my eyes like yea right, dude you're probably trying to fuck me like the other boys are in this retarded school. So he hung up an 8X10 to advertise his photography.

Being black in this country limited me, never knowing that because of the Emancipation Proclamation, which said we were free but were not to be equal socially and economically to the white people, really didn't free us from slavery. Before Mama got her federal job, that was slowly changing her into a control freak; she was working at Sunrise, a place for the handicapped. I never called them "retarded," or slow," because they were special people, too. Mama worked Villa 8. Mama went to work and still came home with love and sweetness in her heart; and now that she's divorced and has this government job telling men what to do day in and day out, she was becoming a stranger to me. I was starting to not know who she was.

I was born in Salinas, California, never smelled California, seen California, know three things about California, besides the San Francisco 49ers, which used to be my favorite football team, the Sacramento Kings, which used to be my favorite basketball team, and the California Gold Rush. Despite being at a new school, I burned day and night with revenge.

It was all I ever thought about.

When I ate my breakfast lunch and dinner, I was plotting.

When I fucked, I was plotting.

When I ran track, walked around the 'Hood exercising, talked with the people I loved, I was plotting. I was ugly when I was in pain.

I'm 32 years old now, reading through that journal brought back so many memories of how I felt at the time. Even typing this in my autobiography seems foreign because some of those feelings I never explored until now. It's been a long time.

When I was crossed I succumb to the finality of silence. I watched you, never spoke, and seldom voiced how it made me feel to be betrayed. Loyalty was EVERYTHING to me.

Once that was gone everything else turned from red roses giving off gorgeous smells to pure shit, dog shit, horse shit, pig shit. Didn't matter, shit was shit.

But one thing saved me from ever acting out. One thing stopped me from seeking revenge on those who hurt me: WRITING.

I wanted revenge for losing my virginity by force, revenge for my female cousins sexually taking my ten year old body and using my dick for their perverse pleasures, revenge for Mama saying some disheartening things to me, revenge for my ex step father, and everything he put me through, revenge for everything, revenge for my grandfather telling my (at the time) 45 year old mother "I am not your father," when he knows damn well he is.

One thing saved me: the WRITING.

Well I should say the writing saved them.

My journals. My diaries. My poetry. I wrote enough journals to have journalism renamed in colleges to the King of Erotica's blurbs, enough diaries to make every woman in America burn theirs, enough poetry to make Yeats, Shakespeare and Langston Hughes rise from the dead and plan, execute and host my book signings. I bullshit you not.

Dying to get back at those who ever hurt me. Maybe it was wrong, and deep down it was wrong. But I really didn't give a shit. Why should I give a shit? When I was hurt, the people involved never thought about my feelings, how I felt and how I would feel when it was over. That burned me day in and day out.

Hurricane Andrew Journal

The wind began howling around 2 a.m. this morning, waking me up out of a deep sleep; and the rain began pounding the windows of the Inverrary Hotel on Inverrary Boulevard around 2:15 a.m., which seemed a stark contradiction because yesterday had been such a good day. The sun was out, birds chirped with as much bliss as a crack head searching the housing projects called "The Village," in Goulds, Florida, where I was raised in Miami, Florida, for his next hit. I felt weird sleeping in the hotel Jackie Gleason supposedly died in. In fact the Skeptical Part of me wanted and shoulda researched this, to see if it was true.

    I wasn't one to win over naively. I've been naïve enough in my young life. I played like I was dumb all the time to find out what I wanted so if someone said something I previously studied and it matched that was confirmation. I wished I could convince my English teacher of that. She was short, stocky and wore glasses that reminded me of Big Bird from Sesame Street. I remember when I was in class last week. She singled me out. My friend Bishop and I were in the back of the classroom talking. About bitches, of course.

He was incorrigible. "I get mo' hoes than you, Pharoah," he said, boasting.

I slapped palms with him and said, "You're right. The hoes don't like me, they like you."

He laughed at me, disturbing the teacher while she was at the chalk board. She looked at us with defiant eyes that didn't do a thing to shut us up. In fact we got louder. Bishop blocked her out.

"You know, Pharoah. I get 'em, what can I say. In fact, I heard Thelma likes you."

Yea, right. Miss Mary J. Blige. Miss Real Love. She favored Mary, loved Mary, and had a tattoo of Mary on her upper arm. This was only fitting because the bitch carried more drama than the screenwriters of every soap on national television.

I blushed. "Thelma don't like me, dawg."

Sparkles in his eyes. "Yes she does!" said Bishop, eyeing everybody because they stared at us. We kept talking.

"Prove it. Show me that she likes me."

"If I do, will you holla at her?"

"Yea, I'll say a lil' something to her."

"Yea, right. Scary ass."

"Mr. Wilson and Mr. Byssi. May I ask why you are disturbing my class and using such language in the presence of everyone else?" my teacher asked, tugging on her ward-looking, knee-length brown shirt. Her hair was a series of graying curls. Big turn off, even though my teacher wasn't supposed to look sexy to me, but it wouldn't hurt to try. I fucked a few of my teachers anyways, keeping it on the hush because they were either a) married or b) had families and reputations and I didn't wanna cast the light of shame on them. I have been the product of abuse since I was a kid, and quite frankly I was used to grown people touching and sexing me in ways that'd turn my Mama to the liquor bottle.

Be that as it may I had the blood of Sicily. Venni, Vetti, and Vechi my feelings then seal it with Omerta. Translation, I never broke the silence.

I ignored my teacher, faking a yawn and Bishop, the thug he was, grabbed his dick, stood up and said, "I was just leaving class anyway."

She tucked her chin back. "Have a seat Mr. Byssi."

"I'ma thug Niggah, I ain't sitting down." Our peers were laughing and poking fun at him. He had a stern look on his face, meaning what he said.

"Dawg, sit down," I tried to reason with him. He pushed me in the head. "Don't bow down to this white lady, we soldiers."

I glared at him. "Don't push me in my head again." Code red in my eyes. My blood boiled. I didn't like men hitting me. Since he was my boy, I let him slide.

"Well stay on my side, dawg. Fuck her."

My teacher walked around her desk, her hand on her hip. "I will call your mother, Mr. Byssi."

That frown turned upside down into a smile. "Now see why you gotta call moms, damn. Ok Miss Lumpkin I'll sit down right now."

She loosened up. "Thank you." Her eyes swung over to me. "And Mr. Wilson, approach the black board."
I snapped at her, in a way that made the class get really quiet. "*Black* board? Why couldn't you say *chalk* board? *Why* does everything have to be about color?" Each word had razors on it. But they failed to cut her because she had thick skin.

"I'm offended, Mr. Wilson."

Fire in my eyes. "So am I, and why do I have to come to…"

"Mr. Wilson, NOW! To the Black board."

I laughed to myself. "I got *one* mother, and you can call her all you want."

"I will, when class is over."

"Here's the number: 954-345-0098."
"Don't get smart, Mr. Wilson, to the board."
She didn't say black board. "Whatever."

I stood up and slowly walked to the front of the room. My friends were snickering; they knew I had an attitude. To be quite honest, none of them were my friends. Except for Bishop , Edgar Retana, Leandra Hayes, Nicole Samuels and a few others.

I was a Hurricane Andrew victim, lost everything I owned. My Mama's federal job got us up to this hotel. The hotel was closed down, out of business; and then it was re-opened for Hurricane Andrew victims, mainly for the families of the Feds. Everything was free, food, lights and water. We were given clothing vouchers; Mama got a shitload of cash from FEMA. And being that I was in Fort Lauderdale, seeing more Jamaicans than the land of Jamaica itself, half of the kids of Fort Lauderdale picked at us.

They said: *You guys are taking away our attention from our parents because they are focused on you. Why did ya'll bring your windy, rainy asses here? We don't feel sorry for you.*

I got into a lot of fights out here. Defending myself. Steven and a few others from Southridge Senior High, my original High School, were there with me as well, so I had a little clique.

Despite the bad, and the continuous press about Hurricane Andrew, and the lives lost, I had a few friends. Edgar Retana, Spanish Thug.

We had the same math class. We were tight. Coolest Spanish/Thug I'd ever meet.

Trina Fletcher, Miss Jheri Curl. Loved her to death.

Nicole Samuels, about five feet tall. Just a sweet girl to talk to. When Mama moved out of the hotel and got a condo in the Blueberry Hills Condominiums projects, I had my own room, had to look after my siblings while Mama drove an hour to work and an hour back home five days a week.

Nicole was the one in the 'Hood I spent the most time with. Leandra Hayes and Aaron were good friends of mine as well. I had a crush on Leandra. Miss all around. She was a cheerleader, active in clubs. She was the one girl every man wanted to have sex with, yet we couldn't help but protect her. She was like your little sister. Always smiling, so loving and loved all people.

For her birthday party, held at her aunt's house (she had money, the house had to be worth $300,000), I bought her a $15 Exclamation powder and perfume set, and gave her ten dollars. Wasn't much, but it was the thought that counted.

But all of that didn't matter. Once I was at the board, my teacher told me to write a sentence. I looked at her, dumbfounded. "About what?"

"I don't know, *anything*. I want to know what you and Bishop were talking about. Write about it, you probably can't even write a complete sentence."

"Whatever." I was nervous. I hated being embarrassed, and I double hated being put on the spot. My hand trembling, I began to perspire. Someone blurted out, "And please don't write about Hurricane Andrew. We know you lost your shit, we don't care about that, please don't go there."

I stared at the board. I was about to run. What do I write, what do I do, and what do I say? Why was she making me do this anyway?

I faced her, sneering. "I'm not doing this."

"Ha," she joked. "Yes you are. Are you dumb? You look stupid as hell."

I tucked my chin back. "And you're better than me?"

"Basically, yes." She rubbed the top of her white hand, like she was relieving an itch. "Write the sentence."

I threw the chalk at her; it missed her by a fraction of an inch. She sat on top of her desk, not intimidated. In fact she picked up the chalk and put it on the chalk holder running along the bottom of the board.

"I'm not doing this."

"Acting out, 'ey? Write a sentence, Mr. Wilson, or I will have you suspended."

"Miss, he is probably crazy. My Mama said hurricane victims are simply crazy."

I looked at her and said, "Shut up, Ho. Before I make you swallow your teeth."

"Write the SENTENCE MR WILSON!"

I stared at the board, all my anger and anguish washing over me like tides. Bishop walked up to me and said, "Write what you're feeling lil' homie. I know you got something bottled up." He pats my shoulder, pulled a chair beside me and had my back.

My homie.

That gave me a boost of confidence.

I felt like ripples, motioning away leaves meant for palm trees yet never left my hands because the infernos in the retinas of my eyes channeled all my pain; all the abuse I went through, feelings of autonomy over a hurricane that devastated our lives rendered me speechless.

I picked up the chalk. Something snapped in me, took over me. I couldn't feel my legs, my hands, I couldn't breathe. My wrist awakened my fingers, the chambers of my heart and I wrote, in two columns:

They expect me to be
something,
nothing,
maybe anything other than
who they have yet to be
which is why I:
Pharoah C.
Drop the Wilson,
add an absent father,
buy the consonant,

and a Vowel,
Fire Vanna White,
Turn the letters my teacher,
racist,
want me to use to piece together
sentences too abstract for my
black mind because white people
think Niggahs don't write.
I am talking,
rather I'm writing
With a white piece of chalk
on the black board,
does that mean that white words
overshadows the black mind?
Why couldn't the board have been white,
and the chalk black, and trace
the very lines surrounding Jesus' pupils,
since he had wool hair.
Is my sentence long enough, short enough
smart enough?
They expect me:
to be something,
nothing,
anything but what they have yet to be
because Pharoah C. searches
for the consonant in the name Wilson
who is making another family with another bitch
come see about me,
before I complete another
sentence.

And when I was done I broke the chalk in half, tears falling down my face and stormed past my teacher, who was reading my poem in complete shock, her mouth ajar, her eyes wide. I slammed the door behind me, running up the hallway, hating myself, hating Hurricane Andrew, hating

Mama for moving us up here, hating life. I was questioning everything God was, everything he did.

When I saw the bathroom I sat on the toilet and I sobbed, to the point my nose stopped up and I couldn't breathe. I didn't understand why those poetic words poured from my soul the way they had. I couldn't explain it. I heard the door open. But I didn't look up. I was on fire, I hated myself I wanted to die, I thought about suicide, ending it all. I felt hands on me, soft hands against my bare arm. I was pulled into an embrace, the smell of faint perfume filled my nostrils.

It was my teacher, hugging me, rubbing my back, crying with me. She told me two words that made all the difference in the world.

"Cry, Pharoah. Let it out."

Her blouse was a wet wash cloth by the time I was done shedding the last tear.

I wanted to be in my old apartment, called the Caribbean Colonies, which was located directly on the side of Caribbean Elementary on 200th Street, Caribbean Boulevard.

But Hurricane Andrew made sure that wasn't possible. We lost everything, from couches and pictures without copies, to our kitchen and security. My Mama's white Pontiac Grand Am, with my Southridge Senior High sticker plastered on the back window was messed up. I loved that car. Mama taught me how to drive in that car.

My boy, Bishop, appeared from behind us and he said, "Dawg, I didn't know you were a writer. I wrote that all down for you, so you can always have it."

He slipped it in my pocket, looked at our teacher and said, "I got it now Miss Lumpkin"

She stepped aside and he hugged me tight. "Boys forever dawg."

"Boys forever."

Σ

I stared at the darkened ceiling, sucking in air. My brothers were in the opposite bed, sleeping.

At 15 years old I worked at the hotel full-time, in reception, answering questions and taking phone calls with the aplomb of a seasoned veteran. I knew how to talk to people. When they called the hotel I always answered with a smile. When they visited the hotel or wanted business I directed them the Manager, Brian, a very nice white man who loved blasting Natalie Cole's *Unforgettable*.

Well I should be honest; I lost the job because the I.R.S. told the Hotel Manager that they didn't want a minor child doing hard labor, that I should be focused on my schooling.

I was running the entire hotel, making almost $600 a week.

Therein my business savvy was born.

In fact inside my head were images of Goulds: hustlers fucking the same bitches, pimps failing miserably to get their fucked-up versions of Jezebel to obey what they were saying. And to be quite honest, the pussy they were selling would have fell off the NASDAQ instantly the minute Wallstreet figured out those women have been whoring for the past twenty years. Working the same ole blocks, wearing the same ole clothes, smelling the same ole way, dick, ass and pussy, and saying the same ole things. I remembered back a few weeks ago, when I paid for pussy. Now I never had a problem getting pussy, back then I never talked about it. I was really quiet. I did my dirt in the shadows with the darkness.

I was fucking like a race horse. I had a lot of female friends, I loved women around me. I talked to them, always told them they were pretty, listened to them talk about life, school and problems. But the more and more my Mama worked, not really spending time with me or talking to me, because she was so hardcore, I was slowly growing to hate and detest women.

But today I wanted to pay for pussy just to see what it was all about. I approached the demon-looking lady, on the corner by my great Aunt Rozella's house. I swear 220th Street was Hoe Central, especially around the Room In House everybody you knew has lived in at one point in their lives. To be back on that corner after trying to buy pussy years ago before I was ten years old sent a shockwave through my balls.

She smiled at me, looked me over and said, "Hay boy, what's yo' name?"

Enjoying High School life, and relishing the fact that I was actually in the tenth grade at Boyd Anderson High School, I just looked at her. She was clad as the Immaculate Hoe in a pair of tight black jeans and Come-Put-Me-Out-Of-My-Misery heels. In fact one of the heels was gone. She looked like a handicap woman walking unleveled towards me. Her blouse was white and her left titty was showing.

A funky blonde wig brought out her horrible-looking brown eyes. I wanted to run, hoping some director screamed cut and the horror movie turned out to be a scene worth shelving on the cutting room floor.

I was looking fly as ever in some jeans a T-shirt and a pair of Nikes. "I'm Harry," I lied.

She was skeptical. "Harry. You sum kin to the Rolle's?" *Nosey bitch!* "Yea."

"I thought your name was Pharoah." *Well goddamn, bitch what else do you know? What size my dick is?* She was licking her lips, creeping me the fuck out. "Your mama name Clara Lynn. I know her; we used to go to Mays together, never liked her."

My life meant nothing to me.

I realized with a jolt this was the same Hoe I tried to buy pussy from when I was younger.

What the fuck?

Σ

I smiled at her. "You know what? I was gonna give you fifty dollars for some pussy."

Her eyes bulged out her head. "Wait, wait. Come here, baby. Yea, I love you, Chile."

"But I changed my mind. See ya' later, bitch."

And I ran to my aunt's house.

I really didn't like coming over Ro house, ever, because I always felt the tension in this family. My Mom's cousin's children always fought me, for some reason. No matter what day of the week I'm fighting my own cousins, and neither ever whipped my ass, I could tell you that much. And as much as I didn't like to fight, because I had to fight when I went home, it broke my heart that my own cousins hated me. Or so I thought. If I wasn't fighting Buddy's son I was fighting Arlette's son. Even I tried to talk to them to figure out why they always fought me, they fired back by cursing me out then throwing blows so hey, I threw blows, too because I wasn't a pussy by a long shot.

And you would think the elder cousins would stop it? Nah, they didn't. They just sat there playing spades and yelling STOP STOP fighting but never came out the door to stop it. Bomb Beeda, as much as I would grow to truly adore him, used to instigate the fights. A grown ass man making kids fight. So for this reason I grew into a shell and just handled it. I avoided going over Roe house for as long as I can, for what good that did.

But don't pay anybody outside the family to touch me. Then my cousins fought with me, which I found remotely odd. They always attacked me, but when someone outside the family wanted to fight me then my cousins stuck by my side, so with that I felt a sense of loyalty. But it confused the hell out of me.

I used to crack jokes so I didn't think of it, but I knew they never liked us. They were wondering was I gay, bisexual or just goddamn fucked up in the head. I had the answer, maybe I was all three. Maybe I was crying out, reaching out. At the moment I was an American kid with American problems. I was Black but not proud. I was fucking women twice my age. I was letting men twice my age have their gregarious, sickly ways with me because my abuser told me and taught me to believe this was my reality. And as a child you're taught to believe in every single word an adult tells you.

I didn't care. Hell, I was going through this shit for a very long time. No one loved me, no one appreciated the heart of gold I had.

When I got home I just went in my room and closed the door. I was in bed by 8 p.m. and wound up waking up around 3 a.m. On my dresser was a small paperback book with poetry by Langston Hughes, darkened by the absence of light. I felt a cool breeze blow over my clammy skin like escaped inmates searching for a glint of freedom. I missed a man I never met; I called him "Daddy."

He was my biological father, residing in California with the second family he made, the family that kept him away from taking on the responsibilities of raising a black child who happened to be living the Ghetto Life times four. In my pants pocket was twenty-two dime bags. Translation, weed. I was selling weed on the side because Mama was struggling. That was the way it was supposed to go: Mama's first born and the oldest, me, needed to go make that money so Mama wouldn't have to work so hard. I got my weed from a "family member." Schooled me, taught me and set my black ass free. I knew this was wrong, but all kinds of wrong things have been done to me in my young life. My soul was exhausted, lost the will to survive and live. And I was only 15 years old.

Disgruntled, I rolled over in bed, staring outside my open window. Janet Jackson was singing That's the way Love Goes. Love Goes where? Where, damn it? Love? *Don't* talk or sing to me about love. Love has been the sole reason why so many people have hurt me, molested me or tried to plainly destroy me. I was a beautiful child, yet today I was an ugly young man, filled with everything but the right thing. Glee has fled from the epitome of my jubilant flair. I'm just a spark.

My legs drumming together, I take up the lotion bottle and I start masturbating. I was all over my bed, the sheets wet and dirty, my hips trembling, my lubed hand gripping, pulling...I was screaming obscenities into my pillow, had to be quiet, Mama was home. I heard Sam Cooke over Janet Jackson, Darling Yooou Send meee. Darrling yooouu thrill me. Darling, fuck you! I was 15 years old. With the mind of a 30 year old.

Darkness enveloped me like cloaks on vampires. I couldn't breathe, something was squeezing my neck so tightly I had to regurgitate. I was floating in the air, kicking and trying to scream, clawing at hands with fish scales, smelling something so horribly grotesque I couldn't think.

The street lights began exploding, one by one, Boom, Boom, Boom, as he wickedly laughed, the stench of his hot breath stinging my pale skin. My clothes were soaked, the wetness against Satan's skin sending smoke snaking in the air. He threw me into the wall, beady red, sulfuric eyes staring deeply into mine.

I saw my ex step father tying me, with leather belts, to my bed. I was 6 years old, naive and stupid. I saw him writing "LOSER" with his saliva on my cheek.

I saw my cousins taking my virginity when I was ten, as Satan, 8 feet tall, strategically kept leaning into my face. I covered my eyes and the farce played out on my hands, reprinting my fingerprints all over my fingers, spilling like a pissed off river all over my arms, stabbing the Goosebumps, tearing into my blood stream, rebuilding my DNA, catapulting, like some plague, into my stomach.

I opened my eyes as I began to shake and cum spurted on my abs, pubic hair and nuts. I couldn't stop trembling. This felt so good.

I felt the butterflies plummeting towards the end of my life as I stood up, gripping the blunt razor knife I used to hide in my book bag. Mama searched everything but my book bag and my AC vents.

My wet clothes was actually my sweaty birthday suit, I stared deeper into Satan's eyes, the fog snaking into the air, the mirror blurring my vision.

Mentally screaming as loud as I could, I kept quiet...I raised the razor, put it on my wrist.

I was so upset, so scared, so tired of living, I didn't wanna be black. A black man raped me. Two black women robbed my innocence.

My hands were twitching, as I lowered myself to my knees, but Satan yanked me back to my wet bare feet.

An opened economy size bottle of Tylenol looked appealing.

Swallow them, Pharoah. I will love you forever.

God help me, I said, closing my eyes.

And when I opened them I was flushing the pills and the weed down the toilet, staggering to stand up.

Sweating profusely I turned on the shower, soaped my body and sobbed like my soul died, scrubbing myself clean.

"Please...God help me, please...take it away, those past images, my childhood, please."

I sank to my knees and sobbed into my hands, my heart burning.

My stomach on fire...

Why do you have a grudge
With churches you've attended

Lord Jennings

Little known fact about me, Pharoah C. Wilson, that is. Period after the "R" following the capital J of my anchored name. Daddy was my Senior and I was his junior yet didn't have one good memory of the man. So that revelation was bittersweet. I bit into chocolate and tasted limes.

I read the Bible while I was high off weed. Yep. That chronic opened my mind fully.

Unbiased, free of ignorance, chop down the bigotry and illiteracy. I read Nostradamus literature while I was high and Shakespeare, studied some Robert Frost and read everything from *Angels and Demons, The Color Purple* and a book on Martin Luther King, Jr and W.E.D. Dubois while I was high.

To get a deeper understanding of my soul. My inner chamber, called The Holy Ghost, was photographed and framed on my nightstand. So I was reminded of love. Self love. Inner confidence. Inner peace. Then I studied Egypt and suddenly, learning Akhenaton did a thousand years before Moses existed the One God theory, as something you know was there but couldn't see and his Ten Commandments a direct rip off of the MAAT Divine principles, the Bible was suddenly compromised.

The 42 Divine Principles of the Goddess Maat

1. I have not committed sin.
2. I have not committed robbery with violence.
3. I have not stolen.
4. I have not slain men or women
5. I have not stolen food.
6. I have not swindled offerings.
7. I have not stolen from God/Goddess.
8. I have not told lies.
9. I have not carried away food.
10. I have not cursed.

That list was created before Moses and the whole Ten Commandments thing. So that left me scratching my head. After finding this out (I heavily researched it) I didn't have much faith in what I read in the bible anymore. So I prayed to God about it. Put it in his hands to give me an understanding and every time I said Amen I was led to google.com and researched it some more. Akhenaton also believed in one God. The Sun God. Something you couldn't see but knew was there and he believed this 1,000 or so years before Moses so-called existed. So you could see my dilemma.

I did believe in God and *yes* with my heart I know in my soul Jesus died for the sins of man, but the contradictions with religion and church and the Bible caused me to rebel because NO PA$TOR I asked gave me an honest answer. In fact every Pa$tor I asked about the MAAT Principles literally shook in their robes. Playing stupid.

So I rejected what lustful, money hungry Pator taught me and read $criputre for my$elf.

Funny how things were revealed to you when you stopped paying regular tithes (frat donations) to church.

The Pator' attitude changes. He started calling your house, questioning your Mama and your siblings. Wondering are you a little off, getting personal and asking you personal questions.

Wow, God! Simply amazing.

Then and only then did I write my next book.

With opened eyes.

Someone once said I was the Male Face of the Color Purple, if a man was cast as Celie. But I told him I was too handsome to play an unattractive woman in a play. And that was the point, he said. Sometimes beautiful things were insecure outside of normal praise and understanding. I said what did he mean?

He told me My Color Purple would be re-titled *The Color Black*.

I was quiet, of course, trying to make sense of this. Queen's Stone Age *No One Knows* rock song pulsating into my ears via my iPod.

"You mixed your purple with the gray of gloom, and the blue of your soul. Yellow and blue makes green so you're black once all that is combined, not a man of color, but a man of multicolor comprising a rainbow, God's promise to the world. Your feet are bronze, you kept your faith and now you reap the benefit of writing books that make people think or change their views on some things or at least analyze it from an angle they never thought about.

"And a few people hate you for that, even some members of your family," he went on. "...They called you faggots and said *you* gay all through your childhood and teen age years, when you used to pop that booty at the DJ all at the Family Reunion and the streets, competing against the girls and sitting them down with your moves.

"How a Niggah like that figured out a way to get his books published and actually generate over 200 (5) star reviews?"

Eye didn't know, but they still scratched their heads about that one. Dancing in your Mama's front yard, pop, lock and drop it at the bus stop and around the Homestead Air Reserve Park like you giving a free benefit concert.

And I hardly get tired. I was very constructive and creative in a lot of ways, not just writing.

That's just what I focus on presently, but writing wasn't the whole scope of my genius. I had the looks to package a bestselling series, the intelligence to sell a book to a person used to reading watered down fiction and I get the dick hard and the pussy wet through the vivid ways I write a sex scene. Then I fuck you up with a character spreading HIV willingly.

Hook, line and sinker.

When Niggahs and females realize the Niggah on that book cover was that same dancing Niggah throwing down in his Mama front yard, on the track and at the bus stop they come up to me, shake my hand, want my autograph and pick my brain asking what inspires me to do what I do.

The answer is simple. I StimYOUlate then EdYOUcate.

That's my motto.

Never throw away your support system. And keep that around you when you get a little notoriety or if and when you blow up and people start to know your name before they buy your books.

When you keep your support system you aren't blinded by the things your wealth brings: groupies, orgies, threesomes and getting your dick sucked by an Asian bitch who talk black.

Bullshit was revealed. You will lose opportunistic friends and you fall on your knees and remind God of where you got the talent from. You look away from God once, even briefly, you will fall from grace, drown in those deep waters that swallow you up like a whale.

I called that Walking on Water for God through your God given talent.

You walk on water as long as you keep your eyes on God.

I was a direct reflection of my thought process. My thought processes my inner voice before I could hear it with my heart.

Writing what I been through and instilling that in the characters I so willingly and knowingly and lovingly created was therapeutic for me. It opens up my writing to the Holy Ghost within me so I could see me through the characters' voices. That's a deeper reflection of myself.

Keeps me enlightened. My writing makes me a narcissist against my talent. That way one's opinion of me remains in the bullshit pulpits and not a reality of myself. I don't give a fuck what a bitch gotta say about Pharoah. We can clear that shit right now before I type anything further. If you're expecting me to lose sleep over losing any of you then baby, pack a tent. Its gonna be one long night for you 'cause I'm gonna fall asleep the minute my head hits the pillow.

I don't worry about my looks.

That's why I can take half naked pictures in the sand with my ass tooted slightly then take some sexy pictures on the basketball court, laying my sexy ass in the middle of the free throw line, with my hand laying like so across my balls (without grabbing them, you didn't have to grab them to make a point) and laying on the basketball like a leather pillow. Giving the camera lens hell, bitch.

That's how you slay.

I market my looks to bring the reader to my books to get the deeper message.

I want your dick hard and your pussy wet while I give my message.

Cause it's gonna be raw, didn't need no condoms for my lyrical challenges. And you didn't have to put 10% in the tithes plate.

My work ethic was modeled after my Mama. If they had overtime at Mama's job she did it. She was dedicated to her job with the Feds. Always winning employee of the month and getting stellar evaluations. So imagine doing something you actually loved and dedicating your time to it. Like I did. I wrote 14 hours a day, 6 days a week. I create create create, with little time for food, showers or sleep. When I do sleep I rest my head on the keyboard, snoring mildly. Often times I didn't even remember how I got into my bed. Books open around me, encyclopedias, dictionaries and thesauruses, I sleep for *four* hours (no less than 3), get up, thank God for waking me up, take my HIV medicine, shower, brush my teeth, sit back behind the keyboard, ask, "God, what do I write now?" Amen.

And the words begin to pour. I write like the Wind blows.

Any wonder E Lynn Harris' *Anyway the Wind Blows* changed my life.

And shaped the writer/author in me?

Mama was Mama and Daddy, a hermaphrodite of experience. She was tougher than any man I've ever known, and more feminine that any woman I knew. Mama went from picking beans in the hot ass son back in the day to getting paid to braid hair to having a job at Sunrise caring for the handicap; then God blessed her from Villa 8 to a damn divorce from the man who caused me so much grief, to standing on her own with four boys and one girl; she then sent off for a government job she never dreamed of getting to occasionally getting welfare. And when we were getting evicted from the pink duplexes behind Lee's Grocery store when I was 12, Mama got an answer from God.

Because of her faith in Him and trusting in Him, he blessed her with a career. Not a job. She went to training in Glynco, Georgia, passed her tests (her reading isn't the best, but Mama ain't illiterate, damn it!) and our whole lives had changed.

Out of Perrine we moved, no more hearing gun shots at night when we tried to get our slumber, no more dope boys on the corner.

Mama was moving on uppp to the East Side, we finally could afford that bread, bacon and Pie-I, baby.

I was overjoyed. I didn't have to listen to Mama cry through the walls, begging God to help her, to make a way for her children then herself because she never put herself before her children when she pushed her children out on different birthdays, showing the true strength of a man.

That was Mama, and I was proud of her. She gave me confidence. She gave me wit, zeal, self-esteem.

We escaped the ghetto and I never looked back. My old friends became distant friends and I became a stranger in a new neighborhood, quickly making alliances by speaking to people (How are you, ma'am...nice dog, ma'am...how are you, ma'am, nice dress) and they slowly told my peers about me and people were coming up to me, saying, "Yo, my Mama told me you were nice to her. Said she had a pretty dress."

"Yes, I did say that. Brought out her eyes. They looked sad, but they were smiling."

"Aw, man. Moms went through a lot. Daddy used to pimp her, now he's dead and she can't even pimp herself because she wasn't soaking up game or paying attention."

"Man, sorry to hear that."

"Naw, dawg," he said, slapping palms. "You good. She got God, you know. Mama may not have money, good sense or good intentions, but she got faith in God."

"The mustard seed effect, ah I likes that."

"Yea, that's true," he said.

I shook his hand. "Well, I gotta get on. I'm on my way to school."

"What school you go to?"

"Southridge."

"I go to the Ridge, too dawg, what grade?"

"Ninth."

"Hell, yea, me too," he said. "How come you ain't in any of my classes?" he asked, rubbing my shoulders. Relaxing me, and kissing the back of my neck, causing the heat to stir the pot of my soul. I released the Holy Ghost and fell in an abysmal hole and the weakness of my flesh was activated and then awakened. *Robotically* controlling me. Dancing inside my asshole till I came all over my sheets.

But once we fucked he tried to possess me. Oh, no buddy, no no no no boo hoo Niggah save that shit I ain't trying to get tied down. Niggah save that picket fence shit I was not your bitch; Niggah I just said that shit to help YOU get a good, fresh nut Niggah I left that I'M YOUR BITCH shit soaking in your sheets, and some of it skeet, skeets on your abs after I was riding it.

You control the very thing you fuck, if you fuck it well enough. And on top of that your dick wasn't shit. I had better. Make me wanna fuck a cucumber for stimulation. Sometimes, Niggahs stick to the lotion bottles, Vaseline and baby oils. Most Niggahs still didn't know condoms got expiration dates and shelf life like milk and cheese but always trying to stick their dicks in something. Duh.

If you're dumb as fuck don't fuck, Niggah pick up a goddamn book.

Put the dime bags down, bitches want your status, car and loot, not your ugly ass, Trick, and learn about your history. The real history. Not that carbon copy shit whites ripped off and selling you that lie in school.

If you still believe Christopher, a murderer, discovered America then you didn't need to talk to me. As a matter of fact don't even say hello. Keep on a-stepping!

Next time at least fuck my *mind* first. *Mentally* stimulate me. Make polite conversation…squeeze my knee cap; tell me I was beautiful and make love to my brainwaves while rubbing my booty hole and whispering what you wanna eat off my sweet, sweet cakes.

Niggahs that fall in my booty get dismissed quicker than a bucktooth bitch with sagging tits, a fierce overbite, smell like piss, on her period and begging for a goddamn handout.

I like females and Niggahs that take their time with me. At least in college or vocational school trying to better himself, got goals and shit; have something to talk about other than suck my dick, eat my asshole, spit your nut in my mouth and kiss, kiss, this kiss on some Faith Hill shit knowing damn well I was on some Lil Kim shit.

I don't want dick tonight eat my pussy right.

Flattery and patience will get you anywhere, everywhere, somewhere with me.

Hello. Get a clue. So Niggahs saying Sup, Wassup, What's good, What's 'Hood and Sup, wifey when clearly fuck Niggah I don't have no goddamn tits get sliced, diced and eventually chop, chopped and screwed.

MOVE, BITCH! Get out the way, you cock blocking and shit I was trying to get at that fine ass Niggah over there with his foot on the wall, hand on his dick, looking from the female shaking her ass to eying me when I bent over to tie my shoe lace. I was a freshman in high school. He was in hi 30s.

Pimping, and shit. I wasn't no Pimp, sooooo I got at him. Bold and shit. Classy and witty. Complimented his ugly ass shirt. Asked him where he got it from? He said he got the number to the place at his crib. I was like Wassup, Wassup, Niggah. Could I get the number? And he said, "Tell you what, I'ma give you my house phone number, call at about 12 midnight. I'll have all the ringers turned off, Mom will stay sleeping through the night and we can jack our dicks together…but can't tell anybody."

"I got you. I don't tell my business."

"I wanna phone fuck you first. You moan like a bitch and stick your finger in your asshole and jack your dick I will give you nothing but dick in the physical sense you follow Daddy's directions."

"I got you."

So I called him at 12:50 a.m. Never call on time for a Niggah. That messed with his self-esteem really fast. Let him know *Niggah as quick as I came is as quick I will goddamn leave, Trick.*

Tell him just like that. A Top Niggah can fuck me all day, if he ain't matching what my dildos and vibrators do then Niggah you're a sorry ass Niggah.

Toys fuck better than you? Are you serious, Niggah? And want me to be submissive to you when I prefer plastic over your under-the-table cash?

"Niggah, you had me waiting."

"I had to do chores," I lied. I did chores hours ago. I was just toying around with this new wind up doll. See what kinda shit it's talking. Never commit to a programmed Niggah.

"Clean Niggah, ey?"

"Yes, sir. I had a dirty house."

"I like to stick my tongue in a clean ass."

"My ass cleaned thoroughly. Taste just like pussy."

"Goddamn, Dawg. I likes how you flow. I got the whip, Mama sleeping and shit. Cocaine binge. I can come pick you up, and fuck you in my room."

In his 30s and living with his damn Mama? "Bet. Do that."

"Shit, I'm on the goddamn way."

He arrived on time. His heart was pounding, matching mine. He looked so beautiful, very good looking and he told me he wanted to taste my asshole to see what my anus was cooking.

On his way to the crib I gave him head, gave his nuts a brutal introduction, sucked him so good by time he turned on his street he had to park his car in the drive way while he was cumming.

Shaking and shit, goddamn Niggah sound like you got shot or coming down with something. I hope I didn't have to burp this Niggah like a baby fresh off Mama's tit.

He could barely breathe. "Damn, stop tripping."

He got out the car, pants half on his naked ass, dick all out, telling me to follow him to the back door.

The house was beautiful but you really couldn't tell because there were no lights on in the house.

We're creeping and shit, into his Mama crib. What 30 year old you knew still snuck in his Mama's house?

"Shh, don't say shit. Gotta sneak you inside. I'm determined to get that booty hole tonight. Make my dick spit, baby."

"You gonna suck it off my hole?"

"Hell, yea, Niggah."

"Yet you won't eat your girlfriend's pussy…?"

"Niggah. I can't tell her I'm allergic to fish."

"Damn shame."

So he silently opened the back sliding glass door. Opens without a sound. Smells like lavender in the living room. A faint glimpse of his mother's hard work courtesy of the moonlight.

"Go to the back room."

I go and he looked around, tip-toed past Mama's room, into his bedroom. He turned HOT 105 Smooth Midnight Jams on, at a moderate tone and lay me on the bed, Ninja turtles sheets and shit. My booty covering Michael Angelou's left eye. I was still stuck on the grown man with Ninja Turtle sheets part.

He pushed my legs back and rubbed my hole, tongue kissed it, and he said, "You're mine, you pretty little bitch!" and I moaned with the pulse of my nipples, reacting to the burn of my loins. Taste me, wet me up, loosen with that slick tongue then slide your dick so far in me bitch make me stutter like I'm from Jackson, Mississippi.

He put me in a buck, taming the booty cheeks, molding me in his lust, creating me and breaking my barrier and recreating me; gave me his understanding while he kept plowing, planting seeds, looking deeply into my yearning eyes; *see* the mist of my reflection?

Shudder on the South Pole while I continuously slide the Black Hole over the dick's Dome and cum burst through the crack of the frescoed ceiling, deep inside me, dripping off my Prostate, feel me, be me Niggah we're One.

I shudder, moan and called his name; he's not even fucking me. He just has It pressed all the way inside, ten inches, three inches in diameter, submissively I succumb to my orgasm, activated, reactivated, molded, sexually programmed.

I would be chasing Upgrades for years to come. Already programmed in the gay experience, trying to hide it because eye was inexperienced. Eye wasn't ready for the world to know, I had to leave it on the low. Put the shoe box holding the rubies on the floor, in the corner of the room and stack a lot of books on top of it. Niggahs didn't read, so your diamonds were safe. Even being sexually abused eye kept my head in a book, reading.

Now my books got a bitch reading, about men on men. Rubbing their wet pussies, oh, oh, oh bitch lemme call my girlz and tell them 'bout The King of Erotica.

And she called Susie, Donna, Macy and Khia...they were the biggest, most gossiping bitches in Homestead and they sold my book, word for word.

Knew my shit by heart; directed people to my profiles; they were in Barnes and Noble ordering them if they weren't on the shelf and hitting me up with fan mail and I always do my best to answer each and every one in the order I get it.

So being in the church, and certain church members asking me why I write the books I do. I said I was doing it Pharoah's way. Giving a blunt message, wrote the nastiest shit, attached my sub plots and plots, gave it unpredictable endings and set out from the beginning to be original.

To make my own way. The future was still a Free Will choice. You could arrive there Satan's Way or God's Way, but you better hurry up and decide who you're fighting for because tomorrow ain't promised, Boo.

People were dying by the numbers. If it ain't AIDS killing half of Africa and confusing 1 in 5 Americans who were walking around with full blown AIDS and didn't even know they were HIV positive it was some people themselves misinforming others on HIV and AIDS and lack of education suddenly becomes the #1 killer amongst the human race.

You could play the saint and the I-don't-do -nothing wrong-game all you want to. Those kinds of people have or could possibly get HIV, too.

There's more than one way to get HIV. And this was what I told my church buddies when they wanted to talk about my books.

Keep their focus off the sex the characters were having, keep your mind off the sex *of* the characters, and tell them of the deeper message in my stories so when they DO read my books they were already conditioned and prepared for sexual verbal assault through the books' openings.

I was the first to do this. My sexy ass on the cover, owning my shit, snatching lace fronts, weave and wigs and afros too, Niggah on my way to that number 1 spot.

Because of God it happened.

Now I was doing my purpose. Attained my mission in life. And baby that's write. Write till I couldn't write no more. If I could think it bitch I could write it, give a twist, shake people up, get a Niggah's dick hard while reading about lesbians and get a bitch pussy wet while she reading about two men fucking each other in the ass.

So now the ways of the world are revealing themselves. Airplanes crashing and earthquakes shaking unexpected places, claiming lives and rap and pop stars dying before they were thirty, children talking back to their mothers and 12 year old's fucking more than forty year olds...

Corporations wanna be rich by keeping the middle class and the less fortunate poor or living pay check to pay check, invading our TV screens and indirectly preparing us for a change in the future, something big was coming and I hope ya'll get right with God...the stakes in the game were raised, I wouldn't be too surprised the government start putting hidden cameras in teddy bears and baby dolls and cabbage patch kids and lamps and light fixtures, car head lights, street lights and your very own camera phones. Those that publicly bash others but were privately living in the sins of the flesh in the darkness, comfortable from the black of light would always be walking, hiding and breathing the edge of darkness.

Those people won't truly be happy. When you deceive your committed lover by fucking someone behind his or her back then you were not a happy man.

Happiness comes with peace and tranquility.

The war against good and evil has just shifted into an entirely new direction, if you truly read and understand in the Bible Revelations. Recording starts throwing up Devil Horn hand gestures, tricking us into thinking that's cool to sell your soul and have your family sacrificed for some goddamn money and fame. That's what led me back to church.

To listen to the same Pa$tor wearing the same shit he wore when I came four years ago talking about the same old, tired Bible scriptures he learned by heart. Come on, when the Pa$tor keep telling you to recite Psalms 23 he didn't know the Bible as well as he thought.

When I was a teenager, that led me to meeting a married man in church. He told me I was fine as fuck and he had me shaking my head. In the church bathroom of all places. He was shaking the weasel, turning to pull up his pants, letting me get a glimpse of that scrumptious dick.

I licked my lips and he walked up to me. I was tall for my age so we were almost the same height. He then wrapped his arms around me like he knew me all my life and locked the church bathroom door.

He sat on the toilet and made me ride his dick till I buss all over him.

I thought I was in love.

I was 15 and he was 35 years old, who was fucking me behind his wife's back, taught me I couldn't put my faith in man because they would eventually let me down. Because when you fail yourself, depending on others you are going to be at their fledgling, dependent on them and you talk too soon or bite the hand that feed you they will throw you out on your ass, and slam the door closed, too.

I have been there.

I was always judgmental of the Word of God, growing up and enduring the things I did on a grand scale.

Inside me something died, with HIM in me I was introduced to a Star Trek of sorts, the Final Frontier as I thought it to be. Was I the only kid going where no man has taken me before? *Mentally* shackling me in the weakness of my flesh to the point of repetition and redundancy, that it became my addiction, it became my guiding light.

There's an old rule of business corporations failed to mention. There was a difference from telling someone what to do versus fucking them deep in the asshole and demanding what you expected of them and with the orgasm of misunderstanding, the perpetrator's views become the submissive view and the one being fucked gets stuck with all the shit. Gotta clean it up. Gotta give GOOD FACE to cover it up, like a bitch in a beauty pageant hiding that ruined pussy behind expensive panties and flashing that killer smile. World didn't see that white out painted over those yellow ass teeth.

Image was everything back then to me. I always loved pictures and reading books with fantastic pictures. I used to pull out my journal at 6 years old and write fantastic stories of the pictures I saw.

One time in an old magazine I saw Martin Luther King, Jr. Speaking in Washington D.C. That was a glimpse of Barak Obama right there. Martin Luther opened up the heavens that day, inspiring even the angels and God sent another one of his angels down to earth settling in Barak Obama's Mama's womb and she gave birth to the future President, a mixture of different cultures, an accumulation of everything Martin Luther King dreamed.

Barak already won a Pulitzer Prize and Martin Luther King became the youngest recipient to win the Nobel Peace Prize in 1964.

President Lyndon Johnson volleyed for the Noble Peace prize and he didn't want Martin to win; he even tried to put out a sex scandal on Martin, sending a tape to Coretta Scott

King in Miami, with Martin supposedly cheating on her with another woman.

But Coretta didn't fall for the bullshit; she knew her husband's voice and what he sounded like when he was intimate. So she went to Martin and they went to the white house and smashed that shit right there on the cutting room floor and Martin won his prize. One of the few times a white man got beat out of something. When you could get a prize over the most powerful man in the country then you're a threat to society.

Here comes the FEDS to monitor your goddamn phones.

In that lesson I learned that we aren't totally free in this county, but I never walked around with a chip on my shoulder about it.

Even when life as I knew it seized. Nothing was perpendicular to my own shattered frame of mind growing up embattled within myself to secretly annihilate myself before my tenth birthday because a grown ass man showed me homosexual things I would grow to like, love and inevitably enjoy along with validating myself through sex.

Nothing and no one prepared me with a preamble to the perils of this earth *till* that day, that unfortunate day, back when I was 6; I was sexually annihilated and gradually manufactured into what I called homosexuality.

I thought of this when I met my dear friend Sharonda. Knowing her since the seventh grade, she was secretly a lesbian and he was secretly bisexual. She really didn't know about Pharoah and Pharoah really didn't know about her. But they formed an alliance against the odds and then a bond once they stayed up all night on the phone, finding out the both of them had gritty tales of the past that redefined a future they never thought they'd see let alone touch or taste.

They went through ups and down together. While a few Pator were secretly fucking Pharoah Monday and Tuesday, with the wife on Wednesday and maybe the gay brother on Thursday, lied on the phone to the congregation on Friday about not showing up for Bible Study Wednesday and by the time Saturday came he went out to Denny's with the wife and kids, had them home by 5 p.m., picked me up at 6 p.m., did what he had to do in the bushes like my asshole was a part of an exotic jungle and once I was touched, teased, smacked, spanked and spent he drove me home, let me out on the corner, said "Make sure you're in church on time Sunday for Bible Study."

"But we didn't go to Bible Study Wednesday, you're not gonna show up early on Sunday either. So I got to sit and feel guilty before God alone while you're curled up with your wife staying up till the wee hours to come up with a sermon for the masses."

"We can't go to church together on Sunday. What will the people think?"

"I don't care *what* people think."

"Well I care. It's my reputation on the line. They already talking, saying they think you're gay so the only attachment you are to my life is a public *Bible* study so they can say Pa$tor is a wonderful man of God and once the guise transitions to a disguise when the night falls Pa$tor gonna be getting his dick sucked butt ass naked with you baby. Everybody wins."

"Whatever."

Pharoah turned to walk off, disgusted. Questioning the existence of God. If he existed, why are these Pator so horny, homosexual and lustful for my young, experienced flesh? Calling me on the phone at night (after I turned the ringers off so it didn't wake Mama) jerking his penis, telling me to moan like a bitch, say it belongs to him and claim he was so hot he came on his fat ass abs, put on some clothes and came to pick Pharoah up.

Well Pharoah got tired, and started pulling from the church. He stopped reading the Bible, he called Sharonda and told her he couldn't keep up or give up the bisexual ghost, that he has prayed, got on his knees and prayed and wound up sucking all over the Pa$tor in the same position then trying to sit through a sermon on Sunday. And what did the Pastor talk about? Homosexuality, how it disgusts God and he kept giving Pharoah the evil eye.

Pharoah was uncomfortable, wanting to run. He felt a few pair of eyes on him, questionable eyes and Pharoah jumped up to his feet, pointed and said, "You seem to be forgetting a very important aspect of the gay speech I am so sick and fucking tired of hearing every time I come to this raggedy ass church, bitch!"

"Oh my God!" someone said from the crowd.

"His mouth in the house of the Lord."

"Glory to the father he knows not what he do."

I glared at the big-lipped, double Decker neck Hoe. "Oh, yea? I caught you sucking the bishop's dick and he fuck more ass then a pair of Fruit of a Loom too sizes too small on a sumo wrestler, bitch."

Shock waves through the church.

"Watch your mouth young man."

"I'M GROWN, PA$TOR! You don't goddamn yell at me. You aren't gonna tell me my sexuality is an abominable sin to man when men cheat on their wives daily, horny housewives daydream about their husband's best friends making them come on their tongues, the homeless ain't trying to find a goddamn job and beg a bitch to death for five goddamn cent and the Pa$tor, yea, you got a few secrets that you don't want me to fucking put out."

"Pharoah, *please*." He held up his hands, giving me the murderous eye. His pupils held up I WILL KILL YOU FUCK NIGGAH signs that my pupils couldn't read because the image of crookedness didn't alert my corneas and my aqueous humor didn't find the gesture funny.

"I know this. If you preach that homosexuality sermon one more time I am going to scream."

"I am going to call your mother."

I was laughing. "I don't give a flying fuck! Don't you understand? People have been abusing my body since I was very young. I had to keep it in the family. Warned to never let it out. So I ran to church for God to save me and I get propositioned by more adults then the people my age. And now I'm being indirectly criticized for looking redundant and repetitious to the aftermath. The carbon copy of his sick soul."

"Pharoah..."

"I'm out, Pimp! Church *ain't* for me. I wasn't ready to get saved but Mama insisted on me getting baptized. And for what? That cold ass water gave me the chills, and froze my old self inside myself like a block of ice. And after all this time I *still* feel the goddamn same. I'm gone."

"You shouldn't leave the church."

"Let the whore leave," said the Pa$tor's wife and I paused, looking over my shoulder with a sneer. "What?"

Oh her balls bigger than mine. Oh, shit! Show me what you got, trick. "You heard me," she said, walking down the mildewing stair case, her hand on her hip like she's a HollyHood superstar. Being ghetto fabulous wasn't gonna get your picture on the White Diamonds commercial. Her head was so high if the atmosphere had an asshole she'd smell like wet pussy.

"No, you didn't hear me," eye said defiantly. I'd snatch this Hoe all up and down those pews she touched me.

She snatched me by the shirt and pulled me to her face. "YOU WILL NOT CURSE IN THE HOUSE OF THE LORD YOUNG MAN!"

"*Tell him!*"

"Praise him!"
"Pray for him!"

The church was in an uproar, even the Pa$tor clapping, wiping sweat from his face. Phew, 'ey Pa$tor?

I looked around, not afraid of any one of them. "Pa$*torrr* you better tell your wife to shut the hell up."

"Didn't I say watch your mouth?" she asked like she's my mother.

"Maybe you should have watched your mouth," I snapped back.

"Pharoah, no!" the Pa$tor shouted.

"Why?" I asked.

The Pa$tor was running at me, tripping over himself trying to stop my lips.

But they had too much on their minds and said, "If you would have been watching your mouth then I wouldn't have been sucking his dick."

The church fell into a deep silence, just as the Pa$tor grabbed my arm.

But it was too late. Everyone heard.

"Don't got nothing to say, lady? Ain't talking that Proverbs shit now, are you?"

Hot tears fell down his face. He felt abandoned even in church. He could do badly all by himself in the world. Didn't need church for that.

"Tell her Pastor. Tell her."

"He's lying. He never even been to my house."

I put my hands on her shoulders and looked her dead in the eyes. Why was her pussy wet? She trembled beneath my fingers.

"You have a king sized bed. A his and her closet. You have a Mahalia Jackson poster on the door of your closet. Your panty drawer is the fourth drawer on your armoire and you have a pink and purple dildo under the nightstand."

"Oh my God!"

"Yes. If I never been to your goddamn house, how the hell I know all that?"

I was DONE WITH CHURCH! "And that's who you all give your money *to*? He's been giving me some of that money. This is the man you hold in high regard, but you all bash each other, bring down each other then wanna plan a function, a party, a flee market, a bake sale or a meet and greet and you can't even stop the negative remarks about each other on a simple Sunday morning. You all are pathetic."

I walked up the hallway, past the wife and her gay pa$tor bitch ass husband and let the double doors creak closed behind me.

The *heels* of my church shoes clucked along the uneven tile on my way towards the exit door.

That was also the church entrance.

One way in.

And one way out.

Note: I changed the names in this chapter.
Pharoah.

*Did a woman ever confront you
Publicly about your sexual
Orientation?*

Lord Jennings

I hate calling women out their names but this one bitch defined the goddamn word and I wasn't with the bullshit, especially from a nappy headed trick I didn't know.
 Um hey, Ho! Yea, you. I seen ya' boyfriend, yea, bitch I seen your Man. Talking all that shit at the Miami Dade Homestead College Dirty ass Skank Central Library. Yea, bitch. YEA, YOU! Cross-eyed bitch. I TOLD you this day was gonna come when I write about that shit but no, Hoe, you test me like I'm pussy and you got fucked morning, noon and night and a Niggah didn't even kiss your lips or part the Red Sea to say hello to Miss Clit.
 I was in the library, homeless I might add but my teeth were still brushed and my hair was still cut and I smelled ZEST FULLY CLEAN, bitch and still looked like a diamond in the rough, but in a rut, ya' heard.
 People were coming around me, talking 'bout, "Girl, this is the King of Erotica. He writing his first book, he posted in his Myspace blog."
 "The King of Erofifa, who?"

"*Not* Erofifa, girl. Ebonics, Chile. The Niggah got like 400 number 1 blogs in writing and poetry and everybody, even ya' Mama reading his shit. The Niggah is bad, Chile."

She walked over to me and I was typing, scoping this Hoe out the corner of my eye via the Peripheral vision, mind you and I didn't miss a beat or a piece of the character's dialogue. In fact the way she was *Easting* me (meaning staring me down in a very confrontational way and bitch didn't even know me or my Gatorade or tea), I was adding the real life Hoe to the fictitious Hoe in my book, enhancing the character's description, hence how Melissa Jackson from The Golden Masks (The King of Erotica book 1 the Throne, check it out if you haven't) was born. I created her loose pussy ass during that brief encounter with a thirsty bitch hell bent on attention.

I was still typing about 62 W.P.M. Bitch all in my air space and I knew she was close by because when she walked in I faintly smelled that Elizabeth White Diamonds bullshit, bitch a flawed diamond wearing some legendary shit, instant fail already but who was I to judge when I was wearing imitation Gucci out of Big Lots for about $3.

"Hey boy."

"I got your Hey, boy, bitch," I snapped, already pissed because her presence broke my concentration, so part of the inspiration was destroyed so I mentally diverted my attention to the attention-seeking whore and suddenly I had a lot to type about. "The day my dick grew past 6 inches, bitch, *this* little boy wasn't in Wonderland."

Her mouth fell open. People were laughing.

The librarians looked up at me, they were wrapped around my finger anyway 'cause I was a tall, sexy bitch reading encyclopedias and dictionaries and concordances and thesauruses while the Niggahs lookin' like a fool with their pants on the ground, checking me out, too.

Her hands on her skinty ass hips. The bitch that sucked dick for the taste. Or so the rumors went.

"Who you callin' a bitch?" she asked, heated.

"U-N-I-T-Y! *You!* Queen Latifah LaStanka."

"Its Latifah, thank you and my man g'on beat your ass."

"It's Latifah, thank you," I mocked, talking like a fag to annoy her. "And my man g'on beat your ass."

The laughter was crazy.

She eyed her man, giving him a You-go'n-just-sit-there-and-let-this-Niggah-talk-shit-to-me look. He glared at me with hate and contempt, about to get saucy up in here and I didn't turn to face him.

I kept typing in my book with onlookers admiring a Niggah 'cause he could cuss a bitch, read something I wrote on notebook paper, type it without looking from the screen and look sexy.

Ow, bitch where they do that at? I know where. Miami-Dade County, Niggah.

But I needed a break so I stopped, and looked this Niggah deeply in his eyes; like Gladiators, and I was Nassau, Bahamian, *bomba clyde*, me no look away from no secret pussy boy.

You see I was NOT SCARED OF NO NIGGAH GET A CLUE BITCHES! I fear NO MAN. God made you, I pray to God, he woke me up daily to endure the financial hardships, a backstabbing ass family, bitter ass cousins, my sexual frustrations and still didn't put no more than I could bear on my shoulders.

So why should I fear those off brand ass Niggahs who were store porch bums and parking lot pimps because they couldn't even spell GED or motherfucking J-O-B, C-H-I-L-D S-U-P-P-O-R-T, K-E-E-P Y-O-U-R D-I-C-K I-N Y-O-U-R P-A-N-T-S I-F Y-O-U L-I-V-E W-I-T-H Y-O-U-R M-A-M-A O-R Y-O-U'-R-E O-N F-U-C-K-I-N-G P-A-R-O-L-E.

Let's assess the opponent, shall we. In *this* corner was a tall, chocolate Niggah with gleaming gold teeth worth more than his unpaid phone bill and drove a candy apple Chevy with silver rims and a booming system for your ass, and your mouth, too, depending on his mood.

And in *that* corner was a 6 foot 5 inch Niggah from Goulds, been through some shit, swinging some thangs, made it through troubled waters, burned my bridges and was homeless, broke but full of wealth with these unwritten books percolating in my heart, body, mind, heart and soul.

I heard he ain't worth the plus tax on a can of tea. So bitch don't act grand. Don't act like you got the catch of the century when he a bum living with his grandma telling everybody she had bad surgery, that she sued the hospital and got a settlement and the bitch couldn't even get Social Security on time by altering the last four on her goddamn paperwork and you had to drop out of college in Jacksonville, move out your apartment and back home to care for her. Bull. Shit. America. With his unrealistically retarded ass. And you believed that shit. Bitch, boo.

I heard his dick ain't about shit either. Your sister, Miss Mistletoe Tonsils with a Giraffe neck, was talking 'bout how she sucked honey out his asshole in your bed while your ass was working the night shift at the old Homestead Hospital (before they tore it down and built a much more elaborate, high tech one), getting paid under the table because you told your man you were going to work but you lost your job as a RN (Sucking one of the patient's dick when you were supposed to be on your lunch break), and was actually turning tricks from 7 p.m. till 7 a.m. in the morning. In your RN outfit, so don't talk shit I know all your business and Hoe you don't even know my first name, but I know your name, trick.

And you all in the library try'na make me look bad?

She said all you had to do was get the Niggah high and squeeze his upper thigh and he would stuff a dick in your asshole faster than a bitch could ring up your grocery at Publix Supermarket because his Other Pregnant Hoe was a cashier at the Ghetto Wal-Mart in Florida City letting anything on two legs eat sunflower seeds from her pussy.

"Why you staring at him, get him, baby. He disrespected me," she demanded, rolling her eyes t me.

He stood up and everybody grew quiet. Librarians, they fiercely protected me. I looked at them and they looked at *me*, picking up the school phone and alerting security.

Homeboy approached me and I looked up at him, turning in my chair, cocking my legs, leaning back in the seat like What, bitch. Grabbing my dick.

He paused, glaring me down like the sun fell out the sky and sat her sulfuric ass down in this chair looking the spitting image of me.

"Why you talkin' shit to my broad."

"Fuck you *and* your broad."

"Gay bitch!" she yelled, and people laughing.

I sat there.

"*You g'on just sit there, Mr?*"

"*He must be gay!*"

"*He ain't doing shit.*"

"GAY BITCH!" She yelled and I looked deep in his eyes while he balled up his fists, gritting his teeth with fire in his eyes and I said, "Tell your Hoe to shut up."

"Hell naw. She my girl."

"That's right. My man 'bout to beat your ass."

"Tell your Hoe to shut up," I said the second time, my legs drumming together at the atmospheric pressure blowing just behind my pipe; trying to find the hole; tying to burst inside; trying to make me release some tension.

He glared at me, meaning business. "*Dawg*. You got one more time to disrespect her. Apologize."

"*Yea*, faggot," she said and I tilted my head down with my eyes up into his face and I put both hands on the chair and I pushed up with my arms, relaxing the muscles in my legs and I snapped, "TELL YOUR HOE TO SHUT THE FUCK UP BITCH!"

"That's it," he said, walking towards me and she instigating and she said, "My man 'bout to beat your ass."

"THAT'S IT!" he shouted, that GOON coming outta him. Yawn. I wanted to laugh.

Security thundered inside and I got on the computer table and I said, "Listen up, everybody ATTENTION ATTENTION! I SAID LISTEN UP!"

Everyone quiet. Ole boy staring, in shock at my outburst and Miss Loose Mouth shut up too, looking at her man.

I was fuming, my hands shaking so bad I had to squeeze them into tight fists.

"I *warned* you to shut your bitch up. I am already pissed you brought your Allapattah looking asses back here fucking with me. Don't nobody want Cutler Manor pussy, bitch. I am trying to fucking write, do you fucking understand?"

"Niggah..."

"Shut up bitch!" I told her, jumping down. I got in her face, then turned and looked in her man eyes smiling. "Since you wanna call me gay, Miss Thang let me tell you a little story. Of a Niggah name Frank, yea you, fuck Niggah. One day his girl," I said, looking at her when I said, "That would be you." I looked back at him. "You pissed him off. Let me describe your bedroom."

Everybody in shock, shock, stunned, she shocked, librarians in shock, security stunned, covering their mouths, students are shock, shock, state of shock gasp gasp gasp I can't breath kinda shock and I didn't give a fuck.

"Your panty drawer is the third drawer on your armoire. You got two dildos in the top one, though, he fucked me with them. A picture of your dead Mama is in a

Dollar Store frame on your fucking nightstand, bitch wearing that tired ass dress with the Whoppie from *Ghost* wig when she reluctantly gave four million dollars to a bunch of nuns, praise God! I got him high, squeezed his top thigh and I sucked his tears away, made him cum from the back, put on your small ass petite ass panties, got fucked looking in your dead mama eyes in her picture bitch while he said this felt better than you and your sisters pussy combined and you in the fucking library calling me gay when you been sucking my pussy from this Niggah's dick for the past 6 months bitch didn't you just check in the hospital last week from food poisoning? Ain't that ditzy Hoe that work at Wal-Mart pregnant with your kid, fuck Niggah?"

"Oh my God!"

"Hell naw he just fucked you up!"

"Hell naw Pharoah keep it one hundred percent real."

"Frank gay oh my God!"

"I knew Frank was a faggot! He always *got a car full of Niggahs from the 'Hood and make his girl catch the bus to work.*"

Frank was crushed. Now the spotlight on him. Take a bow, Niggah, close the curtain last call for alcohol.

"Pharoah, you promised," he said.

"And *you* promised to keep your bitch in check; yet you *can't* even control your Hoe. She running her trap and don't even respect you."

"Pharoah, man how could you?"

"How could I?" I grabbed my shit, took my jump drive (it auto-saved my document) and opened my book bag. I put in my folders and jump drive and my Bible.

I took something out and walked past Frank. He couldn't even look me in the eyes. So called gutter Niggah. Bitch please, ain't even man enough to stop your face from falling on the floor or picking that motherfucker up.

I paused in front of his Hoe.

"I think these are yours, bitch!"

I put her panties on her fucked weave job and walked past her. And yea they still smelled like my asshole. If she woulda been a good lil bitch and left me alone I probably would have washed them using Tide with Bleach and my Downy fresh fabric softener and hid them under her bed or something to keep the bitch mind going.

"My panties! How he get my panties, Frank?"

And I left Frank to his aftermath.

Should have kept his bitch in check.

And I woulda kept my loyalty and my lips in check.

I had to snatch both their wigs, sorry.

I'm from *Goulds*, bitch!

Pharoah *ain't* the one.

*Tell me about a time
A family member detested you*

Lord Jennings

When I was younger, about age 11, 12, I was approached by one of my male cousins; one of those bitter cousins my age that used to fight me and my brothers every time we came to Roe house. If it wasn't one of Roe's down and out sons pushing them up to fight, it was my peers getting that ass stomped because neither one of them whipped my ass. I mean, shit, I was only being raped already in my home, trying to fight a grown adult male authority figure off my ass and now I was over to my Great Aunt's house as an escapism from the dreadful reality that was my young innocent goddamn life, and had to fight him, him, her, him, the little one, the three legged dog and the goddamn old, fat ass instigator WHIP HIS ASS HIS GRANMA KILLED MY GODDAMN DADDY! Bitch in the fucking doorway and ass I slapped Him, and knocked HER ass on HER ASS, the *rest* of them, even the three legged dog, who jumped when I growled at his ass, ran off past the Instigator who sucked her teeth and rolled her eyes when the little one ran up to me and said, "Wawwy why you so sad Wawwy?" (Larry)

My little cousin couldn't pronounce Larry (Pharoah) so his cute little self said "Wawwy" and still got the meaning and content across. Smarter than most the older ones in the house.

"I'm not sad," I said, picking him up and the Instigator said, "Don't baby him. We don't want him growing up to be no punk."

"You know what I'm getting sick of your fat ass."

"Who the fuck you cursing at boy? I'ma ya' elder, I'll beat your ass."

"Bitch please, you tell my Mama all you want, but bitch I saw you in your older brother room sucking a crack head's dick for fifty godddamn dollars 'cause you claimed you were running out of douche, tampons and deodorant and we can't have that, huh?"

She rushed up to me and snatched the baby. "For your information I needed my feminint products."

"Feminine product, damn. I'm in the *sixth* damn grade and I know that shit."

"Take your gay ass home."

"Go buy some feminine tampons, bitch. Lying to that man. Knowing he married. Giving him that fat pussy. Talking 'bout feminine products and you got a drawer full of enemas, douche, Secret deodorant, Dial soap and some goddamn brand new panties."

"I'm gonna tell you one more time. Watch your mouth. I'll tell ya Mama."

"So! Who you think she gonna believe. You or me?"

"She will believe me, I'm the older one."

"Oh, yea?" I challenged her, staring her ass down. "I'll just tell her you said my Grandma killed your *daddy* and she will beat your ass to Alice's grave for an apology. Now go suck crack head dick."

And I pivoted on my heel, said Peace to God, get into your Word when eye get home. Still didn't know why my Kindergarten teacher taught me to spell my name first, gave me a dictionary and a Bible and said, "*Keep* HIM first, son. Don't question me, don't question it. Follow in the ways of his Word, don't let your parent's force you into religion, have open eyes and see the Word for what it's worth."

I rolled my eyes looking at that huge afro eccentric lady in tight brown pants and a Keeping your Head in the Water Temporary Layoff blouse like she was crazy. She damn sure wasn't pretty as Penny from *Good Times* but damn she 'bout to beat my ass if I don't *take* this Bible *and* Dictionary.

Um, I looked at the ceiling, my eyes up forehead down and I said, nervously, "God, hi. I guess I'm stuck with you, huh? I'm Pharoah. Spelled P-H-A-R-O-A-H."

My teacher was overcome with joy, clasping her hands together. Her eyes lit up the heavens and broadened the corneas of our eyes with pupils and trepidation and I looked at her and said, "Ok, I did it."

Her smile was stuck. "What?"

I grinned, cautiously, as to not offend her. "I did what you said."

"What? You just introduced yourself to God."

"Only cause you made me. You looking at me like you wanna punch in my chest, lady I don't know you to be putting your hands on me I'll tell my Mama and her Daddy who is my Grand daddy was an Airforce man, yes ma'am and he will *shoot* you with his big oleee rifle."

She snatched me by the shirt, "You little ghetto fucks."

"Who you cussing at? You just told me don't let my Mama and them force me into no religion. And then you turn around and force me to take what you say about God as the truth. I don't know nobody name God! You crazy, lady. My Mama and step daddy sleep in the same bed, I don't gotta look at the ceiling for no God when he, when he…"

I paused. I wanted to say, I don't gotta look up at the ceiling for no God when my step daddy put his thang in my mouth and hump all on me til that thick white stuff is all over me, yuk!

But I didn't say a thing.
I did know I felt older than my years.
And I didn't know what to do with that.

During lunch in Junior High (Cutler Ridge Middle) school I would sit across from my friends. They had names in front of them and I would always steal somebody's name, put it in front of me, and put Pharoah Wilson in front of another kid when he wasn't looking, so he could indirectly represent who everybody that I was and thought what was to become of me.

Another reason why eye sat across from friends was because I looked in the Grown folks mouths when they spoke. And I was filled with information, soaking up Game and dissecting some shit with my childlike mind.

Mrs. Brandy whispered to Miss Anthony, "Girl, so I sucked his dick right. You know he got a man and shit."

"No girl he a faggot?" asked Miss Anthony in shock.

"Yes! Yes, girl, yes! Would I lie, would I sit my fine pretty ass here and lie?"

"No, girl. You got that fine ass husband at home sticking dick to that pussy, huh?" asked The Fatter Teacher. Four of those gossiping tricks sat together.

Mrs. Brandy warmed to her subject. "Yes, Girl! Check it. Ole brother n law of mine never liked me. It's the 80's, ok. He looks me all in da eyes and stare me down and talking bout 'You better treat my brother right. He has been hurt by Hoes like you.'"

"And what else he said, Gwarl?" asked Miss Jheri-Curl.

They were all into it, so was I.

Mrs. Brandy said, "'Girl I looked at him all crazy Chile and he said, 'I warned you,'" and he walked out.

"And?" they all asked. They were on the edge of their seats.

"I ignored him," Mrs. Brandy. "I went to my husband and told him what his brother says. He say I'ma fool, that I better know my role and leave his family alone or he gone divorce me and shit girl. But the Bible say marry a woman and forsake all others and be fruitful and got his son and he still protecting his family over his wife girl God ain't real."

"Yes he is, girl," The Fatter teacher said, drooling at the mouth, nosey bitch.

"Then what happened?" asked Miss Anthony.

"Girl. I came home last night, my stomach was hurting. I'm pregnant, you know I *ain't* been eating right *and* his brother been running my house bills up, eating up the food and all the cereal and won't buy shit back and my husband make me use my money to replace it and he gamble Across the Tracks with his money and lose it all up."

"Or pay for pussy," said the Fatter One.

"Yes ma'am," Miss Jherri-Curl.

Mrs. Brandy looked crazy. "I burst into my room and guess what girl my husband…" Her tears fell harder.

"What girl," said Jherri-Curl, about to bust this Hoe in the mouth from stalling.

"Tell us!"shouted the Fatter One, Miss Anthony holding her neck.

By now half the students stopped talking at the outburst of "Tell us!" and they're listening intently and I was too, but I was also doing something else.

Grown people surely focus when dey tawk cause man o' man damn they didn't notice shit.

And dey grown?

"My husband was fucking his brother in the ass girl."

"What?" Jherri-Curl was stunned. Kids stunned. Fatter One stunned. Miss Anthony stunned. Mrs Brandy shaking her head in disgust.

"Yes! I was in the door way shocked and stunned and my husband said, 'Fuck this dick bitch you been getting this ass fucked since we were little Niggah now take this dick.'" Mrs. Brandy gave all the dialogue, and eye was writing it all down.

"But brother...please, stop. I'm your brother, what are you doing please!"

"Take this dick!"

"Fuck me brother, no, no I didn't mean it stop! I'm not granddaddy I know what he did to you was wrong but I am not him why you hurting me."

And he broke down.

Kids started wailing, crying and I had tears in my eyes and the teachers were fucked, realizing we all were paying attention. We heard it all, some of our eyes were opened, they rushing around the room like three black tornadoes with fake hair and a Jherri-Curl and overly painted faces trying to shush us. I was writing. I wrote their entire conversation down. Maybe I can write me a book one day. Library got a lot of them

I folded the paper and put it in my closet.

When I got to Roe house after school with my book bag, my friend Quincy came with me. We hung out all the time and Miss Hill, his auntie, was a nice lady when I did see her. Maybe once or twice in my young life.

I saw Cyn sitting at the table and Buddy walking around eating something out of the fridge with his shirt off and those nappy little hairs on his chest.

I looked down at my own chest like I hope I don't get dat shit.

"You need to go home, you," Cyn said to Quincy. "Where your Mama?"

"Um..."

"Go home. Bye."

She was drinking a Pepsi with Peanuts. Some chicken on her plate, half eaten mashed potatoes and too much hot sauce. How much hot sauce did you need?

Quincy never came back over again.

I saw one of my arch nemesis cousins, around my age, who I used to fight. He looked at me and I looked at him and I walked to the back room to see if Wanky was back there and he wasn't. I loved Wanky so much and it didn't dawn on me that he died years ago, when eye was a kid.

    I loved to talk to Wanky. So nice and he always made me laugh.

    Never instigated his nieces and nephews to fight me like the other big bitch.

    When I got back there he wasn't there and it hit me like a ton of bricks that he was buried years ago and eye was depressed outta my mind and my cousin pushed me on the floor and closed the door.

    And locked it.

    Eying me evilly.

My male cousin hated my ass.

    And muthafuckah, I equally hated his ass.

    He all in my face, jealous of my nose and shit.

    "Why you're gay, boy."

    "What?" I asked, wanting to leave and leave now!

He was a cocky bastard. "You heard me. Why you gay?"

"Why *you* gay, Niggah what you tawkin bout boy you don't know me boy."

"I'm ya' cousin."

"My grandma killed your granddaddy *remember*. That's what people keep saying. So we *ain't* no blood."

He started taunting me with laughter that made my skin crawl. "I *know* that man raped you a long time ago."

He hit a nerve. "*Shut up!*"

"You liked it *didn't* you?"

I was stunned. *Yes.* "No, I don't!" I did, and that was a bitter truth that was the basis for the hatred I would later have for myself.

"*Yes* you do. He was getting you in the booty. Faggot! I *knew* I hated you."

He spit on me and I wiped it off my face and slapped him with it and spit back on that bitch.

When he gonna learn he can't beat me!

"You bitch. You ain't gonna spit on me," he said, punching at me and I pushed him into the wall, trembling.

"Don't you tell nobody what that man DID TO ME! IT AIN'T YOUR FUCKING BUSINESS BITCH! And you better not bring my Mama in it."

"What?" he asked, balling his hands into fists.

"You heard me!"

He said, "I *heard* what you told my Mama. That that man getting you in the booty. Nasty, nasty, nasty! Keep your mouth closed."

He punched at me again and we went at it, knocking a lamp off the dresser, falling in the bed…he pulling my shirt and I punched his face and he bit me and Roe calling out our names telling us to stop fighting but we weren't hearing her.

We wallowing, going at it. A Niggah like me and my cousin *ain't* backing down. This was Goulds.

I pushed him off me again and Bomb Beeda and Buddy came in the room grabbing us. And we still reaching out trying to connect negatively and they spanked both our asses.

And left us to sit amongst each other, crying, angry and mad.

"I HATE THIS FAMILY I PROMISE YOU I HATE THIS GODDAMN FAMILY!"

And eye meant it.

"Ya'll behave now, you hear?" said Bomb Beeda.

"Leave me alone!" I screamed at him, and he closed the door.

"I hate this family!" I screamed again, and this time I meant it.

"You gay dawg," my cousin said, looking away from me.

"No I'm not," eye said silently.

"You are. You can't say that man making you gay. One of your uncles keep touching on me and I ain't gay. He ain't poking me in the booty."

"My Uncle ain't do nothing to you."

"Yes he did! Your whole family sick. And I hate you."

"We ain't gon never like each other."

"Let's shake on it."

We made a pact.

When we became adults, we were the best of friends.

Who woulda thought.

Would I continue fighting with my cousins, yea, I would, and every time we did the same ole result. I was getting weary of all these fights, and for what? Over something their aunts and uncles pushed them up to do? Older people who were supposed to be setting the standard and raising the bar in our lives pushing kids up to become gladiators for their own entertainment.

Fighting seemed second nature to the other b.s. of the entire thing.

Cleaning Roe house.

Oh my God, talk about the house was nasty as hell OMG. Floor looks like shit, dishes always piled up towards the roof like God was in a buffet line about to grab a plate.

Roaches, roaches, roaches. Bathroom nasty as hell. Oh my God every time I had to piss somebody left turds in the goddamn toilet. My little brother Kells was terrified of that bathroom. Close the door on him when he pissed he tore the damn door down screaming.

It got to the point I was too afraid to even go in the bathroom myself or close the damn door. My brothers used to piss in the bushes to keep from using that bathroom but my pride wouldn't lead me to the bushes.

Roe opened her house to all. She never turned anybody away. They wanted to eat shit, but never cleaned a damn thing. Roe was a humble, God fearing woman, she taught me some pretty valuable things in life. I used to bring her insulin so she gave herself diabetic shots, not understanding why she had to stick herself with needles everyday. Confused me, and when I inquired about it she told me to stay in a child's place and not worry about it.

One day Cyn asked me to bring her Jackie Collins book from her room.

I was reluctant, but eventually I went. It was right where she said it was, on her cluttered nightstand. She had books all over the room. One thing I could say was she wasn't a dummy. I didn't really know what she did for a living, I think she was a nurse or something because I would always see her in a yellow and white medical uniform.

And could eat? My God. If you didn't wanna share don't bring shit around her.

Oh my God.

One day I came over with two pieces of fried chicken from home. God knew I was a stubborn bitch that day 'cause I told everybody from the flies to my brothers *Hell, no!*

Soon as I get in the house to eat my chicken in peace...

"Hey, Pharoah. Hmm, I like fried chicken, *too*."

I looked at Cyn sideways, frowning. "Ok, that's nice."

"That means give me a piece, now."

"But this is my chicken and you got bones in front of you," I said. Her favorite spot in the house was sitting at the dining table, and her Mom, Roe, sat in the Lazy Boy.

"COME HERE!" She took off her shoe and I looked at her again.

"You don't have to yell."

"You got a smart little mouth."

"'Cause I don't wanna give you my chicken my mouth smart?"

"Come here."

"Man!"

"NOW!"

"Why?"

"Pharoah."

Roe said, "Pharoah, go see what she wants."

"But Roe, this my food."

"Go, Pharoah," said Roe. "Doesn't pay to be stingy."

I sucked me teeth and *yes* I wanted them to hear it.

I reluctantly walked over and she took my food and started chomping on it and I was so mad, a darkness filled me and my fists were balled and I said, "I hope you die on that chicken bone!"

"Bring your ass here!" She took off her shoe and swung it at me and I ran out the house, ran for dear life.

I promised not to look back. I would never go to that house. If they weren't fighting me and talking shit they were trying to make me clean that junky ass house I got my own house and hardly gotta clean that up, my Mama does that.

Before I could turn the corner one of my older cousins grabbed my arm, and the other, a little older, took my legs and they carried me, while I was kicking and screaming, back to Cyn.

She beat my ass with that white medical shoe, a cigarette dangling from her mouth.

"I hate you! I hate this family! I want Mama!"

She beat my ass for the old and the new.

My chicken on her goddamn breath.

How do you develop character development in your works?

Lord Jennings

The second part of The Basketball Court (Part one of the Basketball Court was in my book Some Men Wear Panties) I wrote while I was a little tipsy on Grey Goose and blazing one to the moon. Many people do many things for many reasons. But since my Grandma died before I was born I already felt robbed and was always jealous of my homeboys who had fathers and grandmas. People who knew my Grandma said she was a fabulous story teller. So when I blaze one I am smoking life Grandma pushed up from the core of the earth and writing pieces of literature that are out of the norm, but show and express dysfunction, even from within the family. So my motto is: My Grandma died with a lot of shit on her mind. That's why I'm a bestseller. I can tell exactly what she was thinking by watching the ways and decisions of her grown children.

WASSUP FACEBOOK. REMEMBER; DON'T PRAISE ME FOR MY BOOKS. THAT'S PRESENTING TO GOD A FALSE IDOL. PRAISE GOD FOR MY BOOKS AND THANK HIM FOR GIVING ME TALENT. I'M

NOT BUT AN INSTRUMENT PLAYING MELODIES FOR BLANK PAGES AND PRESENTING A BOOK OF LIFE OF SORTS. ALL OF THOSE STORIES COME FROM DIVINITY, NOT VANITY. AND THAT'S GOD. GOD IS THE TRUTH. AND FROM THAT MY IMAGE WAS CARVED FROM THE LAPELS OF HIS EYE LIDS.

After eye hit "submit" two separate times (because eye had a character limit on my status box update) on Facebook eye decided, that after writing for thirteen hours straight, eye needed a quick break. Been writing for hours, since I first got depressed. And the stuff I've written oh my God. Powerful.

I am happy in my life. I have my nieces to thank for that. I do anything for my babies. I am the best example around them, as a man who has been up and down, been through shit in life yet I remain of sound mind and spread humbleness with fear for God.

Those characters eye created in head were why I called my books The King of Erotica. They were the cream de la cream of their own individual lives. They pretend and they slay, they talk about others and they were sensitive towards criticism in their own lives.

They validate themselves through sex and misconstrue it as love. Just like eye once have. How many of us have done THAT before? That is, if you can truly be honest with yourselves.

The weakness of the flesh was defined as lust. Putting that weakness into action was called sex.

I'm not feeling very well. Just down for some reason. Don't know why. But I tell you one thing, when I'm depressed I write and my characters come across depressed as well. So as I improve through prayer it reflects in my characters, no matter how much sex they were having in my books.

That's character development.

Even some of my characters ask GOD for forgiveness. That was my status update on Facebook on November 30,

2009. Around 7:30 p.m. I was already upset I went to get my HIV Meds and they gave me Epzicom and my multivitamins and Lexiva. But I had to wait a whole day for the Norvir. Some guideline about discernment issues. I get the other drugs on time but the Norvir the next day at 11 a.m. and I had taken my last dosage for the month this morning. So I had nothing for tomorrow except the Epzicom and the Lexiva, but without the Norvir that shit ain't effective. So I told the pill people and they insured me when it opened at 11 a.m. I could come early and get them. But the problem was I took them around 9:30 a.m. Consistency. Taking them at 11? Inconsistency, but tell these braniacs that. I should have known better. They worked in a local clinic in the Hood and not a prestigious hospital, so that in itself should have spelled fuck up.

They playing with people's lives. Some of them already gotta pay for health care. They closed down on Thanksgiving. Clinic personnel at home eating with family and we couldn't get our refills on our HIV medicine on time. That was Thursday. Then Friday hits and the clinic still closed what the fuck? I got four days dosage left. Friday through Monday. And now it's Monday and I gotta wait till Tuesday to get the Norvir?

Then to add insult to injury they fired my case manager Kevin from the UNCARES department at CHI in Goulds. They hired a Cuban dishwasher with no experience to oversee all the Case Managers. I mean this Cuban came in barking orders, demanding everyone show him how to do his job and when his ally attempt failed he treated everyone like an episode of *Survivor China* and Kevin was fired because that position was really his and they hired a dishwasher with no experience to stagnate his promotion.

I'm sorry. But an inexperienced Cuban with pussy on the brain managing people giving my HIV prescription? Um, no! When Kevin was fired I told myself they really didn't care about our health. Files backed up for months Kevin was the man that cleared them all up. He took on so many workloads that UNCARES department was successful because of him. But successful case loads made inconsistent money so they fired him and brought in the inexperienced Cuban and now names winding up on the wrong medications.

All over money? Nah, that's a classic case of people getting fired and in their place CUBANS were being hired right here in great old Miami, that was starting to look like Cuba more and more everyday. We had to be bilingual for a job, but they were One Lingual, Spanish, and hardly spoke a lick of English but muthafuckahs too scared to take their former employers to court. This was sad. So finding out my case manager was fired and some white bimbo with Scrappy Do hair from Scooby Do going to refill my pills? And with those Coke bottle glasses, so goddamn thick I couldn't see her eyes, I gotta take anything she signs off on?

Chile. All this played a part in my being upset and depressed. I knew why they fired him. He didn't play by their rules and refused to help someone that took his promotional spot. If you hired the dishwasher for the job I'm sure that entailed more than just washing dishes. In fact this is helping people air laundry. Then add the fact that I sent Kevin all my pictures from my book signings to his company email and you tube videos of E Lynn Harris receiving my book and giving him a few promotional copies of books I had yet to release and business cards to pass out on the clock. They probably said he was soliciting one of the client's literatures and not focusing on work.

And I didn't send their asses shit and they got jealous and turned his ass in.

So I got a message from someone on my friend list. I talk to all my fans, when I can. And he typed:

Hello Pharoah I don't know you and I never spoke to you. And just now I saw your status post I thought

MAYBE YOU ARE DEPRESSED BECAUSE YOU WISH TO BE LOVED WITH WARM EMOTIONS FROM THE HEART. CHARACTERS OF YOURS THAT THEY HAVE TOO MUCH SEX ARE YOU MISSING THAT TOO? BECAUSE ALL THAT CAN BE PART OF YOUR MOOD JUST DON'T TAKE ME WRONG IT BOTHERS ME WHEN PEOPLE ARE SAD.

I smiled, writing him back. I could tell he really thought about sending me that message, the way it was typed he was careful not to offend me and I thought it was cute.

I said:

YEA THAT COULD BE TRUE AND PROBABLY IS. AS LONG AS MY CHARACTERS ARE FUCKING AND RELEASING THEN I GO TO BED MENTALLY SATISFIED SO IT'S NO BIG DEAL.

Like my characters, they are imperfect, inconsistent and flawed, reflecting my teenage years devastatingly.
    If my characters can suck dick, eat pussy, get fucked in the ass, rob a bitch, talk back to their mothers, fuck their daddy's and keep a secret, raise their children to hate what they love and love what they hate, then why can't you? We're ALL sinners the Bible said, and no man, woman or child is exempt from his rule.
    But the thing was that the Bible has been rewritten and changed so much, people are fucked up. What version did a bitch follow? The King James Version or the Greek version. Sin comes from thought. Thought before action. Weren't my characters derived from my thoughts? I had to think it to write it. But get this. Weren't my characters inspired by my own trails in life, things I seen, things I fucked and tasted, things I experimented and documented in previous journals?
    So was the action truly before the thoughts since my actions and taking responsibility for them inspired me to write this autobiography?

Dapharoah69

I often thought of this when I smoked marijuana or went through trails and tribulations. Some of that shit Mama never saw coming. Some of that shit she didn't prepare me for. Some of that shit my Daddy was supposed to teach me, beat my ass to learn but he'd rather nut up and down the block chasing Hoes with dripping pussy and left me to fend for myself while grown ghetto Niggahs dug me out, slid in deep and told me eye had good pussy and eye was just a teenager searching and looking for love and acceptance. A place eye could be myself. Instead eye was secretly fucked, had to secretly suck grown niggahs and live my life amongst idle threats on my life.

One niggah told me eye wouldn't live to see my 15th birthday if eye told anybody he was fucking me. He always wore his wife's panties and wig. A thug niggah.

He told me later on his Mama used to fuck him with strap ons the minute he thought another man was cute. She beat and fucked him and he never said he was cute again.

Mama couldn't teach me to be a man or show me how to be a man. She had tits and a pussy. Not a chest and a dick. I had a chest and a dick and a pair of balls, getting hairier by the day and frankly I knew what a nut and my nuts were before she thought to teach me because my ex step daddy raped me and taught me Anatomy 101, the Expert Version and my two older cousins used to beat my ass with extension cords if I didn't fuck or eat their pussies right for 8 months.

I captured everything that saddens me when I write. I have been doing this shit since I was a child. I knew when I was very young that I was a Pharaoh, but back then they called them Good Fathers.

Good fathers would never be called the real Pharoah in the media, because they keep overlooking Good Fathers and broadcasting the bad ones, the daddy's that sell drugs to feed their children. Their children go to bed with bellies full from the substance bought with inner city money and with *that* money the consumer buys from the dope man (some of these *millionaires* were bigger drug users and had more dangerous habits than inner city niggahs) takes away from their families and children to eat so now a bitch gotta rob and shoot the armor trucks for some of our money back.

I never was one to write from thought, really. I always created from emotion. If my character didn't suffer emotionally then spiritually they would be frauds. I knew this before I wrote anything.

And being that I was the one in the family that wasn't supposed to make it, I was *also* the one under a Generational Curse from my daddy side.

God took out on me sins of my *father* and it *didn't* matter that he didn't raise me. The grave things Daddy previously done before my birth befell me in Florida and while he went through hell in California I was being bashed, spat on, pissed on, fucked and beaten inside the hells of Goulds, Florida. Environmental voodoo. Satan poked Daddy, Step Daddy poked me.

My daddy's essence was God's voodoo doll. Strike my father it strikes me. I never knew this man but I was a reflection of him and validated it when I looked in the mirror. I had his lips, cheekbones, chin and eyes.

Yet I never looked in his eyes and I was suffering with him.

I used to think this and my Pastor confirmed it. He wasn't my Pastor two whole weeks when I visited Atlanta *after* I became a bestseller. And he told me more than all the Pastors of every church I ever belonged to combined.

He said, "Son, you are under a generational curse on your Daddy's side."

He corrected the lie. I wasn't under it from my Mama's side.

I was under it from Daddy's side. Daddy was cursed to tend Mama's field and when what he cultivated killed us from hunger she left his ass because he reneged on his promise, his Vow. To love and honor and protect her.

Dapharoah69

So God punished him for running out on his wife.

And I had to suffer too. Eye didn't look at that as unfair treatment now that eye am a man with a burgeoning career. Eye look at that as "preparation." God knew what was to come of my life and Satan did, too. Eye had two paths in life. The Good Path and the Wrong Path and we were born with the Free Will choice to travel whichever, whenever; and Mama set me on the Right Path, *but* what she didn't tell me was that the Wrong Path beautifully disguised itself as the Right Path and twisted me through wicked forests and brush fires and sexual orgies and men who fucked me good and women who pussy fucked my dick good and she gargled my nut while she and her married husband/man tongue kissed all over my asshole while eye blew bubbles with his brother's nut as he fucked my hot mouth and once he came again down my throat we all lay spent through the night and eye was creeping out the door as they slept the night away and eye had a pocket full of money, sipping from a bottle of Glenfiddich single malt scotch whiskey and their wallet's left on empty on the side of the road disguised as the bedroom nightstand.

Eye didn't fuck around with niggah hoes, niggahs' Hoes or Hoes themselves. When eye was homeless eye turned tricks to feed myself, even if that meant getting $500 from an Opa Locka pa$tor who drove all the way down south in a black BMW to get all in my mouth with that little pathetic thang he called a dick.

The first night eye saw it eye laughed my ass off like, "*Come* on now. Stop *playing*. Put that thang away and bring out the real thing.

Niggah 6 feet 1 with a five inch cock so sucking him was the easiest five hundred dollars of my life.

He liked to come in my mouth then tongue kiss me and eye pushed his nut down his own throat because if there was one thing worse than swallowing a man's nasty-smelling jizz was swallowing biblical jizz and eye wasn't with the program.

He nearly gagged from swallowing his own seeds and eye would give him a sexy gaze, cupping his sweaty face and while he's saying, "Oh, Jesus that felt good," eye told myself, *My name is Pharaoh. Eye am not Jesus and eye'm so glad you swallowed that nasty tasting shit because UGH eye need to brush and gargle, like now.*

The weakness of my flesh was my blind side; and overcoming that was hell in itself with its own set of rules, flames and cruel and unusual punishment.

Eye got there through writing in my journals, writing books and analyzing myself through how it all played out once a story was done. Eye hardly edit my work. When you edit you take away and you edit and you take away and you take away and you TAKE AWAY and your story then sounded like another story that wasn't truly your intentions.

That's why eye didn't trust editors. Some of them got besides themselves and forgot who the goddamn author was. If eye wanted Melissa Jackson (From The King of Erotica books) asking Hoes and Niggahs "Are you Freaky Deaky?" then goddamn it you leave her untouched.

One editor bitch out of New York with a Master's Degree and couldn't write "This Little Piggy Went to the Market" without struggling and flipping open a dictionary when the computer already got spell check (Eye mean duh, Miss Editor!) suggested eye make Melissa "Less black and more articulate."

And eye looked at her late ass and said, "Um, No. She's a PRC working Hoe that pays rent sucking and fucking a dick and eye know Hoes like that, ain't trying to be shit and ain't trying to count on nothing but those dollars they sucking from the ball bag of those retarded ass cum drunk on the DL ass Niggahs. And some of them already named their kids while they were pregnant. First name PAY-CHILD middle name SUPPORT last name NIGGAH!"

She shut up.

Dapharoah69

Now eye procreate books and say exactly what's on my goddamn mind. If Donald Goines and Jackie Collins could write the kinda books they wanted then damn it lay the fuck off Dapharoah69.

And my writing reflects my anger, frustration, grief and anguish.

A woman eye know, who always hated me, called herself talking shit about me in church one Sunday three years, 2007. She huffed and she puffed and she begged to blow my dick till eye nut in the shadows. Boy you so goddamn fine. Eat my pussy. So eye ate her pussy then she turned around, after massaging me (she made me wear her crotchless thong panties) and she pulled the G-string thingee to the side, spread my ass cheeks and started tongue fucking my asshole. Eye could have told her then she was tasting her husband but sometimes keep your BIG JOKER hidden in the shadow of a four player spade game. Nobody knows who got the BIG JOKER but guessing who got it makes the game more thrilling.

Then she got the ass to ass dildo and she put one end in her asshole then the other end in my asshole and we were ass to ass slap slap slap slap slap slap ohh shit slap slap slap she tossing that black ass cheap ass weave ooh shit Pharoah slap slap slap. Our sweaty booty cheeks jiggling all over a double penis ended dildo.

She came and eye jacked my dick and came.

Never called her again after she paid me $700. Eye paid my parole at the time, bills, then gave some to Mama. Slid my sister $20 and bought her an outfit and a purse.

She gets mad by telling me in church, in front of her husband that eye tried to come on to her during Bible Study at her house and everyone gasping and shit, looking at me weird and eye never even had Bible Study with the Fantastic Four looking Bionic bitch.

He jacked me up and eye pushed him off me.

"You tried to come on to my wife?" he asked, getting saucy and eye pulled out digital photos and threw them up in the air. Me and his wife doing the ass to ass thing spirals to the floor intermingled with pictures of him fucking me deep and eye shut them and the church up as eye pulled out my Black and Mild and lit up walking to my homeboy's car.

That inspired my writing. To show the dysfunction eye sometimes had in myself. Still acting out self-hatred, hurting myself and my spirit.

Getting HIV certainly opened my eyes and made me a believer. Slowed me down and knocked me on my ass. And eye had myself to blame and it took about three months but

Dapharoah69

eye inevitably took accountability for my problems and my reality and took responsibility.

So what eye was yesterday God told me its alright once eye got Baptized and got a fresh start. Eye would still be with sin and temptation. Baptism was a fresh slate, not immunity from sin.

In the form of the characters eye pen eye captured this. So as they improve I improve because I wrote and created them when I got on my knees and asked God for forgiveness and because of it he helped me improve.

So when people ask me, "Have you accepted being a talented writer?"

I say Nah. God is the author. I am the editor. I am not an author. I am a *creator*. I Pro-create with God's blunt way of teaching to reach a hard to reach group of people in denial. He did the same thing with John the Baptist and some woman wanted his head on a platter as a birthday gift and God allowed Satan to do it.

Free will I give my characters. The power to choose. Life or death. Light or darkness. Water or thirst. Food or hunger.

God or Satan? Who's side were you on?

Eye side with Jesus Christ.

That's my free Will Choice and my character development was my Immunity Card.

Did you ever try to kill
Your ex step father?

Lord Jennings

When eye was nine years old it all came full circle.
Wanting it to stop. Wanting him to leave me alone. Wanting it all to end. Yes, by that time eye loved sex, was addicted to sex and craved grown man dick but after all the sexual episodes, innuendos and the curling of my toes I wanted to go away. Eye wanted to die to make it all stop. I wanted him out the house. I wanted to die. I didn't even want to breathe. Eye wanted to be a normal kid again. But even eye knew that would never be.

I was always fascinated with the *Halloween* movie. Seeing Michael Myers as a small child, before eye turned 9 years old, did a number on me. Watching the soulless man, I was never afraid of this movie.

If anything, for me, *watching* it, something deep inside me seemed to make perfect sense.

Over the years that followed, I was 9 years old and *still* attracted to the movie. I watched it over 11 times, knowing every scene and line.

When I watched the movie I studied Michael. The way he walked, killed and moved. I noticed he was emotionally unavailable, didn't feel a thing when he killed someone.

My step daddy didn't feel a thing when he sexually killed me.

I wanted to understand it because—when it came to my step daddy—I didn't feel a thing. I didn't love or care for him.

I just wanted it all to stop. To all go away.

My friends were starting to call me gay, whatever that meant.

A few of them were bold enough to call me a *faggot* and as a 9 year old that was the first time I heard that term in a public setting with that much maliciousness and I still didn't know what it really meant. So eye cut them off as friends.

I didn't know why we moved out of Goulds, but we packed up and moved to South Miami Heights before I turned 10. I was happy to go and really *didn't* object. I mean I was a child, who listened to me?

I was still silently angry about what he was doing to me and believe me being quiet about it wasn't really working. Because I was developing, maturing and I was starting to be outspoken. Watching Mama speak her mind to everyone from her husband to bill collectors gave me some hope that one day I could be *that* outspoken. Tell a bitch to leave me the fuck alone and mind their own "bizzness."

So I started studying Mama like I studied the *Halloween* movie.

The way she walked and talked. I noticed her attitude with her father was different from that of her husband. She seemed to be on guard when she talked to my granddaddy and seemed a little tense with her husband.

When she talked to Laron, my brother (the second oldest) she was tender, loving and reassuring. The way she dressed him wasn't in a way she used to dress me. When she used to dress me it was rushed *and* she barely smiled.

When I was younger, around 3 or 4, we stayed with Cyn, my cousin in Chocolate City (Arthur Mays Villas). We took many pictures there, especially around Christmas. I loved Cyn and I should have told her what my step daddy was doing when it started happening. But the thing that stopped me was simple: what if I got the same response two of her sisters gave me?

What if she didn't help me? What if they already told her what eye came to them with?

What if she told me also that my Grandma killed her daddy?

So I remained quiet and any time someone rejected me in the future I would grow into a shell and never ask the same person for anything else, no matter if my life depended on it or not.

Reject me once, Game Over.

We moved to South Miami Heights, 11335 SW 190th Lane, next door to Jane, who was married to Barry at the time. They had two kids, Andre and Lawanna, his sister.

The year was 1988. Our new home was in housing projects by Miami Southridge Senior High. I remember seeing my future high school when we drove by it, moving into our new home.

I was in love with the building. I knew Mama got her diploma from there and I wanted to get mine from there as well.

My brothers and I played out in the front and back yard, but we were adamant about letting outsiders play with us and the kids knew we were the *new* kids on the block and they wanted to befriend us and I *didn't*.

My brothers made friends quickly. I wasn't sold so easily, I was suspecting of everyone who wanted to talk to me and everyone wanted to talk to me for some reason and the more I ignored them the more they wanted to know my name and I wasn't with the fucking program.

Eventually, Andre and Bert approached me. *Bert* had moved down from Liberty City. His Mama's name was Miss Eartha and I adored Miss Eartha, she was very nice to me.

They asked if I played football and I said "N*o*."

"Would you like to?" asked Andre, already athletically inclined.

"You should," said Bert.

"I'll think about it."

They were cool with that. So we became good friends.

Eventually Barry approached me about playing football. I was making mud pies out of dirt and water in the back yard.

"How are you, son?" he asked, and I kept making mud pies. I wasn't too fond of strangers and if it took me forever and a day to talk to the friends I have what made him think I was going to talk to him.

"Son," he went on.

"You're *not* my daddy," I said, standing up. I turned on the hose and filled the empty milk carton with water, my heart pounding.

"What's your name?"

I turned off the hose. "Pharoah." I didn't look at him. He extended his hand to shake it and I walked my tall ass right by him, sitting back in front of my well put together mud pies.

He was behind me. "My name is Barry."

"I know that," I said.

"How do you know?"

I looked deep into his eyes. He had a curly perm, wore nice jeans and a T-shirt. Athletic build, nice shoes.

"You're Andre's step daddy *aren't* you?"

"Yes, I am."

"You raise him right?" I asked.

"I love him as if he's my son."

"I wish my step daddy loved me." *Enough to keep his hands off me.*

"I'm sure he does. Seem like a nice man."

I looked away. "My mud pies are nicer than he'll ever be. And they have more heart."

I stood up, stretching. The sun beamed nicely and it was a good day. No sign of clouds.

"Do you play football?" he asked.

"No, I haven't."

"Have you thought about it?"

"No." *Because I been thinking about dick.*

"All boys think about football. Don't you *dream* of making it to the NFL?"

"Did you? Why aren't you in it yet?"

He shook his head, I hit a nerve.

"Thought so," I continued.

"You should play ball."

"No thanks."

"Would you like to play?"

"I'm not interested."

"Are you ok?" he asked, putting a hand on my shoulder and I took a few steps back, shaking my head.

"Please don't put your hands on me."

"I'm sorry. I apologize."

"No problem."

"Are you sure you're ok?"

I walked towards my back door. "I'm ok." I opened the door and turned to face him, going back into hell. "I don't think me playing football is such a good idea."

"Will you at least think about…?"

I slammed the door closed, went into the bathroom, closed the door and sank to the floor burying my face in my hands.

"I'm not normal," I said, shuddering with fear. "Someone has been playing football with my body for a long time. Every time his dick turn my ass into a big H he says 'it's good!'"

Exploding with loneliness, I fell asleep.

Σ

After we got settled in our new home over the next few months I was not that talkative with my step daddy. I speak when spoken to, and I really hated him.

He wasn't having sex with me as much, more focused on the family and I was starting to go through withdrawals. He wasn't touching me as much and with that came the panic attack. I didn't know how to handle this kind of dilemma. I wasn't myself, and I was losing myself and hadn't found myself quite yet.

So I told myself one thing.

"If he doesn't fuck me anymore I'll find another grown man to take his place."

I meant it. Going to bed with Barry on my mind…

Step Daddy and Mom were having marital problems and I was happy they were. If he wasn't going to do that trick with his tongue in my asshole then bye, bye. How could you turn someone on to sex and then sexually abandon him once he becomes addicted? And ZANE wrote a book called "Addicted." Chile, don't make me write my version and call it ADDICKTION.

I used to have vivid nightmares about him raping me, over and over and over and when I awakened the next day half the time I didn't know what to do with myself.

I remember one incident my step daddy hit Mom while she was in the shower. Mama beat his ass into the hall closet where we stored the bikes and all you were heard were BOOM BOOM BOOM sounds. Mama tore through his ass like a brush fire.

I was in a new school. Caribbean Elementary. *And* I was making new friends. I met a boy named Mandola, and Chad, my best friend I hadn't seen in a couple years, was there and when we saw each other we ran to each other and embraced like brothers.

"You go to Caribbean now, Pharoah?"

"Yea, Chad. I do."

"You will love it here dawg!"

"It's so good to see you."

He had on a light blue shirt, jeans, clean cut and a thin necklace with Jesus crucifix.

His face was a frown. "Let me guess. Your Mama still married to that monster?"

"Yea, she is, man."

"He still, you know," he went on, afraid to say around passing students.

"Not as much." I was sad now. "I miss it, though."

He took me by the arms. "Pharoah, you don't miss it. What he did and is doing to you is wrong."

"But it feels good, Chad," I said, tears falling. "It feels good. And I hate it all the same, what is wrong with me, dawg?"

He hugged me. "I will protect you with my life, dawg. You're my brother. I will not let anybody hurt you again."

I hugged him back. "I can protect myself."

I had to walk to and from school.

But I didn't walk alone. My friend Bert, Andre and Marlon walked with me. We walked together, which was a good two something miles from our projects, Hollywood Square so if baby snatchers tried to snatch us we would royally stomp that perverted ass back into the shell of sickness he came from: his Mama's pussy. Then go fuck up his Daddy for not making his baby Mama suck and swallow his nut so that little sick baby snatcher would have died in another form of Hell: his Mama's stomach acids.

We had to walk through houses and up the boulevards, avenues and long stretch-of-a-street till we got there. But we always joked, laughed and talked about girls along the way so we weren't focused on time and distance. We spent real quality time together walking and getting to know each other.

Well, I didn't talk about girls with a grown man's dick on my mind. But I said a few things about girls to keep the conversation hot.

One day we were walking to school and we had an interesting conversation.

"I get all the girls," Bert said and I was laughing with Andre and Marlon, who dismissed his comments with waving hands.

"Niggah you don't get shit," Andre said.

We were ten years old talking like grown men in the environment that shaped us mentally and emotionally.

It would help shape me.

I wanted some dick and I wanted it badly and I hated that about myself because I finally found out what gay and faggot meant. A friend of mine in school told me when I asked. He pointed at a girly acting boy and said, "He's a faggot."

"So if you act like a girl you're a faggot? How do you act like a girl?" eye asked, winking at him and a sly smile played his face and his dick was getting hard so he looked at a girl with a big booty and pick tails and regained focus.

"Look at him," he said, with evil eyes. "I hate faggots. He likes a dick in his ass."

Um, straight boy that's a real woman with pussy and tits; why did you just say she's a boy acting like a faggot. Lapse in his thinking allowed me to see the shade. This niggah was gay and only looked at hoes with asses and pick tails for sport. You know the type of niggahs. They alive and fucking you in the booty when the lights off but when the lights turned on and you played dead and left you alone to explain it all he was that kinda niggah.

Shiesty.

I thought about the dicks I already had in my ass and grew into a ball of silence around my friends. I had to know something.

"Can I ask you something?"

"Sure, Pharoah," Bert said.

"I have a friend who told me his step daddy had sex with him. Does that mean he's a faggot?"

He looked at me with his mouth open. "His step daddy is fucking him?"

"Yea, forcing him to. Well, he told me it's not by force anymore. He actually loves to have sex now and he says he hates himself."

"They are both fags."

"But his step daddy raped him."

"I feel so sorry for your friend. But when he started to like it that's when he became fucked up."

So I'm fucked up. I'm a faggot! I can't tell him this. I hate that man OH MY GOD I HATE YOU!

I HATE YOU I HATE YOU I AM GOING TO KILL YOU I HATE YOU.

"Pharoah? What's wrong?"

"Nothing, man. I'm going home."

"We are on lunch break. And right now everyone is looking at you."

I looked around, sneering. "Why they looking at me?"

"You kept saying I hate you over and over and now the entire cafeteria is in complete silence."

I stood up and ran to the bathroom and threw up in the toilet when I got there.

I cried until I had enough strength to go back to class.

You're a faggot!

Eye lay awake that night. My brothers were sound asleep and eye yearned for Step Daddy.

Eye made sure my brothers were ok and crept out the room and up the dark hallway. It was a bad night of heavy rains and the lightning briefly lit up the hallway but thunder sounds never followed through.

Once eye reached the door way Mama was gone but Step Daddy was fast asleep. Beer can empty and contents gone. Slightly snoring, mouth wide open. Eye could smell the stench of his hair up my nose. He needed to wash his stank ass hair.

Eye looked to the kitchen and lightning lit the house again, flashing through the window, making my heart speed up. The ticking of the refrigerator oozed into a soft buzzing and eye tip-toed towards the kitchen, the lightning illuminating me once more.

My eye was on the kitchen knife. The big black one.

Eye inherited it and my body craved Step daddy. Eye wanted to suck him again and eye wanted him to treat me like a rag doll. My legs shook thinking about it, my salivary glands curtly activated.

My dick was hard as hell.

Step Daddy here eye come.

Eye was standing over him, gazing down into his sweet angelic face. So angelic when he slept; eye want you dead, rapist bitch! Eye never saw him sleep before. It was then that eye realized that even the big bad beast needs his beauty sleep to rejuvenate old bones.

Eye started to suck him up but shook my head and whispered "Eye want it to stop!"

But he feels so good inside me.

But he beats you, Pharoah!

But...

But nothing! Remember your blood? The bleach bath that nearly burned your open cuts with stinging pain.

Yes, eye remember that...

Eye raised the knife high above my head, breathing hard, my chest heaving.

Do it!

My nostrils flared and adrenaline shot through my body.

Do it, Pharoah!

And *everything* came alive: *DO IT PHAROAH DO IT DO IT DO IT KILL THE SICK BITCH KILL HIM PHARAOH DO IT YOU LITTLE BITCH!*

The lightning illuminating the room, me slowly bringing the knife down and a loud BOOM sounded and the thunder knocked me to the floor and eye dropped the knife and eye held my breath, looking up and he awakened with a start, looking around and eye lay on my side, with my back pressed against the wood siding of Mama's water bed and eye didn't say anything. His shoes were right by nose and UGH the smell!

Lightning lit the room and a slight rumble sounded and he yawned audibly, looked at the clock and lay back down.

Slightly snoring.

Eye closed my eyes, took a deep breath and crawled out of the room.

Replacing the knife where eye got it from.

My heart about to beat out my little chest.

Mission FAIL!

*Tell me an incident
Involving your Pa$tor*

Lord Jennings

As a 32 year old I went to church.
    And I felt like a ghoul. Sitting amongst the elite, learning about the books of the Bible.
    Even though some books of the "Bible" have yet to be published.
    I came to service to see what bullshit the Pa$tor was talking about today. I hadn't been in a while, and eye had the urge to show my face.
    His tired eyes told me he'd been up all night putting his sermon together. Typed his notes, highlighted scriptures in his big ole red bible.
    I didn't know they made Bibles in Red.
    When he began, he spoke to us all.
    "Hello, and how are you all doing?" He sounded and looked phony, like he'd rather be masturbating.

The usual hey's and Hi's and head nods. Nothing out of the ordinary.

He looked at me and I looked at him.

"So your book is out. I heard congratulations are in order," he said maliciously and eye stared at him with a poker face.

Members of this dismissive, forgettable congregation clapped and whistled. And when they started chanting *The King of Erotica* I stood up, waving my hands.

Nervous. My head low I looked up to the high ceiling.

Then I looked at the church body. "Don't call me a King in the Lord's house. I'm just Pharoah. I can never be a King."

"But we look up to you," an in the closet homosexual said.

"Your books inspired me to wanna write again," said a mother of three, barely making ends meet.

"Because of you I want to be an author!"

"I appreciate the love," I said. "*Truly*. But praise God for my work not me."

It was the hypocrites and haters turn.

"How can you love God writing the books you do?" Sister Harris asked me with contempt.

"How could you give birth to your daughter when you were fourteen before you got married?"

One down.

"Writing about man on man sex, God doesn't give you the talent to write such filth," said another. Eye gazed at her with a smile.

"Did you say that when you sucked one of the usher's dicks in the back on his truck? Wasn't his wife out of town?"

BOOM BITCH! "THE HELL WITH YOU!" She ran out the church so fast rumor has it she never ever returned. Nor the Usher she sucked up.

Another one down.

"I write the books I wanna write, I said to everybody with politeness. "*God* gave me the talent. When he said let there be light and we received vegetation and fish of the waters there came darkness, marijuana and whores. I do the things I do to stimYOUlate then edYOUcate."

I turned and walked towards the Pa$tor.

"I'm giving my ten percent now, and I'm gone. I don't have to take these old whores and ex crack heads judging me. Half these muthafuckahs getting over a hangover; bitches are four hours from the next AA meeting and throwing shade."

"Son, calm down."

"Fuck church. Take the money. That's all your rehearsing ass want anyway. Rehearse scripture before you teach it. I don't believe in organized or rehearsed religion. Jesus never bashed us, so why is your phony ass church? I'm gone."

His wife touched my hand. "Let me talk to you."

Eye snathed it back. "Get flip with me one time eye'm going slap off."

"Agreed. Now let's talk…"

We were sitting in the Pa$tor's Chambers. Shit didn't look like a chamber. More like the hallway closet of a housing projects. Cluttered, unorganized and a Vivica Fox screen saver on Pa$tor's computer.

"Yes, Lady Simone."

"I understand your turmoil."

"You do."

"You have been badly hurt by previous churches. I know your story. I read it online. I heard your Dedan Tolbert interview. About the Pa$tor that had sex with you when you were a teenager."

"OK, and?"

"But there is a way you go about business, son. You're an author. People buy your work. They follow you on Facebook. They live for your updates."

"So!"

"This is church! Cursing doesn't fly here."

"Church, smurch my ass, Lady! God say come as I am, damn it. I had to admit I was sinner before I was dipped in that cold ass water."

She was stuck like Chuck. "Why are you angry?"

"I am not angry."

She tried to reassure me. "You have a lot of tension."

"Is this cross examination?" I looked at my watch.

"You have walls up, Pharoah. Allow people in to love you."

"I did that once. And I got fucked for four years. I couldn't defend myself. I had to fight alone."

"God was always with you."

"Doing what? Getting money out the ATM machine to give to your husband?"

"Damn, who hurt you Pharoah? I see it in your eyes."

"I'm not hurt. Just reverted." I stood up and picked up her iPod. I put the head phones on, skimming through the gospel songs.

"PHAROAH?"

I was like the movie *Child's Play 2*:

DON'T FUCK WITH THE CHUCK!

When I stopped on Plies' Get you Wet song I looked up at her, my hand over my mouth.

"What?" she asked, wondering what was wrong with me.

"You judge *me* and *Plies* is on you iPod."

"I love all kinds of music," she said, realizing she fucked up. And tried her best to dress the wound.

"Plies is talking about smelling your pussy and getting it wet in this song, lady. He said he hates dry pussy in this song, and the Pa$tor's wife has this kind of questionable music on her iPod?"

Her eyes were wide. "*Pharoah, it's not what you think.*"

"Let's see what the congregation thinks when I show them this. Your *members* wanna criticize my books because they are too dumb to spell GED."

I spun on my heels, stamping to the door. This was why I don't do organized religion. They all acted like their shit smelled like last night's supper. And it did. Right after you got off the goddamn toilet.

I snatched open the door and she grabbed me.

"PHAROAH! STOP!"

What the hell? "Stop? Why? What are you afraid of? Mama taught me don't do anything that you're ashamed of."

"You can't destroy the congregation's image of me and my husband. They look to us and follow us. Believe in us."

"That money in jeopardy, huh? What ya'll pull in a week. Come on. You can tell me."

Her hands were trembling. "Pharoah. Give me the iPod."

"A thousand. Two thousand?"

"Please."

I rushed out of the office, pushed past the usher and walked to the front of the church.

"PHAROAH! PLEASE! STOP HIM!" she shouted, startling everybody, eve her husband.

The ushers tried to grab me and I gave them an evil look.

"You touch me I'ma fuck you. If you know what's good for you you'll get your slow asses out my fucking face!"

They retreated. I was at the front of the church.

"Guess what kind of song the Pa$tor's wife got on her iPod?" eye asked everybody. "Since ya'll wanna bash my muthafucking bread and butter. Plies. Get you wet."

I set the iPod on the notch of the iPod player by the Pa$tor's laptop on the podium and crank it up.

"GET YOUR PUSSY WET!" sounded with that bomb ass beat that made a secret bitch in church wanna dance.

And I walked out the doors, leaving her amongst her organized chaos. Explaining to followers why a married spiritual sister had such "filth" on her iPod.

When the doors closed behind me I never looked back.

Might turn to salt.

How seriously do you take writing?
Do you mix real life with fiction?
Tell me a scary moment in your life,
After you became a bestseller?
Was sex involved?

Lord Jennings

I take my writing very seriously. It has become my obsession. To create what I want when I want empowers myself. I hardly eat or sleep and the only time I truly make was taking my HIV medicine on time, then I go back into Creation.

Door locked, phones off and no internet. No TV, so I took it out my room. Didn't care to watch it and as much as I loved Janet Jackson I told her goodbye while I was Creating.

She didn't think of me when she make CD's so I didn't think of her or anything while writing.

Then I turned around and started listening to Rhythm Nation, a 20 year old album, while I write. Now it's always on repeat when I create.

If I have to pee I run to the bathroom and take a leak but I lose writing time. I lost a lot of thoughts between draining and shaking my dick, washing my hands and drying them off.

That was a page of text I could have typed right there and when I sat down to Create, it wasn't the same.

You couldn't start and stop inspiration while Creating. Only God could do that.

Remember, we're an "image."

Now I came up with a better way. I drink a lot of water and Gatorade. So I save the empty bottles.

If I was deep in thought writing and didn't wanna lose a page of text while taking a piss, shaking and washing my dick beaters, then I could do one thing.

Piss in the empty bottles.

Perfect. I write butt naked anyway, with the door locked. Don't fuck with me while I was writing, if you did I cursed you out and gave a fuck about your feelings when my book was done.

I stand up, line the hole with the hole in the bottle and fill the bottle while I continue typing my chapters. I didn't break inspiration, I simply slowed it down a bit…typing with one finger till eye was done taking a leak; gave me time to really write effectively and think deeply.

Once I was done, I set the bottle in the missing slot, and put my fingers on the keyboard and I ASDF JKL; the words out of slavery, creating on the page my form of a completed puzzle every time I write.

I never had Writer's Block. EVER. In my entire life of writing.

I had too much to say. Too much on my mind. Too much sadness, anger, happiness, jubilancy. I was a demon and an angel when I Create, mixing the two entities with The King of Erotica at the helm and when I was done I was satisfied with what I wrote.

I had too much inspiration.

Loving God was all the inspiration you needed.

Self-help books, the Bible, inspirational books and I didn't see eye to eye because I was always one judgmental ass munch when I was a teenager. My fast ass was already sleeping with people well in their 20s and 30s around the fourteen years of age counter. So I had an old soul, hung around elder people because they always talking about something unrelated to me and my peers. I would soak up their knowledge, and it slowly started to become my character.

The environment shaped me from the mold of anger I already was, to the point I lost myself just before I found myself.

And everything unraveled. Everything Mama taught me went right out the window. Everything my grandfather told me about life was contradicted by the things elders around Perrine used to talk about.

Cheating on their husbands and wives. No, they didn't know, shit. Stealing money outta church. Selling drugs. Selling ass, dick, lips and pussy to pay the rent. Rearing children they didn't want.

That shaped me, planting in my mind seeds that would sprout all preconceived notions out of my head, seeds that would blossom all over the stuff my Mama and other important older folks in my family taught me.

I heard somebody's granddaddy say, "My son is going to play football whether he likes it or not. I want my motherfucking money back for raising his ass, and if he makes it to the NFL we're in the money."

"You ain't wrong! You ain't wrong!"

"I already told him…if he doesn't play football effectively oh he gotta get the fuck outta my house. I beat his motherfucking ass if he doesn't practice like he playing a championship game."

"Fuck his skinny ass up, and don't forget us, shit," said the drunken bums, smoking weed or cigarettes.

He made it to the NFL. I know him very well.

But I'll keep his name to myself.

Back then I didn't like PHAROAH, didn't love myself in fact I spelled LOVE like this LUVH.

Luvh. My own way of understanding the human language. White man made this lexicon bullshit, stolen from Italy and they got it from Africa.

But they wouldn't say, so I was always a little standoffish when it came to reading something the white man wrote.

They used to have my ancestors in slavery, and many of the stories the ancestors wrote of empowerment and inspiration was taken, stripped and the big publishing houses put white faces on it with Colgate smiles and well-seasoned kids and called it Inspiration.

That was cemented when, in September of last year, a big publishing firm out of New York offered me 1.5 million dollars for ALL WRITES and RIGHTS (Big difference) to The King of Erotica. Eye'm telling you. Don't read contracts yourself. Get a lawyer. Eye took a class on Contracts and had knowledge of them but didn't tell a soul.

Once eye rejected it, wiping the smiles of those suited white men's faces, they approached me a few weeks ago with a $2 million dollar offer with SAME stipulations: take me off the cover at will, hire white editors to take out the blackness and put a white sexy Caucasian on the cover of the books eye stayed up 14 hours a day for three years writing. Eye'll die first. And the *representative* for "that publishing house" eye blocked his ass on Facebook and told them over the conference phone (they weren't flying my black ass back to New York via their pocket books and murses because of the way eye embarrassed their asses the first time) to suck my dick and pray they smell my asshole.

Click.

Aspiring writers, get a lawyer when it comes to a contract. Those major publishers worded shit so beautifully you'll be signing your life away and they'll OWN your hard work. You'll be known as a "ghostwriter."

Then some seedy white dude will be on national TV, Oprah, Good Morning America and Regis telling the world how they wrote your book but the world will be fooled into thinking it was his book. They wouldn't even know you existed.

Study WRITES and RIGHTS, copyrights, publishing. Who your books compete against, the market in a whole and everything associated with it. Know what "synopsis" means. Many authors out there didn't even know what the word meant and it meant WHAT IS YOUR BOOK ABOUT!

WRITES mean ANYTHING you write in the future already becomes the major publisher's property and RIGHTS pertain to shit you already wrote.

You wouldn't own a goddamn thing, not even your copyright and they will get big time white stars and editors and models to erase your blackness from the project all across the board and your one time payment didn't last forever but they banking off your shit for a lifetime.

Not only that the publisher that approached me (even flew me under the radar to New York the first time) and part of the contract stated that they would slap a fat GAG ORDER on my mouth that states I could never publicly say I wrote these books or was The King of Erotica.

Can you say I couldn't be whitewashed?

But that's for another chapter.

Inspirational books I shun deeply. I meant, what gave these fucks the right to tell me I couldn't like this but I needed to think like the bullshit in those books?

What made their lives better than mine? Because they graduated college and got M.D Ph.D next to their names with a Masters and a Doctorate.

Bitches, I could print that shit off the goddamn computer and put Ph.D. next to my name too.

Now what we comparing? Status against experience?

You gotta remember…inspirational books were edited for brainwashing and clarity, folks. They rewrite and rewrite and rewrite those chapters till they sounded *another* way and *not* at *all* how it sounded at the start.

That was writing nakedly as opposed to writing technically. Naked writing and Technical writing. I write fresh off my dome, fresh off my brain. That's naked writing. No spell check, no grammar check. Nothing. None of that shit. I write it fresh out my head, and no matter how the creation (not manuscript, people) turned out, I knew what was what. But to an outsider, they didn't know what was going on.

That's how I write. Like the wind blows. I think it I write it. That simple.

Once you're done you send it to your editor. He has another name? It's Technical Director. Technically, he's the technical part of your creation.

No, you shouldn't say it this way you should say it this way.

No, this sounds too *ghetto*. This type of shit won't *sell*! Your characters cursing and shit won't fly.

"*Um*," I said. "*You* just said *SHIT* twice."

Rolling his eyes he said, "Oh, no he's *gay* and she licks twat! Oh *no* they won't publish this, Pharoah! She's cooking crack on the stove. Ain't that about a bitch? *But* I'ma change it to this (and he makes changes) and turn this around and put a pot on the stove here and do this like that."

And the finished product? Technical writing, not the author's vision but the Editor's Choice.

And you still read inspirational books?

You wanted some goddamn inspiration? Sit behind the computer and write from the heart, edit your own shit, say what you wanna say and grab your nuts or your tits and represent your shit.

That's what I do now.

I'm my own editor.

I write nakedly. Mind, body, soul and spirit.

That's called the Holy Ghost.

I was resurrecting a form of Jesus every time someone writes or emails me and said my book opened their eyes.

Thank you, they say. You say Thank You to God, didn't you? That's the highest form of a compliment you can get.

People add extra shit to feel a little better, like thank you, you are so good. Oh my God, how did you write this?

Those kinds of people I was weary about meeting. If they are masqueraded by what I wrote and not the man who wrote it then something was a tab bit off on my spiritual compass.

When she says, "Oh my God!" didn't mean she didn't see me as her God, now did it? She could have meant, "Oh, My God! You are so wonderful," meaning she's telling her "God" that he was wonderful. And a woman and a lot of gay men have told me, online, face to face or in private, that I am their "God," and I told them oh, no. I could never be God. I was Pharoah. All praise goes to God. The Creator. Jesus' father. One of them said, "But you did create those books, I read them. So I don't get it. You're God to me. You're sexy, and very intelligent." Trying to blow smoke up my ass and it didn't work.

Now people do this over Beyonce. Calling her Beysus Christ in the gay community.

And a few gay men called me Kingsus in Atlanta, at the Pride.

I said, "What does that mean?"

"You slay for the Gods. You're a King. And my God. Kingsus."

I ran like hell, leaving my books right there on the table.

I was not the one in the Heavens, but the one made in God's image, that writes the books, the one with Him on the cover a few folks seem to think has healing powers and I didn't.

Some people said they worship me and I started to tremble. Eye told them to worship GOD, not me. Eye didn't even entertain that. Oh, no! Didn't play God like that.

Some people said they idolized me and every time I opened my front door I look up at the sky hoping not to dodge thunder and lightning.

Some of the most beautiful women have wined and dined me, sucked my dick and gave me so much pussy they thought it would revert me to being straight. Yes, ladies eye loved tits and pussy and eye loved eating pussy and sticking dick to pussy but eye loved men, too. My appetite couldn't be tamed or controlled by NO ONE.

Some of the most beautiful men have taken me out, wouldn't even let me open the door for myself. Pulled out my chair in public.

Really masculine, business men with money and cars worth more than your house.

One famous niggah, who played for a major NFL team, took me out on South Beach in a Lamborghini.

He picked me up from 5th street and eye stayed with him for the next week.

The way the engine settled through my bones and reverberated all over my body eye was sleep before we got to the restaurant.

Eye fell in love with the inside of his car.

The entire time all he said (and what a goddamn hunk oh my God!) was, "*Pharoah*, you're so sexy. Eye saw your pictures on Myspace. Eye read *both* of your books. Eye love how you write about Hoes sucking dick. Damn."

His dick was hard. Handsome in thug gear. Nothing about this man said he played professional sports but eye knew it was him because eye watched him on ESPN on some of the sports Highlights. He took my hand behind thickly tinted windows.

He stopped at a stop light and tongue kissed me, people walking to and fro on a very gorgeous South Beach night and they hadn't a clue eye was kissing a man worth millions of dollars.

"When you going to let me fuck you?" he asked.

We fucked right in an expensive hotel, a few blocks from Club Twist. We went in together. He told the man at the desk eye was his assistant and he made me wear a black hat and his thick Gucci shades.

Eye was in that room with him 5 days straight.

Fucking.

On the 6th day eye awakened to find him gone. He sent me a text and said he was boarding a plane to go back to his "football state." He told me, "You are an amazing lover. And you have the sexiest eyes. Eye can't see you again because if eye do eye will fall in love with you and eye'm married with kids."

Tears fell down my face and eye pulled the covers over my body and my face and eye cried till eye fell asleep.

He sent one last final text.

"You are talented. You write the kind of books that makes the thugs read in private. God blessed you. Thank you for giving me the pleasure of your body. Because eye haven't fucked my wife in two years."

Eye slammed my cell phone so hard on the floor it shattered.

A few moments later a rapping on the hotel door. Eye wrapped myself in the expensive white sheets and answered.

"Are you Pharoah?"

My eyes were blood shot red. "Yes. Who are you?"

He handed me a Moshino bag. "These are for you."

An outfit worth $7,500. The light brown gator shoes cost 2 grand alone. Goddamn. Courtesy of Mr. NFL. There was a card in it and eye took it out. He didn't put his name and the wording was rushed.

Eye thought you might look good in this. My sweet angel. Eye never let my men leave without a gift. But this is the most eye ever paid for anything. You're worth every dime. Eye can see myself loving and protecting you. Eye read all your interviews. Eye relate to you. Eye was raped as a kid too but eye could never say that in public. So eye live and try to forget it happened. Eye admire what you're doing. Keep writing. And eye'll be secretly reading and rooting you on, Pharoah.
    Warmly,

But eye had other plans.
    After my shower, eye put on my regular clothes and grabbed my book bag and the Moshino bag and eye looked over the gator shoes.
    On second thought eye tried everything on, and looked myself over in the mirror. He bought me some FCUK cologne and eye sprayed some on. Going back to my normal life of writing 14 hours a day. I was about to start my third book in a few months. Tired of being single.

Eye covered my face and shuddered from loneliness. The loneliness writing brings. Eye go to bed alone every night. Eye wake up alone everyday and thank God for another day of being alone, lonely and autonomous.

Eye couldn't go back to my world in those clothes. Questioning eyes would be all around me, not that eye give a fuck.

Eye took the clothing off, put back on my Phat Farm beige sweat pants, my white Tee and my black Nikes and left the room without looking back. Held my breath all the way to the Lobby. Didn't want to remember the smell of the room.

Eye was walking towards the bus stop and decided to walk all the way down the street.

Eye saw a bum. He was black, thick dreads and he slept soundly.

Eye looked at the Moshino bag, and the receipt still inside.

Eye could turn it all in and get the money and pay off bills.

Eye could put together a small book event for the 'Hood to get them reading.

Eye put the bag behind the bum, and covered it with his mildewing blanket.

"Eye can't use this," eye whispered, tears falling down my face. "Maybe you can get you something to eat or a room to stay in. Seven thousand is a lot of money. But money doesn't make me happy. It's a temporary replacement of peace."

Eye made a cross over my chest and walked off.

Didn't look back once.

Might turn to salt.

Some people said they worshipped me then invited me to their church and I was about to burn through the floor and the pew when I went, knowing I didn't believe in organized (or rehearsed) religion because organized religion was technical church, not a "naked" (Free spirit seeking understanding) church.

If I wasn't mistaken the Bible said put GOD first in all things. Yes, even church. And that the TEMPLE, or the church that Jesus built that couldn't be torn down, was my Body, my naked body, so I couldn't praise God at home reading scripture for myself, then I research it on the internet (thank you Google.com) and my eyes were opened.

Any wonder why I wouldn't read self help short story writing books? Or take Creative Writing classes? Creative writing was sitting on your ass and writing your heart.

Now they put a price on this in college, and called it Creative Writing, but it was Technical Creative Writing in my eyes.

I like using my own voice when writing. If I read self-help books I would be writing THEIR STORY, following their formulas and rules.

That ain't fucking writing. That's verbal slavery. When you can enslave words, twist and turn them, give them a new meaning, like I did with LOVE: LUVH, and change the world then and only then are we mentally enslaved.

Something you read has you conditioned in that particular framework. This was why I didn't read everyone's writing. Why?

TOO MANY GHOST WRITERS OUT THERE!

Some of those men on the cover didn't write that book. A ghostwriter did. Someone who signed a contract for the money and not the fame, wanted his shit out anonymously so people were fooled by "technical writing."

You meet the author and shake his hand and give him gifts of praise yet he didn't write it and he knows he didn't write it and his ghostwriter in the shadows celebrating a job well done.

But what he *didn't* know was he lost all writes and *rights* to that book. He got a ONE TIME PAY like a jacked porn star. That's it, Carl.

I knew a writer that was going through that. His book has blown through the roof and he couldn't publicly say he *wrote* the book.

This was why I turned that New York contract down.

I was aware this kind of shit went on BEFORE they approached me.

Michael Jackson said History books were lies and *lies* they *were*.

Some of those text books in school have ghostwriters, too.

But in this case, my homeboy didn't wanna be a ghostwriter. He was approached with a $400,000 contract and was so blinded by his family, who didn't want him having books and wanted to ruin him forever, telling him TAKE THE MONEY TAKE THE MONEY I NEED A NEW CAR BABY WE SO PROUD OF YOU! YES SIR!

He didn't even read the contract.

He signed it, got his big check, told everyone his book was just picked up and when they went to buy it a white man was on the front.

Edited by So and So on the cover, just under the author picture.

"This ain't my book."

And when he did read the contract, he read that he'd been sold to verbal slavery. That's what the Gag order was. A form of it. He was reduced to documentations.

Property again.

You talk they get pricey lawyers paid with the money YOUR BOOK MAKES and sue you for the money you got left.

And you lose the money, your publishing rights, your right for Freedom of Speech (oh you can talk all you want, but you better not talk about writing that book, sir) and your *self* respect because you realize you sold your soul.

To the Devil. For $400,000. After taxes, you didn't even bring home $300,000 and you wondered why you're broke, your house was in foreclosure and your pricey car got repossessed.

They snatched a patch out your ass.

And this "white man on the cover" went on to make over 2 million dollars off my homeboy's book.

I would NEVER sell all my rights like that? Oh, no. Sad.

The King of Erotica™ FOREVER stays with me. Period.

If tomorrow wasn't promised, and people sometimes put off tomorrow what they needed to do today, why DID some people PLAN for their future, assuming they will live to see the day, the time or the experience? That's why I was greedy with my time when I was going through the bitter hells of my past, blaming myself as I go along. I wanted what PHAROAH wanted RIGHT THEN AND THERE! NO EXCEPTIONS.

And this led me to many wrong choices made versus the outcome of a situation I put critical thought into. Eye was laying out every avenue and created false expectations. And when it all fell apart I stopped putting off tomorrow what I could do today.

And on the opposite end, the other side of VERSUS I should say, things still turned out oblique.

Why, I used to wonder, beat myself up over trying to figure out life in one night. I just knew I was that smart back then.

And why shouldn't I dream big? I hated reading books because I was too infatuated with writing in my journals, but I found the more I read new worlds opened up and suddenly my journals read like mini books complete with editor and marketing director.

So now I have no problem sometimes putting off tomorrow what I needed to do today. Because I was focused on time, instead of focusing on outcome. Instead of focusing on realism.

The reality was, I couldn't learn about life in a day, I couldn't complete each and every task or fight every fight in a day, so what I did finish wasn't a total waste of energy and time.

I simply prioritized what I needed to do when I awakened, the most important first and the less important last, and throughout my junior and senior high school experience I would look at this list:

- TURN HOMEORK IN.
- SIT IN THE FRONT OF THE CLASS.
- TELL YOUR FRIENDS WE'LL CLOWN AFTER CLASS.
- MAKE THE REST OF THE CLASSES ON TIME.
- JOIN THE FBLA (FUTURE BUSINESS LEADERS OF AMERICA)
- TAKE A TYPING CLASS
- ONLY GO TO MY LOCKER ON MY LUNCH PERIOD; THAT'S WHEN YOU SWITCH MORNING

TEXT BOOKS FOR THE AFTERNOON BOOKS: ECONOMICS, HISTORY, AND MATH.

Unfortunately, I thought those rules applied to the Bible as well. Putting GOD on YOUR time table.

I would pay dearly with a wakeup call that felt like semi automatics tearing through my ass.

I was in a situation. Another situation I could have avoided. But how could I when I didn't love myself? How could I when I have been asking God to kill me in my sleep since I was a small child with buck teeth. By the time I was done living I was barely 15 years old, didn't want to see anymore, didn't want a future, erase me before it gets here because I didn't LOVE MYSELF. Eye used to write Janet Jackson letters telling her of the abuse I was going through, but the only thing I ever got back was a post card to join her fan club with a price attached.

I came over to a guy name Phillip's house.

He stayed in his grandma's old house. She recently died and left it to him. He cried over her for three days and by the fourth day he realized he had a new house so he started bringing *all* his male lovers over to fuck them, cook for them and send them home after they sucked the nut from his balls.

He never let his Bottom Hoes leave his house with a purple belly (meaning being hungry). All that High Grade beef he stocked in their anal cavities, hanging like vampires. He fed and fucked them good. He had 'em limping out of the house.

They skipped, skipped, skipped to my Lou out of his house.

Couldn't wait till next time.

When we hooked up I knew *of* him but I didn't know *about* him. I heard all the men fell in love with his swagger.

Shit, I just wanted to fuck. I was on some Tina Turner shit. Simply the Best, goddamn it. What's Love Got to Do with It?

So I could validate myself, convinced I was living for me and waking up on my own and hardly reading my Bible remembering I got a muster seed of faith.

He was a gentleman. Picked me up in a Chevy. Cleaned inside, strawberry bagged incense dangling from the cracked rear view mirror. Damn it's a lot of finger prints on that mirror. Little fingerprints and bigger fingerprints side by side, creating some kind of picture I wasn't seeing.

When we got to his place it was dark outside. No lights. His curtains and window, closed.

I was scared but I didn't show it. I was about to dance with the devil, to be sexually sacrificed.

Boy was that an understatement.

He opened the door and said, "Welcum to paradise!"

He pushed the door open OH MY GOD! Rose petals leading into three different trails. One to the bathroom. The second trail to the kitchen table. And the third trail to the bedroom.

I loved it. Candles of assorted sizes strategically set up.

Janet Jackson playing. That's the way love goes.

YASSSSSSSSSSSS! I hadn't started writing The King of Erotica 3 yet, and eye was starving for affection. Tired of being single. Desperate for love. And that's when eye failed.

I turned to him in pure excitement. "You remembered I love Janet."

"Yes. Only the best for you. And I have your dish prepared."

He led me to the kitchen. He raised the rusty tin panned top. *Rusty tin pan?*

"CRAB LEGS!" eye said excitedly.

"Yes, your favorite food." His eyes sparkled.

Fuck the food. You got me, Niggah.

We kissing and shit, biting his bottom lip and his hands was in my pants and my hands were measuring his dick length, girth and width.

It's an all right dick. Nothing to send post cards about. But do-able. This thing had niggahs limping? They must be amateurs because a well seasoned bottom would chop and screw this somewhat little member back to the LOG IN page. Lose your cookies fucking with me.

He spun me around and bent me over, pulling my pants down and licked me up the trail to the bedroom.

Once we got there he turned on some gangstah shit. Bye, bye R&B. He sucked my toes, licked my nipples and vanished.

I lay there feeling good stretching like a cat purring and shit. How does a Niggah purr?

Eat him out and he'll show you.

PURRRR!

He brings two drinks. Root beer mixed with Hennessy and Patron."

I taste the odd mix. Yummy.

"What is this drink called?" eye asked.

He licked his sexy thick black ass lips. "Get the pussy Moist."

Eye grinned. "I like that."

He was tugging on his nuts. "Kill that shit. I'ma bathe you."

I gulped the drink, smacking my lips.

I stood up and he took my hand and led me to the bedroom.

"What about my bath?" I asked, getting unnaturally sleepy. I could barely keep my eyes open. I yawned. Shit. Yawwnneedd again. DAMN! Yawned again.

What's going on?

I had to pee and he helped me to the bathroom, my stomach hurting because I was inhaling all the assholes that been in here before me. And this was supposed to be paradise? With this pissy, ass smelling bathroom?

I wanted to puke. I was pissing all over the floor.

He was grinning. His darkness opening to receive me.

When my head hit the pillow I was out.
Floating in the darkness.
With no light to guide me.
The Holy Ghost wasn't home.

I felt trapped. Restrained. Immobile. Stagnant. I slowly opened my eyes and couldn't focus. Blurs. Ghosts. A voice. Talking. Informing. Advertising.

I had to continuously blink till the picture came into focus like a camera lens with the digital option like Cannon.

"Hello, Pharoah."

He had a mask over his face a zipper along the middle. Tall and sexy. Cock dangling like Tarzan was recently fired.

Nipple piercings. Classical music playing softly. I was scared.

"What is going on dude? How did I get *tied* up?"

The chains holding my arms up were wrapped around the ceiling fan. Candles everywhere. I saw a few cut chicken heads and spilt blood all over white sheets.

I was shaking all over. On my head was a Burger King crown and I looked pale.

He walked up to me and slapped me.

"AM I YOUR GOD?"

What the fuck is going on? Where's my strength? "Hell no! Let me out!"

He slapped me again, dumping cocaine all over my body. Some got in my mouth. This was surreal. I couldn't believe this. I had to be dreaming. This couldn't be real. CAN'T BE!

He slowly climbed on the bed and another man appeared in the room, naked, wearing the same mask with the zipper running vertically to the top of a black shiny scalp.

"Look who we got in the room. The author. The Niggah writing all these sex books, got our women talking and shit."

Oh, No! "Please let me go, man!"

He was laughing at me. "Oh no! Because of your book my wife left me. You described my bedroom in your book Niggah. Don't you know that I don't give a fuck? I don't got 'em all. I am heartless, Niggah."

He spat in my face and put his hands around my neck.

And he squeezed, my head pressed back, half dangling from the ceiling fan.

I couldn't breathe.

"Tell me I'm your God. I'ma take that pussy. I'ma give you something to write about after I kill you. You took my life."

"Please…" I was blinking rapidly. "Please…I've been..been hurt. Enough. In. My. Life. Please…"

The monster of his eyes lay down across the irises like submissive lions. I felt the wind of his breath. Softened. Hardly reached the lapels of my nose. I could barely smell it. He retreated.

"Pharoah I'm sorry. When we met I told you I would never hurt you man. I know what you been through Pharoah." He slapped me so hard my head snapped back. "But you messed up my life."

Huge tears ran down my face. I looked up at the ceiling.

The first man asked me, "Pharoah who is your God?"

I looked in his eyes without fear. No more fear. A burst of light ignited the darkness of my soul and packed its evil and left town.

The glimmer in my eye.

"If I went through half the things you went through Pharoah I wouldn't have made it. You're otherworldly. You walk by straight Niggahs and they whisper about wanting to fuck you. Who is your God?"

God, be with me. Eye'm about to play the game. Just like eye did with The Pail Man when he was raping me. "Take the mask off your face *then* I'll tell you who my God is."

He hesitated. Looked to his friend. Eye held my breath. He slowly unzipped it.

It was my ex boyfriend. The one who gave me HIV.

"Put the mask on my face," I said, licking my lips.

The second man unzipped his mask, the owner of the house, Mr. Sexy Thick Lips. It dangled from his hand. His charming eyes mesmerizing me. As the mask went over my face, then the zipper, I smiled. At my new boyfriend. The one I gave my heart too, the one I just met, the one who said he loved me for me, not my books. The one that picked me up and brought me here. I mean we didn't make it official, but we were both so lonely when we met we made it official without saying a word. And that's where the problem started. Eye was too old to be thinking like a cum drunk fool. When was eye going to grow up?

And I said, "Who is my God? Jehovah is my God. May no weapon formed against me prosper. Now can you get me down out these chains, Niggah? Please. Don't throw your freedom away, man. I can forget this happened."

Both of them reached up and unlocked the chains. They fell to the bed, nearly hitting me in the head.

The sound opened me up. I looked at them and picked up my clothes, unzipping the mask.

"I don't wear a mask in public. I am who the fuck I am and don't give a fuck what a bitch gotta say."

I dropped the mask at the bedroom door, heading through the living room.

"Make sure your masks are zipped all the way up before you go around your kids and baby mama's. My new book dropping soon."

"Which one?" my ex asked me.

I turned and looked at him. "The King 3!"

I slammed the door behind me.

Lord Jennings
And The King of Erotica

It took Lord Jennings a minute to get it together.

He wiped tears from his face, his nonchalant composure compromised.

"I can't believe what I heard," he said.

"I know, right."

"You are an amazing man. Where did you come from?"

"My Mama's puss…"

He laughed, holding up his hands. "Don't say it, ha ha."

"Shit, you asked."

"The things you've been through. He tried to get you to denounce God?" He seemed excited about it for some reason. Child like almost.

"Yes. I get that a lot. A lot of fans hit me up with that nonsense, trying to tell me God isn't real."

"Do you think he's real?" he asked, setting the note pad down and pressing STOP on the mini recorder.

"Yes, I know he's real. Look at the things he delivered me from."

"That's true. And how does he reveal himself to you through what you've endured?"

"The more I struggle, the more I know he's there. Something is *trying* to distract me from God. *That's* why I struggle. If I didn't have a mission in life I wouldn't be going through all the hardships. Satan is trying to get me to turn on God."

"I admire your faith."

"I do, too."

"How did you feel being chained up like a slave?"

"I was scared for my life."

"But you didn't show it on your face?"

"Hell, no. For what? I never let the enemy know I'm scared. When you do they gain their position and destroy you with it."

"Good concept. Before we go any further I would like to do one thing."

"What's that?"

He set the pad down, then the pen. He took off his reading glasses, stood up and walked over to me.

"I just wanna hug you. For a moment."

He wrapped his arms around him.

And I exhaled.

"How about a drink?" he asked, standing up. "We covered a lot of shit. Damn, man."

"That doesn't sound like such a bad idea."

"It amazes me that you're candid and so open. Eye could never be that open."

"Why?"

"It's hard for me to be candid."

"Eye can see. Especially getting paid to listen to people talk about their problems and you have to sit there and act like you give a damn."

"And my mind be on my paycheck. Yea. That's true."

"Don't tell your clients that."

His lips twitched briefly and the reaction confused me. Eye knew then that he didn't like talking about himself.

"That's why eye agreed to be your shrink free of charge."

"And eye am grateful."

He loomed over me, his chest bare, nipples erect and his pajama pants barely staying on his magnificent ass. He had nice abs, a killer body and his eyes lit up the room.

Eye studied him. "Where are you from?"

The sparkles died in his eyes instantly. He was fidgeting. "Colorado."

"Colorado. Interesting. You have any brothers and…"

He spun on his heel, his dick losing its erection and he stomped to the kitchen, trying to remain cool but eye knew he was anything but calm.

"What would you like to drink?" he asked, opening a small wine pantry. He had everything in there, even Sutter House shit.

"Where are you from?" eye asked again.

"Georgia," he said and eye looked at him. Didn't he say Colorado?

Eye didn't press the issue. "Just get me a Budweiser."

"Naw, niggah. You're The King of Erotica. How about some Dom?"

"Sure."

His back was turned to me the entire time he prepared our drinks.

Eye lay on the expensive sofa and put my arm over my face.

Why would he lie and say he was from Colorado?

"Pharoah." Eye sat up, and took the intricate flute glass. Interesting glass, eye tell you. Never saw anything like it.

"Let's have a contest."

"A contest?" eye said, narrowing my eyes.

"Yes. Whoever wolfs down the drink the fastest get to pick his own prize."

Eye was laughing. "Sounds like fun."

"All this talk of your past we need a break. Live a little. Do something other than this."

"Agreed."

We locked eyes.

Glasses clanked together.

We stared at each other.

Ready. Set. Go!

We wolfed it down, some of it spilling over the tips of his lips and down his chest.

Eye smacked my lips, slamming the glass on the low table.

"Eye won!"

"Damn," he said, finishing last.

"And you're spilling some of it. Eye wolfed it all down."

He looked at me. "Eye wish my wife was this fun."

Eye looked at him. "What do you mean?"

"She's so goddamn cold inside. Always in church. Pastor runs my goddamn house. Not me."

"Do you believe in God?"

He said, "Yea," after thinking about it for a few minutes.

"Do you go to church?"

"Hell. No."

Eye yawned. We've been up the past 10 hours. And we haven't been to sleep.

He moved closer to me. "If my wife was half as fun and sexy as you...we would..."

His lips were dangerously close to mine. "We would what?"

Eye couldn't stop looking at him.

He leaned into my face and tongue kissed me and eye was stuck but eye let go because we grew a bond since being in his condo 50 plus stories above the ocean.

He wrapped his arms around me and eye leaned back and he kissed my left nipple, sliding his hands in my drawers and playing around with my tight hole.

"When was the last time you let a Niggah get up in there?" he asked breathlessly. Breathing my air. Eye shuddered along side his willing and able body.

"Before you? Over a year."

"Goddamn."

"What is wrong with me? Why am eye so horny?"

"Because you want Daddy to make love to you. Niggahs don't know how to sex a niggah like you. You require special attention."

The room was spinning. Eye could hardly grasp a thought. *"Really?"*

He turned me over, taking off my pants and drawers. He had me on my knees in front of the couch and he spread my ass cheeks and started tonguing my hole.

He felt so good eye could barely stand it.

He was smacking, letting me hear what he was doing.

He took his time, rolling his entire tongue over my hole, spreading my cheeks wider, tongue fucking me at times.

Then he put on a rubber and he told me to reach back and keep my cheeks spread and eye was moaning and he pushed deep inside me and once he got his entire ten inch dick inside me (it hurt like hell, been over a year) he slowly grinded in me, taking my hands, kissing them. Planting moist warm lips on the back of my neck.

"You even fell better than my wife."

"Lord...we shouldn't do this."

"What's my name?" he asked, pounding inside me, bouncing all in my asshole like niggahs loved to do and eye was stuck, mouth ajar, eyes narrowed, throwing the bussy back, showing this Top niggah eye wasn't easily broken.

"Lord..."

"WHAT'S MY GODDAMN NAME?"

"Lord."

He bounced inside me all night.

After the fifth time eye made him nut he shot blanks. Nothing came out. Eye slept like a baby.

He fucked me even when eye slept.

Tell me about a time you regretted
Being with someone.
How did you feel when you met him?
How did you feel when you left him?
Lord Jennings

Eye met him by accident. Like I slammed into a truck because I was texting a bitch on my cell phone. Some, OH MY GOD I'M SORRY shit. That's how we met. We weren't supposed to meet, but Mama asked me to go to the grocery store and buy her some onions. She needed it for her collard greens. I was huffing and puffing, trying to ignore her long enough hoping her ass forgot.

PHAROAH! I NEED YOU TO GO TO THE STO' AND BUY ME SOME FUCKING ONIONS!

When I tell you I had a major attitude. If the wind blew wrong that day I got upset.

When I was to myself that's the way I wanted it. I was happy alone or around people, didn't make me any difference but that day I was seriously upset, wanted to be alone and it seemed like out of all Mama's near grown kids she kept fucking calling MY NAME OH MY GOD!

So I drove the '95 Ford Taurus, knowing she gave me a time limit. Because she knew I was making detours, going to see people right quick, getting in somebody's business.

When I got there I parked in the back, I liked a bitch to watch my tall, fine ass walk into the store, like I got a purpose.

I saw his handsome ass picking up a bag of grapes when I walked towards the onions and I was like Oh, shit damn he cute in my mind but never betrayed it with my eyes.

I cautiously walked past him, getting a look at his legs, the way those gym shorts fit his ass, the wife beater, the scar under his eyes, the body tattoos.

Damn.

I picked up a bag of green grapes, sulking.

"Damn these fucking grapes expensive as fuck, dawg! Three sixty-nine a pound? For grapes?"

Fuck all that preliminary, what do I do to get his attention shit. You want a Niggah just talk to him like he one of the boys.

"I know right?" he asked, smiling. Damn, Niggah. He's a Thug, masculine and clean shaven. Smelled like Old Spice. "I'm Tommy," he said, sitting the grapes down and extending his hand.

Bingo! "Eye'm *Pharoah*. Nice to meet you."

He looked me over. "How tall are you? You 'bout 6 feet 3?"

"And you must be 6 feet 5."

"I am. You're just as tall as me. Tall ass Niggah. I like that."

That was the signal. I like that, he said. Oh yea! There you go, baby. "Thanks. You ball?"

"Yea, a little. Not much. Niggah gotta work."

He worked so he wasn't a thug. On the clock pay wasn't under the table pay, shit you couldn't file taxes for. And that's a thug's M.O.

"Damn, ok."

"Well, I am headed to a game in the City. You free? Wanna come?"

"Hell, yea. I'm game, dawg. Just gotta buy these onions for Mama."

"You got a number?"

I gave it to him.

Wrote it on his hand.

He picked me up a few hours later in a shiny black Nissan Maxima. Nice, shiny rims. A killer booming system.

He was walking up to the front door wearing no draws under his gym shorts, his swagger stank of masculinity, self assuredness and confidence.

In a T-shirt, flip flops and long white tube socks.

Um, 305 hat pulled low over his gorgeous light brown eyes.

I opened the door, grinning. In my gym shorts and wife beater and unlaced boots. Sneakers around my neck, dangling on either side by the tied shoe strings.

"You ready, Pharoah?"

"Yea, Niggah. Born ready."

He licked his lips. "All right now."

"Niggah, you ain't saying shit but a thang, dude."

I closed the door and he held up his hand so I could walk ahead of him.

"Thank you," eye said.

I walked to his car.

He was looking at my ass the entire time.

During the drive on the Turnpike, North, we talked about everything under the sun. He was a real cool dude. He said I was pretty cool and laid back, too. Loved my smile, liked my bluntness. I matched the potency of his rolled unlit joint nesting in the ashtray with no cigarette butts.

Told me he wasn't a very stressed Niggah. He hated and avoided drama.

He said he was born and raised in the County of Miami Dade. He's the older of two kids. Parents been married since Jesus wore sandals rocking split ends.

And he had two kids of his own, having his first when he was 13 years old from an older cousin and they kept it hidden deep in the family because they didn't believe in abortion. Now his parents pressuring him to marry his baby Mama, a girl he didn't love. He said he was at a stale mate in his life. I told him he shouldn't marry her if he ain't in love or happy, that simple.

"You are so right," he said, relieved somebody was on his side.

"You're the one that gotta sleep with a woman you care nothing for. Do you even know her favorite color?"

"Hell naw. Don't even know her zodiac sign."

"Now that's fucked up," I said, and we chuckled.

"Thanks for seeing things my way," he said.

"Ain't about seeing it your way. If you don't love a person and you're not ready why stand before God? Makes no damn since to me."

"Preach, Niggah!"

He used to ball for Miami Central High School but lost his scholarship to college when he was arrested for selling cocaine and weed to kids in high school and his team mates.

His Daddy, a crazy ass Niggah, was a Vietnam vet who cursed too much, beat his wife once and tried to fuck his step son.

His Mama got a crazy check, was pushing 50 and still went clubbing in the same patent leather skirt her big ass had for 20 years.

Too many of her panties had holes in it so she free clit that night, like a man free balled by wearing no draws.

I told him about me.

He listened. Intently. Staring at me at certain times, mouth fell open a few times, shook his head in anger a few times.

"I got a better idea," he said.

"What?"

He was heading for I-95, via the 836, speeding past the Miami International Airport.

Twenty minutes later he parked by a large bay of ocean water. The Atlantic. South Beach. Further down the road, around the part seldom people went. We sat on the sand, the sun setting, the darkness peaking over what was left of daylight.

"This ain't the b-ball court."

He grinned thuggishly. "I know, Niggah. Just flow with me. I wanted to show you this place. It's very dear to me. People look at me and see a thug. I got a heart, feelings *and* emotions I can *never* show 'cause Daddy didn't raise no punk ass Niggah and he would literally beat me with the butt of his pistol if I show any sign of weakness. So I come here to cry, to vent and let it all out."

"Wow, thanks, dude. Getting deep on me, huh?"

"I look in your eyes, there's depth. I fall in them, in the mystery of them. You have been hurt, my dude. My grandma used to bring me here. Just me and her. Then she died, leaving me alone. IRS took her house, owed too many taxes on it. I became a thug then, selling dope to make money to get by."

"I'm sorry to hear that, dawg."

"It's cool…" He looked at me fixedly, my heart stuttering. "I have something to tell you. Something I wanna do. Please understand."

The temperature changed, the climate started to drop.

Slowly, he leaned into my face, deeper into my eyes and he gave me some tongue.

We were deep French kissing, rubbing each other, building a fire from the rubbing of twigs...

When nighttime fell he was digging me deep in my asshole, while the cold waves splashed over us under the crescent moon.

I came on the sand two hours later...

For the next 3 months we were on a sexual rollercoaster. Then our feelings got involved, and everything changed.

He was possessive, controlling, demanding and questioning my every move.

He analyzed me, like his grandma used to do. He said she suspected he was gay, and she died before she could tell him why she suspected it.

So dating me, he was chasing that, asking me deep shit about how I viewed him, did he look gay, sound gay or act gay?

No, no and no. But he was never satisfied with the answers I gave him, sometimes getting angry and lashing out at me.

I remained quiet.

Sometimes I had to say, "I'm not your grandson, stop trying to be what your grandma was, dawg. She's dead. Get over it. Jesus!"

But I never thought of leaving him.

We made love twice a day. The more he got the more he wanted. He was obsessed with my ass.

Around his crib were framed pictures of me, everywhere. On the low table were my framed baby pictures, on the end table my graduation picture from Kindergarten to the first grade next to my high school graduation picture.

On the entertainment shelf different pictures on me.

Hanging on the wall, poster size pictures of me he had blown up at Walgreen's.

He wanted me to move in so he could manage and monitor my life and I said I didn't shack up in sin.

I was conflicted. I loved sex and dick, loved him but I loved God, and my sexuality, the Pa$tor said, was an abomination. My constant talking about the Bible and God angered him, but he claimed he understood.

Then I found out his Daddy was a goddamn Pa$tor. He's the Pa$tor'$ son.

Oh, boy. After going through two years of this, and his obsession with my body and controlling me darkened, as more framed pictures of me inhabited his bedroom walls, the walls of the hallway and the dashboard of his Nissan, everything exploded.

When the boiling point was reached.

One Sunday we were dressed for church. And he had an attitude. As a Gemini, sometimes you didn't know if he loved a bitch or flipped and wanted to cut a bitch. That evil twin that lived in him was a twisted motherfucker.

"What's wrong?" eye asked, looking sharp.

"Don't wanna go to church," he mumbled. I barely heard him.

Eye pat his shoulder. "Why, we love God."

"I love you. You're my God, Pharoah. I worship you."

"What?" I was nervous. Never have a man told me this.

"You're my God. You're sexy, beautiful, and that pussy," he went on, wrapping his arms around me, grabbing hand fulls of good ass, planting his warm lips on my aggravated flesh.

My dick was hard.

"That hole moist?" he asked, sucking on my neck. Putting hickies everywhere.

"Yes," I said, panting.

"I'm your King, right?" His dick was hard, pressing against me. I felt it throb.

"Yes."

He was fumbling with my hole, his long, thick fingers feeling like dick in training.

"I'm your God, baby."

We kissed. "No you're not. Jehovah is my God."

"Bullshit." He pushed me into the wall and slapped me. "In my house I'm your God. You're mine. We shape our own lives. There is no God. My daddy told me that. He's an atheist and fools everybody but me."

My mouth hung open. Eye was I shock. "*What?*"

"I'm an atheist. I believe in Scientology."

"You done lost your natural mind."

"My Grandma totted that fucking Bible. Everywhere. Pushing her beliefs in my face did nothing but push me away. Beating me to believe in the Word of God did nothing but cause me to *rebel*. She knew I was gay, she beat me for it. She told me I couldn't blame my older cousin for molesting me. That I was born into sin. That my sexuality was determined before my birth. I said she was crazy."

I didn't know what to do. "Baby. She's dead."

He got in my face. He was rubbing my arms, searching my face. "Why did she think I was gay?"

"I don't know, man. I don't have anything to do with that."

"But you love me?"

"Yes, baby."

"But you believe in God? Even with my tongue in your asshole and your dick in my mouth," he said, throwing my Bible at me. "You're a fucking fool if you think God is in the sky."

"He is, man."

"You must choose."

"Choose what?"

"God? Or me as you God!"

"Nothing comes between me and God."

"Did you say that when this dick went between those butt cheeks?"

"My heart did. My lips said something out of lust."

"Me or God?" He was getting in my face, about to explode on my ass.

I shuddered, turning dangerous in this room. His eyes were dead balls of vision. "God, of course."

He was appalled, tucked his chin back with his fists balled up.

"What? God over me? Your *Niggah*?"

I stuttered. "*Yes*."

"Look around. It's everywhere, baby. Your shrine I fixed up. I spent over a thousand dollars on your pictures and buying expensive ass frames."

"Baby...not like this. I love God. Don't put me before God. I am not worthy of that."

"But you scream OH GOD when I'm deep in those guts. Making you run from this dick."

That's where the ball dropped. "Niggah your dick ain't that good. I never ran from that eight inch skinny shit."

His eyes combusted into flames. "You're trying to be funny?"

"I'm speaking the truth. I'm going home, Niggah. You're *weirding* me out."

"No you're not going anywhere, bitch."

"Yes I am, Niggah."

He punched me so hard in the face my head snapped back into the picture of myself hanging on his wall. I was shocked by the onslaught, the brutal attack sweeping me off me feet.

"I said no you're not. I own you, Niggah. When you let me get up in that ass we became one. We connected, Niggah. Any other Niggah fuck you I'm kill you and that fuck Niggah. That's my ass, you hear me?" he asked, spitting in my face and slapping me again.

I punched at him and he pushed me back into the wall, laughing. I was disoriented. He grabbed my arm, spun me around, grabbed the back of my neck and slammed my forehead into my picture, the glass cracking; zigzagging from top to the bottom of the frame.

Pulling my pants past my ass, he slid his dick so far in me I winced from the pain. No lubrication, spit, nothing. It burned badly, and I was trying to push him off me.

He grunted. "You're mine. I won't let *no* other ever have you. I'm obsessed with you. Your beauty. Your looks. All the dope boys whisper about wanting to fuck you. I secretly smile 'cause I'm hitting this pussy…"

He grinded into me, possessing me, kissing my neck, biting my lower ear lobe.

"Please…stop!"

"You need love and direction. People hurt you. I will protect you, baby trust me. Say I'm your God. You're mine, baby. I worship you. Give you my money. Work to give you what you want. Your pain is trapped in your eyes," he went on, fucking me harder, bouncing off my booty cheeks and I was snatched in a vortex, the pleasure engulfing me like oversized wings.

Fluttering through me like falling feathers twirling towards the floor.

"Please!"

"I gotta nut!"

He groaned, and shook and I threw my head back into his nose so hard he screamed, falling out my ass and cumming on his carpet.

I ran past him, to the door, pulling up my pants.

"Don't leave me! Like my Grandma did!"

He sprinted past me, startling me, standing in front of the door. Blocking me. Keeping me hostage. Trapped inside. Kidnapping me.

"I love you, Pharoah. One last time, God. Me, or your version of God?"

"Je. Ho. Vah!"

"You're not even thinking about it."

"I chose God. Niggah, nothing comes between me and God. My faith never waivered. Not even your dick is good enough and if it was God still comes first. He made what you so eagerly use."

"But you're gay. I'm on the Low."

"You're gay, too."

"I'm straight, playah. I love pussy. I just fuck you, bitch. I'm not gay!"

"Bullshit. You're a faggot!"

"NO I'M NOT!"

"Move out my way."

"PHAROAH!"

"MOVE!"

"I hate you!"

"You hate yourself, psycho!"

He punched me again and I fell to my knees. He kicked me in the face and I fell back on the floor, my legs up then falling to the floor.

He was stomping me in the chest, and I crawled into the fetal position.

"I am going to make you chose me as your God!"

He kicked me in the back and I stayed in the fetal position.

"I'ma kill you if I can't have you."

I tried to stand up and he punched me again and I grabbed his foot and with all I could muster I kicked up into his nuts.

He fell down to the floor with me.

I tried to run out the door but he grabbed me, hopped up to his feet, and we were fist fighting, like a boxing match without boxing gloves.

He got some good blows in and my swinging fists deflected some of his blows.

"I'm a City Niggah, bitch!"

He brandished a knife and swung at me and I jumped back, looking around wildly.

I was going to die, oh my God!

I saw a wooden bat by the bathroom. I ran to it and he was on my ass, swinging the knife and the blade slamming into the wall.

I swung the bat across his face, and then swung at his legs.

He fell to his knees and I swung once more.

Knocking him out cold.

"I'm from Goulds, bitch!" I spat blood in his face.

Grabbed my shoes.

And left his punk ass unconscious. And didn't call motherfucking 9-1-1.

Fucked up ass Niggah.

I left the door wide open when I left.

And didn't look back.

Lord Jennings And The King of Erotica

"Did you feel connected to him?"

"Yes, I did."

"What was the connection?"

"His older cousin being pregnant from him. I connected to that, because I've *been* there."

"His family didn't believe in abortions so his cousin carried the baby to term."

"Yes."

"And your cousin lost the baby?"

My eyes watered. It was still so painful to think about. "Yes."

"What if the baby would have lived? Would you have been a father to your child?"

"I don't know. I was just 11."

"I'm sure you would have raised a healthy baby."

"The baby wouldn't have been so healthy. I mean my cousin was pregnant from me. I could have never told my child who his real mother was."

"I understand."

"And that's the part of me I struggle with. If the child would have lived. What would Mama do? Beat me? I have already been beaten enough in life."

"Would you want a girl or a boy?"
"A boy."
"Why a boy?"
"So I could be a better father than my dad was to me."
"And what kinda father was he?"
"A dead beat!" I said angrily. "A bitch! He didn't even try to find me."
"Who left who?"
"Mama left him."
"Did she tell him where she was moving?"
"No."
"She just up and left?"
"Yes."
"So do you still think it's *his* fault, if she up and left and didn't give him the information on your whereabouts?"
"I don't know," I said, confused. I was 32 and still confused about the whole ordeal and I still didn't even know the whole story. Mama and my grand Daddy told me bits and pieces of the story.
"When you sleep with men, how do you feel?"
"Safe."
"That's an interesting word. Safe."
"Yes, safe and secure."
"What do you look for in a man?"
I looked him deeply in the eyes. "A father."
"A father figure?"
"No. A father. That's why I call my man Daddy. I look at him like a father, as someone who takes control and makes decisions for us both. An aggressor who knows how to hold me down and put it down on my ass when I get outta line."
He closed his eyes.
And didn't say a word.

Tell me about a time a straight woman
Wanted to date an openly bi male

Lord Jennings

Mabel and eye aren't friends anymore (and haven't lost no muthafucking sleep either, bitch) because eye had to give our friendship tough love. Been friends for 13 years and some change and she now has an 18 year old son. We're both 32 years old (Mabel and eye) soon to be 33 (my BDAY was a week before hers so she border line Gemini/Cancer, which means her evil twin was also a sensitive ass, like me) and she already had her son's mind all discombobulated to hell. She had complications when giving birth to him. She nearly died delivering him when she was 14 years old. She hardly gained ten pounds when she was pregnant with him, so her pregnancy went unnoticed. She was a tom boy anyway, secretly eating a few cheerleaders' pussy at Southridge and swore she would never like dick because she watched her Mama get raped and even though he's serving life for trying to rape and kill her, she swore she'd never be with a man.

While eating pussy one of the cheerleaders had a boyfriend named Clive. Tall, slim and had a big dick. Eye should know. Clive, two years older than me, used to sneak me through his grand daddy's bedroom window, tip toed to his room and he fucked me all night at times.

When she saw Clive she fell in love. With his smile, his piercing gaze and his swagger. She dressed like a girl the very next day. She was sexier than the cheerleaders and the cheerleaders tried to fight her because she stole their popularity and their shine.

Long story short she gave Clive easy access pussy and when she got pregnant she dressed like a tom boy once more because she didn't want her police man daddy and her court attorney mother knowing she was knocked up by a secret fag.

She was a baby having a baby and she had to live home to home with various family members (that despised her) because when her parents found out she had a baby they threw her out butt ass naked and the baby was butt ass naked, too.

Wrote her ass off.

Then her mom lost her job for swindling funds and the white man told her Mama if she left amicably and paid back the money they would spare her reputation so she paid it back, got hooked on drugs, lost her house in the suburbs and had to move with her third cousin in Goulds and since her daughter really didn't have a home she moved down to Goulds, too and still had to live home to home with strangers she met at the Cutler Ridge Mall and the rest as they say was history.

By the time we did graduate (she enrolled at Southridge my sophomore year) she was raped again by one of her brother's cousins on her daddy side, emotionally beaten from her mother who followed her all over Goulds, everywhere, even every store (even while she was shopping!) yelling, "She's a soon to be 15 year old whore with a baby already, ya'll!"

Eye was with her that day in the mall and Mabel was crying, carrying her baby in low riding tight jeans, heels, and her mother's old expired make up, earrings and panties.

She really struggled. To make ends meet she was a stripper 5 nights a week and wasn't even an adult and she got paid under the table. She made good money.

Her mother, clad in dingy pants, pinkish shirt and a bad wig, smacked her lips with a sunken face and her big toe nearly peeked out her shoe.

Eye was shaking my head. "Don't wanna get an education but on the phone with those mens tawkin' 'bout sucking and fucking cum from a fucking dick, bitch ya' stupid? Didn't eye raise ya' better?"

Eye was mean mugging her mother, slowly reaching a boiling point.

Mabel held her baby on her big ass titties, huge tears of shame and embarrassment falling down her face and she looked over her shoulder, accidentally bumping into people ("*Damn* bitch watch where you going," a white woman said, frowning).

"Mama leave me alone! You're *so* embarrassing, God leave me alone! Why don't you just die, bitch, fuck!"

Eye was around Mabel's age so this type of thing was even new to me. Never seen that before so eye was embarrassed for Mabel. Eye cried with her, feeling helpless, powerless.

"*Mabel is a slutttt! Listen, boys my daughter got easy pussy step right up step right up and take her slutty ass home tonight starting at twenty dollars you can pay me eye'm her Mama!*"

That WAS THE FUCK IT!

Eye snapped on her cracked out, graduated from Howard University ass Mama.

Eye got in her face and snatched her wig off, people laughing. She covered her bald head and eye said, "Eye don't care if *that's* your daughter! *Don't* talk to her like that you bad body bitch!"

"You go to hell. And eye heard you're a faggot. Eye heard you suck dick…"

Eye slapped her across the face with the wig and tried to shove it in her mouth. "Don't throw stones you druggie bitch."

She pulled the wig from her mouth and pushed me into a cart with hanging watches and hats and bangles. That shit hurt.

Eye started snatching pouches, throwing them at her and she ducking, and dodging and eye'm throwing watches, hats, anything eye could get my hands on and hats and pouches hitting her in the face, tits and stomach and eye'm throwing shit and throwing shit; bracelets and costume jewelry and she's screaming, trying to cover her face with her trembling hands and security guards grabbed me and Mabel trying to push them off.

"Let my goddamn dawg go!" she yelled, pushing with one hand and telling a bystander woman to hold her baby and the lady sat in a chair, bouncing the baby on her lap so the baby didn't watch the drama.

"Pharaoh! Stay out of this," she was yelling at me, trying to get me to calm down. Eye was trying to break loose so eye could break dance across the Mama bitch's neck, treating her daughter like that. *What* kinda mother was she? All the women in the world who couldn't have babies and prayed to God for a child and she couldn't appreciate the one she fucking had?

"PHAROAH!"

Eye didn't hear Mabel. Security yelling and holding me and eye'm dangling, my dangerous eyes on the crying, big mouth Mama. Eye was still trying to get to her.

"BITCH! You ever scream my home girl personal business in a mall filled wit' fucking assholes and strangers and nosey muthafuckahs eye will proudly go to jail beating your ass. Eye never hit a girl before never, Hoe but eye will get in your ass."

Eye pointed at her. Eye meant that shit.

"Pharoah!" Mabel got in front of me, getting all in my face, and eye'm trying to push her ass out my goddamn way. When eye'm mad let me be. Try to stop me eye'll fight your ass, too.

"Young man calm down," said a security guard.

"We're going to call the police," said another.

"Let me go!" Eye threw my head back into his face and he released me, toppling over the other guard trying to hold me. Eye pushed him in the huge water fountain with all the pennies. His pocket change jingled as he fell inside. Hell that was about $4 in change worth of wishes. Four hundred Abraham Lincolns; so eye made that many wishes. For Mabel to be saved and protected by God. And that's where eye messed up at because eye should have been praying instead of wishing, but eye was trying to handle it on my own and couldn't quite do it because eye was a minor dealing with adult issues.

Another security guard tried to *grab* me and eye threw a one, two piece at him and he jumped back and eye had up my set, lurking, timing, just *waiting* for somebody to touch me. Eye put Mabel behind me.

Eye glared at her Mama.

She was screaming again.

"Son you will be banned from this mall if you don't stop. Eye'm giving you a chance to tell me what happened."

"Nothing flash light cop!"

"Eye'm calling the *police*."

"Fuck the muthafucking police. Don't talk to me about no goddamn police. When eye was raped as a kid *where* was the fucking police *then*?"

Eye turned to her mother and she cringed and eye grabbed her by the shirt (she swinging her hands at me).

Security grabbed me.

"You follow her around, calling your own flesh and blood daughter a tramp but you failed as a parent. My Mama had a still born daughter and you take yours for granted."

Eye let her go. "You ain't worth the trouble," eye continued.

Eye walked over, and took Mabel's baby.

"Come on, sugar poo," eye said, and told Mabel, "Let's go!"

Mabel and eye and the baby were waiting on the #52 bus.

"Eye can't believe she embarrassed me."

"Eye can't believe it either," eye said, exhausted.

"Thank you for having my back."

"No problem."

"Lord knows eye don't have that kinda courage to face my mother."

"She's on crack, lost her career and threw you out girl don't sweat the small shit. She didn't care if you lived or died."

"Eye know."

"Eye mean, yes respect her that is your mother, but damn she don't even respect herself."

"Tell me about it. Damn it's hot out here."

We saw some shade under a tree by the bus stop so we went over there.

There. Felt better. We sat on the grass and she held her baby on her tits. Baby sleeping.

"Eye..."

She stopped talking.

"What's wrong?" eye asked, searching her face.

"Eye just wanna talk to you, Mabel that all."

Her mother was behind me. Eye hopped up and started to swing and eye didn't know how she did it but Mabel hopped off the ground with her baby and grabbed my hand.

"Get away from her!" eye yelled defensively.

"She's *my* goddamn child."

"Fuck you! You don't deserve to have her as your goddamn child bitch! Get AWAY! Eye will protect her like she's my sister!"

"Mabel, eye love you. Eye really really do. Eye just wanted you to be better than eye ever was. Yea, eye got a college degree. Yea, eye had a husband. Yea, eye was high maintenance, went to church, *paid* my ten percent faithfully; but eye was troubled. Eye never wanted kids and when eye had you eye didn't want you so eye got involved more and more with my career."

"What?" Mabel was in shock. So was I.

"But eye married your daddy and raised you best eye could and eye know eye made mistakes and eye am *trying! Eye* ain't perfect."

"Nobody's perfect," eye said, shaking my head. Yea, she loved her daughter but those drugs had her soul. Had her soul badly. Couldn't break free because she now trying to dig in her daughter's pockets.

"Give me some goddamn money bitch! Eye need my hit!" Her Mama yelled.

Eye pushed her on the ground.

"Rape! Rape! SHE TRY'NA RAPE us help help US PLEASE!" eye yelled, drawing attention.

"Baby forgive me." People started running over to us and she hauled ass, cut through the bushes and never looked back.

"Eye hate her," Mabel said, our bus coming.

A few men ran up to us and Mabel said, "Ugh leave us alone damn we was just playing. Didn't wanna give the crack head five dollars, damn."

And we got on the bus.

The next day Mabel and Eye was on our way to get her baby from Drake, her boyfriend (a high school drop out turned dope dealer, and the boy brought in some serious cash!) when a stranger walked up to us, with huge tears in her eyes.

She was trying to hand Mabel something.

"Here, take it," she said and eye was like what the fuck?

"*Lady* eye don't know you!" Mabel said.

"Take it! Your Mama said if anything ever happened to her she wanted me to give you this letter."

"What do you mean if something happens to her?" eye asked, and Mabel stared at her in disbelief, tears forming in her eyes.

"You ain't heard about your own Mama? She died of a drug overdose this morning. They found her full of dope Across the Tracks, behind Disco South."

"Mama, no!"

She never went to get her baby.

We were on Goulds Park, by the sliding board. Crying together. Eye held her and she couldn't stop. Asking God to take the pain away. Asking God to give her mother a second chance. She was destroyed.

Eye was destroyed with her. Eye didn't hate the woman but eye hated her ways. Mistreating her abused daughter.

She pulled away from her and looked deep in my eyes and eye'm stroking her face and staring in her eyes and she said "Now eye don't got nobody."

"You got your baby."

"But that's a baby, Pharoah!"

"You got me."

And we stared at each other and for some reason my dick was hard as a brick but eye was focused more on her emotional state and she leaned up to me and eye'm still rubbing my thumbs over her wet cheeks and we kissed, some tongue and fell into each other and her man hated me, he hated my bisexual ass and told me eye never got any pussy but hmmm ten minutes of kissing and making Mabel's pussy dripping wet eye fucked her raw dick under the huge oak trees, digging all in that good pussy till eye bust a nut deep in her cervix.

Niggah hated me.

And eye'm getting his pussy.

While he's Mr. Mom at home with no diploma, selling dope and no life eye was granted playing time in his girl's pussy.

And it was some good pussy too, fuck niggah.

And that's all eye would ever be. Comfort dick. She was fucking the niggahs her dope dealer man set her up to fuck, banking the money and when he beat her or mistreated her she running to me giving me Keith Sweat Why Me baby Pussy.

Eye wanted some Let me Lick you up and down till you say goddamn stop, Silkk pussy and she never gave me that kinda pussy, never let me bounce in the pussy. Eye had to be tender, giving her Ralph Tresvant dick when eye wanted to give some It's my Prerogative Dick. Do what eye wanna do.

We would do this off and on for years. Eye fucked her again after graduation. Fucked her some more before eye went to the Army and had Tam's late ass (my, ahem, girlfriend) thinking eye was in love when in all actuality my cousin Jason told me about her whorish ways so eye pretended to wanna got to the Army and marry her. Yea. Right. Ok. When eye chose a dick over you and never hit the pussy then what does that tell you?

Who's the fool? Ain't me like you thought all those years.

Girl. Flattery, eye tell ya'.

Even when eye got out of prison (eye wasn't getting pussy for four years nine months!) Mabel let me nut, nut, nut all over her lips, face, in her asshole, deep in her pussy and all in her mouth for the next three weeks. And eye would get lost in her pussy; then turn around and get with the DL niggahs and get fucked better than eye fucked her and eye got lost in that, trying to make up for lost time.

Eye was convinced eye was happy. Eye wasn't.

Eye had God, thanked him for getting me through prison but eye was back in the *same* environment that had me negative and if you didn't change your environment and everything you wanted, desired or dreamed was a stone's throw away then you haven't matured.

After a month passed, eye let it all go.

And Mabel called.

She came to see me.

Mom was at work and eye was the only one home. Brother's playing basketball on the park and my sister at her daddy's house.

"Pharoah. Can eye come in?"

"Sure." She comes in, looking good but a little fat. Ass kinda on the flat side, but what she lacked in ass she made up for in her tits.

She hugged me and eye kissed her neck, running my fingers down her arm.

"Pharoah, eye like you."

"Eye like you." We kissed.

"And eye can't stop thinking about you."

We kissed. Eye reached in her pants and dug up in her tight pussy. Pulling my hand out eye made her suck her pussy down her throat, then suck all four fingers, stretching that mouth preparing the landing field of the tongue for this big ass hard ass dick.

"Eye love the way you touch me."

"Damn can a niggah get some head?"

"Hell yea."

Eye pulled my dick out and she squatted in heels and started taking it to the throat with no hands, humming her favorite song, rubbing my nuts ("*Oooh wee*, bitch!) and she puts two fingers deep in my asshole and eye am fucking her tight, hot mouth, suction sounds filling my ears and reverberating off my balls and my asshole bouncing on her fingers.

"Goddamn baby you try'na make me nut already."

She sucking, finger fucking me and playing with my nuts...

Eye had to come already goddamn eye didn't say shit she know my M.O. hated to tell a Hoe when eye nut if you a real bitch and real about your shit swallow this unpredictable nut and she did, didn't flinch or miss a beat, swallow, suck, pull balls, fingers in my ass *ohhhh* shit, bitch.

Eye was drained.

We lay in my bed.

Lounging. Eye wasn't worried about getting caught. Just did four years prison so pussy on me or around me surely wasn't a problem with me.

She said, "We should be together."

"Um, no we shouldn't."

"Why?"

"Eye mean, eye like you."

"Like me? You don't love me?" she snapped.

"Eye mean, the head game two points in the paint and the pussy, eye mean..." eye yawned, no pun intended and she hot as a firecracker now! "It's good *but* girl eye'm young. *Eye'm* not trying to be tied down."

"Will you think about it?"

"Eye'm bisexual."

"So what. You ah good man. Eye can look past that. At least you told me."

"NO!" Eye got out of bed. "You need to get the fuck out my house."

"Fuck you, niggah."

"*Get out!*"

"Fine, niggah! Eye just wanted to be your *girl*."

"Half the Hood fucked you and you want me to be committed to a piece of pussy every niggah in Goulds, Florida City and Naranja fucked?"

"Fuck you! You insensitive bastard."

"Get out my house."

"Fuck you, faggot."

"Oh, shit. Eye love when you talk dirty to me."

Eye bent her over the bed and fucked her.

"Touch your toes."

"God*damn*, Daddy! Eye *knew* you wanted this pussy."

Eye bounced in it and for a minute eye imagined eye was a straight man with no gay bone in my body and eye still didn't see me being committed to this bitch.

She's a good friend.

But as a girlfriend? Um, slut.

Bitch!

Eye pissed in her pussy and pulled out, opened the door and threw her butt naked out the door with her clothes hitting her in the face.

"Bye."

Eye slammed the door closed.

Tell me about a bad problem child
One of your friends couldn't handle

Lord Jennings

My homegurl was 39 years old and had the mind of a goddamn 12 year old. For real. Instead of paying rent she buys weave, nails and heels. Her phone line was a bill collector's dream! She has a 23 year old. Subtract 16 from 39 and unearth the tender age she was when she gave birth to the nappy headed, whiny little fucking ass clown. He grew up licking milk from his mama's mouth and being spilt by his brain dead Grandma before he became a problem at the age of 16. His Grandma, married to a man who used to chase rabbits in West Palm Beach, raised her grandson to disrespect his Mama the way Dye, his mother, disrespected her.

    Darshawn, bad ass, knew how to get what he wanted from his mother by throwing her whorish days in her face. She never told him but his Grandma was out of pocket and out of place for raising her grandson to disrespect his own mother. Dye went through 9 hours of labor delivering his bad ass, not Grandma. And eye told her this but she never listened. She liked to pretend a problem didn't exist in her surreal world she built for herself. A world she was Queen and could come and go as she pleased.

Darshawn never took her seriously and eye watched this shit for years. We've been friends since eye was 15 years old and it was the same shit. Darshawn do this, she said. Um, no Mama you goddamn do it, he answered. Cursing her ever since he was 7 years old and his Daddy, with his no good ass, doing life in prison, trying to tell Darshawn what to do from a prison cell and Darshawn wasn't trying to hear that shit.

Every time she used to beat him...his *Grandma* whipped her ass for whipping him and she was too afraid to tell her mother that, even though she should respect her, to FUCK OFF when it came to chastising her SON!

Grandma Pearl hated my ass because eye didn't take her shit. When eye was 19 she told me to stay out the family business when it came to me voicing my opinion about Grandma raising a future thug. He was drinking Henn with his Grandma and smoking weed with his Grandma by the time he was 16. By the time he was 17 he had two kids from two different women, and had another 15 year old pregnant in Houston, Texas (his daddy side of the family was from Houston).

Grandma Pearl was a cop but lost her career when she got into drugs. Selling them then using heroine and she lost it all. Life went up in smoke. Used to be heavy in the church and it blew up in her face when she came home and caught her husband sucking two dicks with another in his ass. Proverbs wasn't apart of the vocabulary anymore.

Turning to the heroine to erase the images brought about her family's ruin.

Grandma Pearl was on heroine when she was raising Dye. Dye hated seeing her mother do drugs and was the butt of a thousand jokes in school. Eye befriended her because eye knew what it was like to be picked at and we became close.

Grandma Pearl fucked up raising Dye, and now Grandma was try'na school Dye about her mistake's child.

She didn't have heart so she never stood up to her mother or her son. She feared her son, and her son used to whip her ass. A 15, 16 year old beating his mother's ass when he didn't get money, food or clothes and he drove her car to hell and she still worked two jobs giving him one check to spend on pussy and Hoes and her other check barely paid the rent and she calling me asking for money for the Dumb Bitch of the Year fund, um, no sweetie.

Nobody in her family stopping Darshawn from disrespecting his Mama because he's spending some of the check on them. As long as he kept buying booze, Popeye's chicken and weed they remained mum.

How was Dye going to stand up to her mother when she couldn't even handle her son or her own inner turmoil? Her mother made her feel like a failure all her life. Making *Dye* pay for her failed police career. Wasn't Dye's fault Mommie wanted a needle in her arm.

Dye and eye had a conversation on the phone recently. Eye was telling her eye didn't trust *then or now* niggahs. Eye trusted *now and then* niggahs because they were go getters, hardly ever *stagnant* and *knew* how to flip a quarter and get fifty dollars.

My family was filled with *now and then* niggahs, that knew how to get money, keep money and make money and no eye didn't do what they did but for years eye always sat back and observed, studied and took notes eye now apply to my life when shit gets a little rough.

Dye wasn't paying attention because she was always jealous of how eye stood up for myself, no matter who it was but like eye told her eye wasn't always like this. People used to run me over, rape me, piss on me and fuck me but Pharoah got muthafucking TIRED!

The day eye told my sexually frustrated Pa$tor "Fuck off, bitch," when eye was 15 was the day Pharoah stopped taking people's shit.

Eye watched Dye try to stand up to her mother. Eye was at the table eating spaghetti, in silence and shock, mouth wide open, fork with food barely in my mouth. It was like watching a poodle fight a lioness. They spoiled my appetite. Couldn't eat my damn food.

Darshawn, 23 years old, playing the PS3, laughing. "Get her bitch ass, Grandma."

Eye'm 31 at this point, last year. Watching this shit for years, something building up inside me for equally as long. Eye'm fuming now, staring at Darshawn.

Eye didn't get in other folks business so eye swallowed whatever it was eye felt and remained as mum as Darshawn, cunning and clever, continued to pay off his family with his mother's hard earned money.

He's not working, she pays his car note (had a black Charger) and takes care of this niggah.

Now Dye was married to Stanley and Stanley didn't love her ass. He used to sell dope from her home but later found a new location after he was raided. They didn't find anything, but the incident caused him to be a little more cautious.

Grandma Pearl took $60 from Dye's wallet, called her a "stanking bitch!" and left her weeping in the living room. Grandma on her way to *Miccosukee*, to gamble.

Darshawn laughing and Dye stormed up to him, and said, "Go to your room!"

"No!" He pressing buttons on the joystick, dressed in the latest urban gear, mouth full of golds.

"Now! And what eye told you about keeping weed in your room?"

He didn't look at her. "There's no weed in my room."

She snatched the power plug to the PS3 from the wall, got in his face and shouted, "Eye found weed in your goddamn room!"

He stood up, all in her face, pointing. He's about 5 feet 6; she's 5 feet 4.

"And eye found condoms in your room! And you're married to my daddy!"

"Um, he's your step daddy and he ain't about shit! It ain't all of that, son!"

"Who are you letting come up in here getting deep in that ruined pussy bitch?"

My mouth still hanging open. Eye pinched myself to see was eye dreaming.

"SHUT UP!"

"Somebody's sleeping in my step daddy's *beddd*, baby!"

"SHUT UP!"

"Bitch you shut up. Dick sucking Hoe!"

Hold the fuck up. That was the fuck it. Stop the goddamn tape, bitch.

Eye pushed back from the table and stood my 6 feet 5 inch ass up. Eye'm 245 pounds. He's about 170 bitch couldn't beat my goddamn ass.

"Apologize to your fucking mother," eye said calmly, controlling my emotions and baby they were pouring out like lightning.

"No." He looked at me, then looked back at his mother and her dumb ass crying and weeping boo hoo boo hoo all in his face and wondered why he didn't take her dramatic ass serious. Bitch grab your pussy and roar. Grab your twat and remind yourself and your goddamn son where he came from.

"APOLOGIZE!"

"Faggot eye said no."

Eye swooped this fuck niggah off his feet and threw his punk ass through the wooden low table. Niggah squirming on the floor like a worm out of the belly of the earth. Eye leaned over and snatched his dumb ass up like a rag doll. Like a skilled carpenter's tape measure, nail and hammer.

Eye stuck my pencil behind my ear and got all up in his grill. Yea, boy. All up in your fucking face.

He was shocked. Never saw me yell or get in their business. But he never called her a bitch around me. Grandma Pearl got your shit smelling like roses and bitch eye'ma remind you those roses smell like boo boo, Outkast.

Now he caught out there, caught his ass completely off guard. Eye did a 360 on this lil' wet behind the ears Similac breath Gerber baby stains in his shirt ass Pull ups niggah.

Eye said it again. "Apologize."

Before he could say anything eye pushed him into the wall and got back in his face like T Rex running up on a goddamn turtle.

"Eye'm not apologizing, niggah and eye'ma shoot your ass for hitting me niggah eye'ma goon."

Eye slapped his bitch ass so hard he's even more shocked, holding his cheek. He's 5 feet 5, 6; eye'm 6 feet 5, bitch and weigh nearly twice your size with a fourteen shoe times two is TWENTY 8 feet up in your young ass niggah.

"You think you bad fuck niggah? Eye don't need a gun or goons to beat your ass."

"Pharoah, eye ain't never had a run in with you. But she dead ass wrong. Fucking niggahs in my daddy's bed. Eye used to want a girl that reminds me of my Mama so now eye'm fucking all women like Hoes."

"No, man. Listen. Don't dictate your life based on your mama's discography. Be better than her and your retarded, dumb ass Grandma. Get you a classy wife. Build a family in the Word, bruh. Do you believe in God?"

"Yea, man eye do. But God don't like or love me."

"Because you don't like or love your fucking self."

Eye had him.

Eye said, "Go back to school dude. You dropped out and got three goddamn children. You're living with HIV. Eye know you be fucking women without rubbers niggah and that's against the fucking law. You got choices. You need to call those two women you infected and get it over with niggah. You never had a man in your life and yea eye'm bisexual and will beat your muthafucking punk ass you EVER call your Mama a fucking bitch in my goddamn face the fuck again Popeye."

He lowered his head. "My daddy locked up for life. Nobody showed me how to be a man."

I raised his face back into mine with my finger under his chin. "That's because your Grandma pussyfied your Hoe ass. Eye watched this for years and never said shit. Get an education bruh. Be more responsible. Eye been through hell and back, even four years of prison and they fuck Niggah's like you in the ass and make you feel like a pussy. Do you really wanna raise your kids being broke and dumb as fuck?"

"Mama takes care of me."

"After today she ain't."

She walked up to me. "Pharoah. That's my son. Eye have…"

Eye snatched her ass. "Wake up dumb ass. You're letting your seed disrespect you. Ain't even woman enough to tell your Mama where to get off. This is your son, yes but not your goddamn obligation or responsibility when he a grown ass man out there fucking up. You're a dumb ass broad. Are you even a black woman?"

"Pharoah you're hurting my feelings!"

"GOOD!"

Eye turned away from her. And looked at Darshawn. Tears flow but he 'Hood with it. He didn't utter a sound.

"Now apologize to your mother or eye will beat your fuck ass all over the fucking projects fuck niggah APOLOGIZE RIGHT THE FUCK NOW!"

"Mama…mama. Eye'm sorry."

"Sorry for what?"

Dye's eyes lit up. He never apologized to his mother a day in his life. She didn't know how to take the apology.

"For calling you a bitch."

"What else?" eye asked, taking up a few knots of money off the low table and shoving it in her big ass titties. Her money. Not his.

"For disrespecting you."

Dye hugged her son and he hugged her back. Eye never saw them hug. Never in my goddamn life. They clung to each other.

Grandma came barging in the door cursing and when she saw them, still embracing and crying audibly together she said, "Dye, bitch what's…"

Eye pushed her old ass out the door, "Go to your own goddamn house you miserable dried up bitch!" and slammed the door closed.

Eye opened the window and she panting and raving and threatening me and eye said it simply, "Stay away from Dye and her son. If you don't eye will call the police and let them know Dye's man is doing life in prison for something you did. He's taking the fall for you because he doesn't snitch. Don't stay the fuck away you just muthafucking watch what the fuck eye do bitch. Wanna test me?"

"Hell naw," she said. "Eye got my own goddamn life."

She was high on heroine. You could tell the way her balding ass was slurring.

Eye closed the window.

Eye walked over to them. Eye had to go home, and probably wouldn't be coming back over to the projects for a while.

Eye snatched him from his mother's embrace and to my face. We coulda kissed he was so close to me, wanted the niggah looking me deep in my eyes.

"Do that fuck shit again, take any more of her money, call her a bitch again and eye'ma be your Bi daddy and beat your goddamn ass like my dick spat you in your Mama's pussy. Got me niggah?"

He hugged me and eye hugged him back.

"Yea, Uncle Pharoah."

Eye picked up her *Bible* and opened it up.

Better yet eye closed it and gave it to Darshawn.

"Open it to Exodus Chapter 20 verse 12."

He really didn't wanna open the Bible. Eye could tell by the look in his eyes he didn't really believe in religion. But religion was a label for spirituality, not spirituality itself.

He had to turn to the *Bible's* table of contents to find what page Exodus started on. That was fine. Eye could count the number of times he cracked open any book to read it: ZERO. NADA. ZILCH! When he found the page he flipped till he saw chapter 20. Dye smiling because her son never opened up God's Word. Eye wasn't no perfect muthafuckah, but, take me as eye am because God didn't make no mistakes when he made my blunt ass.

"Eye found it."

"Read it to your mother."

"Honor they father and mother; then you will live a full, long life in the land the Lord your God will give you."

"Good. Now give the Bible to your mother."

Her hands trembled when she took it. "Eye haven't touched a Bible in fifteen years."

"You're touching one now. Turn the Bible to Ephesians 6:4 and read what that says."

"Eye don't wanna read no Bible."

"Your son did it. Now you do it. Set an example for your son then maybe he'll start to respect your dumb ass. Turn it to Ephesians 6:4. And read it to your son!"

She knew it by heart. "Parents don't provoke your children to wrath."

I said, "*My* advice is to read a chapter of the Bible to each other daily. Eye'm telling you God can do great things in your life if you trust and believe. Darshawn, from this day forth if you yell or curse your Mama eye will fuck you up."

"Uncle Pharoah eye got you man. Eye just wish my father wasn't doing life. Eye wish it was him here doing what you're doing."

Eye put my hand on his chest. "He's in your heart. Just be the man he will never be."

He hugged me. "Eye miss my father, Pharoah."

"Darshawn, be blessed you know who he is. Be blessed you can talk and visit him. Me, eye haven't seen mine since eye was about 15 months old. Eye wouldn't know him if he stared me in the face."

He held me tighter, and my homegirl hugged me too.

"Don't raise your son to hate his daddy. Raise him to love, honor and still respect his father."

And we fell into a deep silence.

Eye never went to visit them again.

My mission, accomplished.

> *Your Zodiac sign is your armor*
> *What does that contribute to your success?*
> *The 6 and the 9*
> *Ying/Yang*
>
> Lord Jennings

Now that eye'm successful and gradually becoming visual in the literary world and on social networks eye trust no one with my career. NO ONE! Eye'm not being mean, but all trust is in GOD. And eye don't need a bunch of God-made images all up in my empire. Watching me work instead of them editing, photographing and planning events. Eye'm supposed to whistle while you work. Eye'm the author and the breadwinner. Eye'm supposed to kick up my heels and call it a day. But eye'm picking up the slack for editors and promoters. Doing more gift of gab then they were. Bad enough my hands had to convince the keyboard to compute my thoughts on Xerox 8x11 paper. Maybe eye need to start writing my books on 11x16 papers.

    The more they watch the more they trying to familiarize themselves with your business, how you talk about business and giving up some of that asshole to tie up that loose transaction. Eye'ma sexy bitch. Ahem, my Facebook fans says that! But eye don't feel sexy. Some days eye cry because eye'm getting older. But another part of me embraces my feminine side and eye do a switch, ball change up Presto! Change-o! Eye's a bitch with a new attitude.

Now eye don't mix business with pleasure, talk about pleasure while conducting business or writing about pleasure while conducting business. Eye took sex all the way out the equation. Dick + no passion = STD.

And kept my mind on God. And my trust in his full armory of weapons.

When you have your own business you gotta crush egos and hurt some muthafucking feelings, even your own: for the sanity and productivity of your business. If a niggah you hated could take you to the next level pay for his services. Niggah may hate you but in the business of making money *know* when to create an ally. Once it pays off pay him, kick him to the curb. No *Thank You* card, keep it gangster, keep it moving.

That's business. Pimping each other for the Grand Payoff. Emotion couldn't get in the way of the business success if, when it hurts you or don't produce the profits you been bragging about you abandoning shit, man down, Chile man overboard. No life jacket? Here's a rain coat.

Eye had to do that. Making editors earn that money and photographers earn that money and advertising people earn that money and web designers build my shit for free and earn that money and eye was giving up the booty to the editor to get it free on the house. The squirrels in his balls paid *me* with nuts and gave me protein shakes all the way to the photographer. He ugly ass *fuck* but got a juicy dick. Rode his shaft, in the darkness. Unplugged all the lamps, turned off all glowing cell phones. Slipping those hundreds out that wallet while he get his nut. Half the time he didn't realize eye got off his dick and said eye wanted it on my stomach and squeezed my sweaty legs together and convinced this late niggah he was fucking me good, oh yea you getting all knee deep in my asshole.

Yawn. You got some wet filet ah thighs. He pounded my squeezed-tight thighs and swore he was "tearing the booty hole up." Sad, dude, that you gotta find out in my autobiology/autobiography that you had got off on my thighs LOL.

And with the marketing director, he was a club promoter. So eye give him a little suckcie suckie pussy and he's happy go lucky. Go home fuck his wife to sleep just to cum back and get his second nut.

Shit bubbling like lava and the more eye shake, shake it he's one pressed niggah and when he get in it he all up in it, saying its better than his wife's mouth AND pussy, combined. Eye was like, yea, right.

Watch that Top lay on his sweaty ass, cock his legs open with his feet flat on the bed, grabbing my ass cheeks and slamming my warmth up and down upp and downnn upp and down. Up! And. DOWN.

Thug ass niggah, can't catch a break. Hired him on the side to fuck me twice a day before eye met Mr. NFL on South Beach. So when fans hit me up spitting game eye already made the hired held spit from his dick all over my face, running down my tight hole. Niggah hi, how are you, good bye God bless. Don't want your number hell no you keep your wife. That's flattering, eye got a man, I lied (didn't have a man and wasn't looking) and *hell naw!* you couldn't see my private picture.

And that was that.

Eye didn't want a relationship. No sweet nothings. Niggah eye'm paying you $100 a week your job is to bring your dope dealing Thug 6 feet 7 inch ass to my room, blow my back out, make me run from it. Then when eye cum jack your dick with my seeds, nut all over your hands, swallow it all up.

You swallow that shit, niggah. *Not* me. You don't pay me enough to swallow. Eye gets more money from you than eye give to you.

Eye calls that insurance. Eye'm actually paying you you own money to do the do.

Chi...sit.

He then got a job at one of the biggest clubs on South Beach, sometimes on Holidays a bitch pay $40 to get up in this dead-looking shit.

Club ain't all that. Eye briefly met Young Jeezy been there before and eye shook Trina's hand.

She wouldn't remember me *anyway*. And she didn't know eye was a bestselling author and eye never said anything about it. Eye knew what and who eye was so eye was good with that.

She a celebrity bitch we speak in passing. *Hay*, bitch. Shake hands, smooch, smooch. *Hey*, bitch, toss your lace front and eye grab my dick, my jeans sagging, walking with my head high past the thugs, ignoring the females, lesbians and good pussy honeys.

Niggahs singing *'bout* the Snow Man niggah this Miami, Florida. Sunny as fuck. Hot as fuck. Humid as fuck. Ain't no goddamn snow that far from the equator and the equator damn near run slap through us. The *Snow* Man? What worked for Jeezy ain't gonna cut it in Miami-Dade County.

Most people couldn't walk up and down ALI BABA BOULEVARD without cringing or flinching. Niggahs down here got metal detectors. Trying to find where they buried their stash. Better not ever snow here. Niggahs will be fucked up. They'll be buried in their houses like up North in New York and their money will be buried beneath the covered earth and under the buried snow.

And we couldn't have that! Um, yea. Eye'ma Snow Man. Nah. Snow Man was the Coke Man by the way and eye never snorted coke a day in my life. Fuck that. Shit, naw dude eye pass.

We building sand castles, not snow men. Watching chickens clucking (Swahili for sucking!) jerking and swallowing nut and catching byrds flying I-95 SOUTH for the winter in unregistered Hondas.

Snow men melt into water. Sand castles turn into shores. Keeping us above water. Sand bagging the waves. Keeping shit cool. Keeping shit chill. Keeping the sharks, whales and dolphins at bay. Eye could deal with the beam of your binoculars. *Haters* look, dream about and daydream about fucking this tight asshole day in, day out; fucking their wives wishing her pussy was mine. Eye make ya' man feel like a nut from whispering in his ear during mental stimulation and conversation feeding him grapes in between breaks.

'Cause you ain't gonna get it so stop flashing your fake infrared beam. Your broke ass couldn't even afford tithes in church so eye know you didn't have guns.

This promoter, Nigga who loves, breathes and lives for Jeezy, took me one time to his place of business. Mighty fine establishment on the outside.

He told everybody on his Facebook EYE GOT THE KING OF EROTICA cumming to Club_____. Oh boy phone calls were made.

Didn't pay attention to "cumming" not "coming."

Got people gutters in rotation, moving like Earth plates all through their minds. Building Hawaii out of dicks and erupting volcanic orgasms from deep in the pussy pool of the female. Now they come to meet me wanting to fuck, not to buy a book.

Hoes' pussies wet. Eye see you, faggot. Niggah's dicks hard but you could never tell with those huge baggy jeans, unlaced boots and overturned baseball caps. Eye fucked with niggahs in Baseball caps, grimy niggahs get up in it and wanna protect their "baby." Ahem, me.

Shit, they the swingers, chasers and catchers. With a short stop catching all balls. If some get past him or get away he still in a squatting stance.

Eye don't fuck with niggahs that wear football Caps. This year at the Super bowl the Saints shined through on the Vikings chasing them around the field like dolphins.

Niggahs in football caps are chasers. But they chasing ass and then the *ball* the whole four quarters. Eye couldn't fuck with a niggah always playing the game in quarters chasing asshole camouflaging it with a ball and tight knee-length pants with pads. Why you think football players shower together. They got all that money, millions of dollars and you mean to tell me NFL player #1 gotta look at suds running down NFL Player 2's asshole? He gotta clean his ass around thirty swinging soapy dicks?

Sometimes going into over time, if the coach could stop the quarter back sneaks (old PLAYED OUT!) and challenging the referees. Referees wear black and white stripes. Vertical stripes. Whenever millions of dollars are involved referees are instructed to wear Ying Yang colors. A state of hypnotism. SNAP OUT OF IT, WAKE UP!

So eye write with enlightened knowledge. Eye understand things dancing with my alter ego *better* than eye could ever comprehend sober and solo.

Nonetheless, the club was thick. Goddamn. It's thick up in here! THICK! Meaning the neighborhood's Whose *Who* was out. Dressed nicely; hair all done up; niggahs on point with colored Polo cotton button up shirts; and women actually had on panties under ankle length dresses.

So eye never understood why a Hoe took off her panties when wearing short skirts? When you dancing you wanted a niggah to notice your ass cheeks? Or the Joe camel toe pussy?

Already people that follow me think eye'm easy. Cum out by the numbers, sign autographs, half of them never heard of me; the other half never read my books. Saying eye inspire them. Chile, *sit*, don't wanna hear that. Eye wasn't prepared, wasn't planning on promoting now eye'm amongst the elite of the 'Hood, and everybody want a book and eye don't even have muthafucking flyers.

Eye'd been had. But eye smile anyway, shaking the females' hands then kissing, cupping the fingers by their fingertips, lowered forehead, eyes casting up into theirs.

Yet the fellas, straight type 'Hood niggahs that slang big dope drive big whips drank BIG drank rock silk suits get good pussy and cum down some throats are always kissing my cheek or kissing my hand, spin me around, pat my ass, whisper in my ear they want some pussy.

When eye say "No," they dangling Bentley and Rolls Royce, Lamborghini and Porsche keys with blinging key bracelets matching their cuffs, earrings and bling, bling, promising me the moon when in their eyes eye see the sun not the stars. And we couldn't stare at the sun with a straight face. Can we?

Those kinda niggahs eye couldn't trust. Eye saw the Sun not the SON and that told me inside him wasn't the Holy Ghost.

Take full advantage on that *Welcome Sale* sign hanging on the windows of his soul. Just look in his eyes deep enough. You'll see his intentions.

Eye got it down to a science. Eye smelled bullshit a mile away. Niggah ran off with my money once. Won't pull a Michael Johnson in gold track shoes on me goddamn twice.

Then when they feel like their sexuality and manhood was in question they retaliated by pulling away, chasing the sexy, sexy Mama walking by in the club, with her late ass, all that ass out, raw and uncovered and they say, "Goddamn baby! Damn, can a niggah fuck."

Females, some of you may be the shade.

Yea you, Ho. Late ass. Fag. Take off that wig. You ain't no Hoe. Don't got no pussy. Haven't used your dick in 29 years and you turned 29 yesterday. Virginal gay ass niggah. Talking shit, trying to stop my books from succeeding.

Eye was dating a thug niggah who was a secret bald headed, flat chest drag queen. Eye wanted to gag when he walked by me at Club Boi snapping and prancing. Talking to the other drag bitch, his/her best friend drag, Hoe. Saying did eye want a shot of ass, but didn't notice me in my get up.

Eye hate wearing shades but that night eye had on knock off Gucci's.

Then eye had on my homebody's old MCM pants suit. You know eye'ma throw back niggah but never wore throw back type clothes around you.

So *eye* was the relationship hoax. You, the dismembered spook.

Eye looked closely, and you said, "You are so sexy."

"Thank you," eye said, wanting to puke. Pink panties up a charcoal ass, niggah you black as fuck. Bright red lipstick? Looking like a burnt pig about to get slaughtered. You didn't wait to get to the slaughter house to slaughter that kind of pig. Disgraceful, disgusting, but eye tuned it out. He/she's were people too, couldn't treat them no different.

One of my deceased best friends used to dress in drag and was born with a dick and a pussy.

That's what changed me. And my writing improved because of it.

So eye applied that my books, writing and my own business minding its own business. Eye hung around those that were writers like me. You got to wine and dine with the successful to be successful. Ain't no niggahs in the 'Hood talking 'bout no damn overseas stock, when they broke as fuck shooting future rent in a daily crap game, knowing one or the other would come out the victor. The overall winner. But a niggah got a pistol in his back pocket for insurance; he gonna *gamble* willing to lose or win; but if he lose he robbing your late ass the minute you get in your Chevy.

Pop! Pop! Pop!

Was all it took when someone killed my hermaphrodite friend. He/she had a heard of gold. Used his dick or pussy/asshole wisely.

Never bothered a nun and never swatted a fly. Went to church every Sunday and admitted publicly he was a sinner. Too ambitious and was a better rapper than T.I.

But the world didn't understand him so the darkness took him out.

Now eye'm looking closely wondering why the tranny look like my boyfriend.

Oh my God!

It was!

"The King of Erotica's dick!" is tattooed on his right side. Oh my God! OH MY GOD!

"YOU BITCH! YOU A DRAG QUEEN?"

He/she was shock, shock oh God he so shock, yes, shocked, bitch! "OH MY GOD! PHAROAH! EYE'M SO ASHAMED!"

"Bitch!" Eye snatched wigs that night. Eye beat his ass and then his he/she girl friend drag Hoe came trying to get her bid in and eye smacked the Hoe so hard, she buckled and eye kicked her in the chin, footing her to the ground by those plastic titties. Late bitch!

She moaning threatening to call the police and eye ran at my secret he/she and eye whipped his ass.

"You don't wear MCM or shades! Sorry Pharoah! Eye love you! You said you'd be my bitch!"

"FUCK YOU!" Eye was betrayed. To find out the man that's fucking you, your true Top niggah was an undercover drag tranny bitch with minus tits and a half clean asshole didn't sit well with me.

He never let you by his ass, touch his ass or stick a finger in his ass when you were the bitch/Bottom in the bedroom of the relationship, thinking the kitchen's equipped and you discover he was taking it in the ass on his night job and eye was the goddamn dummy!

Eye dumped him, changed my number, and stopped taking his calls. Eye did this for months, locking myself away writing books. Mad. Redirected.

Then after my BDAY passed eye looked in the mirror one day and said eye need to stop putting trust in man. STOP IT EYE SAY! MAN WILL EVENTUALLY LET YOU DOWN! HELLO!

Eye tamed all the hired help at that point in my career, Cycle 2, with the booty, since we fucking anyway, ain't shit for free. They think eye'm on lockdown, "they" contradicted all of their individual thoughts. Hey, hey. From the beginning eye told you my motto. What was it? Yea, eye'm from Goulds, Bitch!

Eye run amongst those that run amongst us, zip codes disguised area codes and unmarked cities and countries not printed on the U.S. or World Map.

Underground caves, polished floors, marbled walls. Couldn't enter unless your eyes were scanned.

Running all *through* the Grand Canyon playing golf on marble courses and fancy contraptions; to the naked eye, invincible.

Eye realized this smoking weed while *reading* Anne Rice Novel. About Lestat faggot ass. Vagabond. Queen of the Damned.

Eye read everything for influence, then eye carve out my own niche that's all my goddamn own.

My alter ego when eye got the first two bestsellers, The King of Erotica book one, revealing Pharoah's Throne and the King of Erotica 2, Pharoah's Crown, was a more assertive being. Eye didn't approach things as aggressively and eye actually settled down and enjoyed my writing more without all the pressure.

The King 2 had the same book cover as book 1 but was a different numbered picture from Steve Shires' photos immortalized with well-cleaned and focused photographic lens. HI, STEVE! LOVE YA' BUDDY!

Eye was cheerful, carefree and took my eyes off the fort. Left my post before properly relieved and now eye trust people with my money and cream and with that you think you call the shots, forgetting who helped you rise to the top. My arrogance set in harder than humbleness.

And that action detached me from God, and was the cause of sin.

Eye thought eye was hopeful, eye certainly projected it in the couple interviews eye had, a niggah thought he was grand, got besides himself and boom fall flat on thee face, waking my late ass up.

Eye was publicly humble, thanking God and in private falling to my knees for Adam and Steve; Steve is Eve with a haircut, tamed bush, deeper asshole. Fuck like a man, talk like a man, bouncing in booty holes with plastic strap ons.

Chile, ain't doing that shit to me.

Eye was sucking a Niggah's dick. Closed all the blinds in the day light even dropped down the curtains and tied them closed to keep out the sunlight.

Vagabonds in all our splendor. Night crawlers. Carnivores. Lovers of flesh, weak flesh, love/hate utter summoned catastrophe.

One of the seven churches had my soul again. Bouncing in my waves with a ray of light instead of hope.

Light never pierces the dark in places lacking hope, mustard seeds and the Holy Ghost. Sure, everybody is a Temple, but not every Temple has a vacancy. Some of them far and in between have up No Vacancy Signs, Foreclosure and Land up for Sale signs. Bad economic times hit harder than a prostitute's pockets when niggahs didn't even have enough money to buy pussy.

That's when you know things were fucked up. So we out on the block more now, shit ain't nothing to do. Working all the time kept me driving my car paying the Florida Tolls, taking a bagged lunch to work for a payroll check.

Now the government fucked up everybody's bank account with a Trojan Horse and numbers fucking up people getting laid off and some jobs won't hire you with a criminal background when they hired family under the table with criminal backgrounds and laughed at our black asses when we walked out the door.

"Don't worry we'll call you!" the Cubans and Caucasians say when you're black with a name like James Rodriguez. They throw your application away after you shake their hands, thanking them for their time. Bitch they knew you were married into the Cuban family. All that nappy ass neck hair bitch we don't have hair like that.

Our shit lay down the minute water touches it.

Now eye'm jobless on the block more now, shooting craps again, making that old school money and blaming it on the white man and then the alcohol.

The Noriega Factor enthralled me. Niggah gotta walk picking up pennies now. Fill Zephyrhills bottles now. Couldn't throw punk Lincoln's away any more. Gotta save those tarnished rusty tasting/smelling pennies. Don't leave 'em in the room too long. Liable to leave a stench.

And what did eye do with my free time? *Lay* on my ass; jack my dick; fuck my asshole with _____'s dildo she don't think eye know about; wash it off, secretly pop lock and drop it to Beyonce's Single Ladies and crank it up to Ciara to prepare me for Janet's dance routines eye did day in and day out exercising to stay in shape.

Wear her panties while watching TV and still looked in the mirror looking like the Rock's cousin, the one daddy never told his wife about.

Eye was job hunting with two books out, online keeping up the shade and still had a business mind blundering business savvy.

With off brand niggahs something always came up when they wanted my pussy but eye dropped everything for those Trades getting all up in it, kiss my pussy and beat it out, bitch.

If a niggah wasn't working he didn't get to fuck me but come with a salary and a career, not pay check to paycheck, Pay Day Advanced niggahs.

Courting doctors, massaging the elderly man's feet, pimping these lips to the thugs. Python and good asshole to the elite.

Eye had two NBA stars when my second book came out. Both were fighting each other over me, couldn't stand each other publicly.

He wanted my asshole.

He wanted me to be a side line Hoe.

Was gonna give me loot, money and a beach front condo.

Eye rode that dick, made it spit and took $2500 and said, "*Hell*, No! The King of Erotica ain't up for Lease or Rent. Take mortgage in this pussy but on my terms, my way, or the high way. You'll be filing Bankruptcy fucking with me niggah. To breathe in my presence has a hefty price tag."

NBA balls and NBA dick chasing the author. The author yawning in front of them on secret dinner dates. Check my watch more than eye kiss or pat your dick. Niggah you tired. So's your dick. Ahem, next!

Best believe they paid me beautifully and paid my asshole/slash pussy handsomely.

When eye'm promoting books eye'm Dapharoah69 but my alter ego had a hot pussy and my name was Ying Yang at that point. Not anymore, but back then, on my way to the top, yes.

My skin was black but my cum's white. Eye go hard, eye go soft. Suck to get it up and once eye'm bouncing on it he couldn't keep it up, keep up, panting, gasping and shit like he was having a heart attack. Or he wanted me to stick my finger in his asshole when eye ride that candy shop/chop shop dick.

This was my downfall with men. Telling myself eye didn't mix business with pleasure and the minute a cute face with a cute smile came along eye was a puddle of piss waiting to be mopped up.

Ugh! When my Top turned out to be a secret bottom eye was grossed out. Some say eye shouldn't be mad at him. Because he was what eye needed, but eye wasn't a dyke. Eye didn't have sex with a man who took dick like me. Don't ask me why! It's none of your business!

Eye wasn't bumping booty holes and damn sure wasn't using double ended dildos doing that ass to ass shit. With me eye'm competitive so it would be more like ass vs. ass to me. And eye was a tall bottom. Sexy, tall ass bottom with long arms, long fingers, long tongue and long legs. Wrap around a niggah twice. Eye would bump the other vs. ass bitch right on her goddamn neck.

Only room for one beyotch in the sheets.

Eye was the bitch in the bedroom; which in all actuality was a purchased for two weeks hotel room.

That's the liar of the Trades. Men who have sex with men and don't think they are gay, are on the low, got girlfriends and wives and they only fuck you when they are horny, ain't getting it at home or their women counterparts put a lock on the pussy, making them sleep on the couch. That's when Trades come out to play.

Eye broke a rule falling in love with a Trade. Trades never put their faces online in photos. They find a rapper that fits their personality and use the rapper's picture in it's place.

This particular Trade fit the bill of what eye was looking for. Unattached sex. Eye write books. No time to be tied down. Fuck me good. Get your nut. Keep that cum off my face that's reserved for my main niggah when eye decide to read applications. Keep it business. Eye was like bestselling author Mary B. Morrison, eye wasn't taking care of no grown ass man.

I loved hard. Niggah was all up in deep when he saw me on my grind, taking pictures with my fans and handling my shit. Now he wanted to be something other than a Fuck Stop.

He was a secret bottom disguised as a Top. The worst kind, eye couldn't stress this enough. Versatile, good pussy niggah with somewhat acceptable cock. Tasting that Niggah's asshole made me smack more than drinking a fruity V8. Those days tomatoes were *fruity* now.

Taking booty hair from my teeth. Goddamn, niggah shave your ass. All that goddamn hair. Despite his flaw he was a bad, bad niggah always listening to that she's a bad, bad bitch song on You Tube with Janet Jackson images all over it. He had Derek Jeter's complexion. Loved pumping inside my sponge with his muscle cumming all up inside me.

Made that niggah skeet a hot nut. Two second violation in the paint. Out of bounds, overhead throw.

My Kobe Bryant complexioned ass bottom niggah set up the game winning shot. My ass got feet. They're called My Hips. And eye had this Top niggah chopped, chopped, screwed, screwed. When eye gave him this hot mouth, he fired up a blunt for a contact high. And when eye laid this booty hole on Dick Shaft Boulevard he smoking cigarettes calling up his homeboy on my cell phone saying he think he found The One.

"Um, no. Dick wasn't that good. My loyalty was still to God, despite my sexual escapades. Then eye was loyal to me and my career next.

Eye grip his chest and talk to my niggah at times, seeing where his head was at. The little head deep in the clouds so eye wasn't concerned with that. Half the time he stuttering with words, other times his eyes narrowed and mouth wide open like he retarded.

My booty cheeks bouncing on the roof of his delicious nuts. Sweat trailing his balls. A sweat's single tear colliding down his left ball, surpassing the dotted moisture. Down the split between his legs it goes. Cleansing and rinsing his asshole.

"Oh, shit!" He grabbed both ass cheeks, slapping noises filling our ears faster than the air. Into your eyes deeply eye stare. Control my spine. Dig me out. Eye'm throbbing all over. Eye kiss his moistened lips. He's all up in my face, choking me.

"Ride this dick."

And he still called me his wife's name and tried to take it back.

That was the day eye stopped having casual sex.

That was the day eye told myself eye would never do that again.

And eye meant it.

For the moment.

So he was pimpin' me and the entire time eye thought eye was getting over tricking this niggah into a relationship without confirming or actually asking. Setting my heart up for disappointment and thought eye was invincible. Eye had ill intentions and so did he, though we never discussed it. But the common denominator in our monitored goals was doomed from the get go.

When you monitor and schedule your goals instead of listing them then something isn't right in the Kingdom. Shit blew up in my face. Now eye look like a fool when he got the ass, got me to pay a few bills and hit the road without a return call or a post card.

Fell off the face of the earth. He wound up the victor. But eye'ma Pharoah! Well, eye thought eye was. Got fucked by the peasant and he ran off with a percentage of my royalty check. Probably fucking and dressing up the next niggah. Pretending to be a baller. Losing to a niggah named Victor.

Eye spell *Hay Sus* J-E-S-U-S! Because that's all eye need.

And eye stopped going to church and fellowshipping sucking his Temple till eye swallowed Mt. Saint Helen.

Eye covered my face, shamed, tears falling hard. Eye lowered myself to my knees, my face in my hands.

Eye thought eye was using him and he used me.

And eye rushed outside, up the block. Eye ran and eye ran, ran as fast as eye could, the cold air against my face and eye ran till eye saw some bushes and eye ran through them, twigs slapping me in the face, branches hanging low bumping my legs and ankles and arms but eye kept running.

And eye fell to my knees, and prayed and eye prayed for God to forgive me for *turning* away from him, getting embedded with the weakness of my flesh.

Eye cried for the old and the new, privately, didn't tell a soul. The Trade's dick was good while it lasted, but blinded by it eye was no more.

Eye had to make some changes. Eye had to stop giving up my sweet nectar to just any niggah with a big dick and a smile.

Once it started to rain, soaking my clothes eye ran back to the Trade's place and packed my things. Called up a friend in another state and he bought me a ticket, since he worked for the airline, and once eye arrived in Massachusetts he was right there to scoop me in a polished Hummer.

We embraced. "Pharoah, keep getting in shit, huh?"

"Well eye'm human."

"You're a recognizable face. You gotta stop getting with bum dudes, Pharoah."

"Eye know, man."

He grinned, handing me a Budweiser. "Bottles up, Niggah."

We clanked bottles. "Yea. Bottles up, *Mane*."

"Eye paid for your things to be shipped to me, till you find out where you're going."

"Eye'm going back home. Getting ready to put my third book out."

"Whatever you wanna do dawg its cool with me. Eye got money to burn and more to spend. So it's no thang, really."

"Eye'll pay you back."

He took my hand. "*Mane,* just write those books! You're setting the world on *fire*! You're the real deal and you got it, Pharoah! Ain't nobody fucking with your books."

Eye smiled. "Thanks."

It felt good to always have that one good friend who was your moneyed guardian angel. Moving away from that city as far away as eye could travel, staying temporarily, for 3 days, in Boston was a good thing. Had a chance to recoup, focus on growing up and reinvent myself and my image.

And while eye was there eye focused on writing and never went to a store, a mall or the post office. Eye stayed low in my homeboy's crib, his wife cooking me breakfast and making sure eye wrote my book undisturbed.

When eye did move back home with Mama it was bitter sweet, because she didn't know eye actually moved out. Eye left to live with the Trade and told Mama eye was gonna be gone for a few weeks. But wound up staying three days. Eye wrote The King of Erotica 3 in three days, and eye was back home on the fourth day.

"So you back home?" Mama asked with an attitude.

Eye looked at her. "Yea."

"Eye was beginning to think you moved out. Shit, looks like eye didn't get my wish."

"Eye'm going to write this book, Mama."

She looked at me and eye looked at her and retreated to my room in Camp Clara.

But not for long.

Eye was glad eye went through things and survived them. Eye grew up real fast in the year of 2009. At this point eye openly talked about contracting HIV from a three year relationship, and influenced over 14,000 plus people on Facebook to get tested through my status box testimony.

Over 3,000 people have my status box alerts to their phone. When eye hit "submit" 3,000 muthafuckahs got my words instantly.

Now eye could talk to fans candidly and openly, being as blunt as my books, being real and raw. They love me for that, especially my home girl Eboni King. She always hit me up on Facebook when she want me to keep it one hundred (percent real) and every time eye do.

Eye didn't worry about haters. Haters were late bitches with too much cum on the breath. Sucked dick effectively and still got nowhere. Fucked and still wound up broke, bitter and BGC forum pressed into the wee hours in the morning hiding behind a Beyawnsay default picture and an I Am Sasha Fierce STAN card on your HTML signature bearing your face bitch Beyawnsay didn't know your late ass existed in the world.

Eye keep my head high through anything now. Eye don't bow for nothing, no matter what people do or say. When eye do bow eye'm praying for God to stop me from snapping a bitch's neck. That's how eye maintain self control. Eye've already been publicly ashamed and mentally tamed. Eye'm over and past that. Bitch, do something new. That late shit ain't working, couldn't bring me down.

Now the level eye'm on was simple. If they working and could sponsor my career then we straight. Takes money to make money and eye make and spend money wisely.

Eye'm picking up pennies putting them in Zephyrhills bottles and eye was getting loose change from under the cushions of couches; and saving them too and at the end of the quarter eye am putting the coins in the bank and it all adds up towards something for my new book.

With Niggahs now, if they are too clingy eye stop them from getting some ass by telling them something came up (friend in the hospital, death in the family, tired from 14 hours of writing, you understand) and for the *other* Niggah with all the money, buying my planet tickets, taking care of booking fees, eye would drop everything for the dick. He snapped eye stood at attention. When he giving you $1,500, $3,500 investing in your career then baby money talks.

You' swear he had WD-40 for nut. His seeds kept this Nassau, Bahamian asshole moist and lovingly marinated, and juicy. Put this wet ass before a mirror it'd fog up anticipating daddy. Eye loved when he grinded inside me *making* one hundred dollars bills rain all over me, even sticking to my wet booty cheeks.

Now for the year 2010 and beyond eye am Ying X. Eye dropped yang from Ying, seeing things differently, using my brain in business, keeping my draws up and my legs closed.

Didn't need to look back to see how Yang was living. Eye'd turn to salt.

Ain't gonna get me a second time, Satan. Take off the ski mask, game's over, you're not funny, you ain't no thug bitch give up the jealousy ghost.

Put down your Gat like you're try'na rob me. Gun ain't loaded anyway. Lions roar they don't meow or bark. Nor say Moo, so there you have it. Fake ass girl. True thugs and gangsters don't have Beyonce or Lady Gaga on their iPods.

You could rob me but one thing Satan could never take away.

Despite my pitfalls.

Eye'm still a bestselling author.

We're you ever a $tripper?

Lord Jenning$

(U)
N
A
$
T
Y
Boy!

In a myriad of thoughts about where eye'm going and my future, I stood at the fridge, filling my glass with liquid. The room temperature of the glass gradually cooled as the cold water turned it from full (atmosphere) to half empty (Shore, ocean and half of the atmosphere). Then the house phone rang and all the phones were on *one* line, Mama's line.

I answered. It was Tom, with his fine ass. But he's slow as hell so that wouldn't work with a niggah like me.

Tom said somebody stole the church's money.

"*Nooooo!*" I'm stunned into silence. I forget all about my cold water.

"Yes, sur! Initially they counted about 2 G's, but 1.1 G's has been accounted for by the secretary."

"Oh my God, dawg," I said, bothered by this. *And they wonder why eye'm late paying tithes.* "Damn, yo. Why the secretary counting money? That ain't in her job description!"

"She's the accountant and the secretary."

"*And* the Pa$tor's wife, people keep forgetting that bullshit, dawg!"

"I know I keep forgetting. I guess she gotta take a little here and there to set up in another account."

"I know, man. And they wonder why I put two quarters in the collection plate."

"I know right. You got me doing that shit."

I said, "Hey, what can eye say. Eye put common sense in the plate. When I *was* going to church I used to drop two quarters in the tithe plate. I did this consistently. They know who's donating and who's not; they know who's stealing and who's getting over in church. But the niggah who putting in two quarters amongst all this green we gotta find him. They called me to the office one day."

"No," my friend moaned. "And said what?"

"Yea, they called me to the office behind my Mama's back, questioning her child about what's going on in my house yet Mama thinks she knows more about me than myself. Ok, Mama. Keep thinking that!"

"What?"

"Yea, man…"

The Pator' Chamber

I was remembering that time, when I was 19 years old and was so lost, confused and full of hate, bitterness and darkness and I never told a soul. I hid behind my smile. I used to love making people laugh because it kept me off my problems, and they were disturbing ones.

The images came flooding back in retrospection.

Pa$tor said, "Ya'll that broke? You can only put two quarters in the collection plate? Why half of a whole dollar. That ain't good economics, son."

"You're right. It's English. Two quarters mean you need to get some common sense, get it. Two quarters are in common so I ain't hearing you."

"I never did like your mouth."

You didn't say that when I sucked your dick the other day and nearly vomited because it was a stank dick at that.

"And I never liked *you*."

"God doesn't like unruly children."

Eye narrowed my eyes. "I'm a teenager, and God don't like horny Pator that cheat on their brain dead wives with young teenage boys, bitch!"

"The Lord wants his ten percent," he snapped like a fish outta water and I grinned at his uneasiness.

I stood up. "And God just told you that?"

"Yea, he did."

"Bullshit."

Sarcastically, I'm looking around the office, eyes sliding past expensive carpeting, half done wainscoting chipping at the corners (termites) and real lamps and real plants but out in the church the carpet was made from cheap, fake synthetic and was so low to the floor it felt like you were walking on concrete and fake flowers and fake pictures of a Caucasian looking Jesus beaming down over the congregation (when the J wasn't invented during Jesus heyday, so how was his name Jesus?) and the ceiling fans were the ones Home Depot sold on the clearance shelf.

"Son."

"God? You here?" I asked, ignoring him. My heart was pumping. I knew the day would come when he would talk to me or show himself. Why should pator be the only avenues to God when the Bible states Jesus was the mediator, not Pator. That goes to show that when Niggahs get a little power it goes to their heads. They think they're Batman or Superman yet in bed his favorite game to play was called Lower the Submarine. Just wished he washed that muthafuckah!

I started to walk around, rubbing my arms like I'm cold.

"God? You hear me? Talk to me, father. Please…"

Nothing.

I turned to the pa$tor out of anger. "Why God ain't talking to me?"

"You can't question him," he appeased and it didn't appease a goddamn thing.

"I didn't question Him! I'm questioning YOU. WHY ain't he TALKING TO ME?"

"He only talks through me."

"Bullshit. But you preach that God loves us all, that he hears all his children."

"He does."

"BULLSHIT! IS GOD HERE?"

"Yes, Son!" He was getting nervous, trying to calm me down.

"Good. I gotta get some shit off my chest." I started yelling. "GOD! GOD WHERE ARE YOU!"

Pa$tor was nervous. Now he was worried about his image. In a desperate attempt to shut me up, he rushed up to me, slapping me like a prostitute.

"Niggah shut up!" Small beads of sweat started popping across his wrinkled forehead. "The congregation out there...they can hear you."

I pushed him off me. "You ain't my fucking daddy! Keep your hands off me, bitch. GOD! Where you at? You walk over me to tell this grimy niggah about me? Why not tell me, God? Whisper in my ear let me know you exist, Lord?"

His eyes bulged out his head. "Pharoah shut up! Before I punch you in the face. You're out of control."

"Out of your control, *that* I will agree on."

"What is your problem?"

"I got some questions for God."

"Such as?"

"My Daddy ain't never been there for me nor did he teach me to play ball. Why, God? When I was 11, 12 and 13 Mama always smiled through her problems, worked hard and that built my confidence. Then she betrayed that one night she thought I was sleep and I heard her break down through those cheap walls. Asking God to give her strength to raise her children. That it was hard for a single mother to survive in this world. My own Mama lied to me. Everything wasn't all right. I had a false sense of security. And when your Mama lies to you things change but I'm her child. I was programmed through church and older family and teachers to never question her. To do as she say and half the shit she asked me she didn't do her goddamn self."

"And you shouldn't question her."

"SHE'S NOT GOD! So I can question her if I respect her. Why can't I ask her questions?"

"Because your type of questions aren't suitable for a child to ask."

"But I have an old soul, man. I'm 19 years old! I am NOT a child. I have questions and people can't just keep pushing my feelings under the rug. I have feelings too! Because I'm a teenager means my feelings mean nothing?"

"Pharoah. That's the way it is. Your mother is the boss."

"She's my mother. She's not my boss. If she's my boss where is my paycheck for keeping all her kids so she can work? She owes me some *serious* back pay. Why can't I file taxes on the work I do around the house, cooking and cleaning tirelessly like eye'm some cunt about to deliver triplets?"

"You have internal issues."

"I got questions!" I was tired of talking to him. I wanted to talk to the Creator, GOD. "GOD WHERE YOU AT?"

"You can't test the Lord or question him!"

"Bull. Shit! Why are you lying to me? You question him all the time. *What*...you're better than me because you wear a robe?"

"I'm not lying."

"Yes you are! What are you not telling me about religion?"

"Why are you so fucking smart?"

"Because I read a lot of books. I read books and don't tell anybody. I pretend to hate reading books in public so people don't suspect anything. Plus I write in my journals every day. All my anger and frustration with this sick planet is outlined. I don't wanna live anymore! I didn't ask to be here. I think my parents are SELFISH for bringing me here to this place. I was perfectly fine in the dark of nothingness in her womb. I was just fine!"

"No one asked to be here, Son."

"I am not your son. Stop calling me that."

"You have to calm down."

"I have to stay black in the ghetto and die. That's what I'm taught. That's what these failed black men around Perrine and Homestead and Goulds are exhibiting. Grown ass men robbing each other, making babies with all those Hoes, barely taking care of them or their seeds. These dumb ass niggahs live in the 'Hood, picking pussy over the welfare of their kids and got the fucking NERVE to say they are real niggahs doing real things. Dumb fucks. How you're a real niggah and couldn't even give your baby mama a ride to the store because she refused to hold your dope and be your goddamn punching bag and door mat? Niggahs got the game fucked up, yet throw a fit when a niggah come through and treat his Mama the way he treats his baby mama. Got her catching the bus with your damn bad ass kids in tow, carrying a thousand grocery bags. I see the look of hurt and betrayal on her face. If ANY niggah do that to my goddamn sister eye'm taking his ass off the planet my goddamn self and send his mama a Thanksgiving card Federal Express. Niggahs would rather buy a car with beats and rims over a home for their baby and baby Mama. Don't talk to me about calming down. I don't wanna end up like that!"

"Pharoah. Calm down. This is my last time saying it."

"And if I don't? What are you gonna do about it? Whip my ass? Call my Mama? Tell her I been a bad, bad boy? You do that I will tell her you been touching all on me since I was 14, creep."

"Tell her what you want! She won't believe you."

"Adults love saying shit like that. They won't believe you. Two of my older cousins once said that when I told them to save me from my ex step daddy raping me. I was shaking with fear, thinking I was going to be removed from that home. They said what you just said. They also said my grandma killed Uncle Al, their daddy. Who gives a fuck! I had nothing to do with that. I wasn't even born yet. Why should I have to suffer for that?"

He tried to hug me and I kicked him in his balls. I pushed past him, snatched open the doors and said, "Maybe God is in the main assembly."

People were seated, talking and opening Bibles. Getting ready for the Pa$tor to drain their wallets and purses dry this week.

I pushed through the doors.

And startled them all.

THE MAIN A$$EMBLY

"God, are you in here! Where are you? You talk to the Pa$tor but not me?"

I walked up the aisle, looking all around the church. Causing a disruption inside a controlled, programmed environment and didn't give two fucks what they had to say. Talking about everybody and everything but themselves and their own individual fucked up lives.

"GOD WHERE ARE YOU? I DON'T WANNA BE HERE ANYMORE!"

To say I was angry and loudly cursing and they were in shock was putting it mildly.

"God!" The tears fell. "I can't do this anymore. I want to live. I want to be Pharoah. I got kicked out the Army. My life is nothing. I work at Turkey Point, and I am tired of the Outage. I am losing myself in watching over my siblings. Cooking and cleaning like I'm a woman. I'd rather cut the grass. Wait, I do that, too!"

I fell to my knees, looking at my hands on my lap. People looked at me and didn't utter a word.

"God, can you hear me? I thought you would *never* forsake me. Or is it all lies Pator tell to get your money. Are you even real, God? Are you a myth? Like Greek gods, everybody knows Zeus ain't real."

I was let down. God didn't come. He didn't say anything.

Like Elvis, GOD has left the building. Was he ever in it? I slowly stood up.

I glared at them. "You know what? Fuck church, you crack head looking recovering motherfuckahs!"

Kill the lights; they didn't utter a word or a Word. The church body was *too* stunned by my outburst, totally unexpected.

Sometimes you had to cripple your opponents to win the game. And they would be some paraplegics by the time I was done.

The idea, the image and the spectacle of church was ruined.

"You know what yea I'm bisexual goddamn it and I am a real ass niggah; and *sometimes* I can be a bitch. Are ya'll real? We broke as fuck in Goulds and all up in the church like Sunset Boulevard. This ain't no Sunset Boulevard or Hollywood. Those rich white people don't care about us. And ya'll talking all that back biting ass shit. Tell me in my goddamn face because I am not scared of neither one of you motherfuckahs."

"He is so ghetto, he ignorant," somebody said and I put my hands on my hips and slayed for the Gods they served because it *wasn't* Jehovah…The Pa$tor had us on our knees, praying to.

Pa$tor' Dumb Ass thought *he* was God. People worshiping the Pa$tor, and not Jehovah. Eye knew it and they knew eye knew it.

"You gonna say something, looking at me all messed up potty mouth child," she went on, standing up and eye took a few steps in her direction.

"When you kissed your niggah, bitch, you taste my cum?"

"What? Oh my God!"

"He ate me out my ass, too, swollen mouth bitch!"

"Kick him out the church!"

"His mouth!"

I lovingly looked in her eyes. "Coming from the mouth of the bitch who sucked her husband from my dick just a few short days ago?"

She grabbed her purse, ducked her head and ran like a bat out of Hell out the exit door. Boom bye, bye, bitch.

A few people were leaving, but others were too curious to know the other's business if I exposed it and they forget they are a part of the collective whole of the congregation so their shit getting exposure, too, that's how the Media worked anyway.

I went on. Church has hurt me for the last time. Telling me God was try'na tell him somethin' 'bout me. Let God tell me for himself. I wanted God to tell me about me. Why go to a man that has sex with me with my business?

I got some shit off my chest once and for all, "I want my money back. All the money I gave with a cheerful heart. Half that money I got from turning tricks. Yea that's right. Adults paid for this, not my peers, not people my age. GROWN MUTHAFUCKAHS! Using rent money and utility money to get into my body and eye shouldn't have given you jack shit. I gave you common sense from that money, not ten percent. I should call the Better Business Bureau on this goddamn establishment. Church is a joke. Shit started happening when I got saved, losing money, Pa$tor is rich and I'm hurt, fucked and broke and I'm not even 20 years old yet!"

Pa$tor grabbed my arm and I pushed his ugly ass on the floor.

"Don't touch me. You talk all that homosexuality is wrong bullshit but you fucked me in your wife's bed while she played with her pussy. What the fuck? And I'm going to hell? Where the hell you think you and that slut wife of yours is going? Ya'll been sucking and fucking me since eye was 14. But nobody wanna talk about that shit!"

The church was destroyed.

"What?"

"Pastor, that true?"

"Oh my God!"

"I am in shock!"

I looked the shocked harlots in the face and said, "I know ya'll ain't popping off at the mouth. Ya'll wanna throw stones? Ya'll wanna talk about how the Pa$tor got his rocks off with me?"

Oh, they quiet now. Retreat! Retreat those scared eyes yelled at me. Withdrawing the troops. I had arsenals for that funky ass.

"You popping off?" I pointed at an elder. "I had you." I pointed at his wife, "I ate your pussy 'cause you said your husband can't eat fish cause he secretly sucking my dick!" I pointed at him and his brother, "I watched you two fuck each other so don't go there on me, bitch! Nasty bitches! Ya'll in love with each other and you got the same Mama and Daddy."

And the big girl running for the exit door.

"NO BITCH!"

I ran behind her fat, wobble, wobble, shake it, shake it ass.

"Don't run out that door."

She tried me, pushing it open and I snatched her by her wig and pulled her ass back to me, looking like toppling dominoes on a checker board.

"Don't run. Tell everyone you were my school teacher. In high school. When I was a mighty, mighty Spartan! You used to tell me when I turned 18 you were going to suck and fuck me to sleep because I was fine. You were even at my graduation. I was still 17, a few days before my 18th birthday in 1995 and I snuck out the house and you made me nut eight times that night. After the 5th I was shooting blanks, though."

"Pharoah. Shut up! You lying!"

"I'm lying? Tell these nosey bitches in this corrupt church. I'm not going to lose no sleep."

"SHUT UP!"

"I'm dating your brother right now bitch. Want me to bring his slow ass in here and confirm my story?"

"I hate you!"

"And my dick hates your buck ass teeth. Always grazing my shit. And this folks is why I gave two quarters and not ten percent of my mortgage, lights, water bill, child support check, payroll check to give to these greedy ass people. Ya'll been had! Ha ha, not me! Enjoy your communion. Eat that bread, drank that wine you whoremonging stealing ass hypocrites!"

And I spun on my heel and threw up the peace sign, walking my fine ass up outta that hell hole of a church.

Been robbed blind for years by a Pa$tor preaching that same bullshit he preached ions ago, and still getting ya'll money. They need to run background and finger print checks on Pa$tors, Elder$ and Preacher$.

Church ain't and never will condition me.

When ya'll g'on wake up?

Σ

Tom didn't wanna finish talking about the church's money coming up missing after I told him that story. But, hesitantly he finished talking. Good.

I said, "...That's crazy. Now they stealing in church and want me to believe in organized religion. Niggah. Bad enough I done fucked half the church and all of them were Pastors, elders, older motherfuckers who haven't been fucked in years and looked at me and wished they were 27, 28 and 29 again. One Pa$tor told me, "If I was 27 again, niggah, I would *fuck* you to sleep and make you *nut* on my chest."

I was so turned on he didn't have to wish because he activated my flesh and made me weak in the knees, some SWV shit.

And I made him shoot for the stars all night and misfired, skeeting on his sheets. Didn't want that old ass nut on me, oh hell, No!

Tom laughed so hard he choked. "You crazy!"

"They stealing, I coulda kept my $400."

"Niggah, stop lying! You only gave them forty dollars, all in quarters in those quarter rollers."

Now I laughed. "I know."

"You gave out a lot of common sense."

"Ha, I know!"

"Well shit saying I gave $400 to the church sounded appealing, all about the image. And why are you counting my money for me before I put all those quarters in the tithe plate?"

"Tithe plate, collections plate, whatever."

I said, "I remember last week. You took out about seven $20's, thinking nobody saw you..."

"I had to come up with $140 extra for rent, shit."

We were giggling like hell. Tickled me pink. Niggah silly as fuck. Ya'll ain't got no dawg like that, just make you laugh when he look at a roach.

"You dumb!" eye said.

"When you get an eviction notice and 30 days to leave you realize the government forfeited and reneged on your 40 acres and a mule you had on lease for a year in your sister's name because you were a convicted felon. Even if they gave all us blacks our 40 acres and mules we'd look like complete jack asses when they hit us with all that inheritance and property tax. And niggahs gonna sell out on each other for that ass I meant mule.

"I hear you."

"*Look*, I gotta go. Gotta get ready for school. Financial aid office keeps calling me about paying for fees. *Damn* I just started school."

"They're hating."

"Yea, and my Cuban friend Juan ain't paid a fee or a bill in a year and they ain't called HIM to the fucking office yet."

"You know they look out for their own."

"And how I owe the school when my Financial aid goes directly to the school? How I owe money? They didn't even give me a receipt for spending my government money!"

"They crooked as fuck."

"I'ma call the police and file a complaint about that. Juan goes to school for *free*. I haven't been here three weeks and they teasing my asshole about some goddamn payments."

"You crazy."

"Bye.

I hung up and called my homeboy Cedrick.

"Pharoah?"

"Yes. Let's make this money. I wanna be a stripper. What do I gotta do?"

"I am so pleased. A whole new world is about to open up for you. You're on the next level. They ain't gonna be able to take you, Pharoah. And you write?"

"Shake it, gimme those dollars. Let's go!"

I still wound up calling Tom back, being nosey about the church's money.

My thought process about stripping was a very inner coastal, discombobulating thing. Because I was incarcerated by society's expectations. There I was living it up to society's expectations when I haven't even lived up to my own. And at this point in my life I was a ghoul of a goblin. An egotistical, barbaric ghost rocking the boy next door birthday suit and a sassy, masculine attitude, but nothing too flamboyant. An oxymoron of myself. Playing straight and was one quiet bisexual muthafuckah. I was afraid of the light. I was a vampire of my sexuality; a slave, held at its fledgling and the thought of leaving the darkness sucked the moisture from my lungs and I was thirsty.

Satan knew this.

Oh he knew that shit well.

Promi$cuity

I couldn't even go to the grocery store without fine ass men, men that were my type, athletic types in gym shorts wearing no goddamn draws hounding me. One Liberty City Niggah asked me what time it was and he had on a watch.

Another asked to use my phone when he just got off *his* phone. Claiming his phone died. So I let him use it. No one answered so he gave it back and we went our separate ways.

Later on that night, just after 11 P.M. my phone ring and I answer and it's him, talking 'bout, "I had to call my cell to get your number. I hope you're not mad. I think you're fine as fuck. I'm gonna cut right to it. I wanna fuck you. I'm married. Got two kids. Don't give a fuck. Help me get this nut."

I hung up.

Then they walked up to you and you saw that huge dick print and they semi hard talking to me, couldn't take their eyes off my lips.

And they always nodded at me and I was hard as hell, secretly sneaking in the bushes with them and making them cum all over the wild grass.

If I was as promiscuous as I was back during my self-hatred years, I would have been rolling around the sack with them, validating myself. I would get lost in it, like I had before. Try'na breathe but suffocated instantly when niggahs got up, got dressed and left without a Bye, see you later or a tip.

And even around that time I made out with a few niggahs in their cars. Most niggahs loved to be inside me on the back seat of the Impala or the Charger or the Chevy with the police tints and defunct cartoons airbrushed on his trunk.

One married niggah pulled over on the side of the turnpike, turned on the hazard lights, lift the Hood and he fucked me for two full hours on the back seat with those police tints.

Then I vanished without a trace. *Niggahs* didn't know my name, place of address or my goddamn phone number so I didn't lose any sleep but I did wake the fuck up eventually and decided that I wanted and needed more in my life. I became a ghost to those niggahs. Bitches, too.

I was too afraid to lose the mask, convincing people it's my face when it wasn't even Halloween. So tricks and treats were unnecessary, but that didn't stop me from doing tricks for the treatment of dead presidents. I got fired from Turkey Point. They said I was stealing and I wasn't. Stealing what? Toilet paper. What the fuck. They just wanted my black ass gone. So I left.

Niggah couldn't find a decent job, so I applied to be a Security Guard and was hired a week later. I HATED it! *Being* a security guard at Cutler Landings wasn't cutting it because it was some overnight work and I was growing weary of it. So I put in a change of post with Pro Guard Security, and they moved me to the Florida City Outlet Mall. Gave me a military type hat and some tight ass pants and long sleeved shirt. Eye was walking around all day, bored as fuck because the outlet Mall was slow as hell, located under Jesus sandals (Homestead, just before the start of the road to the Keys). I enjoyed the job now, eating up the food in the

Food Court and buying up all the football cards and collecting them.

I noticed every time I walked past Rack Room shoes a short, sexy bitch with nice tits kept running up to the window waving at me. Initially, I ignored her, just doing my job. I never chased Hoes and I really didn't sweat bitches. All that "You're cute" shit didn't work on me. If I went to the mall with a group of niggahs while 6 niggahs rapping at the same girl or the girl and her girls Pharoah was in the back picking imaginary dirt out my nails and niggahs got mad when Hoes bypassed them and came right up to me because Hoes hated to be ignored. I wound up yawning, looking up and saying, "Naw I'm cool. I'll pass," and nine times outta ten me and the Hoes went at it till I wound up fucking one of them just to shut the Hoe up.

But one day the Rack Room shoes broad ran up to the big window and her tits looked so good under that tight ass black shirt and she had a nice ass and those tight ass pants were eating that pussy up, nice chunky monkey in the center so eye was like fuck Ben and Jerry's.

As much as eye tried to hide it, my dick was hard. Hadn't had pussy in a few months and the season for niggahs that knew how to fuck was lacking so I hung up the freak a Niggah jersey and hollered at the bitch.

So I went in the store and said, "Are you ok?"

She was holding her breath. She had to be about 5 feet 4. I was 6 feet 3 and a half inches. I towered over her.

"Why do you say that?"

"Because you're always running up to the window when I walk by."

"I just think you're cute."

"And so are you. Hungry?"

"Sure. What you'd have in mind?"

"The food court."

So I took her out to eat, and paid for her meal. Cost a pretty penny but she was a dime on her way to silver dollar status real fast. Very sweet, well together girl.

I invited her to my crib so Mom and my brothers could see my catch and they liked her instantly, especially Jarshawn.

She stayed out in the dining room playing spades with the family and I retired to my room, a little left out because she was more focused on them, but it was all good.

I turned off the lights, taking off my shirt, socks, and shoes. Left my pants unzipped. I lie down and fell asleep.

I was dog tired.

$$\Sigma$$

I felt someone straddling my ass.

Two warm hands caressing my back, making me smile in my sleep. Or maybe I was dreaming.

I opened my eyes and Hoe'nita had on one of my shirts, her weave dangling in her face. Her draws were off and her hot pussy wet on my ass cheek.

"Are you still sleeping?"

"No, I'm awake now."

"Are you really?"

"Yes. That pussy hot for me huh?"

"Hell, yea."

I turned over and pulled her to my lips. Her pussy of course. "Ride my face."

She held the head board, with those pretty nails. One by one they snapped off as I tongue fucked her, gripping her sides, controlling her spine.

"Oh my God! Eat my pussy, Pharoah!"

She felt so good on my tongue. The smell of pussy, the light salty taste, 56 calories per gram of fat. Those pretty titties bouncing, she looked down into my eyes, shuddering.

"I'm gonna cum."
I stuck my tongue in deeper.
"OH GOD!"

She came all over my lips, I swallowed, tongue fucking her deeper, handling her petite ass.

"Oh, shit!"

I handed her the dildo. "Fuck your ass with it."

"Pharoah, no...Oh God keep tongue fucking me."

I pushed her off me. I hated disobedient bitches. I was getting up.

"No, Pharoah," she said. She was grabbing my arm. "Torture my clit niggah."

"No."

"WHY?" she whined.

"I don't fuck an independent bitch. If I can't control it fuck you, take your stank ass home, bitch!"

"Pharoah!"

"What?"

She grabbed my dick and I slapped her hands.

"You can't afford that. Don't *touch*," eye said.

"Niggah fuck me!" she said, her pussy getting wetter.

"Damn, it's like that?"

"Hell yeah!"

"Ride my face and fuck yourself deep in the asshole with the goddamn toy!"

"But I don't have any lube!"

I wiped pre-cum from my dick and massaged it lightly on the toy.

"There you go." I lay down, spreading my legs. "Ride my face NOW!"

She got on my face, and my tongue got to work.

"Oh God you can eat pussy! Goddamn! FUCK!"

"Stick the toy in your ass!"

"I'm scared," she said, bouncing on my lips.

"Spread your asshole."

She did, and I slid my tongue repeatedly in and out her pussy. Pussy juice rolling down the sides of my face. I loved this nasty shit. I was a nasty niggah in bed, and didn't give a fuck.

I slowly slid the toy deep in her asshole, her body locking. I didn't care if it hurt her or not bitch take that dick.

"Focus on my tongue in your twat bitch!"

"Oh Pharoah oh Pharoah!"

I had the eight inch black plastic fuck deep in her tight virginal hole. I used to love fucking bitches in the ass for the first time.

She fell back and I let her fall. I pushed her legs back, fucking that ass with the toy.

"Oh, God!"

"Oh, God?"

"YES!"

I spanked her pussy, grinding in her ass with my dick. She didn't even know I pulled out the plastic and gave her this good ass beef.

"Oh, shit! Let me taste my pussy from your lips."

I picked up the toy and popped the top of her forehead. "Say please, Hoe."

"PLEASE!"

"Suck this toy while I get in this booty hole bitch."

She slurped on the toy, tasting her ass. I was fumbling with her clit with my thumb, sliding my middle finger deep in her pussy.

She put an arch in that back.

"I'm gonna cum again!"

"You are?"

"Yes."

"Want me to cum with you?"

"Yes, Daddy!"

I started pounding that asshole, pushing her legs back, putting all my weight on them.

"Oh shit I'm bout to nut!"

I pulled out and cum on her pretty face while she wet up my sheets.

I fell asleep right on top of her ass.

My dick deep in her pussy.

Being with her was going to be detrimental to my frame of mind.

First, she stayed the night with me and funny thing was she never went home. She moved in and didn't tell any of us, we were the slow ones.

She wormed her way into every aspect of my life, and I was so pussy whipped I thought it was love. I was making her fuck my dick day in and day out, sucking those titties, making her catch nut after nut after nut, her pussy juices running down my balls and the crack of my ass.

She was my obsession. I changed posts again and wound up securing some apartments in Leisure City. I would come to work at 8 p.m., manager checked me off and he hopped in his security car and hauled ass till I came back to work the next day. When my shift was over at 4 a.m. he didn't check me out. He trusted me to do that manually and I had.

But I was missing Hoe'nita and her pussy but what I didn't know was that she was fucking my 15 year old brother Jarshawn, turning his young ass out and Jarshawn and I would be fighting over her and I never understood why he would fight me over my girlfriend. She was fucking him under mama's roof in my bed without rubbers and laying down with me without rubbers and I always came deep in her pussy because I hated pulling out.

Thinking 'bout those tits turned me on and my dick was hard managing those boring ass apartments.

And when I did find out I had to hurt her but I didn't *let* her know I knew. I knew before Jarshawn told me over the phone when I wound up in jail. I walked in on them before and tip toed back out the house and never said a thing. I made them think they got over on me.

I was friends with the down low niggahs up in there and we were fucking up something.

Every night my weak flesh was bouncing on another low key Niggah's dick, making him nut, doing to him what his bitch wished she could do.

But they started falling in love with me and I wasn't having it so I cut 'em off, ignoring them.

One by one a niggah would walk up to the car offering me alcohol and weed to get in my draws.

NOPE!

Weakne$$ of the FleSh

One night, after I got off the phone with Hoe'nita, a tall, sexy ass dope boy came up to me.

"Pharoah, damn why you acting flaky with the ass."

"I'm good."

"My female ain't making a niggah nut. Sup with the pussy, niggah?"

"I'm cool. I got an ass, not a coochie."

He rubbed his dick, looking around. Nothing about him said GAY. You could stare at him and he would never give the slightest clue away, those were the kind of niggahs I got *down* with.

"Damn my shit brick."

I yawned, rolling up the window. He got in the passenger seat. "Get out, man!" I said. "I'm working."

"Why you doing me like this? I wanna fuck."

"No."

"Please, Niggah. You got some bomb asshole dude. Make me nut."

"NO!"

"Can I eat you out? Pop it on my tongue, niggah."

"Get out."

The passenger door opened and *another* niggah pulled him out. "That's my ass," he whispered, maintaining that on the low shit.

"Fuck off bitch! Pharoah is mine, fuck niggah!"

Oh, boy.

"Guys," I said. I didn't need this. Not tonight.

"I'll beat your ass, niggah."

He was punched in the face. They started fighting. I turned on my Mitsubishi Gallant and drove my ass home.

Wanted no part of that.

I drove to my God Mama Ronda's house. She stayed around the block and was one of the realest women you'd meet. She spoke her mind, has a nasty mouth and didn't give a shit.

"Damn you off early," she said.

"Yea, I am."

"You *ok*?"

"Yea."

"Go fix you something to eat. I got pig feet in there, I know you love them."

"Yea I do."

"You staying the night?"

"Yea, I am."

Her son came out the room. I was 19, he just turned 18. He had his shirt off, plaid shorts and no underwear.

"You staying the night, Pharoah?"

I barely looked at him. "Yea."

"You can sleep on the couch," Ronda said, yawning. "I'm going to bed."

She retired to her room and locked it. I made my way to the couch.

Homeboy said, "Naw, you ain't sleeping on no couch. I got room. Come on."

"Ok." I followed him to his room.

He closed and locked the door behind us.

I took off my shoes, keeping on my clothes. He got in the bed, and I got on the floor.

I curled up…going to sleep.

He sat up. Pharoah?"

"What?"

"Come up here, man."

"I'm good."

"I don't bite."

I got up and noticed he was under the cover. I got in the bed and turned my back to him.

I closed my eyes.

He came up behind me. I felt the warmth of his hard dick pressed on my ass.

"You know what time it is," he said, kissing the back of my neck.

And he ate me out till I was tender.

Then he fucked me all night long.

"I waited till my 18th birthday to fuck you," he said, kissing my lips, bouncing inside me. I was lost, deeper into the hatred I had for myself.

"I can't believe I'm finally getting this asshole."

He smiled the whole night through.

I hate you, Pharoah. I hate your faggot ass! I was thinking to myself.

Smiling at my reflection in the mirror.

Hating myself inside even deeper and darker.

$TRIPPER

I was afraid to be free, incarcerated in society's expectations derived from mixed religions.

On my way to the strip club for the first time, as an entertainer and debut stripper, I was an inferior fool at war with my heart (irrational), body (sexual), mind (intellectual but lacking common sense) and soul (The Holy Ghost).

When I did my audition I was a definite shoe in for the club's owner, Andy, 6 feet 8, Puerto Rican and Jamaican, temper out of this world with green eyes and long hair like a City of Roses pimp.

Yes, he was ALL THAT!

When a man's dick can make you feel like Julia Roberts then damn it Bob, the Price is Right, Bitch!

But before I get into that I gotta tell you about the Audition held at his house.

I have to convince him to hire me as a stripper.

And he wanted more than talent.

I actually auditioned at his house and realized he was a niggah in one of my college classes at City College, so we really hit it off big.

He said, "Can you dance?"

Can I? "Yes, Niggah. Can you fuck?"

"All night."
"Whatever. Anyways, yea I can dance."
"Ready to audition?"
"Yes."

He picked up the remote and put on some Uncle Luke "Its your Birthday" *hey* I popped it to the floor chanting CANCER!

Is it December, no bitch it's June 26th, 1977.

Go Pharoah!

He stopped the music and I froze in the doo doo brown position, looking over my shoulder.

"What?"

He was grinning. "Damn you got a nice ass."

"Thanks."

"My dick hard."

"I see."

"I don't want you to audition to that. Typical fags can pop to this. Don't require much. If you can strip to this, you will be hired at my club with top billing. You're finer and cuter than those other used washed up niggahs."

He turned on the big screen and pressed play.

Janet's "IF" video came on, women rising from the floor and men lowered by ropes from Chinese ceilings.

I looked at him. "I can't dance to this!"

"Impress me."

"Ok."

I stretched, arms in the air and when the beat dropped I did the entire video, from start to finish, doing everything Janet did, turned the same way she's turned, facing him, the TV behind me and his mouth was open the entire time.

When the song ended he was on his feet clapping, and not once had I stripped off anything.

He took me in his arms and fucked me all over the house.

In love with my talent, not me or my body. But I didn't know that at the time. He would also become my secret, abusive, controlling lover.

My hot, double fudge, passionate, secretly sexy down low big dick aggressively older tender roni lover.

The first day eye took the stage was a scary one. And it wasn't really my first time. This was going to be somewhat of a trail run. To see what eye'm made of. To see if eye could hang with the big dawgs of the strip world. So most of the strippers really didn't take me seriously. I heard a lot of men come through and get up on stage, stripping during their trail run and get scared off into oblivion, never to return. Eye knew eye wouldn't be vanishing.

Entirely new audience of my life, a different stage of my mental and emotional development. Eye was 19 years old when eye stood before Andy, Cederick, Anthony, Bishop, Jabari, Samuel, Big Dick Daddy and Money. Andy being the acting manager of PANDORA'S GATEWAY and the other seven men together brought in over $25,000 + a week. The hottest strip joint in town. Though eye was a "straight" stripper for the ladies, my secret obsession was to men.

Eye was clad in leather cow boy pants, elephant trunk covered dick and a G string on my ass. Felt like eye was flossing my colon when eye walked.

Andy paused behind me, gripping my shoulders, his breath on the nape of my neck. He pressed his dick up against me and said, "Are you ready rookie?"

Eye smiled nervously. "Yea, eye'm ready."

He looked at me sternly. "This is a trail run, Pharoah. If you got what it takes your first night will be in a few weeks."

"I got you."

All the fellahs surrounded me and grinned, smiled, laughed and urged me on.

"Its time to introduce the world to Black Magik."

"That's my name?" eye asked, grinning, slapping palms with everybody. Eye hated the name.

"Yup. Go make some money," said Andy, winking.

The women roared to life when Andy's fine ass took to the stage in a thousand dollar suit and matching shoes. Towering 6 feet 8 with Jamaican and Puerto Rican dick, a few ladies threw fifties on the stage and told him to take it off.

He slid his hands in his pocket, the blinging of the rings on his fingers ceased, and he said, "Coming to the stage is one of the hottest young men out of Dade County. He's fire. And he is everything you want in a young man starving for attention. He is standing 6 feet 4 inches tall. Ladies Ladies ladies, here is Black Magik!"

The lights faded and fake smoke hissed from the side canisters and eye slow grind out to the middle of the stage with my finger tips on the tip of the sombrero, stuck my ass out and gave 'em that Michael Jackson stare.

Lights came on and the Janet Jackson mix Andy cleverly made to Uncle Luck's instrumentals was just what eye needed to get loose.

It's like something took over me, grabbed me by the throat and controlled my body.

Eye hit a spin, popped to the floor with my head tilted, licking my lips. Made the dick thump a few times, snapped my fingers and fell to my hands and knees, crawling, expertly, licking my lips, forehead down and eyes and ass up, crawling to a cute chubby woman who had heart failure and tried to hide behind her girl, laughing uncontrollably.

Don't hide, bitch. Eye'm coming for those dollars.

Eye crawled in her friend's lap and she wasted liquor on my ass cheeks. Eye jiggled them in her face and took chubby lady's broach into my mouth, tilting my head to the right, tonguing the broach and winking at her.

"Daddy need a new outfit and a new pair of shoes," eye told her, putting both hands on the floor, arching my legs in the air and fell, straddling chubby's lap.

"OH MY GAWD!"

"When was the last time a man ate your sweet pussy?" eye asked her, grinding to Janet singing *Nasty* to the One Leg Up, Uncle Al beat.

She was wet, grabbing my ass cheeks, darting her tongue at me and women fanning money all around me.

"She don't know what she doing!"

"Fuck that bitch cum grind on my lap!"

"Grab his dick girl!"

Eye gave her some tongue, took both her hands off my ass and looked deeply into her eyes.

"That'll be $250 for grabbing my ass. And eye want my money!"

She quivered picking up her purse.

"Eye don't cum cheap," eye said aggressively. "*Gimme* an extra hundred."

"Oh my God!" She was about to pass out. And eye wasn't gonna catch her ass either.

She pulled out her wallet and eye lowered myself to my knees, spread her legs and stuck my head up her skirt and munched on her lace-clad pussy and she couldn't take it. She threw her legs up and eye kept munching and she counted out my money and stuck it in my G string and eye took off the hat, my tongue still thrashing chubby pussy and eye put the sombrero on her head, grabbed her tits and tongue fucked her till she cooed, "Eye'm 'bout to cum."

Eye smacked her in the face, fucked off her nut and said, "Did you ask me could you nut?"

And wandered off, dancing and snapping up to a tall woman who wiggled a twenty in my face,

I reached for it and she snatched it back and eye snatched her upper arm, just above the elbow, dropped to my knees and kissed her pussy and hopped back up to my feet, bit her right tit and took my twenty.

"You are off the chain!"

"Eye know," eye said, taking another $20 from her hand and kissed her cheek, dancing off to a white bitch. She snapped and bobbed her head, so off cadence.

"Eye offer dance lessons," eye told her, kissing her hand and grinding my hardened dick all over her.

"How much do you charge?"

Eye threw it out there. "$500."

"Are you good?" she asked and eye took her hand and pulled her on the stage. She watched me pop my booty cheeks up to the stairs. Eye picked her up, put her pussy in my face (her legs dangling over my shoulders) and eye twirled all the way to the floor with my tongue in her pussy,

Eye brought both arms behind her and gently lay her on the stage.

Women throwing panties and money.

Andy was in shock, laughing with the Boys.

They turned on some Jodeci. Grooving to *Come and talk to me*.

She shuddered and eye ate with more finesse. Never ate a white woman, she smelled different from black elegance.

Her nipples hardened, she said she had to cum and eye jumped up to my feet, whisked her off the ground, bent her over and spanked her ass like she's been bad.

No orgasms on my time baby.

"That'll be $500!"

"Here baby!" she threw a cloud of one hundred dollar bills in the air and eye collected them all.

By the time eye was done, and the Boys collected my cash, eye made over $2,400 just that fast.

Andy was thrilled.

After the club closed all the Boys met up in the main assembly.

Andy was glowing, the Boys giggling like school kids.

"Andy! *Wassup*, man? *Why are* you smiling like that?" eye asked, sweating my ass off, trying to catch y breath.

"Goddamn, Black Magik. Do you know how much he made?"

"Naw," said Cederick, jealous of the attention eye was getting. He was the number one money maker. He had a reputation for making money and slinging big time cock. He was Miami-Dade County's go to guy when your husband or boyfriend stopped fucking you. He charged $300 an hour and rumor had it he was worth $900 an hour with his tongue and dick skills. He made women skeet all over the place with his twelve inch dick.

Andy pat my back.

"Eye knew you'd blow em away!"

"How much he make?" asked Jabari, curious.

"Twenty-four hundred dollars. No one has ever made that much money on their first night. Hell, he made more than Cederick and he's the money maker. There's a new sheriff in town," Andy said and we all celebrated.

Till Cederick snatched me by the neck and pushed me against the wall. His body was pressed up against mine.

"Let's get something straight! This was just a trail run! You don't even have what it takes to strip with us you stupid bitch!"

Andy tried to grab him and Cederick pushed him away, turning back to me.

"Man, what did eye do to you? You're the one who suggested eye strip so I could pay off student loans!"

"Eye am the main attraction in this part of town. This is my stomping grounds. The only niggah stomp the yard up in here is me."

I kneed him in the balls and pushed him till he ran backwards then eye punched him right in the center of his forehead and everybody gasped.

"You listen, *bitch!* You must not be all that if on my first night, eye'm sorry on my trail run, eye broke *your* peak. Just like a niggah to be hating instead of congratulating. We all got bills to pay muthafuckah there's room for everybody. What the fuck? Did eye ask for a manicure? Did eye ask for a pedicure? No, then why the fuck you pushed me up against the wall. You like me or something?"

"You talk a good game," he said, running up on me, punching me in the face and eye did a full circle and gave the late bitch a fist to the nose.

Screaming, he fell backward and Anthony tried to grab me and eye punched him over the table and now eye was frightened and when eye was scared eye fought as if my life depended on it and eye was afraid of death so there ya go.

Andy got in front of me with his hands up.

"BOTH OF YOU!" He glared at Cederick. He's huffing and puffing, Anthony was holding him.

He calmed down, but not much.

"STOP FIGHTING! We a muthafucking team up in this muthafuckah, you hear me?"

"Fuck him!" eye screamed, storming out. "Eye quit this shit. Got me fucked up."

"Bring your ass back here, Pharoah!"

Eye turned to face him. "Go fuck yourself." And eye glared at Cederick. "There you go pussy boy. Your *pussy* hot on the block again eye resign, bitch!"

And walked out.

THE RI$E OF THE LU$TFUL BEA$T

When eye got home eye was steaming like mixed vegetables simmering on number 2. Eye'd calmed the fuck down but it still bothered me. Eye went in my room and closed the door, realizing eye didn't get my money. Eye picked up the phone and called Andy. He answered. "Where the fuck are you, Pharoah?"

"Home."

"What the fuck you mean you're home and there's money to be made out here tonight niggah."

"Eye'm good. Look, eye want my money."

"Come and get it. My house. In thirty minutes. Eye got a bone to goddamn pick with you. And when we're done you won't blink straight muthafuckah."

He hung up.

What the fuck was that supposed to mean? Eye wouldn't *blink* straight? Eye swore. Niggahs listened to too much Tupac these days. Just because you knew the words to *Thug Niggahz till we Die* didn't mean you were a stone cold gangster.

So why Andy ass tripping? Do eye love the niggah? Hell yea. Eye loved him because he could fuck well. And that's all the love eye needed because nobody ever loved me in my life; shit, eye gotta get love in any form eye could get it. And dick was the solution to this problem.

When eye got to Andy's house the front door was open. Reminded me of my Mother. When eye was late beating the sun home once. She had the front door wide open. Or if eye did something bad. The front door was open when eye got home. Threshold awaiting me, the floors awaiting the invisible footprints eye left trekking to my bedroom.

But eye never made it there.

"PHAROAH BRING YOUR ASS HERE RIGHT NOW!"

Oh, shit. Eye thought of this approaching Andy's door. He reminded me of Mama.

And that scared me into a block of ice in an ice tray. Stuffed in the back of the freezer. Forgotten about. Never given a second thought.

Eye went to mama, shivering, because eye always got my ass whipped when that front door was open awaiting me to get home.

"Pull em down."

"Mama, what did eye do?"

Eye walked in the house and he took a swig of liquor, threw it against the wall and stomped up to me.

Andy was Mama, and she said, "Pull the pants down and lay on the bed. Didn't eye tell you not to go outside when eye'm at work?"

"But eye didn't go outside, Mama!" eye lied, my eyes wide. Bracing myself.

"Yes you did! My co worker told me! She said she came home and you were outside throwing a ball against the wall with the other kids."

Whack.

"Mama! Eye'm sorry!"

Whack.

Andy grabbed me by the neck. "Aren't you my bitch?"

"Yes, Andy," eye said, appeasing him and he slapped me across the face with his open hand.

"Next time eye tell you to do something you do it," Mama said, storming outta the room…when it *dawned* on me that Andy just said the same thing. Eye shuddered. His dangerous eyes tore through my frightened stare.

"Ok, Andy."

"You think you grown, huh? Do what you wanna do? Eye'm 35 years the fuck old. You're 19. You do what you're fucking told."

He punched me so hard in the stomach eye doubled over. He walked up on me, drunk as hell, staggering instead of showing that manly swagger. He took off his belt. "You quit, bitch?"

"Hell yea! Eye'm not going back to that…"

He started whipping my ass with the thick leather belt with little metal clumps all over it. The shit hurt. Eye had a flash back of my step father beating me, savagely. *You won't tell anybody you hear?!*

Andy beat me, eye raised my hands over my face and he said, "You will do what the fuck eye say. Make that muthafucking money. You will be back to the club tomorrow 8 p.m. sharp bitch!"

And he kicked me in my side.

"YOU HEAR ME, BITCH?"

"Yes!"

Eye was in so much pain eye couldn't move or scream. My wail of discomfort was distorted by my pause in breathing. Wide eyed and scared, eye lost myself.

Eye would do anything he said. But please, please…

Just don't beat me.

THE DEBUT OF PHAROAH THE ROBOT

Eye was nervous about going out, stripping off my clothes before a SOLD OUT crowd. He picked tonight of all nights for me to go out and debut my hot, young sexy body to a room filled with divorced women just discovering the Power of the Dick again. That divorcee who cried for months, days, hours, seconds, minutes and trimesters, swearing on God and swearing off men with slight hints of lesbianism…

Those were the types of women in the crowd tonight. Rediscovering their roots, remembering what their fathers taught them and what Mama couldn't suck from a dick with chapped lips and thick red lipstick.

There wasn't a dry scalp woman in the house. Hair dos on target, hitting the bullseye with their pricey outfits. Eye smelled 60 types of pussy in the air from where eye stood behind the closed BLACK CURTAIN.

Eye inhaled deeply, my dick hard as fuck. Eye was bisexual, yes but goddamn it eye loved some muthafucking pussy and titties.

Smiling, eye inhaled again, pulling out my dick as the announcer shushed the crowd. Closing my eyes, eye spat on my hand, getting that muthafuckah wet and eye bent slightly at the knees, jacking my dick so goddamn good eye screamed out and shushes filled the room. But eye didn't care nor notice.

Might as well jack my dick, get this first nut out the way. Cum right on the muthafucking stage, before the curtain opens on my mobile body with slick hands stealing my clothes from one section of my body at a time.

Eye felt a huge breeze and eye moaned to myself, "Oh, Shit!" My nuts felt rejuvenated swinging through the cool breeze sweeping my body like global praise.

All that was going through my mind was *What if the crowd of divorcee hoes didn't like my performance. What would eye do? Save face and run the muthafucking show? Or grab my balls and run off the stage amidst boo's and tomatoes.*

No time for that now. Eye was so lost within myself that eye found myself and the only thing eye wound up finding was my lost ass trapped in a labyrinth of bullshit.

Eye convinced myself that eye found myself and the only thing eye found myself doing was making divorcee pussy wet for the dollar with good dick on my brain and my asshole quivering for it, yet my dick was hard for pussy, goddamn. That was one fucked up situation to be in.

But eye'm from Goulds, bitch. Eye handled it flawlessly. My body and A game was so flawless Elizabeth Taylor wrote Michael Jackson a goddamn letter and said, "Bitch my white diamonds are *tarnished* from that niggah writing books and trying to dance like you."

Eye spat in my hand repeatedly, moistening my scrumptious, throbbing dick. Felt the pulse of my balls deep in my toes, overwhelming my brain and my heartbeat became sufficient yet irregular.

Eye needed the money to pay off my college loans because mama wasn't helping (or willing) o help me pay for a fucking thing. Talking about she got other kids to raise. So fuck it. Gotta hustle, get it on my own.

Plus eye could get this financial aid Cuban asshole off my damn back. Summoning me to the office every week harassing me to pay for classes. Goddamn, bitch. Castro did it to you muthafuckah, not me.

Eye briefly stop jacking my dick, and slowly opened my eyes and looked at myself in the mirror.

Frowning at what appeared before me. Eye hated that Niggah trapped behind the glass, looking like me, a spitting goddamn image.

What the fuck you're lookin' at, late bitch?
You, you ugly fuck. At least eye ain't no stripper!
Whatever, late trick. You're my reflection.
Yup. And when you strip, I won't be yours!
Fuck off.
You first!

Before the mirror I stood, sombrero pulled low above my saddened, painful eyes. It hurt to look at myself, staring at what eye had become and what eye continuously become daily, when the sun rise. My body's oiled to a shine. Nuts gleaming under silky black elephant trunk thongs housing my hardened dick. Had to stuff that big bitch back in silk. Leather pants grip my legs and ass like so, but nothing too tight.

The other strippers, before walking out to this closed curtain, were behind me in the dressing room getting rid of the scary butterflies/dragonflies in my stomach. Eye threw up three times before coming out from nervousness. The 5 strippers were my moral support system.

Andy winked at me from the stage. Eye winked back.
You can do it.

Eye pulled out my dick and started beating off again, trying to boost my adrenaline. The crowd roared and eye smiled.

It was then eye realized the curtain was already open.
A sea of money flapping from sweaty palms.

Eye kept jacking as slow music came on, narrowing my eyes at all the Hoes through the reflection of myself, yet my eyes didn't focus on that reflection. I choose to focus on the feeling of beating off and getting caught.

May the best bitch win.

I came on the floor without a sound, holding it all in as my toes curled in my thigh high leather boots.

Eye turned to the microphone, women screaming out all kinds of nasty shit. *Fuck me. Eat my pussy, you sexy skinny Niggah. You got a big dick. Let me and me girls fuck you.*

Eye winked, ignoring childish pleas of desire and licked my nut from my fingers with a smack, winking at a fat bitch at the fifth table from the right of the stage.

Eye walked seductively to the microphone and paused, looking it over, popping my ass to the floor. Jodeci *sang I wanna get you sweaty.*

Oh my God. The women went nuts.

A few women jumped on the table, swinging their bras in the air like a helicopter. All eye saw were women alerting me, telling me wordlessly to cum get that money.

That could wait. When you made money wait that was called investing in time, seeing what their money would do for you. Some bitches upped dollars to seduce you to their table, so the stock in my dick and balls took a much needed leap towards future earnings to put in my bank account.

Rule number one of business: never let a bitch with money know you're desperate. Look at their dollars like shit, wink and go get another bitch's money.

Eye popped my ass cheeks on the floor and slowly did the snake back up to my feet, my tongue sliding along the microphone stand, my forehead lowered and my eyes staring at the ceiling.

Gyrating, as I used both hands to jack the stand like my dick. Wanting that nut from the base. Utilize me, beat.

Eye looked to the left, winked, popped my ass, thrust my big dick forward, the trunk of the elephant thongs bouncing with a purpose. A skinny woman ran towards the stage with a hundred dollar bill and begged to slid it in my thongs. I held up a finger, tilting my head. No, no, no, no. That's not enough, bitch. I got cock strong dick. I'm not those Niggahs you won over waving a hundred dollar bill eye may not get.

She pulled out another hundred and eye fingered her to the stage. She ran up the stairs, tripping over clumsy footing.

Eye wrapped my arms around her, lowered her to the floor, kissed her vinyl-clad pussy and stood up, taking both bills into my hands.

I thrust my pelvis forward, bumping the bitch off the stage.

The crowd stood, laughing and cheering.

My nipples erect, eye stroked my dick, narrowing my eyes and a Barry White song came on. *I wanna do it Good to ya.*

Eye worked the room, lowering towards the floor, putting a boot clad foot up on a chair, balls in a Hoe's face, and rubbed her head as she started licking the sweat from my asshole. She skipped my dick and my balls, and eye realized with a jolt she was actually a tranny bitch. Chick with a dick.

Eye got $20 out of her and some asshole head. She sucked my asshole till my toes curled, and that's when eye bumped my ass cheeks in her/his face and danced a few tables over, and climbed on top of it with he/she's spit drying on my hole. Doing my little dance, taking the hat and popping down Doo Doo Brown style *YEE HA!* and putting the sombrero on another thick woman's head. Eye targeted all big girls. Because the light skinned Hoes thought they were all that; bitch my dick and pussy better than yours, Hoe act like you know.

They were steaming, too because eye knew bitches hated to be ignored and talked so much they'd rather be heard and eye wasn't a patient ass Niggah today and eye could care less about pussy right now when money ruled my ass and mind and all eye wanted for compensation was my goddamn money and see ya' later, Honey!

So a few of them wave their cash in the air, half assed snapping and really wasn't feeling the beat and eye danced right past their asses and didn't as much as fart on the bitches.

They ducking behind their cash, lowering their heads and asses back in their seats.

Eye turned to face the stage and eye saw cash all over it. Glistening under neon lights. Money looked different with this kinda lighting, seeing shit eye never thought eyed see. Hypnotized, eye danced up to the stage, wanting more money. Now eye'm being greedy. Instead of getting in and getting the fuck out, eye wanted to rule shit so eye danced like eye was giving a free concert. Janet Jackson music playing and eye realized Andy put on Janet's *Throb* and eye did the entire routine she did on Saturday Night Live, and got not only a standing ovation when eye was done.

But eye turned and lay on my back, sweaty body clinging to the stage's money. Ain't mine yet till eye pick it up. Eye closed my eyes and inhale as deeply as eye can.

Then eye exhaled. Phew!

By the time the club cleared, eye was in one of the back rooms, laying down on the huge black and green sofa. Having showered, my body was still drained and eye counted $1,765 dollars in cash. For a thirty minute strip/dance show.

Andy was looking at me, looking flawless in his suit. He always looked flawless. Blow dried his hair like a bitch and even awakened in the mornings refreshed. Hair always in place, even when he slept.

But he was far from a bitch. Oh, no. Nothing about Andy spelled bitch. It wasn't in his walk, fuck and head game nor his talk. He was one of the strongest, toughest most troubled men eye would ever know.

When a man puts the fear of God in your heart then he has you. He has you mentally, physically and spiritually because eye dissed church, fell out of the church and made him my entire universe. In my heart was a shrine for him, and he became the very breath that kept me alive.

Only eye didn't realize this. Eye told people eye loved God, yet never told them that at the time Andy was my God. I worshipped the very grounds he walked on, and Jehovah wasn't pleased. He showed me many troubled signs of bad things to come in my life through my dreams, but eye would never write them down, never really cared about the revelation and still had Andy's breakfast, lunch and dinner piping hot. He fucked who he wanted when he wanted and eye didn't care. Eye was the young 19 year old fascinated with an older man that had it all. Money, clothes, dick, hoes, houses, cars, and a host of strip clubs. He was my Messiah

And that's when my world started to plummet. At the seams. When he brutally *beat* me after telling him eye fell in love with him. He fucked and beat me so badly sometimes eye couldn't move. And eye thought it was love. Eye thought eye had to stay with him to prove that loyalty, take him as he was, never trying to change a man who couldn't even save or change himself. So eye became his savior.

Anything eye wanted eye had. Access to everything, but he monitored it closely. Anything appeared out of synch within his limitations he beat my ass like a hooker at the Special Olympics.

He looked at me lying comfortably on the huge sofa and he lit a cigarillo, clapping.

He smiled that boyish grin that set me ablaze with trepidation and pleasure. I felt its pulse in the base of my asshole set off by the pundits of my throbbing member labeled "Dick."

"I really enjoyed your performance, baby."

I was glowing. "Thank you."

"You got all the strippers mad."

"Why?"

"Their regular patrons have switched to Pharoah. They have lost money."

"I didn't want to do that."

"You're the baddest bitch on the roster. Who knew you could dance with such elegance. You were nasty, raunchy yet classy and one of a kind. The way your body moves hypnotizes me and all eye could think about while you made 60 types of pussies wet was my ten inch cut Puerto Rican/Jamaican dick deep inside that asshole."

He got on one knee and I gasped from the sincerity of his eyes. Yet eye knew well enough to brace myself because the sincerity of the eyes betrayed the tone of a shaken, angry voice. He did his best to dress Shaken Angry Voice in winter clothes when Halloween had yet to debut. But eye played it off, and smiled anyway, counting my money.

"You love money, Pharoah?"

"No. I don't."

"Then why do you count it over and over?" He was stroking my booty hole, looking deeply into my eyes and eye still didn't look away from the money eye earned through appropriate entertainment. Remember this was a strip club. What eye did was appropriate for the horny just-discovering-their-pussies divorcees that, hours ago, occupied every possible seat, even the seats and stools at the bar.

"I love what it could do for me. But I'm certainly not attached to it, Andy."

He rubbed my scalp with carefully executed fingers through my high top fade. Felt so good.

"How much did you make?"

"Well over a thousand. Again!"

"Well over?"

"Yes."

"No one has made that much money his opening day or trail run!"

"I'm not everyone else. Certainly not Cederick."

"Most *certainly* Cederick. He had the highest opening trail run and debut. You doubled that. He's extremely pissed."

"And you're telling me because?"

"Eye thought you should know. All the strippers support you. Except Cederick, he's your arch nemesis and he wants your head. He already attacked you once."

"Eye barely know him."

"But he was the one that introduced you to this Club. Hell he introduced you to me. When he brought you, before eye found out we go to the same college, he told me to give you a chance."

"I don't owe him anything. Just because he introduced me into the game doesn't mean he dictate my rules. I set rules to govern myself following my own authority. Not yours."

He snatched my money and grabbed me by the throat, shoving it deep inside my mouth. His eyes fire engine red, eye shook with fear.

"You watch how you talk to me. You're my bitch. I run you, bitch." He spit in my face and eye frowned.

"You do what eye say. Listen. You can't just come in here, claiming shit, taking over like you put in all the hard work to make this place what it's retained in profits. Cederick is a major asset to this club."

Eye spit the money out of my mouth and looked him deeply in the eyes. "And now eye'm gonna take it further than that. Nobody wants his washed up ass. And why are you defending Cederick. Don't tell me you used to fuck him."

"As a matter of fact yes I did. He's still one of my bitches. Does what the fuck eye want."

"What?"

"You heard me. You better do as eye say. Your Mama already wants to throw you out and you have no life. You'll die without her support."

Eye was quiet because he was right.

"Eye'm keeping your money," he said.

"Eye earned that money! Eye have to pay off college loans."

"FUCK COLLEGE!" he screamed.

Eye grew quiet.

"I don't even want to go there. But eye have to. My parents are very controlling. Well, my mother is at least. My father…"

"Your father what?" eye asked.

He released my neck. "Can rot in hell."

DOME$TIC VIOLENCE

Eight months of domestic violence eye had to endure. The man eye was in love with has flipped the script and controlled everything about me. Eye had to cut off family *and* friends. So instead of turning my back on them (eye loved them too much) eye just stopped calling, hanging out with them and going around. Eye could hardly spend time with family. He was jealous of them all. So eye stopped being home as much and spent all my time with Andy and he was always at the club so eye had to be with him. Couldn't even go to the bathroom by myself or the store. One of his goons had to be with me. And they told him everything and eye hated them for it.

    Andy believed anything they said. So since eye was at the club early he worked me more than the other strippers. Eye made them a lot of money and eye hardly got $600. Andy would eat cocaine off my asshole after beating my ass if eye didn't cook right or if his house was half assed cleaned or if eye didn't iron his clothes, have his books out for college (we were both at City College in South Miami) or if eye sassed him.

    One night he beat my ass because eye wouldn't suck and fuck his friends.

He smacked me and beat me with the belt with metal clumps in front of them. And, laughing, each one of them took turns raping me and left me on the floor till eye fell asleep. I had never screamed for MAMA to help me so loud in my life. Only thing was...she didn't hear me.

Weeks of stripping would go by and Andy had better ideas. Seemed a few on the low niggahs came to see me strip bringing their sisters or female friends. Mutual acquaintances, business associates.

Andy set it all up and he told me eye didn't have a choice. So eye did what he said.

Escorting. Making top dollar doing sexual services for thirty and forty year olds and Andy got the money and eye never saw a dime.

For over a month eye loved em long time, me so horny. Lost within the incarceration of my flesh. Lost who eye was gradually becoming another part of myself that was...born.

After a few more weeks of escorting eye decided eye'd had enough of Andy. There was an annual award show coming up where clubs across the state sent in their best strippers for Best Body, Best Dancer and Biggest Money Maker for Awards. Andy told me all the Boys had to be there. It was going to be held at a very expensive hotel.

And it was. A hotel on South Beach. On a hot, humid Friday night. 8 P.M. Eye was clad in a white suit and fresh hair cut, miserably sitting by Andy. If eye wanted something to drink eye couldn't even get up and walk across the room. So Andy made Cederick get it and his ugly ass laughed under his breath, enjoying every moment.

When he brought me the red wine back he handed it to me and when my enclosing fingers grasped the stem of the flute glass Cederick released it, saying "Oh, shit dawg. I'm so sorry," and red wine spilt in my white suit coat and eye didn't jump back or goddamn flinch. Eye smiled, laughed and said, "This white suit was tired anyway. It needed some color."

And everyone started laughing, and eye was clapping and laughing too. Stood my sexy ass up in a ruined white five hundred dollar suit and raised my hand towards Cederick, who was clearly embarrassed his plan failed. "And Cederick, the wonderful director," eye said sarcastically, and people cheering and applauding and eye sat down, crossed my legs in a masculine way of course and looked at Andy and said, "Eye'm getting tired of your groupie bitches."

And fell into a bitter silence.

The awards ceremony started and the room was jam-packed. About 600 guests were there dressed nicely in a suit. Strippers from all over Florida (Tampa, Jacksonville, Orlando…) were in the place and eye was stunned that this kinda shit went on.

Some buff Niggah won for Sexiest Body and some in the closet looking five foot midget ass goon wanna be Niggah won for Best Dancer.

A tall, scrawny, buff white boy won for Rookie of the Year and a Jamaican man with long dreads and a huge dick won for Overall Entertainer.

The biggest money maker category was being announced, and they didn't call out any names as nominees. Then it dawned on me they didn't call out nominees in the first place. They announced the category and called out the winner.

The emcee, as handsome and hot as he was, grinned at the podium and said, "And The Biggest Money Maker goes to Pharoah Wilson."

What the fuck? Some folks clapped and others whistled. Cederick had his mouth wide open and as eye walked to the podium to get a gift wrapped box Cederick pushed me into the podium, and jumped on top of me.

"You muthafuckah. That was supposed to be my award."

He punched me repeatedly in the face and eye was growing weaker.

Andy threw Cederick off me and helped me to my feet.

The room was silenced.

"You know what, dawg. Keep that award you want it that bad," eye said, taking the box and opening it. "Let's see what you won, bitch."

Eye pulled out a huge black dildo, filled with jelly and eye slapped him with it and he fell on his back. "What the fuck? Is this some kinda joke? Who gave me a dildo as the prize? Eye thought it was supposed to be an award."

"It was," said the emcee. "It was supposed to be $1,000 and a trophy. Looks like the trophy was broken and stuffed in the box with the dildo, bruh."

He pointed at the trophy on the ground, in the box.

And the $1,000. Gone.

When eye got to Andy's house eye stormed in the room and opened drawers taking my shit out. Eye'd had enough. This has gone on long enough. It was time to wake up. Eye knew eye was 20 years old now and eye know its going on two years eye've stripped for Andy and did this dumb bullshit.

"And what are you doing?"

Eye put my clothes on the bed, walked to his closet and grabbed my suit case.

"Eye'm gone."

"You're not leaving."

Eye glared at him. "Fuck with me tonight, put your goddamn hands on me tonight Andy eye swear muthafuckah eye will gut your Hoe ass. Fuck with it," eye said dangerously, meaning every single solitary word.

He held up his hands. Strangely accommodating. "Let's talk about it, baby. Eye don't like to see you hurt."

"What?" eye said, walking up to him. "What? You beat me! You abuse me all the time and eye let you Because eye'm used to the beatings. Eye went through four years of rape when eye was little muthafuckah do you really think you're hurting me?"

He was stunned. Don't act so stunned now, Niggah. "Oh my God, Pharoah. Tell me you're lying?"

"*Fuck* you!"

"I see it in your eyes that you're fed up. And for that eye will never raise my hands to you again. Pharoah, damn man! Damn! My father raped me when eye was seventeen years old. Because eye quit football and turned my back on an all paid scholarship to Texas State."

I didn't give a fuck. But he kept talking. "Eye realized my family was clinging to me because eye was going to be famous. So eye quit. My daddy called me a bitch and fucked me like one in front of my Mama and she turned her back, rolling her eyes saying, 'You turn your back on going possibly to the Pros, we don't know you! Fuck you!' and she closed the door on my father fucking me."

Damn! "My God."

"So eye know what that's like."

"Why are you telling me this?"

"Because eye want to learn to heal."

"Do it without me. Cederick has embarrassed me for the last time. Something's going on that's deeper than me stepping on his cash cow's toes. There's something going on eye'm not seeing, but eye know its there."

"It's nothing, man. You're paranoid. Look, eye love you baby. You complete me. Eye know eye can act crazy sometimes, but eye'm so afraid of losing you, Pharoah. You're my fantasy, don't you get it. Eye look at you and see perfection. You're gorgeous and eye am in love; eye am infatuated; and eye am in lust. Eye can't keep my hands off you."

And he took me into his arms and tongue kissed me like it's the last time and he pulled off my pants and ate my asshole through my fruit of a looms and he massaged my ass cheeks while pulling my draws to the left and sliding up inside me deep till eye felt the sting of passion and burst open the river of ecstasy and we row with his Ore, deep stroking my colon. My prostate going mad.

He engulfed me, showering my face with gentle kisses. Releasing his being to make me stay.

"Please baby don't leave me baby. You gonna give another Niggah my ass, dawg? You said that's mine? You gonna break my heart like that?"

"Hell no, baby."

"You promise?"

"Eye promise, Daddy."

"Oh, you feel so good Niggah eye'm going in deeper."

He pushed forward and his dick filled me all the way up and eye paused, wide eyed, mouth wide open.

"Don't run from it. Take it baby. Tell me you gonna stay while you take this ten inch pipe."

By the time he was done, eye was in the laundry room glowing, throwing his dirty clothes in the wash.

Then eye put him a TV dinner in the microwave.

And took him a beer.

Being with my manager/boyfriend was an abusive time for me. This man was everything eye ever wanted in a lover. In the beginning, he did everything by the book a lover should do in a relationship. He got to know me inside and out, learned my favorite color, how I liked my eggs, what size underwear eye wore, my shoe size. In return I learned everything about him. His upbringing and where he came from. His life and passion. His failures and successes. We didn't have sex a lot the first few months we were together.

We used to lay holding each other, talking into the night about life, our goals and dreams and our fears.

Everything was perfect. Picture perfect without flaws spells TOO PERFECT. He never saw a flaw in anything I did, always agreed with me, cooked for me, cleaned behind me and wouldn't let me lift a finger to do anything for myself.

When I was on stage stripping he cheered me on, bought me food, took me out and started ignoring the other dancers and they had it out for me. Before I came Andy and the stripper boys fucked women together, hung out around town every weekend and ate out together. Since I been in the picture Andy was totally engrossed in me, and I loved it. I never asked him to cut off his friends and when I told him he should hang out with them he accused me of trying to talk to another Niggah so I dismissed the request and forgot about it.

Everything was kosher.
Till the day I fell in love.

Our fifth month in a heavy relationship I awakened one morning and realize I was madly in love with Andy and that there wasn't anything I wouldn't do for him. Stripping brought me in some major cash and I gave it to my baby and he put it up for me because I was terrible saving money.

I smiled, brushing my teeth, my dick hard. I turned on the stereo, and Patti Labelle was singing The Right Kinda Lover so I jammed a little bit, because I loved Miss Patsy and eye washed my face, took a piss and flushed.

I danced all the way to the house phone and called Andy. He answered on the first ring.

"Hey, baby."
"Hey, Pharoah. What you doing up so early?"
"School, remember?"
"Oh, yea. College."
"Ha. Don't sound so convincing."

"What are you up to, baby?"

"Laying here stroking this dick. It misses you."

"Is that right?"

"I love making love to you. The way you moan in bed sets me on fire."

I was tingling all over. "So come pick me up."

"I'm on the way."

He got to Mom's house around 10 a.m.

He called me and told me he was outside. I rushed out the door, telling everyone goodbye.

When I got in the car he engulfed me, then gave me some tongue. Kissing him made me feel like floating on clouds.

A possessive hand on my upper thigh, he backed onto SW 127th Avenue, and made a left at the light onto Moody Drive.

"How are you, baby?" he asked, winking at me with a boyish smile.

I blushed. "I'm still try'na wake up."

"How did you sleep?"

"I slept good."

"Did you dream about me?"

"Yea, I did."

"What did you dream about?" He asked, speeding past the small blinking light on the corner of Moody Drive and Allapattah, SW 112th Avenue.

"You."

I wasn't surprised. "Oh, yea?"

He winked at me. "Yea."

He turned into a clearing in the bushes, and drove up the dirt road towards a small bend.

He braked, turned off the car, pulled me to his lips and said, "I bet you didn't dream about this."

And he fucked me for the next two hours.

Eye would get lost in this relationship, whatever it was. Eye took what eye could get because of the self hatred eye had for myself. Moving about God's green earth without guidance or acceptance. Daddy paid for my life with a bounced check because he wrote my ass off like a bitch with wasted pussy. Nobody invested in wasted pussy so you fucked a new bitch. Eye needed that male companion for one reason: a father figure. Someone to be an aggressor, taking charge and telling me how to steer this ship called a FUCKED UP LIFE.

Andy became my new drug of choice. What he said went. When he gave an order eye carried it out to the hilt. He hated feisty Niggahs, and eye was spicy. So to tame me he wrestled around with me, took my asshole and went up so deep inside me my eyes rolled to the back of my head as if in a trace, letting his dick guide my spine.

We were together nearly two years. Eye stripped my life and clothes and self respect away like snake skin for nearly two years.

Then eye fell in love, or eye thought eye did. I realized eye loved him when he was so deep inside me with his left hand gripping my neck tightly but lovingly and his right hand pushed down on the small of my back while he was digging tombs inside my Nefertiti.

When eye said "I love you," he fucked me harder, kissing the sweat from trembling lips. Lips smelling of pussy. We always ate pussy and fucked females before he fucked me, without washing the pussy from his dick.

So why wash my lips. Both sets of my lips smelled of good pussy.

He was grinning, with tears forming in his eyes. "Really, baby? You love me?"

The slapping sounds hypnotized me and his dick made his submissive lover.

"Yes, eye'm in love with you, Daddy."

"Eye'm Daddy?" he asked breathlessly, grinding inside me; he pushed inside my flesh deeper, using both hands to bring the bottom of his totem pole to the bottom of my asshole.

"Yesssss."

He pressed my head to the pillow and raised my ass up a little higher and he fucked me long, hard and deep and when eye had to nut he pulled out of me and beat my ass.

He pushed me on the floor amidst my gentle orgasm, and he jumped on top of me, slapping me repeatedly in the face. The evil side of him rendered me speechless.

"If you love me you will do what eye say, bitch! You will cater to me, cook my fucking food, do what eye say and the money you make stripping you aren't allowed to look at, smell or touch!"

He jumped up, grabbed me by the high top fade and took off his belt and beat my ass so badly eye was reverted back to that 6 year old kid, the one who was torn apart and raped, and all eye saw was him, the Thing from my past, beating and conditioning me inside something only he understood.

I was paralyzed with fear and overcome with emotion as the tears fell. Eye raised my arms above my head, screaming out *please* and he gradually stopped, taking a look at me.

"Face me, bitch."

Eye walked up to his face, trembling.

"Will you do what eye say?"

"Yes, Daddy."

He smiled. "Good. Get on your knees and suck my dick. When you're done get ready for your stripping number tonight. Eye got just the thing eye want you to do."

Eye obeyed.

MAMA DEARE$T

Out of the thousand plus dollars eye generated each night eye stripped, he only gave me three hundred dollars. Kept the rest. Eye felt pimped, but I was madly in love with him. So in love I was willing to look past all his indifferences and love him for the realest he was. I was his bitch and it was my job as a bottom to make sure he was comfortable in our relationship. If he wanted to be the Man and run shit then by all means, do so. He beats my ass to a pulp sometimes, and despite the blood lost my love for him shined strong as ever. Eye keep forgiving him because of what he suffered as a kid, and that enables the loyalty I have for him. He buys me things and takes me out on the town in matching suits and wines and dines me in public with so much sex appeal and masculinity people actually think we're brothers instead of lovers.

I became so dependent on Andy eye thought he was my heaven. Everything I did was a direct reflection of him.

But then eye woke the fuck up when my perception of him shattered during an outing?

We were together for almost two years when, one particular place we went to, unraveled the scheme. The restaurant had the heart of Italy in the main assembly. Beautiful tables with silk cloth, lacquered chairs and chandeliers so overwhelmingly breathtaking eye nearly vomited from the climate change.

His mother was a political woman. She knew all sorts of people. I heard she was about to become a senator or some shit like that. Judging from the clientele eating from plates more expensive than my mother's house, this had to be true. Eye saw the purest, cleanest bottle of Hennessy eye had ever saw in my life. Eye never knew vodka shined so expensively from the solitude of a clientele's flute glass.

Her diamonds glistened brighter than any star eye ever saw in the sky and eye got a chill every time she looked at me dine with her son.

I remembered how he looked at me. Like an unstable man trapped in a snow storm. Clearly lost within a realm notwithstanding his current ideology.

His eyes bulged out of his head. "Pharoah. My mother is here."

I rolled my eyes like, "Oh *no*, man. I don't know where to go." Eye was being very sarcastic.

"She spotted us. She's over there by the entrance."

"Eye gotta get out of here," eye went on, stifling a yawn.

"Quick, get under the table."

Now my eyes bulged outta my head. "What? Do I look like a fucking carpet?"

"No, you look like shit. Get under the table."

"But people will see."

"Look around, dumb ass. Half of these people are drunk. Dressed in expensive garb and the gab fest of bullshit trickling into my ears was nothing short of lame. Get under the table, Niggah."

Eye got under the table, and rests my head in his lap. I was mad mad mad. Why are we pretending in front of his Mama? I held my breath when eye heard the chair slide from the table. Oh, no. She saw me.

What do eye do?

Σ

"Where is he?" she asked viciously.

"Where is who, Mom?"

"Don't play fucking games, Andy. I always knew you were gay."

"I'm not gay."

"Bullshit!" she sounded, looking around discreetly with a killer smile. Hair pulled into a tight bun with huge curls framing her face. "Yes you are. Eye never seen you with a woman, as fine as you are."

"Don't remind me, Mama."

"Where is he? I know eye saw a man at this table."

"It was one of the waiters, mother. I told him I wasn't satisfied with my drink and he sat down and asked me what he could do to erase my slight unease."

"Well, the waiters here are very accommodating. Very polite. As they well should be. Our taxes employ these sonsofbitches. Never talk to the hired help. Your drink isn't to par you shout I want to see the manager, and you let your unease unfold on the one in charge. He orders waiters to serve the drinks. The waiter I'm sure had to…sneak you a free drink to pacify your…slight unease, Son."

That teed him off. Aw. He *teed* off. Poor thing. "Go to hell, ok. Bad enough you fucked up my life."

"I fucked up your life?"

I rolled my eyes, squeezing his upper thighs, trying to get him to calm down. They are in the middle of an expensive Italian restaurant, where none of the food and drinks has prices or pictures, talking about family shit. Two blacks. Who gave two shits about their problems? With or without money blacks manage to cum up short.

"Yes, you did. Where's my *father*, mother?"

"Oh, God. And how old are you? He…fell off the face of the earth. And good ridden. He barely lasted ten minutes in the sack. I think we created you in a matter of minutes. When you fucked up that scholarship he…"

"I hate you."

"I'm your mother. I had you. You respect me."

I unzipped his pants and pulled out his huge dick. The muscles in his thighs and legs jerked. I know it hurt with my pulling out his ten inch dick in an expensive Italian restaurant.

"You don't respect me so why should I respect you?" he asked.

"Because you're the black sheep of the family."

"You walk, look and talk like a crackah and I'm the Black Sheep?"

"I resent that!"

His dick hung low like a vine. I started tonguing the swollen mushroom head, taking his dick deep into my salivating mouth, gripping his inches like the sternness of steel, holding my breath and taking it deep to the throat.

Oh, he calmed all the way down. He was twirling his hips slightly, yet keeping his composure.

"Mom. I would like to be alone."

"You still haven't answered my question."

Eye was sucking as loud as I could, taking it from my mouth and spitting on it. Eye wasn't scared of the trick. And quite frankly I was getting tired of being under this table. I didn't even take this shit over the phone. He tapped my head, yet his other hand was pushing my mouth up and down on his dick. Oh he felt it all right. The tops of his toes seemed to mobilize. Eye realized then he was curling his toes in his shiny loafers.

"What is that noise?" she asked.

He looked disgruntled. "What noise?" He held up his hands. "I don't hear anything."

"What is that on your hand?"

"What?"

"Looks like saliva. Oh my God!"

She stood up and looked under the table.

"Oh my God! *Faggot!* Sucking my son's dick under the table?"

I used the back of my arm to wipe spit from my mouth. Glad I was wearing a black suit. Hid all my business and shit.

I got from under the table. I didn't give a shit. What were they gonna do? Beat my skinny ass. I wish a bitch would today.

I said, "I dropped my earring on the floor." I held it up. "See, you nasty bitch."

"Pharoah! That's my mother!" Andy sounded and actually sounded dumb as hell. Didn't stand up to your mother but trying to publicly stand up for her against the strength of my tongue? Chile. *General Hospital* is down the street, on Channel 10.

I looked at him. "She's talks to you like you're the bitch yet I gotta respect the bitch? I heard everything she said to you." I faced her. "You need your ugly ass whipped."

"Are you going to do it?"

"I would. But I let women handle my light weight. I don't hit women, but I damn sure do curse them the fuck out, bitch. What kinda mother are you?"

"You're the faggot!"

"I'm the faggot? That ain't what I heard, you dickless trick."

Andy's mouth fell open. "Pharoah! Shut up! Bitch SHUT UP!"

"I'ma bitch and your Mama snatching your wig in a restaurant? Didn't she walk out on your daddy raping you over a goddamn football scholarship?" Both of them turned white in the face. "Fuck you, Andy. We're so over and through. I'm not committing to a man who lets his mother pull his cock ring. Are you crazy? I actually let you beat me?"

"You can't leave me!" he said, his mother looking on in shame.

"And you said you were displeased with a goddamn drink!" she boasted. "*You* said a waiter was sitting at the table with your slight uneasy ass. And you were lying! All to cover up this faggot bullshit. I denounce you as a son!"

"Mama!"

"I heard his daddy was a faggot!" I said, crossing my arms across my chest. Now what, bitch. Explain it. I'm listening. As well as everyone else in the establishment serving lukewarm food.

Everyone fell silent.

She covered her mouth, stunned.

Tears formed in her eyes and I picked up a glass of water and dumped it on her ass.

"Cool off, bitch. I heard he was gay. You walked in on him fucking your brother, you know…the one you moved away from and abandoned. The one you left to die in the ghetto while you lunch with moneyed muthafuckahs. Yet your son is the black sheep. God or bad he's your goddamn brother. And everything you achieved outside of him his asshole came into your bed behind your back and destroyed. Andy told me your husband, his daddy fucked your brother better than he ever fucked you."

"GO TO HELL! What is this nonsense, Andy? Are you going to allow this?"

"Andy doesn't have a choice." I looked at him. "We're done with. Forever. Hear me. Go fuck your mama. She been butt fucking your ass for years, didn't you tell me that, Andy?"

"What?"

"I'm gone. I'm outta here. I quit all that stripping bullshit, too. I made the money, *keep* the change."

And eye spun on my heel and walked towards the EXIT. "Your dick tasted like shit!" And the doors closed behind me.

And *complete* pandemonium.

I took a cab to his house.

When eye got there eye pulled out my suit cases and started packing my shit. I was devastated. Because I loved a man who emotionally embarrassed me. I was in love with an image. I was in love with the seeds of his success. I wanted to be his so eye could show off and he was beating my ass for showing off. I was reflecting another man's picture of perseverance, neglecting my own blemishing soul.

Huge tears burned the epidermis of my face. Opening and closing drawers, packing my clothes and shit.

I didn't know how I was going to get all this shit to Mama's house. If she lets me come back.

Andy bought me all this shit, letting me keep the bags. Now the baggage was suffocating me and eye was too weak to carry simply just one.

Andy's phone rang endlessly, but I didn't answer it. For what? Reflections couldn't talk so eye'll just keep quiet and quietly pack my shit.

I had over $5,000 in cash in a small wooden box with a lock. I pocketed the key and put the box in my book bag.

I went into the bathroom and stared myself in the mirror. Looking flawless, yet my heart looked terrible. I didn't know who that Niggah was looking at me from the reflection, when I'm still reflecting Andy's failures and passing them off as my own.

What kind of man was I? I was the man Daddy wanted me to be. A failed muthafuckah. That's why his ass abandoned me. Didn't show or teach me a fucking thing.

Now I couldn't stand up and be a man.

I didn't know how to.

I ran cold water over my face, crying so hard I lowered myself to my knees, covering my face. Shaken. Destroyed. Devastated, I looked up and leaned against the wall. Less energetic, and properly silenced.

I managed to stand up and turn off the cold and hot water knobs. They twisted silently.

I walked out into the bedroom, staring at my feet. A zombie of my own design, the design influenced by Andy. We all draw shit, yet others influence the outcome.

I looked up and came face to face with Andy.

Holding a Beretta.

Aimed at my chest.

THE ANGER OF THE BEA$T

He was distraught. The look becomes him really well. My breath caught in my throat, I stood firm and still. Guns scared me half to death. I tired to hide that fear from my face but my cheekbones were weak sonsofbitches and weren't built to hold a single tear. No matter how you squint when you force a tear.

"I can't believe you pulled me and my father out of the closet in a restaurant I've dined for nearly 15 years."

"And you blame me?"

"*Yea* I blame you, Pharaoh. I blame you for everything that has gone wrong. I told you to hide under the table, not suck me up."

"Yet you didn't stop it."

"I wasn't supposed to."

"So you have to take part of the blame for what occurred with your overbearing mother."

"She's not overbearing! She loves hard. She loves her family."

"Any woman calling her son a faggot is one stupid bitch. Where do you think she learned it from?"

"I have a gun, bitch."

I held up my hands. "I can see that. But you can't blame me for your mother's accusation. She said she always knew you were gay. That means she clocked the flavor of your tea before you realized you drank tea, and that's my fault?"

"The things you repeated to my mother were things I told you in confidence."

"And I held you at that regard. Until you withered in public from her icy words."

"I always wanted to tell her just how I felt, yet I didn't have the courage."

"Because she loves hard? Because she loves her family, Andy?"

"Shut up!"

"I told your mother what you wanted to say. It nearly crippled her. She could hardly breathe through those dick sucking lips. I spoke your truth with my voice. It clearly opened her eyes. What happened when eye left?"

"She said she disowned me. Yet when I walked past her and out of her life she grabbed my arm and told me we could go back to the family house and talk about it. That she already lost her husband to her brother, so she wasn't equipped to lose her son."

"A son made through a flawed union."

"Pharoah…"

"Your daddy was always gay, Andy. You told me that one day when you were drunk. You said your father told you he married your mother because his father, a Pastor, suspected him of being homosexual in the congregation. So that was a cover-up marriage, and you were the misled seed. Your only job in this life was to make him feel his manhood through his stern discipline, and nothing more. You're a

Mascot for the Your Daddy is Gay Academy. He still chased dick, Andy. YOU TOLD ME THAT! He even raped you."

He shot a huge hole in the wall behind me, and I shut up.

"That's your problem. You don't know when to shut the fuck up. You went on and on, Pharaoh, telling my business. Making me face something I wasn't prepared to face. I don't want to lose my mother so I hid my lifestyle."

"Why are you protecting a woman who loves her status in government more than the welfare of her own adult son? Are you serious?"

"My father was an incredible man."

"I never said he was. And if he was Mr. Incredible, why did he treat you like shit, Andy?"

"He's a man. He was supposed to be hard on me."

"Andy. You once told me your Daddy beat you for saying a boy was cute when you were in the third grade. You said he stripped you naked, beat you with an extension cord, poured salt all over your body then pissed all over you. You told me that was the worst pain of your life."

"Pharaoh! Shut up!"

He put the gun in my face, pressing the barrel direct center of my forehead. I puked up so badly it got all over him and he didn't flinch.

"I'm gonna kill you, bitch. I've heard enough. I can't take you and that mouth any longer. You stepped all over my manhood."

"Oh, yea? Your Mama tap dancing on it, too. Shoot me bruh I don't care."

"You do care. You threw up all over me, bitch. Oh you care."

"You gonna kill me anyway, so I'ma say what the fuck I wanna say."

He slapped me across the face with the weapon, blood all over my teeth and lips. The pain gave me a dizzying head ache.

"I love you, Pharaoh. I'm not letting you leave. I just gotta beat your ass back in line. I told you. I rule you. You worship me. You do what ever the fuck I say."

I shook my head. "I denounce you. I love no one. I don't even love myself. How can I be in love with you when I don't even love myself? I don't know what love is or what it looks like. I never have seen love. All I ever seen in my life is pain and pain disguised beautifully as love. Tricking me. My father left me. Mama picked a Niggah over me. I had a rough goddamn life, and you bitching over your daddy being gay?"

"Pharoah. I don't want you hurt. I gotta protect you, baby. I already lost my Daddy. Your remind me so much of him. You look just like him, Pharaoh. That's why I fell in love with you and I gotta control you. I am the man for you. Do what I say we won't have any problems, Daddy. I wouldn't have to beat you and make you sell your ass."

"What?"

Daddy, the Illu$ion

"You hurt my mother. Marrying her knowing you could never truly love her because you're gay. You love dick, just like she do. Why did mama have to walk in on you fucking my uncle? Her own brother, Pharoah?"

"What are you talking about? I never even met your Daddy."

"Daddy stop lying. You always told me you were my King, you were the Pharoah of the house. Remember telling me that?"

"Andy? I'm not your father!"

"SHUT UP!" He rammed the back of my head into the wall.

I blinked rapidly, trying to hold my forehead. But I fell deeper into the blackness of his paranoia. I didn't know who I was at the moment.

"You will pay for what you did to us, Dad. You are a weak excuse of a man. YOU RAPED ME BITCH!"

He pressed the gun into my bloody mouth.

"I should shoot you right here." His eyes balls of hate. "Now Mama blames me for her flaws. She calls me what she called you. She blames me for everything that you did. I lost my mother because of you."

"Andy…"

"SHUT UP!"

"I thought you said you'd never intentionally hurt me, Andy."

He blinked twice and held his breath, taking the gun from my mouth. He started taking a few steps back, avoiding my eyes.

"I did say that."

"So you lied."

"I didn't lie.

"Yes you did! You beat me, cause me discomfort in my life. Make me do what you say. You don't do that to those you love."

"My Daddy did it to my Mother, Pharoah. Beat her ass and made her stay in the marriage. Made her represent the image of family. They were both in politics. She feared him so badly she did exactly what he wanted. Even watched him get fucked by other men in their bed duct taped to chair."

"Andy, I hear you…"

"No you don't."

"I'm leaving you, Andy. Right now I don't care if you beat me or not. You're gonna be beating me all the way to the grave. I hate you. I don't want to be here. I'm not taking none of this shit with me. Just give me my book bag and let me go!"

"I'm not letting you go! I possess you. You are my possession, bitch!"

I started to walk past him, the gun fearing me no more and he pushed me on the bed and raped me on his sheets. No matter how I fought he beat me with the butt of his weapon and overpowered me. He came inside me so many times I lost count. I kept falling in and out of consciousness.

He rode me like a wave rides the sea. I couldn't contain myself nor did I ever try. I was so weak inside I forgot what strength was.

When he was done with my body he whipped me. My body jerked, yet I could hardly open my eyes nor move.

I felt my skin tear. I felt the blood.

He threw salt all over my body. The stinging made me scream.

He stood in the bed and began to piss all over me, the wetness dissolved the salt into my open wounds and I yelled.

Nobody heard me.

Nobody but Andy.

I blacked out. I don't know how long I been unconscious, but I did know I was alive. I knew who I was. I was still here, but everything was so dark, Lord. What I've decided for my life has hindered me beyond understanding.

I roam around the blackness, flinging my arms and connecting with nothing. I felt nothing. I was breathing, but I couldn't see a thing.

I started turn, tripping over myself yet nothing lines my darkened path. But I ran faster, sometimes falling flat on my face and I got up and kept running. Didn't bother to dust myself off. For what? I couldn't see a thing.

As I blinked against the darkness the bottom of my eye lids pulled up brief pictures of light and objects. So I blinked faster and everything came into focus.

Andy was asleep next to me. An empty Vodka bottle and a small empty bottle of sleeping pills.

He tried to sit up, but it was so hard. But I kept trying. Each time I moved my arms I got a little stronger than I was before so I moved my feet and my toes and I used my hands to sit up. My arms trembled with my legs.

My body felt like it was on fire.

I stood up and grabbed my pants and put them on. I fell on my ass doing so, but I sucked up the pain and kept putting them on.

I found my shirt by the bathroom door. I snatched it up and put it on. I took one of his fancy baseball caps and pulled it low over my eyes. I took his car keys and made my way out into the living room.

Gripping my book bag, I had to get out of here. His abuse has gone on long enough. I am being beaten for what his father had done to his family. I was being beaten because I reminded Andy of his father, so he said.

I know enough to know that that ain't love. That's obsession. Obsessed with changing a past you couldn't change. What's done was done. Written in the Book and documented with an index and page numbers. Maybe it's catalogued in libraries and shelved next to amazing books like Hitler, Swastikas and the untold stories of battered souls.

I opened the front door and made my way to his car.

I was two hours away from home.

The Wooden Box

I drove myself to my Mitsubishi Gallant Mama helped me get. It was parked at a friend's house in South Miami. Shit, I still had to pay her back the $3,000 she gave me to put down on it.

Once I got to my car I wiped Andy's car of my prints, wiped down the keys, tossed them on the seat with rag-clad hands and closed the door. Just in case he called the police and reported his car stolen.

I jumped in my car, and blasted Tupac's *Picture me Rolling*, fleeing the past.

Leaving Andy's ass behind me.

I drove to the Cutler Ridge Mall. It was around Christmas time, and I grabbed my book bag and parked by the Main entrance. Cloudy day. Not so sunny, but that's ok. It was a little chilly.

Making my way into the mall, I was approaching a shoe store and Kay Bee toy Store. I looked at all the holiday decorations hanging everywhere.

Everyone was in their versions of a Festive Mood. Rubbed of on me in a positive way.

I was walking past the shoe store when I heard, "Shut up, Boy! I can't afford that expensive video game for you. Mama pays bills!"

"Not fair! You said if I made straight A's on my report card you will get me the game!"

"NO, BRIAN!"

"I HATE YOU! I'MA TELL DADDY!"

She smacked him. "Fuck your no good Daddy. He is doing life without in prison! He will never get out. So tell his dumb ass! TELL HIM!"

"I want the game!"

I walked up to her just as she broke down on a nearby bench. She covered her forehead, sobbing. Three other small kids were crying with her, climbing in her lap, trying to stroke her hair or kiss her face.

Brian, had to be about 16 years old, put his hands on his hips, showcasing rebellion. Yet the sight of his mother crying did a number on him.

"I'm sorry, mama."

"Excuse me, ma'am."

She looked up at me with red eyes.

"What do you want, boy?"

"I overheard what you said to your son."

"You stay outta my business!" She jumped up to her feet. "I'm a God fearing woman. I beat my kids, so what! What? You gonna call the law on me? At least I'm trying to raise my kids! Why are you trying to get the crackahs to take my children from me? They are all I have."

"Are you *really* that God fearing?"

"Yes!"

"So that means you believe in him?"

"Yes I do, muthafuckah."

"If you believe in him, why are you cursing me? I'm nearly 21 years old."

"So what? You shouldn't be butting in my goddamn business."

"Pray to him to get your son that game, if you believe in him."

"I will not."

Brian said, "She needs to do something. Because I want my game. I stay home and look after my siblings. I'm not a bad kid. I do good in school. I am the model son. And she still doesn't keep her word."

"Pray to him if you believe in God."

"Leave me alone."

"Pray to him. You can't even pray to the one you claim to believe in. And you show your oldest child this. No wonder he doesn't believe in prayer.'

"How did you know that?" Brian asked, looking me over.

"By the way you talk down to your mother. That's how I know."

She closed her eyes tightly. "God please help me get my son that game! Amen."

She glared at me.

"See. I did it. He doesn't answer. As always."

"Do you always pray to him?"

She got in my face. "Yes. Every damn day and night. I pray for the big and small things, yet he doesn't answer. He ignores me."

I opened my book bag and handed her the wooden box. "What is this?" She looked it over suspiciously. Her kids were looking, too.

I handed Brian the key. "Respect your mother, or you lose it all."

"Lose all of what?" he asked.

"Unlock it."

"Is this a bomb?" she asked.

"No. Open it. You said you believe in God."

"I do."

Brian unlocked $5,000 in cash, Money I made from stripping. Well the residuals were going to help this mother of four with a rebellious son.

The sight of the cash made her slap her forehead. "Oh, God! Oh, God, thank you!"

"Don't thank me, continue thanking God. Jesus died for us all, and I know how rough it can get for a single mother. My mom is a single mother. I used to be Brain when I was his age. Full of hate and anger for the things I didn't understand."

Brian hugged me tightly. "Thank you, Mr.! I can get my game!"

"Thank you, Son!" She hugged me too, kissing my cheek.

"Make your life and your kid's life better. Ya'll need that money more than I do. I stripped to make that money. I don't deserve that."

She took a hundred dollar bill and stuffed it in my pocket. "I appreciate this. I don't know who you are or where you come from, but your mother raised a mighty fine son. Thank you so much. I almost don't want to take the money."

I pushed the box towards her. "Take it. It's yours."

And I took the money from my pocket.

And handed it to Brian. "I want to see straight A's on that report card again. That's my down payment. My investment is there."

"Thank you. What's your name?"

I held my head high. "Pharoah."

I will NEVER put man before Jehovah ever again.

Not after the Hell I just went through.

NIGGAHS, how do you feel about...
THEM?

Lord Jennings

These were opinions expressed by PHAROAH, and wasn't a direct aim at EVERY NIGGAH.

Eye loved NAS' NIGGER album, the one he changed the title to. That was a hard ass album, and one of the best albums eye have ever heard in my life. Definitely in my Top 5. And even with that being said, you know what eye never understood? Yup. You guessed it. NIGGAHS. NIGGAHS said one thing and often times did another. Half of them couldn't keep their word for shit and most of them reminded you that the world wasn't flat or round. It was the shape of a bucket and we were crabs stopping one or the other from escaping whenever one became successful. Or died trying to be.

    The *essence* of a NIGGAH has died away with scholars, who used to be NIGGAHS themselves (abused the word more than I did), trying to abolish it. Chile. You couldn't think for us all. If you chose to discredit the word then that's on you. But don't push your damn views on everybody else. I don't know you and you don't know me. So stay the hel up out my face when eye do what eye do for myself.

    Eye was never into Oreo Cookie eating NIGGAHS.

NIGGAHS were chameleons. They were like roaches, set 'em free they'd adapt to any and everything to survive. NIGGAHS with nothing to live for got into the most shit. When you gotta find something to do that meant you got too much time on your hands. When you got too much time on your hands *that's* when most NIGGAHS get into trouble, wanna rob muthafuckahs because they worked hard for their shit and you didn't.

Didn't you hear of the words GOD and KARMA? Whether you believed in it or not really didn't matter. Want proof either/or exits?

Just look around your present reality. You still down and out, can't catch a break, your Hoe hates you and giving another NIGGAH your pussy, your kids disowned you and you're broke as fuck, don't even got two dollars to catch the bus and all that robbing you did you still begging a muthafuckah for ten dollars NIGGAH wake up.

That's KARMA right there giving you back what you put into the universe. The only one who can change that is YOU, NIGGAH. It's not too late.

Granted, not all NIGGAHS were bad, but we all had our fucked up ways. All of us. Eye didn't give a shit how Holier-than-thou you were. We all had flaws. We're al struggling with something. We all did shit we ain't proud of.

Eye've met all sorts of NIGGAHS. Some had hearts of gold and would really stick their necks out for those they loved, but some were plagued with darkness and needed to be in a mental ward, not the streets around normal everyday people.

Some NIGGAHS hated God and pretended to love Him, others embraced God but still resorted to Gun and Ski Masks to feed their families because those Cuban employers here in Miami-Dade County treating NIGGAHS like we're Castro and didn't wanna give them a job. Rule of thumb: CUBANS LOOKED OUT FOR THEIR OWN FIRST, so NIGGAHS, look out for your own as well.

A while back I watched a Cuban Manager in various establishments throw NIGGAHS' job applications in the garbage the minute they left out the door. NIGGAH was spiffy. He had on a nice suit that emphasized his personality, clean cut low fade that brought out his gorgeous eyes, hid his tattoos, and took out the earrings. Gave a smile. Interview went well. What was the problem? He was black, and nearly every employee in those said establishments were Cubans, that hardly spoke a lick of goddamn English. This was a huge problem in Miami, but its like nobody cares. So now the majority of the NIGGAHS eye knew packed up and moved to other states so they could take care of themselves or their families.

Or they robbed muthafuckahs.

What good was prayer when your children starving to death because nobody wanted to give you a chance. We all gotta survive. And with most NIGGAHS, any means necessary was putting it mildly.

Why did some NIGGAHS live by the code of the streets when the government already gave the streets names and numbers? You lived by the code of something the white man owned? Why was eye scratching the hell outta my head right now?

NIGGAHS killed BLACKS that representing RED and BLUE and the outcome was WHITE controlling murderous NIGGAHS when you're reduced to a state number. BLACK killing BLACK for that Red and Blue makes the WHITE man's job THAT much EASIER. I don't get it. And eye never will. Damn, get a goddamn clue, NIGGAHS. It ain't a coincidence police sirens were RED AND BLUE, damn.

These days NIGGAHS worrying about the wrong thing instead of focusing on the right thing. Eye tell you what the majority of you NIGGAHS NEED to do. Take your soft asses *home* and be a father to your goddamn kids! Better yet, marry the woman that had your kids, the woman that held you down, took your shit, cleaned up after your ass without asking you for a goddamn thang, and help her raise productive kids, so they didn't turn out like you. Life for most of us will never be THE COSBY SHOW. That shit was left in the 80's.

Eye tell you what some of you NEED to do. Stop marrying women and making babies with mislead women knowing you're a secret faggot throwing shade and scandal at the out-of-the-closet gays who were more man that you'd ever be. If you're such a real NIGGAH why the fuck you dissing a gay man every time he walks by you, muthafuckah that didn't mean he wanted your stank booty ass.

If you ask me, that makes me question YOU. Why you so nervous every time one popped up on your radar? Did you fuck him before? Are you scared he gonna snatch your so-called goon ass out the closet. Like my great grandma once said, "Don't do shit you're ashamed of."

And for once, NIGGAHS, if you're so 'Hood, so goddamn STREET, why do half your dicks get hard when I walk by?

Eye respect real NIGGAHS, gays, bisexuals, lesbians and transgenders for being open about who they are so a muthafuckah wouldn't have to play GUESS WHO board games. Those were the hard muthafuckahs, if you asked me. I respect a NIGGAH enough to respect myself at all times. Just because he's gay didn't mean he found your black, greasy, retarded ass attractive.

Don't diss anybody that's real about themselves when you're a GOON NIGGAH sucking and fucking your homeboy in the darkness because you think a bitch didn't know. HIV, AIDS, Syphilis, gonorrhea and herpes was REAL, NIGGAHS. That's some REAL NIGGAH shit. Protect yourselves. Better yet before you fuck anybody else be a REAL NIGGAH and go get tested. Know your status.

A NIGGAH riding around with a car load of NIGGAHS day in and day out what the fuck? While your Baby Mama on the goddamn bus getting your son outta school? What's wrong with that picture, girl? You love women though, huh? Pussy makes your world go round when all you seem to go "round" were NIGGAHS.

I know what some of you DL NIGGAHS *need* to do. If you didn't want a muthafuckah worrying about you then mind your own goddamn business. Eye didn't care what you did, DL NIGGAH.

Do you and Pharoah will do me. Stay the fuck outta my business then we won't have no muthafucking problems. Who am eye to judge you, so don't goddamn judge me. NIGGAH you ain't, won't and will never be GOD.

You so HARD NIGGAH give your life for the world and get hung on the cross. Sacrifice you life for the greater cause of good. Until then, JESUS is the hardest man that has ever lived and if you couldn't DO or TOP what he did then miss me, take your bee bee gun back to the dealer and get a new goddamn hobby.

JESUS healed and fought enemies in a very non-violent way. He used the Word, not a bullet. He wore sheets and sandals, didn't even have a computer or the internet, yet he didn't go around robbing people, did he?

And you DL NIGGAH PaTOR eye got one thing to say to you: take your dick out his ass and don't say a goddamn thing to me. Simple. If you think you're getting my ten perent, think a-damn-gain. If I'm going to hell fuck NIGGAH you're going to Hell's Hell in gasoline draws with WD-40 on your asshole, bitch.

DL NIGGAH if you getting fucked by NIGGAHS you meeting on BGCLive.cim, ADAM4ADAM.com, MEN4now.com don't you EVER say TWO WORDS of negativity about the PHAROAH.

All on the PARTY LINE hooking up with other DL TYPES, begging for them to hook up with you. Some PLEASE BABY PLEASE James Brown shit. Get a new hobby, horny muthafuckahs.

Ladies, you may think your pussy was the bomb, all golden, crispy brown, but your NIGGAH fucking your gay ass DL brother, your homeboy, and was on the PARTYLINE finding NIGGAHS to dick down in your bed when you're a) outta town and b) at damn work. And NIGGAHS, don't think your dicks were the shit when behind your back your bitch getting her pussy sucked and clit pinched by a butch bitch.

Goddamn shame this bisexual NIGGAH can still pull the ladies, Hoes, Tricks, sluts and the women. I'm a charismatic sonofabitch. Eye didn't have many gay friends because gay NIGGAHS kept shit going, were always in some shit and always hated on a muthafuckah because you didn't like Beywansay's played out ass.

What eye look like doing the Single Ladies. I got a Single Pair of Nuts so cum and Put a Tongue on it, bitches. If you couldn't make me nut from giving me head don't think eye'm putting a ring on a goddamn thang!

Most of my homeboys were straight NIGGAHS. REAL NIGGAHS. NON-JUDGMENTAL NIGGAHS. NIGGAHS I respected and that respected me. Those were NIGGAHS keeping me grounded and supporting me in my literary career.

They accept me for who eye was as long as the boundaries were never crossed. They understand PHAROAH didn't want their ass at all.

We hang out together, go out on the Beach and have drinks. Their wives and girlfriends were there also and even they accept me.

Sometimes their wives took a NIGGAH out to eat just to get me away from the computer sometimes. Feels good to know that PHAROAH has that kind of love.

Eye think the most flawed thing that was *ever* invented were *NIGGAHS*. Because they couldn't work together, fucked each other's Hoes and went after another NIGGAH's success with hatred and vindictiveness. Always talking about a NIGGAH yet having sex with the same garbage pail kid-looking Hoes they've been fucking for years. Damn, 400 years hasn't opened none of your eyes, huh? We did sell ourselves to slavery, and continue to daily, even now. Slavery ain't over. Know your History, NIGGAHS.

Ain't tired of wasted pussy yet? You see a NIGGAH dating a garbage Hoe trust he couldn't pull a decent Hoe. Why did some NIGGAHS flirt with the same bitch for over ten years and made like he's pimping.

NIGGAH you ain't pimping. You public pretending, like jail house Lawyers. Everybody fucked the Hoe you been yapping off too for ten years, get a clue.

And just because you dating and married a white bitch didn't men she was better than a black chick. You better look at O.J., Kobe and Tiger Woods. Those white women will clean your ass out.

A NIGGAH that never has money is the main one begging for your Four Loco and SKOL vodka, talking shit about you to your family then got the gall to smile in your face begging to smoke some of your Black and Mild cigar. NIGGAH, puleaze. Winn Dixie was hiring for overnight stockers right as we speak. Take grandma's advice and go put in for a goddamn JOB.

Once hired, pay me back all my goddamn money you "borrowed" and stop asking for my shit. Get your own. Damn.

Couldn't even enjoy your shit these days without garbage NIGGAHS begging for your shit. Please let me hit the blunt, please give me some liquor; damn could a NIGGAH get a piece of that chicken wing.

And wassup with NIGGAHS cruising NW 79th Street (yea, NIGGAHS, I be scooping *all* your asses) picking up Tranny's and fucking them all over Dade County, talking about they weren't gay? Huh? Doesn't the tranny got a dick? Aren't you bouncing GOON dick in TRANNY asshole?

Nuff said.

One NIGGAH asked could he fuck this jazzy Hoe that was out with me after one of my book signings and eye was like sure bruh bruh but the Hoe packing a dick bigger than you and your senile daddy's and he/she likes to fuck NIGGAHS in the ass, too. And the NIGGAH actually got with her on the Low and took her/he to the nearest Hotel and had it out for a couple hours till he got a nut.

Eye was cool in the gang, he/she was a fan of mine, bought one of my books but I passed the sexual advance with respect and told the tranny Hoe eye didn't get down like that. Eye was bi, but not that goddamn bi. That's too much bisexuality for me. Letting a NIGGAH with bigger tits than the ones eye was breast fed on get *Bout it! Bout it!* in my ass ain't happening. *Bout it! Bout it!* played out like Hammer's money.

Come with some new shit for the kid, ahem me, then maybe we'll be in business.

And if you wasn't gonna pay a NIGGAH back NIGGAHS stop asking to BORROW money then when eye give it to you and a week later the pied piper knocking on your door for my shit don't act retarded.

Reach deep in those pockets, pass the lighter and your weed and give me my green. Just say could you get five dollars, then eye'll say fuck no and send you on your merry way, NIGGAH.

All Pharoah wanted to know was…

What kinda NIGGAH were YOU?

HOME GOING SERVICE FOR:

Sunrise:
August 1995

Sunset:
July 1996

The U.S. ARMY

Pharoah C. Wilson's being
PROGRAMMED
March 1998
11:30 a.m.
Sweet Home Baptist Church
69 S.W. DOOMSDAY Lane
Rev. Dr. God vs. Satan

John 11:35 *Jesus wept.*

A Time to be Born: Pharoah Wilson, Jr....I don't wish to say right now.

Love, Pharoah

A Time to Grow: ...eye withered into a reflection of blackness after she, after...she...

A Time to Reflect: ...never manifested, because of the death of...

A Time to Die and be mourned: I was suffering the deepest depression of my entire life. Nothing I have nor would ever go through, experience, what the fuck ever would AMOUNT to the damage and the way I suffered at the price of my reflection...

That's the day I became an image, taking my writing more and more seriously.

Love Pharoah.
If I even know what love is...

|THE U.S ARMY OBITUARY

*Tell me about your
Time in the army*

Lord Jennings

THE U.S. ARMY

*Joining the Army was one of the
Worse decisions of my life!*

Military and law enforcement officials run in my family. My cousin Connie worked for the FEDS as well as my mother  and a lot of my good friends. My cousin Thomas was a seasoned police office with Miami-Dade and my other cousin worked for the Florida City Police Force, though I never met or laid eyes on the man in my entire life. Thomas, who I absolutely love and adore and respect, met the likes of Nelson Mandela. My Granddaddy, who I looked up to and tried to model myself after, and my Uncle spent more than fifteen years in the military and had more awards than Michael and Janet Jackson combined. My cousin with the last name of Rolle worked for the Florida City Police Department. And since I looked up to my Grandfather (because he and Alfred were the only two father figures I could actually trust) I naturally gravitated towards the military as a way out of the hell of a life I had in Miami. But at the time I joined the Army I hadn't known I had *that* many family members in Law Enforcement. Nearly all of them let me go in blindly, not fully preparing me for the shock of my life. Except my Grandfather. He schooled me. He told me the ins and outs, and that saved me from brutal ruin to life as I knew it at the time.

    I loved my grandfather. He was one of the most prestigious, intelligent men I have ever encountered. In my eyes my grandfather's shit didn't stink, he could never do any wrong (despite people in my face telling me what he did do wrong, and I NEVER listened) and I used to model myself after him. But not anymore. He could speak several languages, loved watching the *History* and *Discovery* channels, could tell you the different parts of a car and truck, and turned around and told you what kind of plant was growing in your yard better than a text book.

    My love of books came from him. And my ability to be my own man and be a leader came from his twenty years plus Airforce career. He retired a Master Sergeant and he loved that Airforce blue.

    The old saying goes don't run away from your problems because they will be at your new destination waiting to throw a block party, but that didn't stop me from running to the Army to escape Mama's house and stern iron fisted rule. I didn't have any more fight in me. Spending your entire life fighting perverted motherfuckers took a toll on my soul. I was exhausted from living by the time I got in the eleventh grade. During that time I really didn't want to know what the future brought.

I was in the 12th grade when I reluctantly swore into the U.S. Army. At first I didn't tell anybody I was even thinking of going, and when my Mom found out she was kind of against it. Well, she was fully against it.

I didn't even believe in this county when I joined The Army. Hell, shit, I didn't even believe in *myself*. I was so programmed by society and being beaten and raped before I went to the Army that, when it came to enlisting, I really didn't think anything of it.

My Army recruiter was talking, happily giving me paperwork and promising me the sun and the moon if I joined. In my mind I already joined. I made the decision months ago. What this white lady talking about, with those black ass teeth. She was into that Copenhagen snuff stuff and it disgusted me. She then spit inside an empty Zephyrhills bottle and handed me an Army pamphlet.

Weren't you supposed to give me the pamphlet BEFORE I signed my life away?

Bitch thinks she's slick, but it's all good. Keep it cool, Pharoah. In my life I've had so much adult pussy while fingering dysfunctional nipples that I could sense, feel or see a snake from a mile away without losing a nut. I still get my nut, no matter how many snakes lurking along the marble floors of the mind. Adults taught me every damn thing about life I knew.

Life was filled with images, photographs and untold hallucinations. The Untold were forgotten and locked up inside mental wards. They're pumped with drugs and kept in a surreal dream state, to the point they really didn't know who they were, where they come from or what they've done in life.

Mental wards were human laboratories. I call it The Chambers of Satan.

But what never dawned on me, as I signed and joined, was that a) my body no longer belonged to me. It belonged to the Government. I was a part of the Property Room, trained to kill and protect the government's investment: MY BODY.

And b) 30% of those locked in mental wards was dishonorable, recently retired, retired, or Vietnam war veterans who have lost their minds.

Those 30% used to wear Armed Forces Uniforms.

The thought sent a chill up my spine.

My Army recruiter treated me nicely in the beginning. She was always there at my beck and call before I signed the dotted line with a nervous John Hancock. Whatever I needed I had it. If I needed a ride to the store a government car was there to chauffer me to where I needed to go. I was treated like royalty in exchange for my signature into their organization. My Signature was a vow. A vow on the Oath. An Oath regular society didn't know about. Unless they were military veterans or rejects.

Yet after I signed and was sworn in, she hardly took my calls, she came around even lesser than the weeks before and then it had gotten to the point she simply vanished off the face of the earth.

Why?

Because I was one of the last ones that enlisted.

Quota, fulfilled.

Orders, changed.

I was a little mad about that, though. Because she was a nice woman. But the more and more I thought about it, she was getting PAID to be nice to me and that meant all her phony bullshit snowballed me.

I should have known something was up with her when she first met me. Came up to me one sunny day before I graduated from Miami Southridge in June of 1995, trying to hand me a pamphlet, but I wasn't interested at the time.

I looked her over. Well dressed. Class A's pressed much? Hmm. Too goddamn pressed, and so was her attitude and my attire has been pressed enough, didn't need some seedy white woman with a blackened smile pressing me into taking the pamphlet about something I had yet to experience or understand.

I was already in the Airforce J.R.O.T.C. I was one of the element leaders, and with Tashena Sutton (the baddest chick in the J.R.O.T.C. Program), we won a lot of Drill Competitions in High school. So I had an idea what the military was about. Or so I thought.

But that's all the military was.

Trophies and competitions.

With humans being the trophies.

I loved everything about the Airforce, and that's where I really wanted to go because of my Grandfather. I kind of wanted to follow in his footsteps.

I used to pray to God about it all the time. But it would never happen. Because eye'm Pharoah. Not my Grand father.

I couldn't get a high enough score on the ASVAB for the Airforce. One of my best friends, Marcus Sands, was going to join with me so we could be stationed together through training.

We were already in R.O.T.C. together. He'd been in it since his freshman year of high school. I joined during my senior year and I always regretted waiting that long to join it.

But when you're the oldest of five kids in a single parent, controlled home things like that you never thought about.

You rolled with the punches and took life as it came.

Marcus and I joining the Airforce would never be. I couldn't score high enough on the ASVAB, despite having a 2.9 G.P.A. in high school.

So I switched gears, joining the Army. With the help of a horny, much older Sergeant.

Who thought my asshole was his wife's pussy, often times calling me...

Her name.

$$\Sigma$$

So the thought of my recruiter giving me a phony friendship in exchange for my signature did a number on me. I was angry with myself when I met up with her and joined. She came up to me in school, in front of the Main Office at Southridge again. Consistent midget bitch. Grinning politely, she offered to take me out to lunch. I said "Sure." Hell, I was hungry. Needed the free meal, shit.

We became friends over pricey food at Red Lobster. Wanted me to join your organization feed me while I sit and roll my eyes at half the shit you're promising me. You're on my time. I wasn't on yours. You needed my signature in exchange for life as I knew it.

I never had lobster before, and she told me if I joined the Army I would get a guaranteed pay check like clockwork every two weeks and I could buy all the lobster my little ole heart desired.

They would help me set up a bank account because we got paid through Direct Deposit.

I couldn't stop looking at her fancy little ole ring. Unlike anything I'd ever seen. Intricately carved into the gleaming metal was an arch over a letter, the letter being 'G.'

Where I was from, I didn't know too many people with a bank account. And I damn sure never seen that kind of ring.

Seemed like everybody had bad goddamn credit and couldn't so much as get a good TV or bedroom furniture on credit; so they started getting utility bills put in their children's names.

Unfortunately, they fucked that up by not paying the bills on time and in the end shit was cut off, leaving their family in the darkness with no running water or electricity.

Their kids' credit and social security numbers were so fucked up that when they turned 18 and graduated high school and were starting college, any and everything they tried to get in their names they were rejected, declined, not authorized, shut down, paused, idle, game over, you lose, bwahahaha, thanks for your time, and there was nothing they could do about it.

I knew a few of my friends going through that. Getting ready for college and couldn't even qualify for financial aid because their parents fucked their credit up.

And when they asked their parents to co-sign on the loan so they could get higher education the parents gave their asses to kiss. Hell naw, bitch. Not me. I never went to college and I'm getting by so you can do the same thang, too.

I couldn't let that happen to me.

And I'll be damned if anybody open any shit up in my name without my permission. I'll take their asses to court, try me like that. Didn't give a shit if I wasn't out Mama's house yet. Open a light bill in my name and you didn't tell me I'm calling the crackers and pressing charges. Crackahs loved mingling in black shit. Made them feel like God to kick in your door waving the Glock.

And I wanted a bank account and most certainly wanted to know what having a bank account felt like. I told the recruiter that and she smiled, cleared her throat and said I could buy shit with my ID card at the PX like a credit card and I would have the best roof over my head; better than the one I was raised in as a regular member of society, the one controlled by ten percent of your paychecks and Pa$torS publicly preaching to congregations, focusing more on homosexuality and barely bringing up infidelity, adulterers, cheats, crack heads and stank pussy stripper bitches, but worship two M(m)aster behind closed doors..

I noticed, while we ate our selected choices (lobster was kinda nasty, ugh. Crab legs tasted better!), she didn't offer me the pamphlet the second time. I wanted to ask her about it but I swallowed my lobster via pride and kept my mouth closed—mashed potatoes were kinda good and those free garlic biscuit OH MY GOD!

A few days later, when I decided to go to her office to sign the papers, she ran a criminal background check on me.

That really made me shudder. Why would she do that? I was only a teenager.

She was switching shit out of a sick need to fill a quota. Enlist as many clean niggahs as you can. Their sides would be determined. They represented a part of THEM.

Any felony on your record you are a part of SOCIETY. The regular society. But not the one you've become accustomed to.

So she's babbling on, spitting—*PUH! PUH!*—in the empty bottle and sprinkles of brownish Copenhagen-clad saliva found my hand and one of the pamphlets (which had a soldier jumping out of a helicopter in full army regalia; but what got to me was the color of his eyes-—they were dead to the world (no soul left) and damn near red).

Frowning, I feverishly wiped the back of my hand over my jeans, creating friction, which kills her lurking goddamn germs.

Bitch didn't even cover her mouth nor say "I'm sorry for that."

She went on. Business as usual.

That set off alarms in me. *What* alarms? I didn't have a goddamn clue. So I did one other thing.

I proceeded.

After signing some forms she's still talking about the promises of having a fulfilling career with the Government, yet all I heard was blah blah blah blah BLAH BLAH. Ok bitch shut up!

I'm so over adults promising me the sun and the moon then turning around and taking turns fucking me and I wasn't an adult yet.

So miss me with the promises. But I stayed quiet, smiled, nodded like I had a hidden shiny red apple for her (and didn't have jack shit) and played along, remembering what my Grand Daddy said.

When I have to make major decisions, I called my Grandfather. Then I would go over and talk to him face to face. Just the two of us. I valued his opinion. His word was worth gold to me.

He gives me an unbiased view. Blood raw, no short cuts nor breaks. You decide to get on that FREEWAY you better be equipped spiritually and mentally, yes, also physically and gun it at 100 MPH on that very FREEWAY all the way to your destination. If the tire blow you better not slow down. If your engine running hot you better keep that foot firmly pressed on the gas pedal and if the muthafucking engine blow BOOM you better jump out the speeding car, tuck and roll, high scrawl off to the side of the road and low crawl through the bushes. But never stop.

Resting was *never* really an option.

Around that time I was reduced to ruble and debris in my own life, living out the perception of being a sex slave for older people all through my teenage years. And now that I was broke, left with nothing, I was growing weary of the lustful and expensive catering…in exchange for my complete silence.

Why should I give joining the Army a second thought? Couldn't be any worse than living on the other team. Society vs. Them, the Government. That's the only two sides on planet earth. Follow the rules and respect the law, or suffer an agonizing prison sentence, or worse, be put to death.

And they say Hell isn't on Earth? Who lied to you, 'cause, ahem, it IS!

After the way my ancestors were dragged, kidnapped and beaten across the slavish, evil waters of the hellish Atlantic Ocean (The Devil's Sea of the Gateway) you really think for one second that wouldn't hinder the respect I would endure for Caucasians?

After my ancestors were separated from competitive tribes (each kidnapping each other and selling for a few gold pieces into slavery, The Wall Street of that Era), they had to have Bibles and Gods and religions shoved down their throats and half of the slaves couldn't read nor write so now eye suffer the loss of separation from family and I gotta try to read a Bible and convert to the Catholic views of my white slave owners and masters?

Every time I saw those old videos of beautiful black souls being sprayed down by racist ass Police, shrieking from snarling dogs and pressurized water hoses nearly tearing the skin from their bones, I grew angry inside. I felt so much rage I would literally squeeze my nails into my closed fists drawing blood and not feel a goddamn thing. For some reason, before I signed the papers, flashes of my ancestors being sprayed with water hoses came to mind.

When the Bic ballpoint pen touched the line where I signed my John Hancock, images of Martin Luther King, Malcolm X and dogs snapping at the ankles of my black folks colored the retinas of my eyes.

Was I selling out, I thought? Was I joining the ranks of the enemies? Was I going to be a part of THEM, separate from SOCIETY and life as I knew it?

Was I selling out on myself? I used to say the Pledge of Allegiance with so much contempt, I used to lip-synch it with everyone else in school, but the breath in my larynx never formed the words. Too many images of my ancestors being helplessly beaten contradicted that shiny sea shit.

As my paperwork was being processed, awaiting ASVAB scores, we hit a snag. All kinds of shit came up on my name. It showed that I went to prison and had felonies on my record.

She glared at me. "Why didn't you tell me you had a criminal record?"

I glared at her late ass. "Bitch I'm only 17 years goddamn old, what goddamn record I got when I'm still in high school and am about to fucking GRADUATE?"

She calmed down. "I'm sorry for snapping."

"Take me home."

"Pharoah…"

"NOW! I gotta tell my Mama about this."

She grabbed her keys, wallet and walked towards the office door.

"Come on, Pharoah. Let's go talk to your mother."

Mama wasn't an easy woman to talk to. Sometimes I thought had a robot for a mother. She was so hard and stern and set in her ways she hardly compromised. She made all of our decisions. Well, at least she thought she made mine. I always, in the end, did what Pharoah wanted to do because I did know that this was my life. Not hers.

Mom shifts on the chair in her living room, giving the white lady the once over. Her eyes were full of knowledge. She pulled on her cigarette, leaned her head back a tad and blew smoke in the air. The recruiter was on Mama's stomping grounds now.

"You don't look like an Army recruiter," Mama said. She wasn't playing games.

My recruiter smiled, spitting in her water bottle. Black snuff-clad spit trailed along the sides, towards the bottom of the wrinkled bottle. It used to be a water bottle till she sucked all the water and air down her throat.

"I am."

"Where were you stationed at?"

The recruiter, who I'll call Directory Assistance, said, "You have knowledge of the military?" looking around

Mom's house at the different things that made our house a warm home.

"I'm one of Them."

I listened intently. "What do you mean?" A muscle on the side of her face flinched, and her left leg nervously shook. She smiled again, like a gushing blonde, and Mama wasn't with it.

"My father did over 25 years in the Airforce and I work for the government. I am a military brat."

"You do?" Directory Assistance asked. I guess she thought we were on welfare. "What's your line of work?"

"A correctional officer."

"I hear the state corrections offer incredible pay," said Directory Assistance and Mama crossed her legs.

She tucked her chin back with a phony half smile.

"I'm Federal. The Feds."

She remained silent.

After a few moments of silence, Mama told me to go get her a glass of water. I didn't hesitate, pout nor back talk.

"Yes, ma'am…you want ice?" I had some resentment in my eyes. Even though joining the Army was my decision, Mama rained on my decision making by reminding me who was the boss.

Mama's head snapped at me. "Pharoah, you know how I like my water."

"Ice it is," I smiled; clearly embarrassed and Directory Assistance was watching me flash the fakest smile of my goddamn life. Yes, I was upset.

When I opened the freezer to put ice in Mama's glass, I whispered, "Oh, yea." I stopped smiling. Anger stung my eyes to the point they welled up with tears. "I'm joining the Army. Tired of being treated like this. She was closer to the goddamn fridge than I was."

"Pharoah, you said something?"

I released a large gush of air.

I forgot the robot had radars for ears.

Hesitantly, I handed Mama the water. The ice tinkled in the cool, moistened glass.

Mama smiled. "Thank you." She looked at Directory. "So why did you wanna see me."

"We have a problem with your son joining the Armed Forces."

"Who's we?" Mama asked, sipping her water. Her hair meticulously framed her face. A series of silky curls. "The President is also my boss. That's who I work for."

"Then we understand each other."

"Get to the point." Mama set the glass down with attitude. She was not fucking around. "I got things to do."

"I ran a background check on your son."

Mama dismissed the comments with the wave of her hands. "He's never been to jail a day in his life. I made sure of that."

She handed Mama a folder with papers in it. Of the search itself. The conclusion of the investigation.

Mama tossed it on the table. "I don't need to read that shit. My son has *never* been to jail. Did I say that in Spanish?"

Oh, boy. Here it comes.

"Ma'am, you don't have to curse…"

"This is my goddamn house. I pay the bills here. You don't like it there's the door!"

"I'm sorry. I didn't mean to imply." Directory Assistance looked at me like a lost dog, and I handed her a pamphlet.

"Have you thought about joining the Army?" I joked, smiling at her and everybody laughed, even Mama lightened up.

Nice save, Pharoah!

"Pharoah's silly," Mama said. She picked up the folder. Quietly flipped through it.

"This is not my son," Mama said.

"Yes it is."

Mama glared at her with an attitude. "No it's not. Two different social security numbers. And my son's birthday is June 26, 1977. This is someone else's birthday." I didn't like the look on Mama's face. What wasn't she saying?

"Let me see that?" Directory asked, reaching for the folder and Mama dumped all the papers on the table.

"This paperwork doesn't belong to my son."

"Well, we'll *redo* the investigation."

"Dumb ass, this is his father. This is his father's paperwork."

I held my breath.

"Let me see that?" I shuffled all the papers up, reading over them excitedly. Mama sat and silently watched me.

My recruiter tried to take them and I stood up, reading as much information on my father as I could. Why he went to prison. The circumstances. *Everything*. I learned more about my father and his life in ten minutes than I had ever known or gathered during my entire existence on planet earth.

Briefly, the memory of me cursing out my teacher for trying to make me watch *Roots* in the fourth grade at Bel-Aire came to mind.

Her name was Mrs. Bamford (eye changed her name) and I called her a racist because she told me we were only slaves, and I had believed it, totally forgetting what I learned in the first grade with the book on Africa the Librarian hid under the book shelf.

We were Kings and Queens as well.

And the few white kids in class used to secretly chant it.

"Your *daddy* was probably a slave, Kunta," and Mrs. Bamford didn't utter a word to save me or chastise the moneyed white kids.

Mama didn't enroll me in schools in the 'Hood, except for Pine-Villa Elementary. Mama put me in good schools.

Cutler Ridge Middle. Southwood, Home of the Stars, a future Magnet School.

I heard Pine-Villa was even a Magnet School now. I should know. I went there as a kid, before it was a Magnet School.

Looking at Daddy's life in black and white printed on government paperwork, I was angry all over again. How much of this information did Mama know? And if she knew this shit why didn't she tell me from her own mouth? Why did I have to find out this way?

When most men and women felt unloved, they joined gangs. Bloods and Cripps, Vice Lords and the others.

I felt by joining the military, all my problems would be vindicated. I could write the chapters of my own fatherless life, and be a better man than his retarded ass would ever be.

I thought that way at the time. Present day, I love my father, though I haven't met him face to face in 31 years.

I'd read enough. I gave the recruiter back the paper work. I was numb inside.

"So, Pharoah, do you want to join the Army?" Directory asked.

Mama looked at me. "If that's what you wanna do, more power to you, Son."

I kept looking at my recruiter.

"Hell yea."

"Don't curse in my goddamn house."

"Sorry, Mama."

A few weeks later, I raised my hand in a room filled with a few other society members, raised my hand before the flag, and promised to protect the United States against all enemies.

Foreign and Domestic.

From a society member to a future soldier.

WHOOOOAAA!

I just wanted to escape, get away from Miami, Florida. I wanted to see new people and experience new and exciting things. If I hadn't joined the Army I would have taken my life. I really think I would have eventually killed myself. It ain't like nobody was checking for me anyway, with the exception of the adults that have been enjoying the beauty of orgasm via my body for years. The further away from them I put myself the better my development.

I grew to detest my own hometown of Goulds. Thank God for the writing. My writing in those journals day in and day out truly became the martyr of my life. And that in itself was an epiphany.

I wouldn't go so far to say I hated the place; my Army experience I truly enjoyed. I had the time of my young life at the time. I didn't have to worry about being CUT from the Army, like regular society members losing their jobs or being laid off and losing medical benefits.

My shit would be automatic. For as long as I stayed in the Army. And if I did 20 years, I could retire with benefits regular society members would never obtain.

So I said "NO" to a career early on. I loved the Army experience, but I HATED the people who abused me in the Army. Regular soldiers like I was. Protecting the U.S. against all enemies foreign and domestic, yet I still got gang raped in Boot Camp with a hand over my mouth, a knife to my back by 4 of the Niggahs in my Battery and threats against my young life if I didn't oblige their sick need for pleasure.

At that point I learned that you couldn't run from your problems, especially if you never faced them and had closure. When I got raped in the Army, I learned this ten fold.

I used to hate it. I was too afraid to tell officials, because of the law of the streets. You never snitch, no matter what happens to you, yet those niggahs that raped me took an oath to protect the United States against ALL ENEMIES, foreign and domestic just like I had.

That meant I had to obey the rules of the Brotherhood. Protect them at all costs.

I was property of the U.S. And getting sexual gratification from my warm hole penetrated that oath, and they became my enemies. Enemies against government property: my body.

If you so much as suffer a heat stroke in the Army, you better hope, wish, beg and PRAY they don't give you an Article 15 or a Court Marshall.

So telling them I was being raped, at what price would it cost the stipulations of Don't Ask, Don't Tell? That order in itself kept me controlled, programmed and quiet. DON'T TELL! Meaning, keep your mouth fucking shut!

Shit real in the field. I hated the negative motherfuckers. I hated the oppressors. At a time I did love my entire blood line, at a time my own Mama was warning me about my older cousins and their backstabbing ass ways, at a time she told me "One day your eyes will be open about your cousins," the day would come sooner than expected.

I also wanted to go to the Marines, even when I was doing my army Time, but my Mom's fake ass friend Sonja Shit-face (also Mom's co-worker with the FEDS, with her big mouth ass) said, "If you make it out of the Marines even I will come to your graduation."

It wasn't so much of her hinting that the Marines was the toughest of the military branches (I heard motherfuckers go straight ballistic, full metal jacket in there…suicide), but I stared at her.

She was sitting at Mom's dining room table, snickering.

Snickering and trash talking was what she did best. Now this was a woman I used to adore. If the tile man was laying tile in her house or if any house work was being done to her crib I would set aside my own life to watch over everything while she worked because I loved her like a mother. I knew her since I was about 13, when Mom first started with the FEDS.

But her mouth, and the things she say about folks (I used to overhear) turned me off, because my biological mama wasn't that sick and twisted. I mean goddamn. A fat bitch walk the tightrope too well Shit-face was going to say something.

I was thinking to myself. If I could survive four years of rape, my cousins fucking me, a haggard teenage life, feelings of autonomy and survive suicide attempts, self-loathing and self-hate and learning about my goddamn Daddy via government paperwork, then the Marines wasn't shit. I was already older than my age. I used to shed tears long after lights out because I realized with a jolt I made the wrong decision joining something I didn't believe in. And if you didn't believe in *something* surely you wouldn't follow the rules of the engagement nor share their personal views.

Marcus and I joining the Airforce, we believed this with everything in us. Be it would not be.

We even had it all mapped out. We were in constant contact with an Airforce recruiter by the name of Sergeant Jackson. He was a short, stocky guy, very intelligent and had it all together. He wasn't the best looking man in the world but his attitude and his compassion for the Armed Forces made me feel like I was joining an elite program.

That, folks, was why I respected my Grand Father. The Airforce fit him like a fine leather glove tightening against a sweaty finger on an M-16.

Marcus and I took the ASVAB, but I didn't score high enough to go to the Airforce. Why I was thinking about this in Boot Camp beats me, but I knew even then that any decision I make I will weigh the pros and the cons AFTER I research what the fuck it was FIRST. So there are NO REGRETS when I make a decision. Don't join ANYTHING if you haven't performed research. Do a criminal background investigation on what you join or what you're a part of. After all, companies and businesses use the government when they do background checks on you.

Be smart.

Shunning research on the Army hindered me and the decision I made when I joined. And that's where Marcus and I fell apart as far as career goals. His mind was set on the Airforce, since he did the R.O.T.C. thing Airforce throughout high school.

But as the years separated me and Marcus, walking individual paths, I would later learn he joined the Marines.

That, right there, showed me just how LOYAL he was. If I didn't join the Airforce with him, he would join something else.

Freethinkers we always were.

I would think about all the drill competitions me and Marcus went to together while in Basic Training, climbing obstacles, pulling myself across thick tight ropes in mid air and forest land. Those were the times of my life. The Army showed me just how tough I was. I never knew I had so much toughness and strength. They had 13 weeks to convert 18 years on God's earth as a regular society member into a shoot-to-kill soldier WHOA who knew how to follow orders and carry out demands and commands.

If your Drill Sergeant told you to do it you do it. The Drill Sergeant's job was to DRILL the ARMY deep into your conscious and subconscious. The soldiers come first. Family could wait.

That wasn't UNITY to me, so I never felt UNITY in the Army. It was more of *every man for himself* in there. That's why so many of the male soldiers were fucking other male soldiers in the asshole in the darkness. The Oath of the Military they were sworn into protected that darkness.

Don't Ask, soldier. And Don't Tell either, Private.

Privates were the lowest of the totem pole in the Army. They just starting off at the beginner's level. A rookie. They get fucked and fucked over day in and day out by those with rank and status.

One of my homeboys, who came with me to Fort Hood, was propositioned by a Staff Sergeant and a Sergeant. They told him if he didn't let them fuck him they would put all kinds of shit on him. And they did. As they slowly destroyed his military career by turning them down, his girlfriend wound up pregnant and with a baby on the way everything changed.

So he called me in tears, crying. He said, "I think I'm going to do it."

"Do what, niggah?" I was half asleep. What the fuck?? But I didn't say anything, since he was a dear friend and a WARLORD.

"I am going to Staff Sergeant Dick's house right now."

"Oh, no, man!" Turning on the light, I jumped out of bed. I had two sleeping room mates. Snoring. So I lowered my voice, in my boxers and long white tube socks.

I thought about Marcus then, and the times we went out of town to Vero Beach and other places like that for high school drill competitions.

Our drill team did the most mimicked and sought after performances in Florida. When our buses rolled in everyone knew who we were.

I learned about doing ANYTHING to win, even then. DRILL competitions drilled one thing in my mind.

DO WHAT IT TAKES TO WIN.

Simple.

With my friend on the phone and a baby on the way, he changed sides. He became one of THEM, letting the Staff Sergeant and Sergeant take turns fucking him in the ass, and all his worries vanished.

He rose up the ranks faster than I.

And that's when I had had enough.

One moment that stuck out in my head from high school JROTC was when we were performing our much-worked on Drill routine in Vero beach, Florida, and my ex girlfriend,

Collier, missed her mark and we all dropped to our knees and she was left standing up. My heart broke for her, but she was gangster. She kept it moving and I loved and respected her for not crumpling.

But on the bus going home, she cried like a baby and I hugged her and told her it'd be ok and Marcus was right there, cheering us on.

But now we wouldn't be going to the Army together, and that was fine. Sometimes, even with friends and brothers, you have to walk on your GODDAMN OWN on your journey. Couldn't be protected 24 hours a day. Gotta fight on your own sometimes. And he is a very loyal friend. He wound up going to the Marines instead.

And I STILL felt betrayed.

I just never said anything.

Despite it, my Army recruiter was a very caring woman. I'll call her Sergeant Caring now. She wasn't all that bad. Just hated seeing her spit snuff in empty bottles all the time. We actually took some photos together when she came over after I graduated high school. I learned then that having family outside of family sometimes saved your life. Even the Bible states that your biggest enemies will come from within the family, even though I didn't believe everything written in the Bible. Some shit I seriously questioned with the heart of a warrior.

She was nearly the only friend I had who didn't try to rape or molest me. It took a while for me to trust her. But once I did, I trusted her with my life.

I didn't know that, in the years to come, I would become family with a few friends and we would all be a close knit family because all of us had been raped as children and that's what would keep us bound for life.

Forever.

When I graduated high school, my cousin Alfred bought me a Fahrenheit cologne set complete with free duffle bag. I had never owned my own bottle of expensive cologne before. I used to own to knock-off flea market shit, but never the real shit. I cherished that bottle of cologne till this day; and it remained my favorite cologne of all time.

I needed the bag because I didn't have enough for all my stuff. I tried to pack every belonging I had, not knowing that half that shit I would have to put up during the 8 weeks of basic training and the other 5 weeks A.I.T.

I was so excited about leaving Miami, Florida I didn't eat a proper meal. Part of me hated the fact that I entered the Deferment Program, choosing to leave Florida in August instead of June. Despite wanting to escape the place I was badly raped, I had my grandfather here and he was one of the most important people in my life. Ever since I was a growing boy, every time I saw his face, my face lit up like a Christmas Tree.

And despite me and mom's love/hate relationship, I loved her more than life itself, so to actually be flying the bird nest and leaving behind a place I was man of the house was hard. It was hard leaving my brothers and my sister. I pretty much raised them. I was more than a big brother. I was their father, disciplinarian, teacher and friend. I loved them like they were my own kids.

But I knew in my gut I had to go. I hated Miami, Florida and every abusive bitch in it.

The night before I was to leave I was all packed. Mama had a different attitude. I think it was hard to see your first born son, a boy who stayed home rearing your kids and cooking for them so you can work and not think about babysitters or paying them, getting ready to spread his wings and fly away. It was a very tearful thing. And since Mama was a fiery Scorpio and never showed a tear or emotions, to finally see some type of emotion reminded me that she was human after all and not a fucking space alien.

I laid in the darkness all night, just staring at the ceiling fan. When I had to piss I didn't move. When my bowels moved I didn't move. I thought of my girlfriend, Collier. I would go to the Army, come home a brave soldier, marry her, give her anything by Whitney Houston (because she looked up to her) and we would have a lot of kids. My delusional ass actually believes that. I remained faithful to her, but I was fucking a dude on the side. I just had to have the best of both worlds. I never fucked Collier. We kissed here *and* there.

We touched and rubbed. But with my fling on the side we fucked all over Dade County. From his Mama's house and couch to the bushes leading to Turkey Point.

I didn't really wanna commit to anybody. I had a huge problem with it. I slept with so many married people and had threesomes with married folks my idea of marriage went to hell.

I used to sleep with men who watched me fuck their wives. I was with married men who told me to show their wives how to suck dick, and the wives, in tears (grown ass women twice my age) would sit there and watch me, studying then sucked the dick with me till they got it right.

I slept with husbands who had wives who played with their clits watching their men fuck me like there was no tomorrow. They were too afraid of leaving their men with money that they satisfied his thirst for male asshole just so they can keep their Benzes and Mercedes and Acura's and their big ole houses and the credit cards and money.

I covered my face at odd times and my body shook with fear. I was so scared to leave home. Then a realization hit me. What if there were more abusive fucks out there? What if I go to the Army and I get raped again?

I sat up, sweating profusely. I didn't want to go anymore. I changed my mind. I reached over and picked up the phone. The numbers glowed in the dark. I called my

Army recruiter, just knowing she wasn't going to answer because, after I was sworn in, she vanished into thin air.

She answered on the third ring. My heart stopped.

"Pharoah? What's wrong?" she asked and I was looking around my bedroom, making sure I wasn't being watched by hidden cameras. How did she know I called with a problem? She didn't say "How are you doing!" She asked, "What's wrong."

I was quiet for a long time, trying to figure this riddle out. I was *so* quiet I heard the ceiling fan spinning and the wind blowing past my ears. "I don't wanna go."

She was laughing. "You're scared."

"Yes!" My eyes were wide with fright. I crawled under the covers and tried to wrap them around my body so nobody could get to my ass.

Felt like the dark wanted to fuck me and I didn't wanna be touched.

"I was afraid also. But you will have fun."

"Fun? Nothing about life is fun."

"You're young! You should be having the time of your life."

"I'm a young man trapped in an adult's frame of mind. I had to grow up fast!"

"That's what I used to say, child. You'll be fine."

"Maybe you aren't hearing me. How many young men you know can spit poetry?"

"I don't know many. But spitting your own poetry doesn't mean you're not young and having fun, Pharoah."

She doesn't understand. "Two roads diverged in a yellow wood. And sorry I could not travel both. And be one traveler, long I stood. And looked down one as far as I could to where it bent in the undergrowth…"

"Oh my God, Pharoah! You're quoting Robert Frost's the Road Less Taken."

Tears spilt from my eyes. I just wanted to die. I recited this poem over and over and over. Every time they fucked my young body, I recited it.

Every time adults touched my ass or licked my nipples, in my mind I recited this.

Two roads.

Gay or straight.

One traveler.

Me. The abused.

Which do I choose?

"Again, how many young teenagers recite Robert Frost when half of them never heard of him?"

"There's something else bothering you, Pharoah. What is it?"

"I don't wanna go. What if I get raped?"

She was really quiet. "Pharoah. You can tell me anything, you know that, right?"

"Whatever."

"You can, young man. Talk to me."

"Nah. I pass. If my older cousins didn't believe me *why* would you?"

"Believe what?"

"I used to try to tell them where he was burying the treasure map, but they wouldn't listen."

"Pharoah, you're scaring me, baby. What's wrong?"

"I don't wanna go," I said, looking to the side and the sight of him made me jump out my skin. I screamed, dropping the phone. Covering my mouth, I bit down on my tongue.

"PHAROAH! PHAROAH! PICK UP THE PHONE I'M CALLING THE AUTHORITIES!"

Shit.

It was just my reflection.

I picked up the phone. "I'm good."

"But you were…"

I was getting agitated. "I just don't wanna go."

"But you signed your name on the contract."

"Well I'll go to prison, fuck the Army! I can't risk being *raped* again."

I heard her gasp. "Pharoah. You were raped?"

"Yes. Ever since I was little. More than one time. So many times I started liking dick by the time I was nine years old."

"Oh sweet mother of Jesus. I'm so sorry."

"Sweet mother of Jesus don't give a fuck about me. I'm scared. I just don't wanna go."

"Pharoah. That's all the more reason to go. Get out of dodge. Don't look back. I love you Pharoah. I'm coming to take you to the airport."

"That's fine." I lay down, my head pounding. Why did I tell a white woman my turmoil.

"Have you told the police?"

"Please. They can't even answer a 9-1-1 call in the 'Hood on time. Too busy dressing as prostitutes trying to fuck people. I have a better chance of taking care of myself."

"Who was he?"

"He used to be my step daddy. He was so fucking drunk I don't even think he knows the monster he becomes."

"Pharoah."

"Calling you was a mistake. Good night."

And I replaced the receiver.

The day came for me to leave for Basic.

I was all packed, and Mom was up and ready to see me off. My cousin Alfred just had to say some smart asses remark. Made me smile.

He said, "If you make it through boot camp I will come to your graduation."

Did they think I was a pussy or something? Just because I rebelled against high school sports didn't mean I wouldn't grow into a strong man.

It would come at a price.

I had never been on a plane.

Mama said I had, when I was very little. Back when she left my daddy and flew back to Miami.

But I had no memory of that. I heard it was the safest way to travel. Umm, yea right. If I had to choose 20,000 feet in the air over big tires on the ground I think I'd stay on the ground.

But that was not to be. When I got to the airport. I was looking nice. Fresh hair cut, fresh sneakers and my crisp white T-shirt. A few chicks spoke and I spoke back. After checking in my bag and gripping my carry on, I settled down in the waiting area.

A cute chick sat by me and she said, "Damn, baby."

I looked at her. And I didn't smile. "Sup, chick."

"You fine."

"Cool."

"You got a girlfriend?"

"Yea, but we ain't gonna make it."

"Why?"

I licked my lips. "She won't suck my dick and let me eat her pussy."

"Oh my God," she said, fanning herself. Her pussy was wet. "Goddamn, baby. Shit, let me suck that shit."

Typical. "When and where?"

"Go into the bathroom. I'll be right in. Go to the last stall."

"Shit, why not." I looked at my watch. Had forty minutes to spare.

I grabbed my bag and went to the last stall.

After I cleaned the seat and put one of those seat protectors on it, I pulled my pants down and sat down.

She tapped on the stall door and I said, "Its open."

She comes in, closing and locking it. She had her hair stuffed under a cap and she had a huge sweater on. She looked like a boy.

"Take off that hat," I said and she did, putting it on my head. She got on her knees and ran her tongue over my dick. It got hard instantly. She had to be about twenty-four. And she had a wedding ring on her finger.

Taking my dick into her mouth, she thumbed my balls and pushed her finger in my asshole. Oh my God it felt so good.

She finger fucked me and sucked my dick, and I grabbed clumps of her hair and fucked her face.

She wanted to play Poker so I will Poke her Face.

Moaning at a moderate tone, she pulled up her skirt and played with her pussy.

"Let me taste that shit."

She reached up, my dick still in her mouth and I sucked her pussy juices down my throat.

I had to cum faster than normal. Mainly because she was fucking my ass.

I didn't say shit. Damn, felt so good. I tensed up, grabbed her head and fucked her mouth faster. Spit trailed my dick, ran down my balls and felt cold racing down my asshole.

I burst deep in her mouth and she tried to lift up and I fucked her face, pumping nut down her throat.

After it was over I stood up, pulling up my jeans.

She grinned, licking her lips.

"I never swallowed before."

The cum stain in her black sweater told me another story. It was dry, so it couldn't have been my cum.

She sat on the toilet and pulled off her panties.

"Time to eat my pussy."

I buttoned my jeans. "I'm gonna suck the clit into a famished bitch."

"DAMN!"

I fixed my shirt. "Ready for this tongue?"

"Oh, hell yea. This is gonna be fun, oh wee, baby!"

Damn, she got some huge titties. I reached down and pinched a nipple. "Close your eyes."

Licking her lipstick, she closed her eyes.

I got between her legs and played with her pussy for a minute. I looked at my watch. I had fifteen minutes to get to my plane.

She was grinding on my finger so I put in two, then three. Bitch was looser than the atmosphere.

I looked closely. Dried nut was on her pussy hairs. Some Niggah fucked her before she met me.

I stood up and said, "Keep them closed."

"Yummy, yay!"

When she opened them I don't know what the bitch saw because me and my bags were persona non fucking grata.

My lips work per diem. So get your head before I get mine 'cause when I get mine first, Chile, the first one cum wins. Like it's a title match, bitch.

I walked up to the cute receptionist.

His name was Hank and he said, "Ready to board?"

"Yes." I looked to the side and saw ole girl looking around wildly for me. I pulled her hat low over my eyes, gave ole boy my ticket and boarded the place.

Never to see Easy Cum, Easy Go again in my fucking life.

Desperate bitch.

$$\Sigma$$

I put my carry on in the cubby hole above me, and, trembling, took my seat. I was so afraid of this damn plane, but I think the world outside of Miami, Florida was even scarier. Before leaving Miami, I had only left the state once. When my grand dad lived in Lane, South Carolina I had visited him there. Me and my cousin Sandra. But after I came home that had been the only time I left.

So embarking on this entire new adventure was frightening.

And I had to do it alone. Without Mama holding my hand.

I put on my seat belt.

God, don't let this be a joke.

When the plane thundered into the skies, I burst into tears, and was comforted by an elderly woman.
"I know you're scared of flying," she said, stroking my head like a loving grandmother. "I was scared during my first plane ride."

My tears soaking into her blouse, I hugged her tighter. "I'm not scared of planes," I said mournfully. "I'm crying because the bad people and my family can't rape me again. My body is free! I'm FREE!"

The elderly woman told me to, "Cry, baby," her gentle voice trembling. I felt her shaking from anger. "Let it out and don't look back."

And for the first time in my life I truly mourned.

I finally got to cry and mourn the loss of my innocence.
I cried till I fell asleep in her arms.

I awakened when the announcer came over the loud speakers. It took a minute for me to remember I was on an airplane thousands of feet above the earth.

"We're now in Dallas/Ft. Worth airport. At this time we request that you fasten your seatbelts as we prepare to land…"

I was in Texas. Holy shit! This was really happening. Yay! For some reason I thought of the Pee Wee Herman movie "DEEP IN THE HEART OF TEXAS!" And you clapped two times.

I clapped two times after singing it at a moderate tone. People started laughing and the little old lady touched my hand and said, "See you are awake."

"Yes, I am. Very alert."

"You slept soundly."

"I felt good too. Best sleep of my life."

"Maybe because you were so many feet in the air."

"Yes."

"So what are you going to be doing in Texas?"

"I'll be hoping on another plane to Ft. Sill, Oklahoma."

"Ft. Sill. Military man."

"Yes. I'll be there for the next 13 weeks."

I felt the plane dropping in altitude or however you freaking said it. The closer to the ground we were the better.

"Make the most of it."

"And what are you going to be doing in Texas?"

"Working."

"You aren't retired?"

"No, son. My line of work calls for me to work."

"But you are supposed to be retired. How old are you?"

She beamed. "Seventy-eight."

"Wow." I rolled my tongue making catty noises. "You don't look a day over 40."

She touched my cheek "Sweet young man. I wish my son was still here."

"Where is he?"

"He joined a gang because I was always too busy for him."

People were getting ready to unboard the plane and it hadn't come to a stop yet. A few moments later the tires hit the pavement and a thunderous noise filled my ears.

"Why would he join a gang?"

"I may look homely but I wasn't always the best mother."

"Nonsense. I'm sure you were."

"I wasn't. I was too wrapped up in my husband and it drove my kids away."

"So what do you do now?"

She smiled. "I'm a prostitute."

My mouth fell open in shock.

I leaned back in the seat, staring at my lap. A prostitute had been comforting me. I cried on the shoulder of a prostitute. Why did I feel so used and cheap?

But I thought about it. I didn't know she was a hooker but she was a nice person, so who was I to judge her. She comforted me when I needed a friend. She didn't know me and I didn't know a thing about her.

"At your age?"

"I have nothing else to go to."

"Where's your husband?"

"He's deceased. Been dead for thirty years."

"So...how long have you been doing the hooker thing?"

"As I said I was so wrapped up in him I didn't have an identity of my own. I couldn't do for myself. I didn't have a job because he worked and wouldn't allow me to. So when he died I had to do it all on my own. So I started selling my body to ease the pain of my loss and wound up becoming one of the seediest prostitutes in Texas."

"I'm so sorry to hear that."

"We all have it bad in life. No one deserves God's grace, son."

The plane stopped. She said, "When you leave this plane, your life will get much worse than you'd ever known."

I shuddered. "Why would you say that?"

"I look in your eyes. Pharoah, you're the chosen one."

"Huh?"

"Great things await you in your future. I don't know what it is, but you will be praised by many. Remember this old prostitute told you first."

"So if I'm chosen, why did I go through all the bad stuff growing up?"

"Because you're being initiated on two levels. On one level, God is allowing Satan to test you to see if you keep your faith in him. Read the Book of Job. And the second reason is because Satan doesn't want you to become this great man you will be. He hates it because he knows what it is and you don't. He will try to destroy you. Promise me," she went on, cupping my hand and kissing it, "That you will press forward. No matter what. Never give up."

People were leaving the plane. "I promise."

"We will never see each other again. I wish I can be here to witness your greatness."

I was chuckling. "I'm not going to be great at nothing. Plus you'll be fine."

She kissed my lips. "I'm dying of AIDS. And I'm an old school rebel I don't believe in doctors and treatment. I'll be long gone before you rise to the top of whatever it is God has planned for you. And judging from the book on your lap, on Egypt, you are probably chosen to be a big time author." Her eyes lit up. "Yes! That's what it is! You're going to be a fantastic author! Everyone will be talking about your books."

"Now I know you're really psycho. Me, published? Ha, fat chance."

She unbuckled her seat belt. Nothing about her told me she sold her frail body. She looked like a nice grandma who baked pies.

"Remember I told you first."

"If I become some big author, I will remember you told me first."

After getting her bag she took one long look at me, shook her head and said, "Read the Book of Job. And prepare yourself."

And I never saw her again.

I was sitting in the lobby of the airport, cool as a breeze, going over in my head the conversation between me and the elderly white lady. I marveled over how fast a book's cover could peel away to another book cover, as was the case with us. To her, I was a young black kid afraid of planes, till I cried on her shoulder and said I was actually crying because my asshole would no longer be tormented and tortured by grown ass preachers and other sick bitches.

She appeared to be a homely old woman with a cookie cutter life, until she revealed she had to sell pussy to make ends meet, and that poured into her retirement years.

When my flight was announced for boarding I saw a tall, handsome dude with a duffle bag. We kept staring at each other. He nodded and I nodded. That was the confirmation I needed to talk to him, to see where his head was and not the one in his pants.

I walked over and introduced myself. "I'm Pharoah."

"Nooo," he said, smiling. "My name is Pharoah."

"Yea fucking right dude. Ha ha ha."

He pulled out his I.D. It said Pharoah Low.

I pulled out mine. It said Pharoah Wilson.

"Well I'll be damned." We shook hands. "What's up twin."

"Shit, man I can't call it," he said, cheesing.

"Where are you from?"

"I'm from Georgia, man, where you from, man?"

I noticed he said "man" a lot.

"Miami, Florida."

"The state with citrus pussy."

"Shit, give me peachy pussy over shit that stings any day."

"I like you, man. Where you headed?"

"To Ft. Sill, Oklahoma. The Army."

"No way man! I'm going to Ft. Sill, Oklahoma."

"Well, lets board."

"I'm taking the next flight."

"Damn, I'm taking this one."

"Fuck, man. You can't get it changed to mine?"

"Well, let's see." We walked over to the receptionist.

"Hello, sir."

"Hey," I told the lady, Pharoah Low crossing his fingers. "Can I change my flight from this one to the next, so I can travel with my brother. We both in the Army."

"Why sure," she said. Twin and I slapped palms. "Since you're both cute, why not?" she asked rhetorically.

And she changed my flight.

We would be good friends through my whole Army experience.

Even if it only lasted a fucking year.

The Army was the worst experience of my life. There were more in the closet fags in the military than there were roaming free in the civilian world. Eye swear. So many homeboys of mine in the Army begged to fuck me or wanted me to suck their dicks and eye was just shocked at the forwardness.

No one wanted to lose their career so the Don't Ask Don't Tell policy a lot of them used as a shield. Fuck men all in the ass. And leave emotions soaking in mattresses and sheets. Better make it to formation on time, niggah. We ain't cool on the clock. In fact niggah eye couldn't stand your faggot ass. So in public you shut the fuck up. And after dark,

Big Daddy will low and high crawl all through Pharoah pussy.

Eye knew Army niggahs that went to the local mall and fucked local men in the ass or had orgies with church niggahs, fucking them like POW's and sending them home with sore assholes. Army niggahs used to brag about it drinking beer and watching Hoes shake ass in the videos. Even when we went to the strip clubs and Mr. DJ's (where eye met and took a picture with then comedian TP Hern) in Killeen, Texas (Fort Hood), niggahs had to pretend to be mesmerized by the female ass with my ass on their minds.

It was funny to me at the time. How Army Niggahs bait and switched themselves lock, stock and barrel to keep UP with their EGOS and IMAGES.

Sweating bullets. Never really being totally free. Some Niggahs had wives. Wives that fucked other men when my niggahs were in the field for two weeks, sleeping in tanks and loading 60 pound rounds and turning, pulling the string BOOM you didn't see what you blew up or what you were shooting at but that little call transmitted through the radio let us all know if you hit or miss the target in the field.

So with another set of eyes eye studied military niggahs while in the Army.

Started at boot camp. Fort Sill, Oklahoma. A place eye never heard of, had wicked interchanging weather and during the winter it wasn't nothing nice. Eye was:

13 Bravo Field Artillery WHOOOAA

CADENCE:

Warlords, warlords smooth this is how we do it BOOM War Lords War Lords shout your left your right it's FUNKDAFIED! Warlords WARLORDS! SHOUT! Hold em up (we all cupped our dicks and balls together in sync on this part) then move out. ARTILLERY! Break Down, kneel get em up GET EM UP, SHOOT! KILL!

Eye lived for our morning cadence when Drill Sergeant Hemple or Drill Sergeant Martinez (who had a crush on my mother and hadn't a chance in hell) called the Platoon to attention.

But before all this…my arrival into Fort Sill confused the fuck outta me.

The purpose for boot camp was simple. It was designed to turn you from a regular civilian to a 100% SOLDIER! Period. No ifs, ands or buts. So making my way to the Transition Center when eye got there, we were given pills to swallow (Salt Petter Pills) designed to stop you from getting an erection, but eye crushed mine under my boot. Eye didn't trust the government like that, even though eye was government property. My very body belonged to them.

After half the niggahs swallowed their erections away, my dawgs, WARLORDS that came with me to Fort Sill (and we were closely knit like a family) followed my lead and didn't swallow the pill.

We were then loaded on cattle trucks. The Drill Sergeant, especially a tall ass niggah Sergeant, were very accommodating and nice. They spoke politely to us. Made us feel welcome. Yes, welcome to the United States Army. Sure, you could go on to make a brilliant career outta this! Where are you from young man? Goulds? Where was that? Miami, Florida? Oh, snap. Never heard of it—Goulds that was. He shook my hand. He said nice to meet you.

Eye said likewise.

So we all stuffed on the cattle truck and stopped by a photography studio and the Drill Sergeants smoked us. Meaning made us drop down and give them fifty. And you better do fifty two.

Dirty and sweaty, we're pushing up and down unexpectedly, and eye'm thinking ok what part of the game was this? After we're done we're ushered into a photography studio. We had to put on Class A uniform jackets and the Class A uniform shirt over BDU pants, put on that retarded, funky ass McDonald's looking hat and say CHEESE in the camera like we weren't just smoked.

Eye was breathing so hard eye had to say GO GO GADGET GIVE GOOD FACE and give the camera a seldom gaze. FLASH. Over.

We're ushered out of the building, back onto the cattle trucks like we were actually cattle. No one said anything as it all sunk in. Tires biting into the bumpy pavement, causing us to shift ever so often. We're holding rails and above railings for balance or leaning on each other for support.

Once the cattle trucks crossed the tracks, we entered another

DimΣnsion.

A dimension very different from the world eye was brought up in. And eye was brought up in Hell, making it to the Fortress of being my own man. And when eye thought eye'd broken bondage eye was alleviated to another realm of social consciousness.

Along the roads huge buildings began to rise from the horizon, like college campuses. Our eyes were wide with excitement. Drill Sergeants' eyes narrowed with maliciousness. Masters with whips was their mental frame of mind. Government property we soldiers were to be.

Once the trucks stopped, brakes squeaking, the DEMONS surfaced.

GET OUT OF THE FUCKING CATTLE TRUCK RIGHT NOW GET THE FUCK OUT NOW!

Drill Sergeant barked orders that put fear in our hearts. Gone was the welcoming spirit they possessed on the opposite side of the tracks, just before the photography studio. My heart pounded through the pulse of my asshole sending shivers down me spine. Yea, ME SPINE!

Eye was *that* fucked up.

Grabbing my bags, we all scattered off the cattle trucks as if they were on fire about to blow in three, two, one seconds and the barking orders ceaselessly stopped our hearts.

YOU SEE THE WHITE X'S ON THE PLATFORM LINE UP ON THE GODDAMN X MUTHAFUCKAHS! PICK THOSE BAGS UP DON'T LET THEM TOUCH THE GROUND IF YOU DIDN'T WANNA CARRY ALL THAT BAGGAGE YOU SHOULDA LEFT IT IN YOUR PAST PICK IT UP MOVE IT MOVE IT PRIVATES!

Eye found the nearest X, struggling to hold my bags and stood at attention. Goddamn it what a goddamn strain, muthafuck!

Out of my peripheral, all my dawgs found an X and stood on top of it, struggling like me to hold all our personal property up. On the outside realm, when eye was a regular civilian the shit in my duffle bags was material possessions eye told myself eye couldn't live without. Yet on the opposite side of the realm, as a SOLDIER those beasts, Drill Sergeants, basically let me know that my material possessions were worthless because my possessions possessed me.

After we all lined up we were separated into FOUR different batteries. Eye was sweating because eye could be mixed up and separated from my DAWGS eye met at the airport and on the cattle trucks. Eye was a part of the DOWN SOUTH NIGGAHS crew, since eye was from Miami. And James was from Georgia, so was Wilcox.

Once their names were called they were to go to the WARLORDS. Cool. But eye wasn't picked. Goddamn it. Eye couldn't go to any other PLATOON. DAMN!

Wilson, WARLORDS.

Um, in that case yes the fuck eye will.

Follow my DAWGS that is.

The first few weeks were grueling. We were "smoked" for every little thing we did wrong. If we didn't work as a team we were smoked. Group Punishment yes they believed in wholeheartedly. One fucked up the entire PLATOON fucked up.

We jogged for miles every morning with skinny, hick ass Drill Sergeant Hemple. He was the skinniest, coolest hick white dude eye have ever met in my life. He ran those miles like they weren't shit, tiring me and half the PLATOON out.

But we made it.

Eye figured out that it was about mind control. For instance you crying about missing your mother or your girlfriend or wife the DRILL SERGEANTS rode your ass.

"Jody fucking your Mama in the asshole boy!"

"Jody eating your wife's pussy boy! You're a soldier!"

"We're soldiers 24 hours a day!"

"Fuck your wife and your retarded goddamn Mama boy!"

All of this angered us, but we had to stand at attention and not mimic, say or breathe a word. You better not even blink. Stand like those Russians in furry hat and red coats. Even if they spit in your face or sucked your dick you better stand at attention like ain't shit happening.

When eye realized that eye was good. Eye didn't let them anger me anymore. Eye was one of the element leaders, so my squad was the shit.

Eye remember two blanket parties that were given out to two different soldiers. One for Rogers (eye changed his name) and the other for a white dude eye couldn't remember his name for the goddamn life in me.

Rogers was the whiner. He whined about everything. He was the best at everything. He was a donkey looking niggah sporting Caucasian pussy around in personal photos. Caucasian pussy being his girlfriend and he drove us goddamn crazy with the bullshit.

They put a pillow over his face and beat him with soap inside blankets. You're trapped in the darkness while heavy bars of soap slammed forcibly into your body for fucking up. If you got the entire group punished you received a certified BLANKET PARTY on the house and you better not snitch because that was your ass.

So eye knew then to keep my mouth shut. Eye never had to go through that shit.

Lester one day got a pair of panties from his girl and he put them on running through the barracks with that fat ass. He was making muscle gestures screaming GAS GAS GAS, which was what we said if gas was in the area and we had to put on our GAS masks. You had about what 6, 7 seconds to put it on. GAS GAS GAS symbolized the mask was put on properly.

To further train us in that we were put through a gas chamber with real live CS gas. My God. When eye tell you that was hell! To be chocking to death on gas and forced to say your social security number and Platoon name standing at attention with a straight face was hell. They got us on video running outta the gas chamber with snot and spit dangling from our nostrils and mouths.

Eye nearly died oh my God.

But the experience taught me to appreciate clean air a little more than eye used to.

Being a soldier would have its turning point.

Boot Camp went by smoothly (except for the few times I was gang raped), and making our way into AIT (learning our military jobs) things seemed to return to normal. We weren't being smoked as much, and Drill Sergeants gave us a little more freedom. I wasn't raped again. Drill Sergeants didn't come awaken you every single morning anymore, weekends were cool as fuck and we eventually received an OFF BASE pass to go to the mall or to the Gunner's Inn (on base) where we got tipsy and drunk as fuck. The Niggahs that raped me were suddenly Biblical muthafuckahs that asked me to forgive them. I told them eye did with a smile, but eye hated them to the very core of my soul.

Nonetheless, we were now one of THEM! Soldiers. The other side of society.

Eye loved some of those fun times in the Army, overall. For me it represented the first time eye actually belonged to a family. A family of soldiers. Trained to kill, yet loyal to each other despite our past or differences.

And that had me fooled.

When we graduated AIT, mama and my cousin Sweet flew to Oklahoma to see me walk across the stage. Mama was so proud of me. Beautiful in a cashmere sweater and light blue jeans, her radiant smile was so strong half the Drill Sergeants took off their wedding rings and stuffed it in their pockets looking at my mama's ass and eye was mad as fuck.

As a platoon, all four of the platoons eye should say got into one huge formation and we, newly trained soldiers, marched to the Gunner's Inn before our friends and family that flew or drove to see us graduate, and Mama was waving at me and clapping.

Eye winked at my cousin because he swore me down eye wouldn't graduate boot camp and eye had.

So he gave me props.

The Army was off the chain in the beginning.

Finding out that half my platoon got orders to go to Fort Hood excited us. We weren't separated. Yes!

Around Christmas of 1995 we were on planes flying to our respective hometowns for a two week break to spend with family. And after the New Year we boarded planes to Fort Hood, Texas from our respective hometowns. The Army was so damn lame we had to buy our own tickets to our permanent duty stations. The catch was that if you didn't go home for the holidays and went straight to your permanent duty station then the Army paid for that.

When we arrived it seemed like another world yet again. Cabins and shit. Houses on base looked different. Or were they houses.

The barracks we stayed in was so grimy and dirty as fuck. Bathroom floors mildewing and shit, and our first sergeant, a ghetto country couldn't read above a third grade level ass niggah, was some MC Hammer reject that drove a green truck he polished twenty four hours a day just so he could brush his hair in the reflection.

Real dumb ass, oh my God. Eye didn't like his horny ass at all.

He fucked half the boys in the platoon. Helping them get rank. Eye walked in on him getting his dick sucked by two horny ass thug niggahs in BDU attire. They tongue kissing the swollen mushroom head then themselves. Both had the same last names. Eye think they were biological brothers. Yup. Two blood brothers sucking the same First Sergeant dick.

Kinda gross, but looking at it…it was thrilling to see the secret lives unfolded in the darkness, when the rest of the world didn't give you a second thought.

They were sucking his nuts, spitting on his asshole. First Sergeant didn't give two shits about me standing in the doorway. All of them were ranked above PFC. Eye'm just a private.

First Sergeant slid his condom-less dick inside the Staff Sergeant's tight hole and gazed into my eyes.

"Either cum in and let me fuck you or shut the fuck up and get the fuck out."

He pushed ole boy's face into the desk and his booty cheeks applauded the genius of his stroking ability.

Eye was trapped by the dimension presented before me, entering and closing the door. Walking up to him running my finger over my asshole, sticking my fingers in his mouth while ole boy pulled down my pants and gave me some head. First Sergeant fucking ole boy from behind, ole boy bent over sucking my dick and First Sergeant slurping my hole from my fingers.

Hell yea.

One of the brothers grabbed his wallet, keys and hit the door without looking back.

"So does this mean eye get rank?"

"No. You're new on the block. Doesn't work that way. Bitch," he went on, slapping ole boy's ass. Cheeks jiggled deliciously. "Show him what he outta do for rank."

"Yes, Daddy."

He stood up, wrapped his arms around my neck and eye kneed him in the balls and he doubled over on his knees, first Sergeant falling out tight boy pussy and eye said, "Don't try to size me up. Let me show you what you think you were going to show me."

Eye pushed First Sergeant on top of the bottom bitch and eye rode his dick. Ole Boy being crushed underneath First Sergeant. First Sergeant grunting in my asshole. The best he never had.

Till now. Ole boy couldn't move. All our weight on top of him. Lemme show him how you get down to the floor.

Eye held First Sergeant's chest and worked my asshole to the bone, grabbing his balls and gazing into his eyes.

"Goddamn you feel better than Gregory."

His mouth ajar eye trailed my saliva all over his lips, watching him lick it off and eye said, "Shut up and fuck me."

And fuck me he did.

Right into an earth-shattering orgasm.

All three of us asleep on the floor.

Breathing my homeboy's air.

The one with the baby on the way.

And this was where the story takes a turn.

When I encountered Chantell Bynum, a thick girl I would fall in love with. No, she wasn't fat. She had a thick ass, deep pussy and tight jaws. When she smiled I saw God taking rib from a sleeping Adam to make the Woman.

Full of life and lust, eccentric and aspiring inspiration.

I felt this when I was in the PX, looking for Alanis Morrisette's Jagged Little Pill album, to see what the buzz was about this angry You Outta Know chick.

I paused before the display of CDs with Janet's Design of a Decade under my arm.

Chantell smiled at me and I frowned. Had to play it cool. Never let a woman know you're anxious to get with her. That's when they get bitchy and besides themselves, comparing you to their Daddies or other men they may love and look up to.

"Is that CD good?" she asked, and I put the headphones on, pressing PLAY.

Listening to the entire album free of charge.

She tapped my shoulder and I snatched the headphones off like, "Why are you touching me?"

"Damn, it's not all of that."

"Bitch it was enough for you to touch. Get away, thank you. I don't give out free samples and heard left over's are for bums."

"Fuck you."

"Bitch don't you wish!"

"UGH!"

"Ugh!" And I put my head phones on, jamming to You'll Learn.

I decided to buy the CD.

I bought one other thing before I bought the CD's. When I paid for my item, I told the male cashier to hold it for me. I had to go look for something else, another CD. Plus ole girl was on my mind, I shouldn't have talked to her like that. I just hate strange bitches meeting my acquaintance. I was very snobbishly standoffish.

Another cashier booth was open next to me, but the light was turned off. But I saw a water bottle and a James Baldwin book under the register.

I thought nothing of it.

I'm headed for the check out to buy the CD's. Didn't find the Barry White one I wanted, so Alanis and Janet would do.

I didn't have cash on me, so I handed the cashier my ID and the CDs.

"This muthafuckah."

I looked up. God.

It was her.

"You work here?"

"Yes, I do," she spat, dropping my CDs into the bag.

I took them out. "Bitch you're crazy!"

I rung them up for her, eyeing her evilly. "Don't be trying to get me locked up for shoplifting. Don't make me get ghetto in this bitch. Goddamn, the AC broke in here?"

I was hot in my BDU's.

"You need to get out my line."

"You need to ring up my purchase."

"Get out my line. You're rude."

"I'm not rude to your fat ass, what the fuck? Because I'm not begging for your phone number or trying to get some pussy don't mean I want your simple ass."

"Go away!"

I reached over and hit the TOTAL button myself, then swiped my ID coded card through the slot. It rung up.

I hit ENTER and the receipt came out.

"Shit, I need your job. God bless."

"Go to Hell!"

I smiled, taking my recently purchased item from the male cashier that held them for me.

She covered her mouth. I held the roses.

"I think you're a sight for sore eyes. I would love to take you on a date."

"I would love to."

She took the flowers and slapped me over the head with them. "Fuck off."

"Fuck you, bitch!" I was mad.

She smiled then, walking up to me. "You can't take me out without getting my phone number first."

When I kissed her I tasted sugar.

The sweetest taste I would ever know.

Even sweeter than her pussy.

But that cums later.

Getting to know her was invigorating. I already didn't want to be in the Army, and I was telling my homeboy that, who had a sister who moved up from Georgia to live with him. So he had a baby on the way (another two months his wife should be giving birth to his first son/child), that I think I was falling in love with Chantell.

She was fun, silly and full of life. She was sexy, even with hair rollers in her hair. She didn't need make-up to be beautiful, and she never depended on a man to take care of her. She had her mother's deviant ways and her father's knack for life, love and business.

We spent a lot of time together. When I had free time, and was off duty I left the barracks, without telling anyone, and hung out with her. We used to get hotels and spend hours together. I never wanted to meet her folks because she said her father disowned her after she lost her virginity with an older cousin that raped her (her Dad blamed her for the occurrence), and her brother barely talked to her.

We went to the movies, out to eat, and I paid every time. We clicked. I told her of my sexuality, and she handed me a James Baldwin book.

"I love James. Giovanni's Room is an incredible book."

"So why did you give it to me?"

"I read a journal of yours. I found it the day I saw you in the PX."

"The day we met?"

"No, a few days before we met. You were in here carrying a book bag. You bought some Jordan shoes and I guess one of your journals fell out your bag when you were putting your old shoes in there. I picked it up, intending to flag you down but I opened it, curious, and read your poetry and a few stories you wrote. In one of them you mentioned this book. So I went out to the bookstore and purchased it."

"Are you serious?"

"Yes. The day we met I was going to introduce myself as a new fan of your work."

"My God."

We were so very close. She was more than just a girlfriend, she was my soul mate I felt. Being with her, I wanted her and only her. Her skin tasted so sweet it kept niggahs and dick off the brain relentlessly. I got to talk to her about me, my past and my life. She used to rub my head when I told her of my childhood. We used to eat popping corn talking about our ambitions and goals in life.

I was so into her I became her eyes, a reflection of the woman who birth me.

In a lot of ways she reminded me of my mother.

But a nicer version.

I stopped going to clubs with my friends on Fridays. Mr. DJ's it was called, and I used to dance my ass off. Sweating like a pig on that liquor and marijuana.

With Chantell I stopped it all. I wanted to be a better man, and through her patience I was carving out a new image of myself, something that became habit, then my character.

One day before February of 2006, Chantell invited me over to her cousin's house. She said she had gotten in a fight with her mother over her career choices, and her brother called her every bitch name in the book. I wanted to fuck him up, but decided to stay outta something that really didn't involve me. If she asked me to get in it, then *Yes*, ok that was different.

She came to pick me up, since I didn't have a car. When I lay eyes on her the sun rose all over again. I saw love.

We kissed and embraced, inhaling our body auras. She smelled of expensive lavender. I smelled of cheap supermarket cologne. I only put the expensive stuff (Fahrenheit) on my nuts.

Holding hands, we talked about everything under the sun.

But it wasn't her cousin's house we went to.

She pulled up in front a hotel that was larger than life.

We were 20 miles outside of Killeen, Texas. Where were we, I didn't know and I didn't question it.

She paid for the Presidential Suite with her mother's credit card before she picked me up.

"I'm tired of living for everyone else," she said, smiling.

"What's wrong?"

"Nothing."

"I can see it in your eyes, baby."

She took my hand. "Its hard for me to open up to anyone."

"You can trust me."

Darkness befell her face. "Can I really trust you?"

"Yes, you can."

"Lets go up to the room, and watch TV. Maybe cook a little something. Hell, my mom's credit card footed it all. She always trying to control and change me. And since she expects so much of me, then maybe her paying for this room is the compensation I need right now."

"You're something else."

When we got in the room I looked around paradise. This was a very breathtaking room, and I'd never seen nor experienced anything like it in my life. She sat on the huge sofa with big off white throw pillows and crossed clean shaven legs. I smelled her pussy in the air, blended in nicely with potpourri inside huge wicker baskets.

"You like the room?" she asked, pouring some wine. I hated wine, never really got into drinking like that so I passed.

She still poured me a glass, handing it to me. I looked at her like she was an alien.

"Taste it, Pharaoh. Don't knock it till you try it."

"Is that what Eve said to Adam when she bit the forbidden fruit?"

We were laughing.

"That's why I love you. You know how to make a woman smile."

I didn't look at the drink once. "Is that why you love me? Because I make you laugh?"

She walked up to me, her nose on mine. Our lips extended, made the gentle connection yet eagerly retreated.

Her eager fingertips trialing the epidermis of my arms sent chills all over my balls. My dick was solid, yet, mentally, I wasn't ready to be sold into the gentle folds of sweet gushy pussy.

I was uneasy for a moment because I've become accustomed to sleeping with niggahs.

I slept with them as a form of executed fatherly love. When I lay with a Niggah I want him to be strong for me, guide me, fall all over and through me until I cum his perception of utilization.

I shiver all night. Nothing was sweeter to me than my toes curling during orgasm. That's when I'm vulnerable, and most susceptible.

With Chantell I closed me eyes and slowly inherited her plump ass. I was calmly rubbing, creating the much needed chemistry for this form of friction to work.

I pulled her pelvic bone up against my body, and I kissed her slowly and passionately, letting it build into edifices too treacherous for the amateurs.

She put her shaking hands in my pants and squeezed my meat.

"You know that's one big dick you're gripping," I said, trailing my slick tongue along her slender Swan-like neck.

"I know what it is."

"Saying hell to my little friend?"

"Yes."

"Well, I have to say hello, Kitty." I fell on my knees, pushing her skirt past her womanly-shaped hips. Pussy smelled so good, but does the taste provide a much needed collaboration?

My tongue melted into her wet, juicy, gushy pussy, my lips correlating with her vaginal walls. She shuddered in her heels, her legs bending at the knees. I pushed her against the wall and her arms go up and over her head while I push the pussy back, revealing a silky, pinkish clit and sucked her pussy till she started to cum.

I kept feasting, swallowing her, running my tongue along her tight asshole, pushing a dry thumb deep inside her ass.

She gasped, wide eyed while I munched on filet ah fish.

When she said she had to cum the second time, I stood up, and slid my big dick so deep in her pussy she had to wrap her arms around me.

Cumming on my dick.

While I fucked the shit outta her.

The pussy felt so good and I realized just how much I truly loved and needed the warm body of a woman, that when I had to cum I didn't pull out.

I leaned into her silky hair, grunted, said, "I gotta nut, baby," and came deep inside that wet pussy.

Best feeling in the world.

Then a funny thing happened.

We drew even closer after our sexual transition into each other's lives. The physical aspect (getting to know her, learning the ins and out of her being, learning her zodiac, respecting her mind before enjoying her body and having real conversations about the future) intertwined both our psyches as one, so when eye gave her my body I was giving my body to her spirit as a sacrifice.

Only I didn't know this. After the first night we made love, fucked and grunted till the neighbors screamed, "Okay you ugly muthafuckers enuff is a goddamn nuff!" we started having sex more and more and eye loved it because eye got to nut deep inside her pussy walls on the regular. Her pussy was my addiction…combining the lust of my hips with the conundrums of her tits.

I became One with her, my dick deep inside what my rib made giving me the feelings of a complete circle because everything became crystal clear. Pussy was the most generous gift God put on this earth. Therefore eye treat pussy as if it's precious, I cherish a good bitch with good pussy and a juicy clit. And if she got a brain, goddamn.

That was Chantell. Eye used to sleep with my dick thumping in her pussy. Didn't grind, move or fuck her at all, but my dick deep in her incubator, keeping shit warm and fuzzy till eye beat it up after my slumber the next day was my true reward. Having that kind of morning orgasm had me on cloud nine.

We would do this for two months. Make love. Go out. Fuck some more. Suck my dick in the PX parking Lot inside her car. Listen to her wails of mistakes made in the past.

I fell in love with her. Everything about her was perfection, reaching perfect tens on every human scale on earth involving looks, brains, guts and beauty. She was that bitch a niggah said he could never get, no matter how confident 50 Cent was on eventually getting Alicia Keys. And she wound up taking another woman's husband and now about to drop the baby in a few months.

But during this time there wasn't an Alicia Keys in the industry nor 50 Cent. TuPac was alive then, even though he would get murdered around the time eye got out of the military.

And with anything good in your life manifesting into something you could cherish, Satan made his move and everything vanished.

Literally the next day, after laying with her half the night trying to get her to open to me about something that seemed to be bothering her, she disappeared. She didn't call or accept my phone calls.

I ran around Fort Hood like a chicken with my head cut off. Being late to formation in the mornings because I stayed up half the night traveling with my boy all over Killeen, Texas, going to every store she shopped asking employees about her whereabouts or if they seen her and getting a NO answer every time.

Eye couldn't eat nor sleep, my dick getting hard for her pussy and it wasn't there so eye had to revert to masturbation to keep the pressure from bursting the tubes in my testicles.

I got an Article 15 for disrespect. And didn't give a damn. I was high on weed with some of the soldiers eye hung out with (they had that Cali Crypt oh Lawd hammercy!) when eye did extra duty. Had to clean those mildewing ass barracks on Fort Hood with a goddamn toothbrush. I mean get with the times. People hardly brush their teeth in the mornings yet you want me to scrub the floor with some 1950s technique?

Eye pretended I was cleaning the floors and crusty shower walls. If this was the Army why these raggedy barracks look like a bunch of bullshit? Couldn't even walk around this shit barefooted. You liable to get athlete's feet or a goddamn fungus.

After I was relieved of extra duty I went looking for Chantell again.

I was a wreck.

A few weeks would go buy before I saw her again. I was shopping at the PX with red and black patent leather Jordans, a red Steve Young sweater with a big #1 on the back, and black NIKE shorts. I felt good that day, deciding to get back to living and be the best man I could be, despite my unease about Chantell.

I was heading out (I didn't buy anything) and decided to grab a slice of pizza. The place wasn't that crowded and the janitor was wiping down tables with an attitude.

Before I could walk up to the cashier, I saw her. Approaching me with a half smile on her face. She looked radiant, as always. Her skirt below her knees, and her cream colored blouse fitting her perfectly.

"Pharoah."

My heart racing, I stared at her. I didn't even blink.

"Where were you? You vanished off the face of the earth."

"I had issues to deal with."

"Issues? That's the excuse you're giving me?"

She smiled, cupping my hand and I snatched it back. "I have been looking all over for you."

"Stop being dramatic."

I walked past her, heading for the door. "Peace."

"Pharoah! I need to talk to you."

I held up my hand. "Talk between my fingers because my hand is protesting your dumb ass."

"Pharoah!" She was running behind me. When I walked through the double sliding glass doors, she grabbed my arm. Just above the elbow. "Please. Hear me out."

I snatched my arm back. "What, Chantell?"

She stuttered. "I had to disappear for a while."

"Why? And not call me? I thought we were better than that."

"We are. And I apologize. But I had to deal with an emergency. One I wasn't prepared for."

"A family emergency?"

"Something like that."

"What exactly was the emergency?"

She was quiet. She took my hand again and this time she was trembling. I was worried. "What's wrong, girl?"

"Come inside, out of the hot sun. Lets grab some pizza. And talk."

I nodded quietly.

She paid for the food, despite my protest. I was going to pay. I never let a woman buy my food. I feel whether they asked me out or not I should flip the bill, as long as she didn't go overboard ordering shit then I wouldn't have to flip out on her ass.

She held both my hands, her head lowered. Her hair hung in her beautiful face.

Licking chapped lips, she looked up and said, "I'm pregnant. With your child."

I closed my eyes.

My heart drumming ferociously, I opened my eyes with a huge grin. Hell yea! I looked down at my dick and said, "HELL YEA!"

Not the reaction she was expecting. She relaxed a little.

She smiled then. "What are you saying?"

"I'm saying hell yea I'm going to be a father."

"But you're getting out the Army."

"Yes, I am!" I was kissing her hand something terrible. She chuckled. Standing up, I pulled her to her feet and picked her up, turning in circles.

We were both jubilant.

"Ya'll she is going to have our baby!"

I was so happy I couldn't stand it. Inside I felt like butterflies over a mountain top during the first break of spring. I would be the best father. I would read to my child and I didn't care if it was a boy or a girl. I would be to my kid what my father wasn't to me.

I couldn't wait to tell Mama. And I know my family would be in shock because they have been calling me names for years.

Now they could suck it.

I put her down, and she got serious on me after everyone applauded.

"I don't want the baby."

I died inside. "What?" I grabbed her arms. "Please don't take this from me. Enough have been taken from me in this lifetime."

"What are we gonna do? I can't have a baby. I got college, and my parents will freak out. Plus you're getting out the Army."

"So what. I will still take care of my child, Chantell."

"I might have an abortion."

"That is a definite No. Are you serious? It's my decision too."

"You can't even tell me how you're going to support this child."

"OUR CHILD! And we will be just fine."

"I don't want it."

"But I do. Kids are a blessing from God. If you don't want it give him or her to me. I'll raise it myself."

"I do want to give you a child. You are a good man. I don't want it, yet I don't want to kill it; but as long as it exists my future is compromised."

Please, please, PLESE, Lord help me! "Please don't kill our child." I shuddered. I have never been so terrified in my life. "How many months are you?" eye asked, trying to get in her good graces.

She tried to smile. "Going on two," she said uneasily.

I was desperate. I was willing to say anything if I had to. I had to change her mind. "Will you promise to talk to me before you make any rash decisions?"

"Yes, I promise," she said harshly.

"So you need me to buy anything?"

She grinned. "No, man. And don't be buying up all the shit in the store."

My eyes lit up. "For my child hell yea."

"What do you hope it is? A boy or a girl?"

"It doesn't matter to me. I'm going to be a goddamn father. Wowee!" I was so happy I couldn't stand it.

"You can drive me to your room so we can talk some more."

"I got a better idea. Let's go out somewhere private so we can really talk about this."

"Fine by me. But I am sure of one thing, even though I am nervous about it."

"Shoot."

She wrapped her arms around me. "I know you'll be a good father."

Oh my God oh my God! "So does that mean…?"

She kissed my lips. "*Yes*, I'm keeping the baby. I will turn our kid over to you because I have a life and there are things I wanna do before I take on responsibilities of raising a child. I can barely raise myself."

"Oh my God. I love you thank you so much!" I picked her up again, turning in circles.

This time she let me, laughing along with me.

But we wouldn't be laughing for long.

The next few months proved to be something of a mockery of my very existence. Because eye nurtured and caressed her belly during my every waking moment. I started spending time away from the Barracks, and staying the night with her. We lay up all night munching apples and oranges and pineapples. And I fixed her my favorite guilty pleasure.

Sliced bell peppers, mild lettuce, and thinly sliced tomatoes with Italian salad dressing (my favorite YUMMY!) and bacon bits. Mix it together and sit back and relax and munch on the concoction. She said she loved it.

Getting her to try it was a feat, though. She was the kind of woman who thought she controlled her every move, when she couldn't control anything God created, not even the weakness of her flesh. That weakness never came with a Surgeon General's warning, directions, instructions or assembly rules.

I was seeing my friends less and less. And that was a good thing because they were still on playing musical beds with their wives and undercover homosexual fem bottoms and tops, dancing inside a deadly obsession so with the coming of a baby, my first child, I had to lead by example so I changed myself instantly.

I was so excited OMG. I wanted a kid so badly I couldn't *think*. I wanted one because I loved them, because my father wasn't much of a parent, guardian, provider, protector or Daddy to me anyway so I wanted to correct the past with my present day reality. My child was going to get nothing but love.

One of my friends asked me what I would do if mother didn't accept my kid. "You know she's mean as hell," he said, shaking his head. "Have you even told her yet?"

"No," I said, telling my friend Starks, Staff Sergeant, getting weary of him trying to worm into my boxers and private affairs.

"Why not?" he asked.

Goddamn get you a life, something, shit! "Because I don't have to report to my mother with a goddamn progress report, referral, detention or an evaluation. I'm a grown ass man and if I want a goddamn kid I will have my fucking child."

I was offended. My mother wouldn't and couldn't stop me from becoming a father. At least she could give me some credit for waiting until I graduated high school and was in the Army before I got a bitch knocked up.

"I think you should tell her."

What is this Niggah's problem? Why the sudden interest in my life all of a sudden? "I don't *want* to tell her."

He walked up to me, putting both hands on my shoulders and I flinched. Eye hated muthafuckahs trying to change my mind.

Looking me deeply in the eyes ain't gonna get me to tell my mother or anybody else that ain't ready to know I got a baby on the way. That's my *goddamn* business.

"Pharoah. Listen, man. You are about to get out the Army soon. You told me you're not reenlisting. You still angry about that General calling you a nigger and no one believed you because you're a Private. That still eats away at you."

"Why did you have to bring that up? That was a very hard time for me."

"I know it was, man. We stayed up over drinks talking about it. We chilled that night. You found out that I got your back."

"Oh, yea? That was till 5 a.m. hit and you decided to put your hand in my draws and fumble around with my asshole. I jumped up on your ass and left. You violated me."

"We both fuck around with Niggahs."

"I'm a Quality over Quantity type of mofo, you diggin' me man."

"So now you talkin' all hip now, huh. Niggah with the two ton balls because he got a piece of pussy pregnant. I must admit the Hoes love you, but you don't sweat them."

"I am about to go home my dude."

"Stay over, man. Think it over. How are you gonna have a baby when you getting out the Army, you haven't told your mother, you don't got your own house, you don't have a car, and barely got a bank account and the account you got is filled with two dollars and lint. You can't afford to have a baby."

"I'm leaving."

"I gotta drive you home."

"I'll catch the goddamn bus!"

"Bus ain't running after 11 p.m."

"Fuck it then man I'll walk. I don't have to stand here and listen to what you're suggesting."

"What am I suggesting, Pharoah?"

"You think my baby mama should abort my seed?"

"Exactly. You're both young. You told me she wants to go to school and really don't want to have the baby."

"But she's having it for me. She will let me raise my child."

"And that ain't any reason to have a child. A kid has two parents. Eventually he or she, whatever, gonna wanna know about his mother. Then what you gonna tell him? That you on lease and set up on a payment plan through the child support agency."

I stormed to the door without uttering another word.

"PHAROAH! Don't mess up your life."

I paused, and spun on my heel, pointing. "Like you? A Niggah with seven goddamn kids from five broads? All getting child support. Leaving your ass with barely a percentage of your military pay. And you're giving me advice."

"That's why I'm telling you this. So you don't make the same mistake."

I grabbed his arms and shoved him into the door. A flash of anger bit his eyes and I smiled and said, "I will kill myself before I kill my goddamn child. I'm having that baby, muthafuckah. And I don't want to have this conversation again."

"Get your hands off me Pharoah."

"I hope you heard me."

He threw my hands off him and stood his ground. "I said get your goddamn hands off me."

"Go to hell bitch."

"Get out my house. You can walk."

"You're gonna drive me home. I'm not walking 20 miles back to Fort Hood and I'ma Goulds Niggah."

"Get out."

I grabbed my wallet and keys. "Fine. I'm gone."

"Have the abortion. Don't be a fool."

And he slammed the door closed.

I stared at the door and said, "Don't your spoiled ass kids need to eat?" I yelled, rolling my eyes.

He thought I was about to walk? Chile. I unlocked his car, hopped inside and drove to Fort Hood.

I parked by my friend Granger's truck.

And called it a night.

But the next few days I couldn't sleep. No matter what I did. I had insomnia out the ass. Wondering was I making the right decision. Was my reason for having a child accurate?

I knew I didn't believe in abortion. That's murder and I'll be damned I murder something my dick created. I was just being real about it.

Mama said if you make it take good care of it. And she meant it.

I decided that *yes*, I was doing the right thing. My family would love my kid. Having the baby would delete the gay suspicions mother has of me.

But then again that ain't any reason to have a child. Kids are not smokescreens. My kid would have it all. All my time and attention. I would probably spoil his or her ass and wouldn't let anybody watch them but me because these days you couldn't even trust your mother or your brother with your kids. When it comes to raising your kids look to God.

That way your eyes were cast away from a very wicked line up of ailments waiting to tear your family apart.

I would stand up and die for my child. And one night, over steamed crabs, Chantell and I talked about it. We were both in matching tube socks, black boxers and T-Shirts. I was never a fan of dressing up like my woman or my lovers, but with her I was a very compromising man. She was going to have our baby, and I would cherish her, no matter if we wound up together or not. I would always be there for her, give her my last for my kid. I made a vow to God. And I meant it.

She already vanished on me once when she found out she was pregnant. I was afraid she would vanish again with my child and I could never see him again and that right there would drive me to the barrel of a gun. If I couldn't have my child, how could I live for myself or want myself?

As the next month passed I was reading and talking to her tummy all the time. She used to roll her eyes at me and say, "The baby can't hear you. He's probably sleeping."

"You don't know if it's gonna be a boy."

"Its gonna be a boy. I just know. And I never saw a man this excited about having a child. The men I know and even my brother were about to die when they found out their women were pregnant. Hoes they were fucking from the 'Hood winding up giving birth to your kids would piss any real Niggah off."

"Well I'm glad you're night like that," I said, closing a book of Langston Hughes poetry.

"Well I do know this: your boy is gonna be a very warm hearted man."

I blushed. "*Aww*, shucks. You mean that?"

"Yes."

We kissed, rubbing each other into a slowly grinding frenzy of lust. Her nipples absorbed the atmosphere and stood erect upon its completion and my dick swelled to all new heights, with a small pain in my dick head because too much blood was pumping into one center a little too fast. A dick wasn't built to handle as much blood as the brain. Too much going on.

She rubbed my balls and I spread my legs, kissing her lips. The faint taste of fruit she ate earlier activated my fingers and I tip toed across her abdomen. Her thigh jerked.

"Our baby wants to feel some love."

"Yea, ok. Mama just wants some dick."

She rolled her eyes. "God. You're *so* romantic, Pharoah."

I bit her tit. "So you're saying that pussy ain't ready for me?"

She kicked at me and missed. "DAMN BE ROMANTIC!"

I dove between her legs, pressed my lips hard against her pussy and held the top of the clit with the flatness of my palm, blowing in the pussy.

She sat straight up. "Oh, shit."

And I began to feast, sucking down the salt and tasting cream. She came quite early, but that didn't stop me.

I ran my tongue across her pussy then separated the folds, teasing the labia menora, caressing the labia majora and getting a few tremors. My lips were receptive to her frequency, and I started to suck on her clit and stroke my dick. I was pre-cumming like a muthafucka.

She took my head and pulled me to her and said, "Put that dick inside this pussy," and I didn't protest, anticipating her warm engulfing…wanting and needing her opposites.

We gave each other some tongue. Then a peck, and another, then another. The instant the tip of my dick slid in the pussy my body locked and I began to nut.

I squeezed her tits together and buried my face, slow grinding inside her as my orgasm intensified, then began to gradually cool.

I didn't say a thing. I stayed hard in her pussy half the night.

She burst 9 times in three hours.

I burst twice.

Then rolled over and snored into dreamland without a second thought about Chantell.

But I smiled for my baby.

When I got in from the Motor Pool I called Chantell, but she didn't answer.

I just got to my room and was dirty as hell. I smelled like oil, sun, dried nut and ass. I jacked off three times at work today. When were they going to understand that working in the heat kept me a bitch in heat? It ain't everyday physics.

I hung up the phone and took a quick shower. Warm water felt good against my skin, rinsing Dove soap down the drain. Dove smelled so goddamn good.

I heard the phone ringing.

Shit.

I grabbed a towel, did a quick dry off while hopping out the shower and wrapped the towel around my waist, nearly slipping down on the tile.

Fuck. I answered. "Hello." It was Starks. "What, Niggah."

"Meet me at my place man."

"So you can kill me for taking your car."

"I ain't trippin' on that Hoe shit. You did a niggardly thing."

"*Niggardly?*"

"Any Niggah would take my car before walking 20 miles to Fort Hood."

I shook my head. *He's too nice. Something is up.* "Man I don't think this is such a good idea."

"We're friends, Pharoah."

"*Were* friends, yup that's about right."

"So you ain't my boy?"

"Nope."

"Man, fuck all that. You're my dawg. I'm your boy. I'm not supposed to always tell you what you wanna hear, dawg. I'd rather lose you as a friend by telling the truth then keep you as a friend through lies and deceit."

That's who I learned that from. "Ok, man. You're *right*. But I don't want an abortion. She's about four months now. Ain't it too late to do that?"

"Let's not get into that. Let's go get a drink at the Bar."

"Cool. Just bring me right back home, man. Don't want a repeat of last time."

"I like you too much. I ain't on that old shit dawg, goddamn. Let your guard down and let a Niggah do something for you sometimes. Make a Niggah like me feel really special."

I actually smiled. "Fine, man. But no funny stuff."

"I promise.

We never made it to the Bar.

He bought a bottle of Hennessy and when we took shots till we dropped he fell so deep inside my asshole I couldn't think.

My head swimming in nocturnal bliss, I became One with his body, moving to the pulse of his biorhythm.

He held me captive in his hairy arms, wrapping his legs with mine, bouncing in and out of me while I was lying on my stomach. I felt every throbbing inch. Filled me beyond reproach.

"I love you," he said. I cringed. Dick wasn't that good, man. Plus I got a kid on the way. All my love will be for my baby. "I'm 'bout to nut, Pharoah goddamnnnn!"

He came deep inside me. Then it dawned on me why he wanted me to have an abortion. He was in love with me.

And wanted me all to himself.

I lay next to him that night. He was snoring and I was staring at the moon light. It was a full moon tonight. The glow against my face, upper body and skin had me floating in thoughtful bliss.

I smiled with tears forming in my eyes.

I squeezed both my fists together and said, "I am going to be a dad."

The snoring stopped.

Starks slowly opened his eyes and wrapped an arm around me.

The breath caught in my throat. I looked in his eyes and he pierced through mine.

"You're gonna be an excellent father," he said earnestly.

I kissed him. "You know after tonight this will be no more."

He closed his eyes. "I know. Trust me, I'm counting the seconds. The thought of never laying up like this again Pharaoh, why you do a Niggah like this?"

"This could never be, man. I'm not ready to be out the closet. I'm not ready for my family to know about this. I don't care how many suspicions they're having. Don't mean I have to confirm them. I'm on the Low, man respect that. I don't wanna lose my family. I don't want my son coming into the world while I'm having one night stands with you."

The words tore through him like poisoned knives. "I'm not mad, man. I'm not ready for my family to know, either. My daddy would kill me. Shit, we're Jamaicans, remember?"

"Yup. I know. And Niggah I'm Bahamian, thank you. *Look*, I'm going to bed. In the morning I need to go home."

"I got you."

He slid deeply inside me, held me close.

And started snoring again.

I was walking around a park outside of Fort Hood with Chantell a few days later, trying to put Starks outta my mind.

"I feel sick," she said, rubbing her forehead.

"What's wrong? Is it something you ate?"

"Probably that seafood. It's not agreeing with my belly."

I was worried sick. "You gotta regurgitate?"

"Feels like it." She found a nearby bench and I helped her sit down. The sun wasn't as hot as the day before, and a little cool wind danced across my skin.

"Want me to drive us to your home?" I asked.

"Nah, let it pass."

She held the tops of her thighs.

And not *once* did she rub or hold her belly.

When we got home I sat on the living room sofa, thinking to myself. Any expecting mother would rub her womb if she was sick, hoping the shit didn't upset her baby. Just a maternal instinct my homegirl once told me. I thought back to a conversation me and my homegirl, Daisy, had after high school graduation in 1995.

She was coming down with the flu and she rubbed her belly before she rubbed her forehead, thighs or hands.

I was so awed. "Why are you rubbing your belly?"

She tried to smile, but you could tell she was feeling down. "I don't know…but when you're about to be a mother you are protective. Even before you give birth you're protecting your baby. I can't explain it."

"So what if you catch a cold or something?"

She started rubbing her pregnant belly again.

"I don't even wanna think about it."

Daisy went on to have a son, and currently he's a year old.

Now I'm 19 years old with a baby on the way. I was getting out the Army. I didn't wanna be in this shit anymore. I stole one of my roommates check book and wrote up some checks to myself and went to the PX and bought up some shit because they wouldn't let me take the easy way out. That General calling me a Nigger really ate away at me day and night. How his rank saved him. Ugly pink-faced bitch!

Before resorting to theft I really tried to do it the old fashioned way, by telling my 1st Sergeant I didn't wanna be in the Army anymore, but he laughed at me and said, "You barely got a year in. You got three more to go."

"I want out this Army shit. I got a kid on the way. And I don't wanna follow orders when it comes to my kid and I can't be in his life."

"You got a baby on the way?" he asked, smirking.

I licked my lips. "Your grab-a-dick-by-the-balls-gay-ass got a goddamn wife, trick?"

He frowned. "Low blow, man. I'm not gay. I am a man fucking a man."

This country muthafuckahs needs to shut up! "You're a gay man fucking a gay man in the ass you in denial ass bitch."

He shoved half the shit off his desk, and I sat there smirking. Just the way he smirked at me when I said I had a baby on the way. "Get out my office private before you get an Article 15."

"Maybe I should send those pictures of us fucking to the Board of Military Directors, whatever you call it. Chain of Command, something. And then we'll see who the hustler is. I'm from Goulds, bitch."

He started to tremble. "Get out my office." His voice was shaking.

"With pleasure." I looked him up and down. "It's starting to smell like…" I sniffed. "Fish in here."

"Fuck you!"

"Enjoy the shade, 1st Sergeant Dick in the Ass. Have a good day. Get me out this Army shit."

"No, Pharoah. You owe Uncle Sam three more years."

I stared at him. "Have you met George Bush?"

He rolled his eyes. "No. What does that got to do with anything?"

"Stop thinking for him, then. He ain't checking for you and he ain't checking for me. Isn't the Gulf War, Desert Storm going on right now? By the way I stole my friend's checkbook. I'll just wait for the MPs."

A few hours later the MPs showed up at my room door.

"Private Wilson, Can you come with us please. You're under arrest."

If they weren't going to let me out then I'll show myself the door.

I also said I was a faggot and they gawked at me like I was an escaped lab monkey running rampant in an elderly front yard.

Like I was despicable.

But for some reason they didn't believe me.

I didn't even want to go to court and fight it. Give me an Other than Honorable Discharge and set a Niggah free, shit.

Working for Uncle Sam when Uncle Sam didn't give a fuck about me or know who I was wasn't a career choice for me. Fighting for a man I couldn't see. The only man I foguth for and couldn't see was God, Jehovah. And that it, Private.

I didn't want to be a part of nothing that kept deep, dark secrets.

I was fingerprinted and charged. I was found guilty of theft and thus my road to recovery began. I wasn't a part of THEM anymore. I was a part of regular society. The Civilians.

I met up with Chantell a few days later. I had to beg her to come over.

When she did she was high on marijuana, and I was furious.

"You're smoking weed, pregnant with my goddamn child?" eye asked.

She was laughing. "So *what*, Niggah," she said, pointing. "I'm stoned. I had some angel dust."

"Oh my God, bitch!" I snatched her by the arm, my heart bleeding for my unborn child. "Have you lost your rabbit ass mind?"

She snatched her hand back. "Don't touch me Niggah!"

I snatched her ass into my face. "I'm calling the goddamn police on you if you ever do that shit again bitch now goddamn try me, Hoe."

"I'm going home. I didn't come over here for this shit!" She opened my door, and stormed out.

"Go to hell, bitch!"

And I slammed the door closed.

We didn't talk for a few days. I wasn't checking for her or checking up on her. I didn't even want to see her right now. Smoking dope while pregnant with my goddamn baby. Bitch crazy or something?

There was a knock at my room door. A faint knock. Like someone wasn't too sure of the door they knocked on.

I slid into my slippers, clad in shorts and a wife beater T.

I opened the door and it was Chantell. She looked a mess.

Mascara running with her tears, lipstick smeared into her white blouse.

She shook in her low heels when she hugged me. I didn't understand what was going on, so I pulled her inside, washed her face for her and asked her to take a deep breath.

"Tell me what's wrong, Chantell."

"I can't tell you."

"You can tell me anything. You know that."

"A few days ago you lashed out at me. Am I supposed to forget about that?"

"I'm sorry, but you did drugs with a child in your womb. That's just wrong. My baby didn't do anything to you. Don't hurt my child like that. That hurts me!"

"You called me a bitch."

Oh my God! That's all she's focused on? Me calling her a bitch? What about smoking cocaine and pot while you're pregnant? Did you care about that, bitch? "I said I'm sorry. I already hate apologizing for anything."

"Pharoah. I don't wanna have a kid."

The fear of God crept into my heart instantly. "But you promised." I was so nervous I didn't know what to do.

"I know. But the thought of going through all that pain? And I wanna go back to college."

"You can still go to college!" I was about to have an anxiety attack!

Something in her eyes died. I was losing her! "No I can't. Who am I gonna get to watch my baby?"

The hairs stood on my body. "I will. You don't even want him."

"I got a confession to make."

I held her arms. "What, girl?"

She stared at me for a long time. And the silence fell on my ears with a ton of hatred. I glared at her and tilted my head, looking down at her belly.

A belly that hasn't grown an inch.

Since she's been pregnant.

"Tell me you didn't..." I closed my eyes so tightly I wanted to scream my discernment and feelings of abandonment.

"Didn't what?" she challenged me. "What? Say it."

"You had an abortion?" I still kept my eyes slammed shut.

"YES YES YES! I did, I did!" she yelled with no emotions.

I sunk to my knees and wrapped my arm around her waist, pressing my ear against her stomach. "You're lying. You have to be."

She rubbed my head with trembling fingers.

"It's true, Pharaoh. I'm so sorry."

"BUT I HAD A RIGHT TO DECIDE TOO!" I exploded, squeezing her to my ear tighter, huge tears spilling over my eyes and was evilly running parallel with the most devastating feeling I have ever encountered in life. "HOW COULD YOU DESTROY ME LIKE THIS?" I shook so bad I nearly threw up.

Her tears fell into my low fade and I was rubbing her belly, wishing and praying she was jerking my chain. I mean I know she was angry with me for exploding on her ass for smoking dope while pregnant with my seed. But to go out and rip my fucking soul out?

"I'm sorry. I'm just not ready."

"Shh, shh," I said, squeezing my eyes even tighter. "I'm trying to hear if I could hear my baby moving. He doesn't like a lot of noise and he loves when I read him Langston Hughes." I shook with fear. I WANTED TO DIE!

"PHAORAH HE'S GONE!"

"I've been talking to an empty stomach? Are you shitting me right now?"

"No I'm not shitting you, Pharaoh."

"I read him poetry and short stories and told him all my dreams and goals and you allowed me to make a fool of myself?"

"It touched me that you gave attention to what you thought was our child. But I had already killed it, even before you read the first sentence to my child."

Angry and betrayed, I slowly stood up.

Opening my dark eyes.

"I can't believe this."

She tried to hug me and I pushed her so hard into the TV shelf she fell to her knees.

She was holding her back and I was holding my black heart. Lay in my hands like burnt ashes. Like Satan took my future with my healthy son and crushed it into cremation with the palm of his hand.

I was a demon. I slapped her and a few of my friends came into my room grabbing me and I was trying to run at her, trying to get out of my shirt and pants but they kept holding and pulling me and telling me to calm down but I wasn't hearing it. I was so deep within myself I didn't even feel them touching, grabbing or pulling me.

I was numb.

"Why did you do this to me?" I screamed, as they started to pull me down the stairs. I was trying to climb them, like a sprinter running against the force of wind up the stairs.

"I'M SORRY!" eye heard her yell.

One of my friends comforted her and I spat at her, trying to stay on top of the stairs. I didn't take my red eyes off her. I hated her with my soul. Fuck her soul. Bitch die. Fuck you. You killed our fucking child you sadistic BITCH BITCH BITCH!

"You have no heart, Ho. You know that?" I started swinging at my friends. Three of them took a few steps back, holding up their hands.

"DON'T FUCKING HOLD OR TOUCH ME!"

"We can't let you fuck up your life," one of them said.

I turned towards her and my friends ran in front of me.

"Somebody gotta be praying for you, slut because these fuck Niggahs standing in between me and you. They let me go Hoe I'm gonna give your soul an abortion. Kill you the same way you TOOK MY FUCKING CHILD BITCH!"

She covered her mouth. "You never talked to me like this?"

I was trying to get past my friends. One tried to grab me and I threw a two piece at his face. He ducked them.

"Pharaoh!" he shouted. "I'm on your side!"

"*I SAID DON'T TOUCH ME!*"

By now Niggahs coming out of their rooms, or climbing the stairs, trying to see what was going on.

I stood in one spot and looked into her eyes. "Why did you break your promise?"

"Pharaoh, please. This is painful for me too," she said, sobbing. I could barely make out the words. "I'M SORRY!"

"GO TO HELL! What made you back out of your promise?"

"I had too. He was putting too much pressure on me."

I was confused. "Who? Your *father*?"

"No, man, no! My brother. He kept putting pressure on me, saying don't be having your baby. That you haven't told your mom about it and you were getting an other than honorable discharge. I can't bring a child into the world with his father failing already."

I was stunned. "You're judging me?"

"No, man. Have some empathy."

"Did you do that for our child, bitch?"

"*Pharoah*! I have to protect my future! I can't have a kid. It would interfere with my plans."

"Who protected our baby?" She fell silent. "Who protected him?"

"You don't even know if it was going to be a boy."

THE NERVE OF THIS BITCH! She's worried about that, after killing our child and telling me nothing? She didn't even let me tell my child goodbye. I woulda tried to talk her out of it till I passed out. And even in my slumber I would still tell her to reconsider. Don't take my life like that; don't crush my manhood, the little I had to myself, away from me. Don't fuck it. It doesn't have an asshole.

"Who is this man that convinced you to kill my child?"

"Pharoah."

"WHO BITCH WHO WHO WHO WHO?"

"Starks, Pharaoh!"

I fell into a deep silence, the fight zapping from my body like a heaven bound spirit cursed with the fires of hell.

The wind left my lungs.

CODE RED! CODE RED!

She was mentally and physically drained.

"I'm sorry, Pharoah. My big brother was right. I can't have this baby."

"Starks, Staff Sergeant Starks, my good friend is your older brother and neither one of you thought to tell me this?"

"It's not that we didn't wanna tell you."

"What did you call it, Chantell? I mean, ya'll played games with me?"

"I needed to know everything. I wanted to know all your plans."

"So you had him get in good with me. And everything, every concern I had, he ran back and reported to you?"

"Yes. That's when I had an abortion."

"When, exactly?" I asked.

"Three weeks after I told you I was pregnant."

"What a low blow. How could you sleep at night?"

"How could you? I'm the one that got a low blow."

"What are you talking about?"

"My brother told me you two are fucking." Gasps filled the room and outer hallway.

People were wide eyed, soldiers covering their mouths.

"We are doing no such thing," I said with a straight face.

"I don't wanna have a gay man's son. What an oxymoron, are you kidding me?"

"You need to die a horrible death. May your soul never rest. May you suffer for the way you killed our child. Pain took our child out of the world, a pain initiated by selfishness and arrogance."

"Please forgive me."

"*The day Jesus INVITES Satan over for breakfast would be the day I forgive you. Until then, rot inside your dark ass soul, bitch!*"

And I flipped the middle finger.

I looked at my friends, ignoring her.

I would hate her. For an eternity. Maybe. Hate was a strong word. But abortion was an even STRONGER word. Because that was an action word. Hate wasn't an action word. It was a human emotion that we're all plagued with. Whether we're using hatred or not.

Hate is needed to keep love balanced.

"I'm going for a walk," I said, walking past them and down the stairs.

I unlocked her car.

Got in the driver's seat.

And hauled ass towards Starks house.

When I got there, I parked by his ride, and hopped out with the car running and in "park."

I left the door open.

I knocked on his door and when he answered it he said, surprised, "You know I like for people to call before they come—"

I punched him in his face and he stumbled backward into the living room.

I saw nothing. But red. Red for blood.

I didn't even think I blinked.

I slammed the door closed and locked it.

He ran at me and punched me good in the gut. I didn't have time to react. I stumbled backward into the front door and he ran at me and I pivoted out the way and his head slammed into the door.

"I HATE YOU FUCK NIGGAH!"

"Go to hell, faggot!" he yelled back.

I kicked him in his ass. He caught my foot and pulled me to his head as it slammed into my face.

Blood was everywhere. In my clothes and on his tiled floor.

He grabbed my neck and squeezed real hard.

"I never liked you."

"How could you betray me?" A knee to his balls. He doubled over on his knees, holding them tightly.

I kicked him in the face and stomped his chest.

"YOU HELPED KILL MY CHILD! I DIDN'T KNOW CHANTELL WAS YOUR FUCKING SISTER YOU BETRAYING BACKSTABBING ASS FAGGOT!"

He looked up at me. I stumbled forward then backwards, like I was drunk but I wasn't intoxicated nor tipsy.

I held my stomach, bending at the knees.

I never sobbed so hard in my life. "My kid is gone. You helped kill my dreams. That kid was my immortality. My goddamn future. AND YOU KILLED IT?"

"Man. I'm sorry."

"YOU HELPED KILL MY CHILD YOU BITCHHHH!"

He was reaching for me. "I love you man I never meant to hurt...you. I was jealous! That you would share a kid with my sister when I'm in love with you!"

"Fuck you!" I spat blood at him. Some got on his shoes.

"PHAROAH!"

I slowly walked up to him, and fell down to my knees. Face to face. I grabbed his face and planted my lips square on his and he held my face and we're stroking each other's face, breathing each other's air and I said, "I will never forgive you. I will never forgive her. I will never forgive neither of you."

He was kissing my face. "Pharoah. Abortion was the right thing!"

"That wasn't your child, Pharaoh."

"GO TO HELL!" I head butted him so hard the back of his head slammed into the wall.

Staggering, I stood up. Looking at his pathetic ass.

"After today our friendship is over," I said, meaning every word. "Don't talk to me and I won't talk to you. I hope you rot, bitch! I hate you so much."

"No you don't," he managed to say, trying to regain his composure. He rose to his knees, avoiding my eyes. "Your heart is too big."

"You don't say that! You DON'T SAY THAT TO ME!"

"Whatever you wish. Leave now, before I call the goddamn police."

"I don't care to be here anymore. Fighting you ain't gonna bring my child back. You took my soul, you little dick bitch! You killed my soul, man. You got your fucking five kids bitch! Alive and well! FUCK ALL OF THEM! FUCK EM!"

He was crushed. "You don't mean that. They adore you."

I looked at him so darkly he trembled. My forehead lowered, my eyes peering into his. "You killed my child. The *hell* with yours."

"I can take that man. Now please leave."

He looked down at the floor and I ran at his ass.

His head snapped up at me and before he could do anything I put all my anger, frustration, betrayal and disloyalty into the discrepancy report called FIST and rammed it into the middle of his forehead.

He fell to the floor.

And didn't move.

HOME GOING SERVICE FOR:

Sunrise: Sunset:
January 2009 January 2009

Lord Jennings

THE FINAL CHAPTER
THE FINAL OBITUARY

Pharoah C. Wilson
Vs
Satan
January 2009
12:00 a.m.
Sweet Home Baptist Church
69 S.W. DOOMSDAY Lane
Pharoah vs. Satan

<u>Luke 22:3-6</u>

Then Satan entered into Judas called Iscariot, who was of the number of the twelve. He went away and conferred with the chief priests and officers how he might betray him to them. And they were glad, and agreed to give him money. So he consented and sought an opportunity to betray him to them in the absence of a crowd.

<u>Ephesians 6:10-18</u>

Finally, be strong in the Lord and in the strength of his might. Put on the whole armor of God, that you may be able to stand against the schemes of the devil. For we do not wrestle against flesh and blood, but against the rulers, against the authorities, against the cosmic powers over this present darkness, against the spiritual forces of evil in the heavenly places. Therefore take up the whole armor of God, that you may be able to withstand in the evil day, and having done all, to stand firm. Stand therefore, having fastened on the belt of truth, and having put on the breastplate of righteousness…

A Time to be Born: Pharoah Wilson, Jr.…

…When your neighbor trespasses against you, you must not trespass against them…

A Time to Grow: …Meeting up with a therapist to deal with my past was supposed to be a new beginning…

A Time to Reflect: …would it become the end of Pharoah Wilson, Jr.…?

A Time to Die and be mourned: A part of me died when those therapy sessions ended. He said they were free, but as I should have figured out…they came at a price.

|LORD JENNINGS VS PHAROAH

ARMAGEDDON

Pushing folders, yellow tablets and notes aside, Lord Jennings stood up in a zombie state, stretching. I smiled, feeling good about doing these therapy sessions. Allowed me to look at my life and see myself through the reflection of memory. I have been through a lot, survived a lot and even I didn't realize just how much I've endured. Survived every brutal and subtle plight that came my way. I was a lot stronger than I thought, and looking at my pictures in frames all over his house and realizing I cared about Lord as a friend did a number on me. Yes, we had sex and I still didn't understand *how* that happened being I was in a committed relationship with my significant other. And no matter how I tried to analyze it, no matter how I kept telling myself that Lord keeping me locked in his condo was *harmless*, I knew that deep down something was there, whatever it was, and it beckoned for attention. Something wasn't right.

"Lord. What's wrong?" eye asked him. He seemed different.

He smiled, his eyes glossy. Shirtless, his jeans barely stayed on his amazing ass, but I tried not to look. I kept looking in his eyes.

"I'm happy right now," he said, but the tone of his voice

betrayed his words.

I smiled. "You are? Why?"

"You've *successfully* admitted to me all your faults, truths, lies and endurance. I am so proud. And to think when you first came here seven days ago you were afraid to ride the elevator."

I know, right! "I conquered that fear."

"I know you have. You've covered a lot in seven days. And I know it's a start. I know you still have work to do on yourself, but I commend you for your strength and for remaining humble."

"And God fearing!"

He looked at me without blinking, handing me a drink. Hypnotiq. Straight. "This drink is for you. To *celebrate*."

"Celebrate what?" eye asked

"Conquering your life in seven days," he said. Dan he was happy, or was he?

I studied him. "Ok, sounds good." I wasn't a huge drinker. In fact liquor was nasty as shit, but I guess in this instance I could oblige.

Reluctantly, I sipped, smacking my lips, barely swallowing it. It tasted nasty, but I didn't want to appear amateurish in front of him so I sat up straight.

Turning on classical music, he sat next to me, looking deeply into my eyes, his right hand resting on my left knee cap. He sipped, and said, "Taste good."

Ugh! "Yes, it does," I lied.

"We should play a game."

I'm not in the mood. "I like games. You got Scrabble?"

"Yes, I do. But I'm not talking about board games. You're much too sophisticated for that," he said, setting his drink down. "We should play Wolf."

"Wolf?" I sipped the drink once more, frowning in confusion. "What the fuck is a goddamn Wolf?"

"Wolf is a simple game. It has only one rule. Whoever can wolf down the drink first win a prize."

Sounds harmless. Why not. "Ok, I can swing with that."

He smiled coyly, leaning over, kissing my cheek, his nipples and dick hardening. I pretended not to notice. Something seemed different with Lord. His eyes didn't seem or feel the same.

In fact, looking deeply into his heavenly eyes I didn't see heaven at all.

I saw the darkness.

I held my glass midair and we made a toast.

"To the future of Dapharoah69."

Dude, I don't even know if I have a goddamn future. These books may never touch a single person or see the light of day. "To a new and burgeoning friendship," I said, clanking my glass against his and I wolfed down my drink, slamming the glass on the expensive low table. A few of his yellow pads containing my life fell on the floor.

"I won!" I stammered, smiling, jumping up to my feet in victory, my fists raised in the air.

I was laughing and Lord hadn't even touched his drink. Instead he pulled out a small package of cocaine from the arm rest, a small glass topped mirror and sipped his drink.

Had that been in there the entire time? I was perplexed. "I thought you didn't smoke weed or do drugs," I said, yawning. I was getting tired, and I should be. I have been staying up for hours and hours telling a shrink my life and my demons. And telling him my Jehovahs and Lucifers did a number on me because I was in a position to examine myself and see what needed an oil change, tune up or what needed to be donated to the Good Will and given to the less fortunate.

I yawned again, and when I tried to walk towards the kitchen I tripped over my foot and fell over the low table, hitting my head on the floor. That shit hurt. Moaning, I rolled over on my back and Lord picked up the cocaine and dumped it all over my face, pressing his bare foot on my chest, leaning into my face.

"So easily one can get into your life and become a permanent fixture."

The room was spinning. "What...what the...hell is going on Lord?"

"Helpless little bitch aren't you? I don't understand you. I really don't."

Oh my God! "What...what are you...doing to me?"

"I put a lil' something in your drink. Pharoah, haven't you learned a thing from your life? You sat in this condo for seven days pouring your soul out to a therapist that isn't even a therapist at all!"

"What?" I was in shock, my energy draining from my body. I could hardly move my fingers and Lord knows I tried to sit up or stand up but my head was spinning me deeper into a vortex.

"I am infatuated and obsessed with you. I always have been. I think you are the most beautiful man in the world. I always wanted to fuck you. I have your porn videos and I been an admirer of yours for five plus years. I never spoke to you or sent you a message."

He stood up, kicking the side of my face. Blood spurted on the white tiled floor and I turned on my side and he kicked me so hard in the back I winced from the pain, and felt helpless because I was too drugged up to react let alone breathe properly.

He laughed the most evil laugh I have ever heard. This sexy man I thought was a new friend, a man I thought wanted to help me deal with my past has turned out to be a crazed fan.

"Helpless, 'ey Pharoah? You are a dream come true. I have always been madly in love with you. You are so sexy, you're very handsome and you have an incredible body. You suck and take dick well," he went on, unzipping his pants, appearing manic. It was hard to focus on him, my heart pounding through my chest.

He got on his knees and helped me to my knees. I nearly fell back on the floor.

"Come on, Pharoah. I'll help you," he said, his eyes dark red. He put cocaine in my mouth, pulled me to his nose and he held the left side of it, snorting it. His head yanked back, his face flushing beet red.

"AHHH SHIT I LOVE IT!"

"Please…"

He studied me, his head tilting side to side cautiously, guardedly and slowly. He gave me some tongue, my lips unmoving. He bit my bottom lip and I screamed. "Kiss me bitch!"

"Please."

"I wanna love you. I want you to be my fucking slave. You will never leave this condo, Pharoah."

"Oh my God, Lord. Please."

"You are not allowed to go outside, which is why I changed the locks on my door. I will feed you only bread and water. Oh, and you won't be needing these," he said, snatching up the blue plastic bag with my Meds and throwing them towards the sliding glass door.

I shook in my skin. "I need my Meds, Lord. I will perish without them."

"That's the plan, faggot. I will fuck you as you slowly perish."

I closed my eyes. "God, please help me."

"THERE IS NO GOD! Are you stupid, bitch? Your GOD sat by and let a man rape you as a child. He sat by and watched you suffer when Chantell aborted your child! He watched. WATCHED! Probably eating the best popcorn he could muster. And you still pledge allegiance to him?"

"Yes, Lord…why is my head pounding?" I asked, attempting to rub my temples and he slapped me so hard my head snapped back. He spit in my face.

"God watches you now. If he truly exist. He doesn't, Pharoah. He doesn't."

"God is not doing this to me. You are."

He pushed me backward, my back slamming hard against the tile. It hurt so bad I puked, nearly chocking from my own vomit.

He slowly walked up to me, one foot over the other, the sky filled with stars I could hardly see. Everything seemed to turn into blurs, then ghosts, then the most demonic ghouls I have ever encountered. I had problems thinking or breathing and I thought I was going to die.

"Miamilicious. Mr King of Goddamn erotica. The one who writes books that got muthafuckahs praising you. Do you realize you are GOD to some of your fans?"

I couldn't form the words. My body felt like it was shutting down.

"Are you ignoring me?" he asked dangerously, straddling my neck, trying to shove his dick in my mouth. He started pissing and I tried my damnest to push him off but I was so weak. I was gagging, then chocking. His hot piss filled my mouth. Then he leaned forward on his elbows and started fucking me in the mouth and I puked again and he kept fucking my throat, moaning and laughing and I puked again as his huge dick filled my esophagus.

"I love when your sexy ass choke on my dick."

My body shook on the floor, my hands finding his sides, weakly, and I dug my nails into him and he screamed so loud he rolled off the top of me and slapped me repeatedly.

"Time for the revelation, The King of Erotica. Pharoah. This isn't a book. You won't live past tonight to write another one. You took something from me, Pharoah, something you didn't realize you took and you must pay the price."

"What…what…price, price what…."

He laughed again, this time even more sinister than the last. He was getting off on my grief and fear.

He walked over to one of the tall bookshelves, took every book of mine and dropped them in a pile on the floor.

"You are an amazing talent. A very talented man." He was butt naked, his huge dick swinging freely. "It is almost an honor to fuck you. Thousands of men jack their dicks to your pictures. I love the picture of you on South Beach with that pretty boy pussy tooted slightly towards the waves."

He opened a small counter in the pricey kitchen and pulled out a small leather pouch.

He unzipped it, approaching me. He pulled out a needle. My eyes widened with fear. I tried to roll on my stomach and push up but he got on his knees, spread my ass cheeks and he began to feast. Loosening me up. It felt good but I made myself go numb.

He kept eating more effectively, running his tongue all over my opened hole, then sliding his fingers and tongue deep inside.

"Give in to me, Pharoah."

"Nooooo…..please…."

"When I am done eating, I am going to fuck you till the sun rise. Raw. I have herpes, Pharoah. Oh yes I do. And I will give it to you." He turned me on my back and injected a needle into my arm.

Smiling evilly. His glassy eyes devoid of life. I shook so hard I couldn't breathe.

"This my friend, my dear Pharoah, is heroine I am pumping into your body. I will pump more and more into you as the night dawns into the break of day. I will then fuck you while you slowly die. I will watch you suffer."

"Why are you…doing this to me? WHY WHY?"

"Pharoah. Look deeply into my eyes and tell me where you remember them from."

"I never met you…before." My throat burned and my stomach felt like it was on fire. I had to moan, but I refused to cry.

"Yes you have. Think long and fucking hard, Pharoah. WHERE DO YOU REMEMBER ME FROM?"

"I DON'T KNOW!"

"WE HAD A ONE NIGHT STAND, BITCH!"

"NO WE DIDN'T!"

"My father used to be one of your...Pastor$ when you were a whorish little teenager."

I grew painfully silent. Looking deep into abysmal eyes.

"I don't know your father."

"Sure you do. You know my mother, too. You had a threesome with both of them. You destroyed their church with your revelation to the congregation and that broke up my family."

I was rendered speechless."Oh my God!"

"Yes, your God is a fraud. Church isn't real, Pharoah. God isn't real. My father was a faithful follower of your God as long as the people gave their hard earned money to his faggot ass. Do you know how it feels to have a gay father and to walk in on him and your mother fucking a teenage fag in the ass? They fucked you so well you hadn't realized I also fucked you, Pharoah. In the darkness. All the lights off. I had to have you, Pharoah. You thought I was my father. You fucked my dick good, bitch. You were my first."

I grew silent, listening to this.

"Can't talk? And watching you on this couch opening up to me, listening to how you explained my mother and father touching and sexing you angered me but I hid it from my face. I knew who you were. I just wanted to hear you say it. Because of you my family was destroyed. The congregation ripped my family apart and my mother divorced my father and he committed suicide in his bathroom."

"Oh my God!"

"THERE IS NO GOD!" He jumped up and kicked me in the side over and over. I crawled into the fetal position.

"YOU HEAR THAT ALLAH. JEHOVAH. BUDDAH, WHATEVER THE FUCK YOUR NAME IS. YOU'RE NOT REAL, ARE YOU? YOU ARE DESIGNED. CREATED BY CAUCASSIONS INSIDE THOSE FICTIONAL

BESTSELLING BOOKS CALLED THE HOLY BIBLE! JESUS NEVER EXISTED!"

He was spinning in circles, with his arms outstretched, committing blasphemy. I cringed inside, because nothing I go through tonight would turn me away from God.

It was then I realized why I didn't sign the book deal with that publisher. It was then I realized why they laughed at me for coming to New York without legal representation.

They were going to give me a million dollar payment if I denounced God. They probably would have given me the world.

But then again that's the world today. Entertainment figures selling their souls to the devil for fame. Did I want to do that? Did I want to go that route just to make enough money to feed my mother, brothers, friends and my nieces?

Did I want fame that badly? Um, no.

And now I was going to die. And I was ready for it. I was scared of the way I may be checking out, but I never feared death itself because it was inevitable. It was going to happen whether I wanted it to happen or not.

He grabbed my feet and started pulling me towards the ceiling glass door. I was weak I couldn't even grab the low table legs to give some form of resistance.

"You took my family."

"Your mother and father took your family. I was a goddamn minor!"

"SO WHAT!"

"Go to hell, Lord."

"Wrong choice of words." He turned me on my stomach and slid his dick up inside me. "You talk a lot of shit, Pharoah. Is this how Thugzilla fucked you on camera for the world to see?"

"Please!"

"I got a better idea!" He pulled out of me, and vanished into the bedroom. I tried my best to crawl towards the front door, but then I realized he locked it and the key was on his person.

Wildly I looked around, and decided to get a knife from the kitchen. But before I could crawl towards it he appeared with a white Jason mask over his face.

He set up a digital camera on a small tripod before me, then opened some lighter fluid and squirted it all over my books.

He struck a match and dropped it, my books going up in flames.

"Please, Lord."

"Beg me. I am your Lord. I am more real than your God."

"You are not God!"

"WRONG!" He pressed record on the camera and he raped me, repeatedly for the next couple hours. I passed out a few times, and didn't know how long I was unconscious. When I came to he was still fucking me like I wasn't worth anything.

When he had to cum he pulled out of me, yanked my face to his dick and came on my cheek, wiping nut all over my mouth and eyes and I spit on the floor.

"You're on camera, Pharoah. My face is covered. Yours is exposed. I am going to upload this video on every social network that I could possibly think of. I am going to destroy you from the inside out. I may even send your mother the video with your heart as a Christmas gift with a Happy Thanksgiving card attached."

"Please, man. If you're gonna kill me…just do it, man. GOD JUST DO IT!"

"No, that's too easy. I want you to feel exactly what I felt when I cried over my father's casket."

"Man give it to God."

"GOD ISN'T REAL!"

"HE IS, LORD!"

"Pharoah. Your mother forced religion on you and forced you to go to church when you were a child. You didn't have a say in the matter. My mother and father forced me and their parents forced them. See the vicious cycle. The human race gotta be forced into serving a God they can't question let alone see. And even when my mother grew up and away from church my Pastor father married her and beat her ass back into the church. My father used to beat me till I saw blood. Told me I better not wince or show any sign of weakness so I endured the shit with a poker face. I prayed to a God that had forsaken me. I lost faith then. Then the state took me from my parents because they barely fed me. Eventually my parents won me back, but they had to prove they could take care of me and they did. My father got worse. My dad fucked me the way he fucked mama. He had to control his household and fucking Mom and I relinquished our control of our lives. I hated myself for it, Pharoah because, like you, I grew to love it."

"Lord…God heals."

"No he doesn't. My father fucked me then beat me and my mother's asses and made us go to church and serve God. I used to vomit from his public display of humbleness to his neighbor yet destroyed me as his son. One time he beat Mom and I so bad he fucked us both, lay Mama on her stomach with a pillow below her stomach so her pussy tooted towards him then he put me on top of her, making me put my dick in her ass and he fucked me then pulled out and fucked mama in the pussy while I fucked her in the ass. I HATED IT!"

"Oh my…I'm sorry…you went through that."

"And you think you had a rough life. There is always someone going through something worse than you. You don't appreciate your life. You are selfish. You are arrogant. You think its all about you!"

"God heals angry hearts, man."

Hate colored his face. He was about to snap on my ass and there wasn't a thing I could do about it.

"GOD IS A HOAX! MY OWN FATHER SAID THIS TO

ME! CHURCH IS A HOAX, DESIGNED TO KEEP US AS A PEOPLE CONDITIONED. DON'T YOU SEE? CHURCH IS AN EVIL MELTING POT OF LIES! IT KEEPS SOCIETY OBIDIENT. REQUIRES YOU TO GIVE TEN PERCENT OF YOUR EARNINGS TO A FUCKING PASTOR TO SPEND ON UNECESSARY SHIT!"

I was silent, listening to him.

"Don't you get it? Can you claim your church donations on your taxes? You eat the flesh of Jesus and drink the wine, his blood during communion with a room filled with sinners."

"Lord, listen…you don't have to do this, bruh. You are not your parents."

"Yes I am. I am just like my father. You have feelings for me and I am not your father."

"I care as a friend."

"This condo belongs to me. When my father died I collected insurance. When my mother died I collected insurance. My father was also a shrink. When he killed himself I kept up his certificates and doctorates. Those aren't my accomplishments, Pharoah. I used them to get to you. I wanted to understand the man who not only write good books, but I wanted to understand why you allowed my parents to use your minor body for their sick perverted pleasure."

I tried to sit up, and shockingly he didn't attack me. He appeared sleepy, almost tired. "I was 14, man! A goddamn kid!"

"YOU COULDA STOPPED IT!"

"NO I COULDN'T! My mind tried to save my flesh, flesh that loved and lived for your father's tender touch. He paid attention to me. He listened to me. My own mother never listened to me."

Blood stained my face. He was calming down, but danger was *still* in his dead eyes. Eye was still dizzy.

Then it happened. He snapped, attacking me, taking me

completely off guard. He snatched me up and punched me in the face, and I slammed into the book shelf. I tried to raise my fists, but he ran into me, the book shelf rocking and books fell to the floor.

He pressed the side of my face on the cold tile.

"You see the book on Pharoahs under the shelf, like you found in the first grade?"

"Nooo, man! No!"

"Niggahs can't even stick together, so why do you call yourself Pharoah? You aren't royalty. Niggahs don't want shit in life. They just wanna smoke pot, sell drugs, fuck people in the ass or pussy or get some head. That's it."

He pulled me to my feet and I swung at him, hitting him in the face and he pushed me, and I ram backward, falling into the bathroom. Toilet filled with feces and piss. He shoved my head in the commode and I held my breath, grossed out, flinging my arms and he pressed my head further in the toilet, my forehead resting on the bottom of the commode and bubbles rose to the top of the water. I used everything inside me, everything that comprised my heart, mind, body and soul to breathe yet I couldn't.

I was suffocating, my life flashing before my eyes. I know what that shit meant now. And it wasn't a good feeling at all. I tried to press up with my hands but he slid his dick back inside my ass and started fucking me, pressing my head down harder on the porcelain.

My body began to fail me. Everything started gradually shutting down. But I wouldn't give up just yet. I wasn't gonna go out without a goddamn fight. No matter how unrealistic it seemed.

Pulling me up, he bounced inside my asshole, chocking me. When he said he had to nut I threw my head back into his face and he yelled so loud I damn near went deaf.

He punched me, over and over and grabbed my feet and started dragging me to the balcony. I was trying to grab hold of anything that I could, but couldn't grab a fucking thing.

He opened the ceiling to floor glass door and pulled me out onto the balcony. The cool breeze blew across my body. Half moon up, the smell of surf below. Fifty six stories up into the heavens, 56 stories above Hell below.

I was going to die.

He snatched me up, this cock strong bitch, and he pushed me against the railing.

"I'm done playing with you. Check out time. Since God is so real, let's see him save you."

He wrapped his hands around my neck and slowly pushed me over the edge of the railing. My feet were no longer touching the floor. And I died right there inside. I completely gave up, let it all go. My body shook so badly I couldn't breathe, my hands trembled profusely. My heart beat so fast eye was surprised eye didn't have a heart attack. I refused to look down. I couldn't because if I did I would die from traumatic shock alone.

"On the seventh day of therapy you realized eye was a fraud. A fake. I wasn't who I told you I was. You need to be careful who you let in your circle. Everyone doesn't like you. Everyone don't like your books. Some people hate you just because you're successful. Those who failed at what you do so well envy you. Closeted gay men wanna fuck your books and your talent, not you. They hate you. They wanna fuck your resources then once they obtain the keys to your kingdom they try to destroy you. And you make it easy."

The darkness was consuming me. It snapped throughout my body, my heart and my mind and I said, "I hate…" And I caught myself.

"You what? Say it. You hate me. SAY IT! You hate me!"

I stalled. Hate was such a strong word. "You know what? I don't hate you. Hating you is easy. I love you, man. Despite it, I love even my enemies. I pray for you. I really pray to God to save your soul."

He squeezed my neck, chocking me with so much hatred on his face. "*How* do you do it? How did you survive all the shit you have and still have faith in a God you never lain eyes on? I could never be that strong."

I was weakening. Losing consciousness, giving up the fight. Living life was too much for me. Too many rules. Too many things I had to obey. Laws and sanctions. Tired of changing for others to be what they wanted me to be. Tired of being talked about, scandalized and battered. Tired of it all. I was exhausted. Maybe taking my life would be a good thing. I wouldn't have to pay rent or taxes. Creditors could get off my back. I could be free. I dangle 56 stories above the ocean, or whatever body of water that was. Bayside behind me. I felt light as a feather and as timid as a ghost. The wind was picking up, gently and inviting. He leaned into my face. "I'm gonna make you pay for taking my family."

This is it, Lord. This is where my decision making has led me. To chaos and destruction. When will it ever stop? Or will it stop right now? Fuck books. Fuck a literary career. To be successful comes with too many people holding you down out of envy and jealousy. Because they couldn't do it they won't allow you.

Eye looked into the face of evil and felt myself letting go. The tears fell down my face with finality.

"Tell God to save you," he whispered, my eyes fluttering closed. "Better yet denounce him. I want to hear you say the words. Tell me he isn't real. Tell me you are your own individual God. Tell me you are the maker and creator of your destiny. And I will let you live. Tell me, Pharoah."

Eye closed my eyes...and gave it all to God. *Everything*. Life, love, books, pain, misery, things I could and couldn't control, this scenario, the pain and torture. I gave it to God. I had complete faith in God. Whatever happened would be his Will. If Lord pushed me over the balcony and I fell 56 stories towards the water it would be God's Will. I wouldn't question it, because God wasn't evil. He was love. Purity. I didn't deserve any of the blessings he bestowed on me.

He was the true living God and it didn't matter if I never

saw him. What mattered was that my praying and believing has gotten me through HIV, suicide, rape, prison, deceptive lovers, crooked county officials, backstabbing family.

God has delivered me through it all, and if I die tonight my life will be immortalized through my books and that will be a testimony.

God, forgive me for all those I have hurt. When I was much younger, God, yes I didn't truly love you because I was forced to, so I rebelled and questioned it and denounced it and thought I could do it alone. But God I can't do it alone.

"Pharoah, denounce him."

I need help, God. If I die tonight I pray you give Mama strength to carry my family, rid her heart of the bitterness she denies.

Protect my nieces, God, because I won't be here to be their protector. Enter my brother Laron's heart to move back down to Miami and raise his daughters and leave that girlfriend of his alone. Touch Darshawn's heart and rid it of the anger and hatred he may or may not have towards the things he's gone through in life.

"PHAROAH DENOUNCE HIM! AND I WILL LET YOU LIVE MUTHAFUCKAH!"P

Protect my family, God please.

I believe in you, God and I know Jesus died for all sins, even my sins, even my bisexual sins Jesus paid for with his life, I am not worthy, Lord.

"SHUT UP, PHAROAH! God is not real! SHUT UP!"

I spoke aloud, yet calmly. I love and believe in God and would not denounce him for nobody and whoever wanted me to could suck a raw fart out my ass.

"As a man I love you God and I am thankful to you for helping me endure my trails and tribulations. I know you're real, God. I feel it in my heart and soul; I even feel it in my bones. I am NOT my OWN GOD!"

"YES YOU ARE, BITCH!" He spat in my face and I felt nothing. I didn't even feel his saliva touch my face.

"I was only made in God's image. Satan's greatest trick is to teach the world that he don't exist, when he does. I don't wanna be my own God. Being your own GOD comes with mansions and episodes of MTV Cribs with you as the narrator and tour guides before an envious world and pricey cars and millions of dollars in endorsements and the world praising you for your talent instead of thanking Jehovah for the blessings. Being your own God comes with #1 New York Times bestseller status and #1 Pop and R&B hits and multiplatinum albums and publicly bragging about the charities you donate your tax write-off money to and it feeds egotistical souls embedded with the wrong type of spirits and money hungry cash cows that represent false idol worship.

"God help me, please. Whatever happens to me it is your Will.

"Amen.

"So be it.

Complete silence. I could hear the surf below; feel the wind on my body. Eye slowly opened my eyes, albeit being drained and exhausted. Lord still held me by the neck. I smiled at him, and the tears stopped falling.

"You felt alone when and after your father abused you. I know the feeling, but your pain is all your own."

He didn't blink. He stared at me.

I went on. "There were nights you couldn't sleep because it played over and over in your head what your father demanded and what your mother allowed to happen. She failed to protect you and your protector was screwing you and your mother. You can't count the tears you shed. I can feel you right now, feel the times you wanted to end it all. You contemplated suicide numerous times yet couldn't bring yourself to do it because you wanted to find out the purpose for your life. This is not your purpose. You sought vengeance against me for the distorted thoughts of your parents.

"Your father stripped you of your human traits and disguised you as another form of society's lie. Eye understand Mr. Jennings. I will no longer call you Lord, because you are not the King of Kings or Lord of Lords and you will never be. But you can be a reflection of his image, for you were made in it, bruh."

"Pharoah." His tears flowed. For the first time he showed emotion. "I don't believe in God…"

"Your father abused you and as a man you think you can go back and protect the little boy or the confused teenager he used to dismantle with his aggression, confusion and penis. You know my life, Mr. Jennings. I poured my soul out to you, a complete stranger that had the motive of killing me the entire time. Was my pouring my life to you as meaningless as you made it out to be? Is your misguided vengeance that important you will support black on black crime, as if enough systems aren't against the African American race?"

"Yes…yes," he stuttered, confused. Trapped. "I mean, um, no, shit. No, Pharoah. I do have a heart."

"I forgave myself for the abuse I suffered. I forgave myself for those I hurt after I asked for their forgiveness. I sleep with a free conscious nightly. Blame your father for what he went through and acknowledge your part in it all. Victim or not, reclaim your life by forgiving yourself. Let it go, and it's hard as fuck I know, bruh. But *I* did it. And so can you. If you don't forgive the perpetrator he still has control over you from his grave. He's resting in peace, you're living in Hell."

He loosened his hands around my neck, his eyes clouding over. His body losing the tension, his muscles relaxing. I had him. Right where I wanted him.

"I understand your situation, but I don't feel your pain. Its all your own. You're the only one who can feel and deal with your pain."

"SHUT UP!"

"God is real. As real as snow. He's the rays of the sun that energizes life to aid productivity amongst the human race. He's the form of procreation. We are the best evidence that God exist. We are living proof of his existence, bruh. Were we not once a sperm cell/Mama's egg? Look at us now!"

He took his hands from behind my neck and he was like a little boy shaking in the cold and I didn't have the urge to kill him or push him over the edge. His soul needed saving and it didn't know how to ask for it so the answer was destruction and vengeance.

"How do you remain so strong, Pharoah? I literally deceived you, beat you, raped you, drugged you and tried to kill you. Yet you stand here like nothing happened. I don't get it. You still love God?"

A flash of anger beckoned me to do his ass in, but I fought it. I refrained. He wasn't worth my freedom. I already lost my freedom once, 12 years ago. "Yes, bruh. I do. If you put a gun to my head I will still love and honor God. If you put a gun to my nieces head or my mother's head I will never denounce God. I have his full armor. I love God. And then I love not people next but myself. I am learning to love me. I am learning to love *everything* about me. I embrace me, bruh. You can't break me. I wouldn't change a thing about myself."

He attempted to hug me, yet he withdrew his arms as if I was on fire and he was gun powder. He cleared his throat, wiped his face and leaned against the wall. He stared blankly into the sky. "If you had to do it all over again, living the life you lived, knowing what you know now—would you have broken up my family?"

I said, "Yes," without hesitation.

"Why?"

"Because it would lead me to this exact moment, this instance. To tell you it's never too late to turn to God, and let him work in your life, bruh. Prayer, effective prayer I should say, changes things. If you allow it. Prayer takes practice. The more you pray the easier it gets. He's patient. He understands. That doesn't mean you won't sin, bruh. You'll live in sin till the day you die. I, too, resorted to vengeance, bruh, in my life, trying to correct a past I didn't understand nor create. I thought anger was an answer. Lashing out got me nowhere. I felt worse than I did before I attacked. I met a new type of devil every time. Urging me on. Giving me the tools to destroy myself and everything I hold dear in my heart. Aren't you tired of losing yourself to another's plan of destruction?"

He was quiet for a long drawn out moment and I was so tired I just wanted to go to sleep. But I was seemingly getting through to Mr. Jennings so I kept silently praying in my heart and mind and kept talking and calming him down.

"Pharoah." It was a whisper as it dawned on him exactly what he did to me. He seemed to withdraw into himself.

"God is love, bruh. I like me. Everything! From the color and shape of my eyes to my slight buck teeth. My bisexuality resulted from experience and curiosity and circumstance. It was not predetermined from Mom's thoughts during painful child birth. I was not born with nuts on the brain. Embrace you, bruh. I don't believe the entire Bible. I question a lot of it. I don't trust what Caucasians rewrote and edited. But I do believe in God, the son and the Holy Spirit. And I believe in myself."

"Pharoah." He reached out to touch me and I took his hand and squeezed it. "I don't know what to believe."

My eyes fluttered. "I'm so tired, Jennings. So tired of this. I'm exhausted, bruh. I'm high. I'm scared. I'm tired of arguing and fighting with people." I felt weak. I sunk to my knees and lowered my head because my head was about to spin.

"Pharoah, what's wrong?"

As if he had to ask. "I don't wanna write anymore books. I don't want this gift anymore. This is just too much."

"Pharoah." He tried to help me stand up but I wouldn't budge. My body was gradually shutting down from shock.

"Do you think I enjoy being bisexual or gay, whatever

you wanna call it? No! I hate it. There's a time I wanted a wife and 12 kids because I have a huge family. I used to dream. Wanted the baddest bitch as my mate. But that's all it was. A dream. A fantasy. Imagery. Make believe."

I stared at my hands on my lap, about to fall on my face.

I continued, my voice weakening. "...I've been writing ever since I was a small child. Fourteen hours a day, right now of my life, goes into Creation. I've done this for the past three years! I'm done. I'm drained. I'm tired. I just need to rest."

He got on his knees in front of me, cupping my hands and kissing them.

"Pharoah. I'm sorry, man. For all of this. For deceiving you. For abusing you. I'm so sorry, man." He seemed genuinely sorry, but how do you just forgive and let go of something that nearly killed you? Ultimately, I had to forgive him, and that's the bitter truth.

He attacked me, brutally did shit to me and now what was I supposed to do?

I WANNA KILL HIM!

I WANNA BASH HIS FUCKING FACE IN!

But I didn't, because I matured in a lot of ways.

"Let me tell you about Job," I went on, looking up into his eyes. "He lost his health, land, animals, kids, money and family. But not once did he lose his faith in God.

"I know the story. My daddy used to be a Pa$tor, remember?"

I struggled to stand up. He tried to help and I denounced it. I then stumbled past him. Growing weary of life and family and the art of war and the bickering and the arguing. My life ain't worth the handle Oprah flushed her piss with.

"I just want to be Pharoah again," I said cautiously. "I lost myself."

I started snatching books off his book shelves, throwing them on the floor. "I hate this shit! I hate writing. Free me of this shit! I AM STARTING TO HATE WIRITNG OH MY GOD! I give this shit up, Lord! Why did you choose me?"

I pushed over book shelves, watching them break apart. Books falling all over the place. I was kicking them, picking them up and ripping them in half. I was screaming, ripping out the pages and tossing the loose leaf pages over my head like they had minds of their own.

"PHAROAH! STOPPP!"

"I will NEVER write another book. I just want the voices in my head to stop talking to me. But I'm too obsessed with writing books!"

"Pharoah, man." He wrapped his arms around me. This time full of love and acceptance and understanding. I wasn't receptive to his touch. I was getting even sleepier. Drained. If he was gonna kill me then do it while I'm sleep. I have been through enough pain. Please, God.

"Pharoah," said Lord, holding on to me. "You are a strong man. Gifted. Talented. You help so many and give them your all. I'm sorry, again, man."

Didn't you just try to kill me? "I just wanna go to sleep. Mama hates me. Daddy didn't want me. People use me. But God loves me. I wanna go where God is."

He laid me on the floor.

"God protect me while I sleep. Just for a little while."

I closed my eyes.

It took a while to convince myself I was awake let alone still alive. But I had a migraine headache and warmth engulfed my face. My eyes weigh more than documented weight loss. I inhale deeply and slowly, with great resistance, open my eyes. They were itchy. Took awhile for the room to come into focus. I lay there, still and quiet. Taking the room in. My photos gone from the frames. The place was cleaned to a shine. Floors were mopped, bathroom cleaned and all the statuettes and books were put on the shelves. The ones I destroyed were in the trash.

Standing up, I was naked. Where were my clothes?

I kept hearing beeping noises. I looked over in the kitchen and I heard it again. The dryer had stopped.

I checked it and it was my clothes he washed. I smiled for some reason.

"*Jennings...*"

Then it all came back to me. The heroine. The cocaine he dumped on me. Drugging Hypnotiq and tricking me into playing a game called *Wolf*. Pushing my head into a pissy toilet. Dangling me over the balcony.

I was nauseated. Holding my stomach, I walked throughout the condo, pricey shit. There was no sign of him.

"Damn it! He locked me in this prison again!"

I approached the front door and tried to knob.

It turned, but I didn't get excited because the bolt lock was locked.

I pulled on the door.

It opened.

It was unlocked.

I didn't know what the future held for me, or if I would continue to write and create books or not. I left Lord Jennings condo and took nothing with me. I left all the memo pads, the recordings and the photographs. Left it all behind like a pissy mattress on a street corner. I never heard from him again nor do I know what ever happened to him. I don't know if he believes in God or if he's still losing sleep over his thirst for vengeance. I never pressed charges nor did I call the police. The heroine he pumped into my body has been eradicated and everything I endured in that condo I wrote out of my mind and told myself I would never talk about. Yet sitting here typing this and reliving those candidly sinister moments, I have to admit that I cruise the Internet giving people the benefit of the doubt rather than being cautious about who I talk to.

Lord Jennings taught me something. He told me I'm too

trusting. He told me everyone doesn't like me or my books, and this was confirmed when my cousin Y'vonia Payne sat me down and told me the same thing, back in July of 2010.

So it took a few months of practice, but I changed it. I don't allow everyone in my circle and I don't try to get in everyone's circle.

I didn't know if my books will ever make the New York Times Bestseller's list, but I'm not going to sell my soul to get there. That shit ain't happening!

It used to be a goal of mine; you know we all should have goals. But going through and surviving the latest chapter in my life, battling Satan himself for my life, my goal has changed.

I may never sit on *Oprah's* couch nor shoot a movie with Tyler Perry. No one may be interested in my life story. But one thing was for damn sure. I pray and then carve my own way.

God guides and protects me. I am his instrument and he plays the Sax incredibly well. With Jehovah watching me, I will travel this road whether it twists onto the wrong path and have me doing Yields on One Way streets.

As I continue to write and release books, I will live by one code.

May no weapon formed against me prosper. Haters and false idols, wizardry, Astrology, voodoo and witch craft, the weakness of my flesh and my ass, mind and dick are weapons of Mass Destruction SATAN uses artfully.

After all…

It's his Free Will.

LORD JENNINGS
SELF DESTRUCT.
DUST.

www.ingramcontent.com/pod-product-compliance
Lightning Source LLC
Chambersburg PA
CBHW031538300426
44111CB00006BA/104